The Firm
and its Environment

Industrial Studies Series

Series Editor: J F Pickering

Industrial Studies Series

THE FIRM AND ITS ENVIRONMENT

R H Barback

Philip Allan

First published 1984 by

PHILIP ALLAN PUBLISHERS LIMITED
MARKET PLACE
DEDDINGTON
OXFORD OX5 4SE

Reprinted 1988

British Library Cataloguing in Publication Data

Barback, R.H.
The firm and its environment.—
(Industrial studies)
1. Business enterprises
I. Title   II. Series
338.7   HD2731

ISBN 0-86003-526-3
ISBN 0-86003-628-6 Pbk

Typeset by Oxford Publishing Services, Oxford
Printed and bound in Great Britain by
T.J. Press (Padstow) Ltd, Padstow, Cornwall

Contents

Preface

This book deals with the structure and activities of industrial firms as productive organisations in the economy. The approach comprises an analysis of the economic aspects of industry, but I have tried to give proper weight to the forces, additional to those forming the subject matter of economics, which go to make up the explanation of the behaviour of firms and the working of the labour market in the real world. The book has been written with the needs of those taking the new A-level in Industrial Studies primarily in mind. It will also be suitable to those pursuing kindred subjects at A-level or preparing for BEC and similar examinations. For those with no examination in view, it is hoped that it may provide a readable introduction to the economics of industry.

I am grateful to Mrs Jill Henney, Mrs Pat Middleton and Mrs Sally Bremer for their skill with word processing equipment and their ability to read my writing, to the Controller of Her Majesty's Stationery Office for permission to reproduce material from the Standard Industrial Classification 1980, and to Professor J. F. Pickering and Dr A. A. Williams for their patience and helpful advice. Any shortcomings which remain, however, are entirely my responsibility.

Acknowledgements

Photographs are reproduced by kind permission of BBC Hulton Picture Library, Camera Press, ICI, Merseyside Development Corporation and the Milk Marketing Board.

The various stages of milk production

1
Industry and Economic Activity

The **standard of living** in any country depends on a number of factors, such as the country's natural resources, the skills of its people, the degree of efficiency with which its production activities are organised, and the extent of its technological knowledge. It may also depend on the size and the age structure of its population, and on whether the population is increasing or declining in numbers. In addition, a country's living standard is affected by the strength of its trading position in relation to other countries: on the one hand, how competitive it is in relation to countries producing the same kinds of goods; and on the other hand, on its terms of trade – how much of other countries' products it can obtain for a notional unit of its own exports. The latter is determined by the relative price levels of the things it exports and those which it imports. In a modern developed economy these factors make themselves felt with conspicuous effect through its industry, which in the United Kingdom accounts for about two-fifths of the country's employment and output.

What is Industry?

We need to be clear about what we mean by the term '**industry**'. It is not at all easy to define, and its use in everyday speech can be misleading in various ways. It will not do, for example, to say – as is sometimes said – that industry is the productive part of our economy, upon which all else therefore depends. Since we do not usually include agriculture in what we mean by 'industry', we had better not define industry by reference to productiveness. To do so betrays a mistaken notion of what we must mean by 'productive' if we are to see our economic organisation in a rational light. The activities of the service trades are also productive in an economic sense. We need not discuss whether it is the cow or the farmer that 'produces' milk, but what is certainly important to the consumer – whose satisfaction is the whole object of economic activity (except for the satisfaction which may be obtained from productive activity

1

itself) – is that the milk is not produced until it is delivered on his doorstep. The services of getting it there in a bottle are also productive. The test of whether an activity is productive is simply whether anyone is willing, out of his own limited resources, to pay a sufficient sum for anyone to do it. To emphasise the great importance of industry to our economy, with its special features and problems, is entirely proper; indeed it is unfortunate that it is so often necessary to do so; but to claim a monopoly of productiveness is itself counter-productive. The parts of the economy are interdependent. (Of course, that does not mean that they are always and necessarily the right relative size to each other. Their *marginal* products may very well be unequal. The meaning of the word 'marginal' will become clear later in the book.)

We may notice another confusion. There has arisen a tendency for expressions like 'the insurance industry' and 'the entertainment industry' to be employed. Perhaps this tendency will persist. Perhaps, even, it arises from an understandable desire on the part of leaders in these groups of businesses to emphasise that insurance, banking, entertainment and the like are productive activities. Indeed they are, but not because they are industries. The usage is confusing: activities such as those just mentioned are different in significant respects from what can be, and usually is, understood by the term 'industry'.

Productive activity can be divided into primary, secondary and tertiary production. **Primary production** is thought of as a kind of first stage, wresting from nature her fruits and extracting materials from the earth. Thus agriculture, mining, fisheries and forestry are the principal examples. Much of the output of primary producers forms the raw material for **secondary production**.

Secondary products are of three kinds:

(1) Some are those which, when distributed, will be ready for final consumption; these are consumer goods like chocolate bars, jeans, washing machines and video equipment. Things like the latter pair are called consumer durables, and consumer durables like washing machines and household refrigerators are sometimes called '*white goods*'.

(2) Some secondary industries produce components and other products for sale to manufacturers and assemblers in making their products. These are intermediate goods (sometimes called, perhaps a little confusingly, '*industrial products*') like speedometers and petrol gauges, packing materials, steel and protective clothing.

(3) Other secondary industries produce machinery and equipment for use in manufacturing and other productive activities.

These are capital goods, such as machine tools, combine harvesters, computers, filing cabinets and ships.

Tertiary production consists of the provision of services and is not directly concerned with the production of physical commodities. Examples are banking, insurance, advertising, transport, wholesaling, retailing, hairdressing and the services of doctors, lawyers and accountants. Some of these services are provided direct to consumers in final consumption, whilst some are like intermediate goods and are provided to other producers – primary, secondary or themselves tertiary – to whom they are valuable in assisting their productive processes. Tertiary production tends to represent a large and growing proportion of total activity in the developed and industrialised economies. We have already noticed that such activities are sometimes erroneously looked on as 'unproductive'. This notion probably arises from the fact that the output of tertiary producers does not consist of material objects, together with the mistaken idea that real income can only consist of such objects. This mistake is known as 'the fallacy of misplaced concreteness'.

The classification of production into primary, secondary and tertiary is helpful in our search for what we mean by industry. It does not, however, remove all ambiguities. Consider mining and quarrying: they are primary production activities, yet have a recognisably industrial character. Consider also an actor playing a role on the stage and thereby providing a service: then consider him doing the same in a film studio, with the end product on reels of film which will be sold or hired as a manufactured product. Puzzles like this are quite plentiful. There is, quite simply, an arbitrary element in setting the boundaries of industry.

The Standard Industrial Classification

Nevertheless, it is undesirable to be vague about what is included when we make statements about industry. For example, in the first paragraph of this chapter we noted that industry in the United Kingdom employs about two-fifths of the working population. We need to know what is included, especially if we want to compare this between one year and another, or with another country, and more especially still if our purpose requires us to be more exact than saying 'about two-fifths' or the like. We use statistical information to make statements like this, and the principal source of such information for industry in this country is various statistical series collected and published by the government. The available statistics cover a very wide range and are collected by various government departments. To ensure uniformity in their basis, and also as far as possible to obtain a degree of international comparability (especially within the European Community), statistics are presented according to a Standard Industrial Classification (SIC) which covers all economic activities. This classification was revised in 1980 and the full range of activities is now divided into ten broad Divisions numbered as follows:

0 Agriculture, forestry and fishing
1 Energy and water supply industries
2 Extraction of minerals and ores other than fuels; manufacture of metals, mineral products and chemicals
3 Metal goods, engineering and vehicles industries
4 Other manufacturing industries
5 Construction
6 Distribution, hotels and catering; repairs
7 Transport and communication
8 Banking, finance, insurance, business services and leasing
9 Other services

These Divisions are sub-divided into Classes, the Classes into Groups and the Groups into Activity headings, of which there are 334 altogether and which are therefore very detailed.

Now, one of the series of official statistics using this classification is what, until the 1980 revision, was known as the Index of Industrial Production. It gives us a measure of how output from certain activities is changing over time. Its coverage is used for presenting other statistics (e.g. employment) as well. It comprises Divisions 1 (Energy and water supply) to 4 (Other manufacturing industries) of the SIC (80) set out above, for which an index of production is compiled. An index of production and construction (corresponding to what has hitherto been known as the Index of Industrial Production) includes Division 5 (Construction). On practical grounds we can do no better than to follow this arrangement and say this is what we mean by 'industry', with the addition of Division 5 (Construction) when that is relevant. It does not remove the puzzles: they may remain to amuse us and to tease the official statisticians; but it gives us clarity.

Sometimes a context requires that we confine our attention to that part of industry which is engaged in manufacture. Manufacturing industry comprises Divisions 3 and 4 of the 1980 SIC together with those Classes of Division 2 which manufacture metals, mineral products and chemicals. This may seem surprisingly small for such a significant and wide-ranging part of our total industry, but Division 4 (Other manufacturing industries) contains as many as 91 of the total number of 334 Activity headings.

It will be apparent that this way of finding a workable solution to the problem of defining industry automatically throws up an answer to the problem of defining a particular industry. It is an answer based ultimately on the Activity headings of the official statisticians, brought together into Groups, Classes and Divisions according to the degree of detail which a given problem may require. In order to illustrate this, the industrial Divisions which have already been listed are divided into Classes as follows:

Division 1　*Energy and water supply industries*

Class

11 Coal extraction and manufacture of solid fuel
12 Coke ovens
13 Extraction of mineral oil and natural gas
14 Mineral oil processing
15 Nuclear fuel production
16 Production and distribution of electricity, gas and other forms of energy
17 Water supply industry

Division 2　*Extraction of minerals and ores other than fuels; manufacture of metals, mineral products and chemicals*

Class

21 Extraction and preparation of metalliferous ores
22 Metal manufacturing
23 Extraction of minerals not elsewhere specified
24 Manufacture of non-metallic mineral products
25 Chemical industry
26 Production of man-made fibres

Divison 3　*Metal goods, engineering and vehicles industries*

Class

31 Manufacture of metal goods not elsewhere specified
32 Mechanical engineering
33 Manufacture of office machinery and data processing equipment
34 Electrical and electronic engineering
35 Manufacture of motor vehicles and parts thereof
36 Manufacture of other transport equipment
37 Instrument engineering

Division 4　*Other manufacturing industries*

Class

41/42 Food, drink and tobacco manufacturing industries
43 Textile industry
44 Manufacture of leather and leather goods
45 Footwear and clothing industries
46 Timber and wooden furniture industries
47 Manufacture of paper and paper products; printing and publishing
48 Processing of rubber and plastics
49 Other manufacturing industries

Division 5 *Construction*

Class

50 Construction

Group

500 General construction and demolition work
501 Construction and repair of buildings
502 Civil engineering
503 Installation of fixtures and fittings
504 Building completion work

Note: This Division consists of one Class only; its Groups are therefore also given here.

Ultimately, as we have seen, the Classes break down into Groups and then the latter break down into Activity heads at the most detailed (4-digit) level. A specimen extract from the 1980 Standard Industrial Classification is shown as an appendix to this chapter by way of illustration.

The general logic of SIC (80) is pretty much the progression from primary to tertiary economic activity which we have discussed. However, even this is not without its problems. It is possible to define individual industries in different ways, and different problems may require them to be looked at in different ways. Does an industry consist of firms producing the same product? It is often useful to think so. Yet a light-weight three-wheeled motor vehicle is something very different in its purpose from that of a four-wheel drive Land Rover (also produced by the motor vehicle industry), and the potential purchaser of the former may well weigh up the merits of purchasing a bicycle instead, and not remotely consider the Land Rover as a potential purchase. Here, the similar technical processes or components of producing what are two motor vehicles form a reason for considering them to be in the same industry. However, what constitutes an industry can also be looked at from other points of view. Many products of quite different kinds are made from a common principal raw material. This idea lies behind much of the Standard Industrial Classification: thus the manufacture of paper products ranges from the production of cardboard boxes to wallpaper, from stationery to books. Again, some different products are made by a common process, for example jute and polypropylene yarns and fabrics: such an industry has a range of different markets, as do also the metal goods industries.

Lastly, it is possible to look on an industry as being a group of firms engaged in fulfilling similar wants on the part of its customers. In such a case we should be defining an industry by reference not to its principal product, its principal raw material, nor its process, but by reference to its market. It is still rather common to take too narrow a view of what constitutes a firm's market, and many companies which have seen the implications of taking a wider view have thereby reaped success. Take brewing as an example. It has, certainly in the past, been considered simply as the production of beer (classified under food, drink and tobacco in the SIC), and its distribution has been left to traditional channels. The advent of television and the shift in income towards a younger age-group have modified the pattern of demand to an appreciable extent so that, with correspondingly modified marketing practices, brewers will now frequently regard themselves as part of the 'leisure industry'. We shall have more to say about 'market orientation' at a later stage. Meantime we may note that all producers of consumer goods are in competition not only with firms in the same 'industry' but, to a degree which may be very large, with those in other 'industries' as well. All are competing for a share of consumers' limited spending power. The intermediate industries lying behind them are also affected by this competition from which the demand for their products is derived. Clearly the less 'specific' they are, the more they can switch their production between articles demanded by different industrial customers (e.g. as with packaging materials), the more fortunate they are in this particular respect.

The Standard Industrial Classification (1968)

Before the introduction of the SIC (80), official industrial statistics were based on the Standard Industrial Classification of 1968, and there had been previous revisions before that time. The reader will inevitably find that many of the figures which he will wish to use, and which he will see quoted, are on the basis of the earlier classification. The 1968 system separated activity into 27 Orders rather similar to the 1980 Divisions: the Orders were sub-divided into Minimum List Headings which were the smallest groupings of activity, and of which there were 906 as compared with the 334 Activity headings we have noted in the 1980 Classification. It will take some time for the 1980 Classification to completely supersede its predecessor, though statistics on the earlier basis are capable of being reassembled on the new.

The Significance of Industry in the UK Economy

There are various ways in which we may attempt to gauge the degree of importance of industry in the economy. In the first place, industry is the source of livelihood, as we have already noticed, of about two-fifths of the working population.

Table 1.1 shows the numbers in employment in the various industries, with the total for the 'Production Industries' plus Construction shown separately. The outstanding importance of industrial employment is apparent. At the same time note should be taken of the growing importance in total employment of the professional and financial services.

Table 1.1   *Employment in Britain, 1971 and 1981*

	1971		1981	
	(000)	*(%)*	*(000)*	*(%)*
Agriculture, forestry and fishing	734	3.1	657	2.7
Mining and quarrying	397	1.7	345	1.4
Gas, electricity and water	377	1.6	347	1.4
Manufacturing industries:				
Chemicals	483	2.0	471	1.9
Metal manufacture	558	2.3	402	1.6
Textiles, leather and clothing	1,147	4.8	831	3.4
Engineering	3,650	15.2	3,150	12.9
Food, drink and tobacco	777	3.2	690	2.8
Other manufactures	1,565	6.5	1,385	5.7
Construction	1,594	6.6	1,672	6.9
Services:				
Transport and communication	1,639	6.8	1,582	6.5
Distributive trades	3,088	12.9	3,159	13.0
Professional, financial, scientific				
and miscellaneous services	6,512	27.1	8,081	33.2
National and local government				
service	1,509	6.3	1,596	6.5
Total	24,031	100.0	24,367	100.0

The 1971 rows for Mining through Construction are bracketed together totalling 43.9; the corresponding 1981 rows total 38.0.

Source: Department of Employment.

Another way of gauging the significance of industry in the total economy is to compare the value of its production with the total output of the activities of the economy as a whole or what is called the **gross domestic product** (see Table 1.2).

The place of industry in the UK's trade in exports is a third way of looking at its significance. For practically the whole of the present century so far, manufactures alone have accounted for over 80 per cent of the country's visible exports. The remainder have comprised materials, of which coal was at one time an important export. Again, the proportion of industrial output which is exported gives a further indication of the place of industry in the economy: this proportion is about one-third. For the US economy, however, that proportion is much less, as the USA's range of resources make it more self-sufficient and less dependent on international trade.

The composition of these exports has been far from unchanging. Whereas machinery and equipment accounted for about 10 per cent

Table 1.2 *Gross Domestic Product by Industry*

	1971 (£m.)	1971 (%)	1981 (£m.)	1981 (%)
Agriculture, forestry and fishing	1,435	2.9	4,867	2.3
Petroleum and natural gas	18	0.0	11,972	5.7
Other mining and quarrying	668	1.3	3,455	1.6
Manufacturing	15,712	31.7	49,916	23.7
Construction	3,431	6.9	13,545	6.4
Gas, electricity and water	1,575	3.2	6,670	3.2
Transport	2,932	5.9	10,935	5.2
Communication	1,166	2.4	5,858	2.8
Distributive trades	5,321	10.7	20,088	9.5
Insurance, banking and finance	3,631	7.3	19,251	9.1
Ownership of dwellings	2,627	5.3	13,869	6.6
Professional and scientific services	5,044	10.2	28,467	13.5
Miscellaneous services	3,747	7.6	20,057	9.5
Public administration and defence	3,385	6.8	15,988	7.6
Adjusting items	-1,154	-2.3	-14,150	-6.6
	49,538	100.0	210,788	100.0

(Note: the percentages for Petroleum and natural gas through Gas, electricity and water are bracketed to totals of 43.1 for 1971 and 40.6 for 1981.)

Source: National Income and Expenditure, 1982.

of visible exports early in the present century, this has grown steadily, with a very marked jump after the Second World War, to about four-fifths of the total. There was also a steady, if somewhat less spectacular, growth in the proportion occupied by chemicals. It must be stressed that we are talking here of proportions of total exports. At the beginning of the century textiles formed nearly four-fifths of our total exports (approximately the same proportion as machinery and equipment recently), but this has dwindled to less than 5 per cent. The falling off in textile exports has also been a drop in absolute terms, though only to about half the volumes which were experienced up to the 1920s. Exports of machinery and equipment have increased in volume approximately twenty-fold since early in the century.

Industrial Change

The pattern of economic activity is always changing, in response to technological discoveries, discoveries of new resources (a conspicuous recent example of which for the UK is North Sea oil and gas), increasing scarcity and hence cost of other resources, changing tastes and demands on the part of consumers, and as a result of the mutual reactions of the economies of the developed and less developed countries of the world on each other. This implies that over any given period some industries will be expanding while others decline in relative and, it may be, in absolute size.

Some such examples of broad changes have just been noted above, though we are not yet here in a position to delve deeply into their particular causes. The pace of industrial change has been particularly rapid during the past two hundred years, at first in this country followed by Western Europe and the United States and then by Japan. It was in its origins much influenced by the liberalisation of modes of thought about nature and about society represented by the Enlightenment of the eighteenth century, and the application of science to productive processes accelerated and wrought deep changes in the social fabric.

The industrial pattern of the UK, based at first on water power and later on coal to power steam engines, took firm shape in the nineteenth century both in terms of its structure and its geographical distribution. Large shifts in population were involved and by half way through the last century what had been a predominantly rural society had become 50 per cent urbanised. Increases in agricultural productivity occurred, but so large were the changes taking place that imports of food were increasingly required, as well as imports of raw materials for the new manufacturing industries; both these were paid for through the processes of international trade by exports of the new manufactured products to the world at large. These were by no means all consumer goods, and one of the most spectacular exports was railways.

The phenomenon of Britain as 'the workshop of the world' could no more last for ever than can any other particular set of economic circumstances – though doubtless some of those of our Victorian forebears who benefitted from it most thought that it could, would and should. There lay in store two catastrophic world wars, the Great Crash of 1929, the prolonged economic depression of the 1930s and two main groups of industrial rivals. The first group was already making itself felt in the nineteenth century. After the initial phase of the Industrial Revolution Germany and the United States in particular – the latter aided particularly by its abundant resources and large, fast-growing home market, the former by its energetic development of applied science and technology, though in neither case were these the only favourable factors – were able to initiate their industrial development with new ideas and without the disadvantages, including obsolescent equipment, which adhered to this country which had been first off the mark. The *relative* industrial decline of Britain dates from this time, and its share of world trade in manufactured exports began to fall at the beginning of the present century. It recovered for a time after the Second World War, but resumed its downward trend after the recovery of Germany and Japan.

The second group of industrial rivals consists of what are known as the newly industrialising countries (NICs), of which Korea, Brazil and Taiwan are examples. Their impact has been felt during the period since the Second World War, and not, of course, by this country alone. Since the level of their wages is low compared to those in the developed industrial countries of the West, and since they not infrequently impose import quotas or other restrictions on imports from developed countries of products whose manufacture they are themselves fostering, they tend to become the subject of complaint by older suppliers and to be involved in international trade disputes. It can hardly be doubted, however, that in general and in the long run, world industrial production patterns will adapt to the existence of new sources of manufacture, provided the new sources meet the requirements of consumers in terms of a combination of price and quality.

The Location of Industry

Some industrial activities are carried out in places fairly evenly spread over the country or, rather, among the population of the country. Bakeries and jobbing printers, for instance, compete by offering fresh bread in the one case and close consultation about customers' special requirements in the other, so that physical proximity to their markets is important to them. Some industries consist of plants in various parts of the country simply because conditions favourable to their prosperity may exist in various places. Some others, however, are to be found localised in particular areas or regions. Clearly the extraction of minerals can only occur in places where the minerals are to be found – which is not to say that it will always occur when the existence of mineral deposits is known: the most productive deposits will be the first to be worked. Clearly, also, shipbuilding requires to take place not only near where coal, iron and steel are available but where there is suitable water for launching the completed hulls.

A complete geographical and historical explanation of the way industry is distributed and concentrated in certain areas would require the identification and assessment of many factors whose relations with each other are highly complex. We may, however, notice some broad types of factor that operate with fairly general effect and we have, indeed, already noted that early in our industrial development industries such as textile spinning and weaving which required power to drive the new machinery in their mills, located themselves by running water as a source of this power.

This was plentifully available in the Pennine streams of Lancashire and West Yorkshire. The relatively humid atmospheric condition of Lancashire was an additional geographic feature favouring cotton spinning, causing threads to snap less frequently. Water as a source of power is no longer a widespread factor in new location decisions, but it can still be crucial as a coolant in some industrial processes and as a means of disposing of effluent in others. Again, industries which use bulky raw materials tend to be located near the source of that material, especially if considerable weight loss occurs during conversion of that material in the industrial process; a material is 'bulky' if it has a high ratio of volume to value, and transport costs are reduced if such materials are carried for shorter rather than for longer distances. In the case of the steel industry, as the richest deposits of iron ore became depleted and sources of less rich ores came to be used, the calculus of transport costs was changed and new plants tended to be located at Corby and Scunthorpe, near the new sources of ore. Another example of the influence of raw material availability on location is provided by the part of the chemical industry producing alkali at various places in mid-Cheshire using nearby supplies of salt and limestone as well as coal.

The universal availability of electricity has tended to reduce the effect of the proximity to coal as a source of power, and proximity to a market for an industry's products, with the saving in transport costs which it represents, has assumed greater importance. The relative strength of this factor depends among other things on how bulky the other raw materials are and where their source is, and whether location close to one market will greatly increase transport costs to other markets.

Proximity to a plentiful supply of labour, especially skilled or semi-skilled, may be an important cause of particular industries being located in particular places. It may in some cases be an overriding consideration in location decisions. Very large-scale movements of population following new employment opportunities have, as we have seen, taken place in the past. Although some sections of the working population are still highly mobile, particularly but by no means solely in managerial and professional occupations, various social factors have tended to reduce mobility below what it might otherwise be. It has been said that 'of all baggage, human beings are the hardest to move'. Be that as it may, available labour supply has been an important consideration in industrial location decisions particularly in the period since the Second World War, and even since before that time Government policy towards the distribution of industry has been based mainly on the idea of taking work to the workers rather than the other way round. It has done this by offering financial inducements to firms to locate new plants in designated areas of high unemployment.

Location decisions based on labour supply often imply location in a large centre of population, which means that in the case of consumer goods at least, and perhaps also in the case of intermediate goods, the criterion of nearness to a market is also satisfied. The effect of this may be cumulative if a plant is large enough on its own (or in combination with others making a similar decision) to attract more people to work there: they automatically enlarge the local market for consumer goods.

Once a tendency for industrial specialisation in a particular area has been established, the process may often be reinforced by the emergence of external economies of scale which are themselves the result of spatial concentration. External economies of scale are advantages which accrue to an individual firm, which may itself be small, from the fact that it is located in an area where there are other firms in the same industry and the total size of the industry in that area is sufficient to attract ancillary services or industries to the same locality. These advantages come about from the scale of the localised industry as a whole as distinct from the scale of the individual firm in that industry and are thus external to the firm. An example is the attraction of specialist banking and financial services

to the cotton area of Lancashire. Again, improved transport services often result from regional concentration of an industry,
benefiting firms already there and providing an attraction for
further firms to locate in the area. The existence of such external
economies may constitute a reason for new firms to locate in a
traditional area even when the original reasons for the industry
locating there have disappeared. Neither water nor coal matter any
longer as power for textile machinery, and mechanical means of
humidifying the air are sometimes now used in cotton spinning
establishments to counter the vagaries of the natural atmospheric
conditions. Furthermore, man-made fibres have replaced cotton to
a considerable extent. Nevertheless, concentration of textile manufacture persists in the traditional areas, though its total size has been
much affected by foreign competition.

The localisation persists because of the traditional skills which
have been built up among the workforce in the area and the other
external economies which have been mentioned. Indeed, even when
in changed circumstances a particular industry would not be located
in its traditional area if starting again from the beginning, the costs
of transfer elsewhere may keep existing enterprises where they are.
The tendency for industries to remain in their established locations
is known as '**industrial inertia**', which is not intended to imply moral
failing, though it may be a sign of sickness. The calculus of costs
making for inertia or overcoming it can be very complex, but the
siting of new steel plants at Scunthorpe in Lincolnshire and Corby in
Northamptonshire were conspicuous examples of how it can be
overcome; in this case the savings on costs of transporting iron ore
by locating near new sources were reinforced by technological advances economising dramatically on the quantity of coal required to
produce a ton of steel. On the other hand, the Potteries remain as
such despite the discovery of sources of superior clay in Cornwall
where, as a result, the industry is now also represented, and from
where clay as a raw material is now also transported to the older
centre of production.

The fact that some industries are localised is really an application
in geographical terms of the economic principle of **specialisation** or
the division of labour: it is the territorial division of labour. The
principle as applied to individuals is that the production of commodities can be very greatly increased if instead of one person carrying
out all the processes required in the production of that commodity,
the whole process is split into its component tasks and people
specialise in those particular tasks. The extreme example of absence
of division of labour is a subsistence economy, instances of which
have always been poor, i.e. not highly productive. Modern industry
abounds in examples of, and is based on, a refined degree of the

division of labour. The occupations in which people are employed are in principle those in which they have the greatest comparative advantage. In this way the economies derived from the division of labour are maximised. It should be noted that under this dispensation, individuals are not necessarily to be found working at that task at which they are best, but at the task at which their advantages compared with others are greatest. For example, a man may be the best double-bass player for many a mile around, yet if there are others nearly as good and he is also a very good industrial chemist though not the best in the area, his occupation will be determined by where his greater comparative advantage lies. This will be reflected in the relative rates of pay that the different employers find it worthwhile to offer him, and so will determine his occupation (always supposing that he does not have a preference for the lower-paid activity sufficiently strong to outweigh the difference in incomes). The territorial division of labour operates in a similar manner. Regions tend to concentrate on those industrial activities in which they have the greatest comparative advantage, or least comparative disadvantage. This explains why parts of the banks of the Thames, which by nature consist of some of our best arable land, are used to produce motor cars, beer, packaging, refined metals – almost anything but wheat.

The cumulative advantages to an area of concentration of an industry in that area are felt when the industry concerned is growing or operating at a prosperous level. There is the other side of the coin. By definition, such industries have the bulk of their markets outside the regions where they are concentrated. When, for reasons of new competition from elsewhere (e.g. newly industrialising countries), general world economic depression or technological advances rendering their products obsolescent, localised industries experience falling levels of demand, the consequences are felt sharply in the region of their location by businesses generally. Loss of jobs in the basic industries means a reduction of incomes and spending power among the workers immediately concerned. Their consequent reduction in demand for goods and services in the locality has a multiplied effect and whole areas become depressed.

Summary

The search for a definition of industry can be illuminating, though it ends in something rather arbitrary. Industry is a very significant part of the whole British economy. It undergoes changes in response to competition and changes taking place in the international economy. Some kinds of industry tend to be localised in certain areas.

Review Questions

(1) Draw pie charts showing the shares of the main groupings of economic activity (agriculture, manufacturing industry, other industry, services, or any other groupings you care to make) in total employment and total output.

(2) Is the area where you live one in which firms in a particular industry tend to be concentrated? If it is, can you account for it? If it is not, can you identify a few firms in your area and explain their location?

(3) How 'logical' does the Standard Industrial Classification strike you as being?

(4) How would you assess the significance of industry to a country's economy?

Appendix

Detail from Standard Industrial Classification 1980, to show Specimen Activity Heads

DIVISION 2 EXTRACTION OF MINERALS AND ORES OTHER THAN FUELS; MANU-
FACTURE OF METALS, MINERAL PRODUCTS AND CHEMICALS

Class	Group	Activity	
21	210	2100	**EXTRACTION AND PREPARATION OF METALLIFEROUS ORES**

Mining and extraction of metalliferous ores and their preparation (e.g. crushing, concentration, washing). Preparation
of indigenous or imported ores at separately identifiable establishments is included.

22			**METAL MANUFACTURING**
	221	2210	IRON AND STEEL INDUSTRY

(Note: Iron and steel industry as defined by the European
Coal and Steel Community in the Treaty of Paris, 1951.)
Units producing iron and steel products described in Annex 1
to the Treaty. This includes the manufacture of pig iron,
spiegeleisen, high-carbon ferromanganese, primary liquid
steel for casting, steel ingots for remelting and forging, semi-
finished products such as blooms, billets, slabs and bars, hot
rolled wide coils other than finished products, hot finished
products such as rails, sleepers, soleplates, joists, heavy sections 80mm and over, sheet piling, bars and sections of less
than 80mm and flats of less than 150mm, wire rod, tube
rounds and squares, hot-rolled hoop and strip, hot-rolled
sheets under 3mm, plates and sheets of 3mm thickness and
over, and universal plates of 150mm and over. The manufacture of coated products e.g. tinplate, terneplate, blackplate
and galvanised sheets is also included as well as cold rolled
sheet under 3mm, electrical sheet and strip for tinplate. Subsequent work on the same site such as tube making, other cold
forming, casting and forging should be separately identified
and classified to headings 2220, 2234, 2235, 3111 or 3120 as
appropriate.

	222	2220	STEEL TUBES

Manufacture of all types of steel tube and pipe, and fittings
thereof, including conduits, gas cylinders and flexible tubes,
from purchased or transferred materials.

17

223   DRAWING, COLD ROLLING AND COLD FORMING OF STEEL

2234   **Drawing and manufacture of steel wire and steel wire products**
Manufacture of ferrous wire and wire products such as fabricated steel reinforcement for concrete, wire nails, wire netting and wire gauze. Upholstery springs are included, but all other springs of wire are classified to heading 3137/2 (except motor vehicle suspension springs classified to heading 3530).

2235   **Other drawing, cold rolling and cold forming of steel**
Units engaged in cold rolling steel hoop, strip or sheet (over 3mm) from purchased or transferred hot rolled sheet; cold drawing steel bars and shapes from purchased or transferred hot rolled steel bars; and the manufacture of other cold finished products (except wire and wire products) not specified in the ECSC Treaty.

224   NON-FEROUS METALS INDUSTRY
(Note: Production of castings, forgings and pressings is classified to Class 31.)

2245   **Aluminium and aluminium alloys**

1. Primary and secondary aluminium and aluminium alloys unwrought
Refining and smelting primary and secondary aluminium and aluminium alloys.

2. Rolled, drawn, extruded and other semi-manufactured aluminium products

Manufacture of plates, sheets, strip, foil, bars, sections, tubes, wire and wire products, powder and similar semi-manufactured products of aluminium and aluminium alloys. Manufacture of aluminium castings and forgoings is classified to headings 3112 and 3120 respectively.

A meeting of shareholders

2
The Nature and Organisation of Firms

Production is carried out in firms of various kinds. In industry by far the greater part of output is accounted for by companies in the private sector, and by the public corporations or nationalised industries in the public sector of the mixed economy. The private sector consists of firms which are privately owned and controlled, i.e. by individuals either on their own or in combination with each other, and their objectives and behaviour reflect this fact, subject to any legislative regulation which may apply to them. The public sector consists of productive organisations owned and controlled by the state; their objectives are set for them by the government and are arrived at by criteria which may differ from those applying in the private sector. Further consideration of the public sector will be deferred until the last chapter.

Apart from companies, there are a number of other forms of productive organisation in the private sector and it will aid our understanding of companies if two of them – sole proprietorship and partnership – are described first.

Types of Firm

(a) Sole Proprietorship

A **sole proprietorship** or one-man business is the simplest form of organisation possible, being one which is owned and controlled by the one person. He (or she) may have employees, but they are not members of the firm as such. The owner carries on the business entirely at his own risk and is liable to the full extent of his personal assets, even his house and furniture, for the debts of the business; the law makes no distinction between a one-man business and the man himself. On the other hand, if the business prospers, the profit is all his. This prospect is a great magnet to some and, with the value attached to independence from others except through impersonal market forces, is sufficient to draw many into starting or continuing on their own account. It has been observed that sometimes there is

21

an illusory element in the calculation of prospective or realised profit in such a business, consisting of failure to charge the business with the full transfer earnings of the proprietor (what he could earn by selling his services elsewhere) before striking a figure for profit. In other words, there is only a genuine profit if the earnings of the business are more than enough to pay the working owner a virtual wage or salary at his market worth.

There is no legal constraint on anyone becoming a sole trader. However, firstly, if he wishes to carry on his business under a name other than his own, under the Companies Act of 1981 he must disclose his own name on the stationery used in the business and in a prominent notice in all the business's premises. The requirement to register business names was abolished by the 1981 Act, but there are certain kinds of names which may not be used. Secondly, although apart from activities which are illegal in themselves anyone may conduct any kind of business which it is legal to enter, there are legal barriers to entering upon some kinds of activity. Thus the government reserves to itself or bestows upon others a monopoly of certain activities; examples may be found in postal and telephone services. Again, a licence is required before undertaking certain productive activities, such as conveying passengers for a fare, keeping a pub, or practising some professions.

Although there are but few hindrances or formalities in starting a sole proprietorship, this form of business organisation cannot at our present stage of industrial development be considered very important in the context of total industrial output. It is much more commonly found in retailing, farming and the professions, but a relatively small number of specialist manufacturing firms, some of which are sole proprietorships, may play a key role in some industries; and the frequency of sole proprietorship in the construction industry is clear enough. The great advantages of this form of organisation are that it is very responsive to the needs of customers, and that decisions can be reached and implemented with a minimum of delay. Its great disadvantage is that it is constrained to operate on a small scale, a constraint set by the availability of finance.

The financial resources of a sole proprietorship are the businessman's own personal assets, the profits he can make and reinvest in the business, and what he can borrow. He may well be able to borrow from his bank, though not necessarily the amounts which his plans for growth require, nor for a long enough period; if he does not already have a record of growth and success, he may not find it easy to borrow from this source. In the past people in his position frequently turned to someone like 'Aunt Agatha', a maiden aunt in comfortable circumstances and with no commitments, or to a successful local businessman quite glad of an investment opportunity which he could oversee personally and whose detailed management would be in the hands of someone known to him and whose abilities he could judge. Such sources of finance are now very much less common than they were in the past for a number of economic and social reasons: a period of high rates of personal taxation and an era of inflation have whittled away the real value of their resources and the real rate of return from existing businesses has fallen drastically from earlier levels; for what remains to them, Aunt Agatha and relatively successful businessmen may prefer the apparent security, and sometimes the tax advantages, of new types of financial asset rather than take the risk of lending to an individual proprietor.

(b) Partnership

A **partnership** is in many respects like a sole proprietorship except that the business has more than one owner. The main resemblance is that the business is unincorporated, i.e. is not a legal entity (which is not the same as saying, as we shall shortly see, that the law does not recognise the existence of partnership arrangements), so that the partners have unlimited personal liability for the debts of the business. Each active partner has power to bind the others in any contract made on behalf of the business. It is therefore apparent that a very high degree of mutual trust must exist between business partners if their firm is to run successfully. Normally, the maximum number of people who may combine in partnership is twenty, though more are allowed in certain professions.

Forming a partnership may be a way of securing the expansion of a one-man business by bringing in one or more partners who put an amount of capital into the business and who also bring with them their own credit standing or borrowing ability. They may also strengthen the business because they have different kinds of skill or experience, enabling the partners to specialise in different aspects of the business and so reap the benefits of the division of labour. A partnership is usually formed by drawing up a Partnership Agreement, though there is no legal compulsion for such a document to be compiled. In the absence of a Partnership Agreement the arrangement is known as a **partnership-at-will**, which has no restriction on a partner deciding to withdraw at any time (though he would be wise to give adequate notice to the firm's creditors in view of his unlimited liability), and which is regulated by the Partnership Act 1890. If there is an Agreement, then it primarily regulates the obligations and the rights of the partners between each other, with the Act applying on any matters on which the Agreement is silent. Thus, for example, unless there is an Agreement, and unless it states how the profits of the business are to be divided, they are shared equally according to the Act. Again, if the partners wish to pay themselves salaries out of the business, they must say so in a Partnership Agreement, as none are payable under the Act.

It is possible to have one or more sleeping partners. In this context a **sleeping partner** is one who provides capital but takes no part in the running of the business; otherwise, his rights and obligations are those of any other partner. It is also possible to have a **limited partnership**: a partner may have his liability for the debts of the business limited to the amount of capital he has put in; such a partner must be dormant, and may be a company. There must always be at least one partner with unlimited liability. It will be apparent that the greater the proportion of the firm's capital that is protected by limited liability, the more exposed to risk are those partners whose liability is not limited. Such an arrangement is therefore not very common, but it does have certain advantages. It may encourage an active partner who retires, not to withdraw his capital; and it may be a useful way, on the one hand, for a partnership to increase its capital and, on the other hand, for an individual or company to invest in a partnership without taking an active part in its business.

The costs of forming a partnership are less than those of forming a company and this is an advantage if the business is small, and it may sometimes be seen as an advantage that – unlike a company – a partnership need not publish its annual accounts. In a partnership it is usually possible to maintain personal contact with customers or clients and with employees, because of the relatively small size to which partnerships are usually constrained. It is an advantage shared by small companies. The advantages of sole proprietorships, which we have noticed, are shared in greater or lesser degree by partnerships. In addition, partnerships tend to have a greater measure of continuity than do one-man businesses; this applies over both a short period, because a partnership can more easily absorb absences due to, say, holidays and illness, and the longer run, because a partnership has a better chance of surviving the death or retirement of a member.

The death of a partner can, however, make it difficult to maintain the partnership. If his interest in the partnership formed the bulk of his personal assets, then the requirement for his estate to pay Capital Transfer Tax may require a withdrawal of capital from the business which, depending on its liquidity at the time, may place a very great strain on the firm if a suitable person is not readily available to come into the business with capital of his own. It is in general not always easy for a partner to withdraw and if he does, it may be very damaging to the business.

Whilst the expansion of a business is usually less constrained by the limitations of finance if it is a partnership than if it is a one-man business, the financial factor can still be a severe limitation on growth because the number of partners is limited by law and, even if it were not, it would in practice be difficult to organise partnerships of the size and in the numbers required for a modern industrial economy. The fact that the large glass-manufacturing firm Pilkingtons was until a few years ago a partnership provides an exception to prove the rule. Partnerships are most commonly found in commerce, the professions and the service trades. They are no longer quantitatively important in industry, although, as with sole proprietorships, their role in some industries is not negligible.

(c) Companies

The limitations on the size of enterprises imposed by the financial constraints of individual ownership and of individuals acting in partnership were felt in foreign trade as long ago as the thirteenth century, a very long time before the accelerated growth and development of industry which began in the latter part of the eighteenth century and which we call the Industrial Revolution. These pressures resulted in the formation of companies, which were the forebears of the kind of organisation which we know under that name today. The earliest kind were the Regulated Companies, which were given exclusive trading rights with a particular area by the Crown and to which the members, who carried on their trade individually subject to the rules of the company, made contributions to finance common services such as trading stations overseas and ambassadors to potentates. An example was the Company of Merchant Adventurers.

In time, the size of the tasks confronting these organisations became larger than they could manage and there emerged Joint Stock Companies to take their place. Such companies were created either by Royal Charter (as the Regulated Companies had been) or, after the Revolution of 1688 which brought the ascendancy of Parliament, by Act of Parliament. They were incorporated as legal entities and might have the privilege of limited liability on the part of stockholders for the debts of the company. The Bank of England, which was founded in 1694 by Act of Parliament, also obtained a Charter later in the same year (it was nationalised in 1946), and was given limited liability by a later Act. The Hudson's Bay Company and the P&O Steam Navigation Company are other examples of enterprises still operating which were founded as Joint Stock Companies.

The power to limit stockholders' liability was much sought-after as the Industrial Revolution gathered pace and with the need to amass together larger amounts of capital from a wider spread of shareholders than had been known before. Railways, for example, did not come cheap. The method of obtaining limited liability, however, was both slow and costly since it meant promoting a private bill in Parliament. Industrial enterprises were therefore widely and simply taking the form of unlimited liability companies and the inevitable incidence of failure among industrial firms at such a time of rapid change brought distress to many people who had entrusted their capital to them. In 1855 a Companies Act was passed which, with its amending Act of 1862, made limited liability available to any company incorporated by registration with an official to be called the Registrar of Companies. This immediately made it easier for those promoting companies for industrial and other productive activity to find subscribers of capital, for the latter could henceforth measure the extent of the risk they were undertaking by the amount they subscribed. It made it easier for businessmen and those with industrial skills to join with those with capital, and legal recognition of companies incorporated by registration meant that investors could spread their risk with greater assurance.

The broad pattern for companies set by the Acts of 1855 and 1862 is that which still exists, though there have been many amendments since then. The two most recent Companies Acts, those of 1980 and 1981, are of great importance and bring in changes required by agreed policies of the European Economic Community. We need not concern ourselves here with the detail of changes over the last hundred years and more, nor with how much of the present position is due to domestic initiative for reforms in the UK and how much to the European Commission in its desire for improvements and more uniform practice throughout the Community. The Acts which at present apply, range over the period from 1948, when the legislation was codified, to 1981; the legislation is now being codified again and industrialists and their professional advisers who have to see that companies comply with it will no doubt be glad when this has been accomplished.

The central features of the company form of productive organisation are, and have been since the Acts of 1855 and 1862, firstly that they are corporate bodies and that they obtain this status of being legal personalities by registration with the Registrar of Companies; thus a company has an existence independent of that of its owners. When a shareholder dies, the business continues; this is much less likely to happen in the case of a sole proprietorship, and in the case of a partnership at the very least the partnership agreement has to be redrawn, and the difficulties may be more severe as we have seen. Secondly, the liability of shareholders is limited to the amount of capital they have subscribed or agreed to subscribe. We have already noticed the advantages of this arrangement from the point of view of the ability to raise capital. It has the effect of transferring some risk from those supplying the firm with capital to those supplying it with goods and services, and it is for this reason that companies are obliged to reveal at the end of their name that their members' liability is limited. Thirdly, the company's profits belong to the shareholders, as does the company itself, and profit which is distributed is divided between shareholders proportionally to their holdings; that, at least, is the basic position which applies to shareholdings of ordinary shares.

In seeking registration for a proposed company there must be submitted to the Registrar of Companies for approval a Memorandum of Association and Articles of Association. The Memorandum states the name of the company and its registered address, i.e. the place where its affairs as a company are dealt with as distinct from the carrying on of its business (the two addresses may or may not be the same); the amount of share capital of the company; and the objects of the company. A company may not do anything not included among the statement of the objects in the Memorandum and therefore the objects are usually expressed very widely so as to give the directors of the company freedom to expand or modify the company's range of activities if profitable opportunities should present themselves in the future, or to adapt the scope of the company's activities as a defensive measure in changed commercial circumstances.

The Articles of Association comprise the rules governing the running of the company as a company. They deal with the rights attaching to the holding of shares or different types of share in the company; the issue and transfer of shares; the frequency of and procedure at company meetings; any provisions as to the keeping of accounts beyond the requirements laid down in the legislation; the powers and qualifications of directors; the appointment of the company's officers; and like matters.

The minimum number of subscribers of capital who may form any company is, since 1980, two; and there is now no maximum for any company. Companies may be either public or private. A **public company** is one with limited liability, whose memorandum states that the company is to be a public company and whose allotted share capital is not less than the minimum authorised by legislation, at present £50,000. Shares allotted must be paid up to at least 25 per cent of their nominal value plus the whole of any premiums payable. Thus the paid-up capital of a public company may be as little as £12,500. Any company not fulfilling each of these conditions is a private company. A **private company** may not offer its shares for subscription by the public, nor allot any shares with a view to any of them being offered to the public. A private company may in its Articles restrict the right of shareholders to transfer shares, but it is no longer required to do so. A public limited company must use either those words or their abbreviation plc or the Welsh equivalent at the end of its name: a private limited company must use the word 'limited' or its abbreviation ltd or Welsh equivalent at the end of its name.

When a private company, having submitted its Memorandum and Articles to the Registrar, receives approval in the form of a certificate of incorporation it may thenceforth commence business. Not so a public company: after incorporation it must first comply with the requirements as to allotment of shares and paid up capital which have been mentioned above, and then be issued with a trading certificate; this authorises it to commence business.

Public and private companies alike are now obliged to file their profit and loss account and balance sheet with the Registrar, which is equivalent to publishing them, and all shareholders must receive them. However, small and medium-sized companies (which for this purpose are defined by reference to their turnover, their balance sheet total and the number of their employees, but which must also be private companies) are exempt from the obligation to file full accounts, though full accounts must be provided to shareholders. A small company need not submit a profit and loss account and its balance sheet may be in a shortened form with fewer supplementary notes. A medium-sized company may present its profit and loss account to the Registrar in a slightly abbreviated form and particulars of turnover need not be given, though full information must go to shareholders.

Final accounts (i.e. profit and loss account and balance sheet) must be set out in one of a choice of forms laid down in the 1981 Act. Thus, for example, it is permissible in the profit and loss account either to show the company's costs according to the kind of item on which the costs were incurred (e.g. raw materials, wages and salaries, rent and rates) or according to the part of the company's activity for which the expenditure was incurred (e.g. cost of sales, distribution costs, administrative expenses). Another kind of choice permitted is that between historical cost accounting and current cost accounting, the latter being designed to remove the distorting effects of inflation on figures purporting to show a company's profit and financial position. This choice is a matter of accounting rules rather than forms of presentation and analysis. The Act lays down for the first time certain accounting principles on which the accounts required by statute must be based, though most of these were already common practice because they had been the subject of accounting standards adopted by the accountancy profession in this country. Nevertheless, their inclusion in legislation is a departure from the traditional approach to company accounts in the UK, which has been not to specify detailed principles but to insist that the accounts must present a full and fair view of a company's transactions and financial position. The latter doctrine is ultimately still preserved, however, as departures from the principles and the forms of presentation laid down are permitted in special circumstances in which a full and fair view requires this to be done; in such cases attention must be drawn to it and the reasons given. In this way the uniformity of practice sought in the EEC may be overridden where it is sensible to do so, and this British concept is being adopted in the other member countries of the EEC also.

Another major change has been to give all companies the power to purchase their own shares, which is a complete reversal of the rule existing hitherto. The Act also requires disclosure of loans by a company to directors, and restricts them; and it requires disclosure of any material interest a director or officer of a company may have in any transaction undertaken by the company. An individual or group of individuals acting together to buy shares in a company, and whose holdings reach 5 per cent of the company's shares, must disclose this fact; this is in order to give a company warning of a situation from which a takeover bid could be mounted.

Since the minimum number of subscribers is now the same for public and private companies, and since the paid-up capital requirement for a public company is so small, the main differences between them are, firstly, that a private company may not offer any of its shares or debentures to the public, nor allot any with a view to their being offered for sale to the public; and, secondly, that only a private company may seek qualification as a small or medium-sized company for the purpose of gaining exemption from the requirement to file full accounts. The latter may sometimes be seen as an advantage, the former as a disadvantage of private company status. There are also a number of other differences, which in general are advantages enjoyed by private companies. It seems very likely that because of these, many companies which were public in 1980 may now have chosen to become private, particularly those which are wholly-owned subsidiaries; equally, the circumstances of some previously private companies in relation to the new legislation have persuaded them to re-register as public companies. In 1980 there was an average of approximately 800,000 companies on the register. During 1980 the number converting from public to private was 27, a fairly representative number as compared with the previous few years; during 1981 and 1982 this figure rose to 885 and 2,340 respectively. Conversions from private to public have also risen, but only to a relatively small extent.

Company Shareholders and Boards of Directors

The first decision made in a business is whether or not to invest in it in the first place. Having made the decision to invest, life for a sole proprietor or active partner is thenceforth a continuous round of policy making, decision taking and carrying out of those decisions within the business.

In a company, however, a shareholder as such is not in this position. If he happens to be a director or an employee as well, his active role derives from that fact alone. It would not be possible in a company with a large number of shareholders for them, its owners, to be actively involved in its running. The holders of ordinary voting shares do have legal control of their company and one of the ways in which this is manifested is by voting at the election of directors at company meetings. Usually, though there are sometimes spectacular exceptions reported in newspapers, the shareholders play little if any role in proposing names. The board of directors elects its own chairman, who thereby also becomes chairman of the company.

The directors of a public company may be required to be shareholders provided that this qualification is fixed at a general meeting of the company. The function of the board is to be responsible for the company's policy. It is now, since 1980, a duty of directors in deciding policy issues to have regard to the interests of the company's employees as well as those of its members, but they owe this duty to the company alone. Its members may serve either part-time or full-time, in which case they will also undertake an executive role. This has the advantage of combining a due part in policy making with the carrying out of policy in a particular department or area of the company's activities. Intimate knowledge of what the policy is intended to achieve in a particular area, and of board policy over the whole field of activities, ensures that executive action in the various fields is closely aligned. The corresponding disadvantage is that such a director may become immersed in executive detail to the detriment of thinking about company policy as a whole. Part-time directors frequently hold other directorships as well, and this may bring a breadth of experience and vision to bear on a company's affairs.

A chairman is sometimes also appointed to be managing director, in which case he is in a very powerful position indeed and is usually a full-time executive director with responsibilities to his board commensurate with his powers. Otherwise, another person may be appointed as managing director; he will take his policy line from board decisions, but at meetings of the board has the same rights to argue the case for or against a proposed course of action as does any other director. In addition to a managing director there may also be appointed a general manager directly responsible to him for the day-to-day running of the business. It is possible for there to be a general manager with no managing director, in which case he would require to attend meetings of the board without being a member of it. Such a situation can only be expected to work well if none of the directors is in a full-time executive position with the company.

The executive directors are, by the nature of things, in fairly close contact with each other and, in addition, may meet together at frequent intervals for the purpose of co-ordinating executive action. Daily or weekly intervals for this purpose are not uncommon. There is always a danger of executive directors, perhaps unwittingly and by imperceptible degrees, making a policy decision on their own which should require board sanction or at least the agreement of the managing director. Meetings of executive directors help to obviate this as well as being conducive to efficient co-ordination. Particularly if there are non-executive directors, however, such meetings are not a substitute for formal meetings of the full board, at which policy questions are settled and recommendations drawn up for presentation to company meetings of shareholders. These may be the annual (or more frequent) general meeting, or extraordinary meetings to deal with particular kinds of business concerning the company as such and as specified in the company's articles of association.

The annual general meeting of shareholders votes on such matters as the appointment or renewal of appointment of directors, the adoption of the company's accounts, the declaration of dividends to shareholders and the appointment or re-appointment of auditors. Changes in the capital structure of the company and amendments to the memorandum and articles of association usually require an extraordinary general meeting to be called. It is most common, however, for such meetings to take place immediately preceding an ordinary meeting on the same day and at the same place.

The shareholders of a large company are almost always large in number and scattered throughout the country. Many individual shareholders, especially if their stake in the company is not a very large one, feel that there is little practical point in their undertaking the costs and spending the time on attending company meetings; if things do not go to their liking it is always open to them to sell their shares. Small attendances at meetings are therefore common, though by no means universal. Voting rights at meetings are proportional to the number of ordinary voting shares held, and a shareholder may appoint a proxy to vote on his behalf and either according to his instructions or at discretion. Directors commonly provide an opportunity for proxy voting by means of forms which are sent out with the statutory papers calling a meeting, inviting shareholders to appoint the chairman or one of the other directors as proxy. It is uncommon for an individual shareholder to have sufficient knowledge to form a reasonable view contrary to a board recommendation, and if he has, but he is not a large and influential shareholder, he may feel it better to sell than to oppose. In this way the board may muster a large total number of votes in addition to those derived from their own holdings. Some companies are clearly controlled by their directors because the latter own more than 50 per cent of the voting shares, and there are some very large industrial companies in this position. It is evident that actual control does not, however, require as much as 50 per cent of the shares on the part of an individual or group acting together, whether that group be the board or some other group of shareholders. In fact, the total holdings of the board members in many large companies is very low indeed and is sometimes of the order of 1 per cent.

In this way the growth of large limited liability companies has given rise to what has been called the divorce of ownership from control, or the managerial revolution. This is a phenomenon which was first observed clearly in the USA half a century ago (by A. A. Berle and G. C. Means 1948), and has been studied again more recently in this country. In addition to this development, another has arisen to erode the position of the individual shareholder. The demise of Aunt Agatha has already been referred to. Personal shareholdings of the ordinary shares of UK companies listed on the Stock Exchange have been falling steadily as a proportion of the total market value of those shares for the last few decades at least. This reflects an increase in holdings by insurance and pension funds, unit trusts and other financial institutions. In 1957 personal holdings amounted to over 65 per cent of the total market value; by 1975 they had fallen to under 40 per cent; and by 1980 the rate of fall had accelerated to the point where such holdings were about 25 per cent of the total. This does not mean that the market value of personal shareholdings in total shrank in absolute size; on the contrary, it increased in the context of a more than seven-fold increase in the total market value of shares. Some of this increase arose from an expansion in the number of companies and shares listed, and some from the rise in their average market value. The obverse of this picture is that between 1957 and 1980 there has been a steady rise in the proportion of the total market value of ordinary shares held by financial institutions such as insurance companies, pension funds, investment trust companies and unit trusts, from something under 20 per cent to something approaching 60 per cent.

It has to be remembered that the figures we are considering are of total market value, not number of shares. It is conceivable that part of the marked difference in the trends may be due to higher capital growth of the investments of financial institutions as compared with those of individuals; this could be the case either because the institutions have had a greater propensity to steer their investments towards capital growth rather than income, or because institutional investment has been generally more successful than personal investment, or both. However that may be, it cannot account for the very large change in the relative positions of personal and institutional shareholdings.

This change has implications for the control of large industrial companies. Financial institutions have become large shareholders. They are not infrequently in a position to influence a company's board should they wish to do so. They do not always wish to do so, partly because if a company's progress is turning out much as they expected when buying the shares, they feel no need to do so, and partly because of a belief that their business is investment and that there is something undesirable about their exercising control (or, probably more important, being seen to exercise control) over industrial companies. It would be easy for critics to say that they are not qualified by industrial knowledge and experience to do this. Nevertheless the financial institutions are becoming more active in their involvement in those affairs of companies which are board-level matters. For example, a very large 'golden handshake' roused the open opposition of a pension fund holding shares in the company concerned. Most of the influence of the financial institutions is, however, exercised privately. This can be very effective because the board of a company with large institutional shareholdings has a sword of Damocles over its head: companies prefer the price of their shares on the Stock Exchange to be kept at reasonably high levels because this makes it cheaper for them to raise further capital should the need arise; and the disposal of large institutional shareholdings would permanently shift the supply and demand position for the company's shares on the market, and in a disadvantageous direction.

It is a debatable matter whether the influence of institutional shareholders should be more frequently and more openly exercised. Their presence is a check on the control exercised by boards of directors, but from the point of view of the individual investor they may be seen as another concentration of power which may not always act for his good. In this connection, however, it has to be remembered that the funds of which the financial institutions dispose consist of the savings, for the most part, of perfectly ordinary people – they are the funds from which private pensions are eventually drawn, and life and endowment insurance policy benefits are eventually paid. They also include investments made by large numbers of people through unit trusts rather than directly in the shares of companies. Pension funds have grown very rapidly during the last few decades, and there is now an investment element in much insurance business. The decline of the personal shareholder as such represents in fairly large measure a change in the medium through which personal savings are routed and assets held. But it has brought a higher concentration of financial investment decisions into a few hands and is affecting the control of a good many industrial companies.

The Organisation of Firms

Productive activity is carried out in firms by, in the first place, reaching decisions about what is to be done and, secondly, carrying out these decisions. We are not for the present concerned with the principles upon which decisions of various kinds are reached, but with the organisational structures within which they are made. In the typical sole proprietorship or partnership, the formation and execution of policy are relatively simple; that is not to say that it is necessarily at all easy to reach some of the decisions which have to be made, but simply that the number of people involved in making and carrying them out is smaller and that co-ordination presents fewer problems than in a larger organisation because few people are involved. In a larger business, however, whether it be constituted as a company or not, those who carry out decisions are different members of the organisation from those who make them, and there will be different levels of management to which various kinds of decision can be delegated. Once decisions are made they must be communicated to those whose function it is to implement them, and a reverse communication process is also required, one of reporting or feedback. This is for two reasons: first, to satisfy a decision maker that his decisions are being correctly carried out; and second, to inform him of any new developments which may cause him to wish to modify an earlier decision. A further requirement of a smoothly functioning organisation is that the responsibilities of each of the various managers at all levels shall be clearly delineated and understood by all concerned. All tasks must be allocated to someone's sphere of responsibility; there must be no duplication in the allocation of any task and no one should be responsible to more than one other person.

The existence of delegation gives rise to hierarchies and organisational structures. There is no one single structure, the best in all circumstances, to which firms either ought to or do conform. Rather, firms engaged in different activities will need different modes of organising those activities; and an organisation's objectives, its legal status (e.g. a public corporation as against a private enterprise) and the course of its past development may all influence its organisational structure. To illustrate the last point, a firm which had grown to a certain size by building on a small beginning in the production of a particular kind of article is unlikely to have the same structure as a firm of similar size which had grown from a similarly small beginning, but whose growth had in large part taken the form of entering diverse lines of production, possibly by the absorption of other companies. Organisational structures are not absolute and fixed, but are dependent on various circumstances which may be relevant to particular firms, and a structure may change as a firm's size, range of activities and objectives or key decisions change.

The establishment of lines of authority, delegation, responsibility and communications may be expressed in the form of an organisation chart which sets out these relationships. Such a chart in a simple form might be as set out in Figure 2.1.

This particular chart sets out an organisation based on line management; that is to say it lays down clearly separate departments with one person in charge of each and these persons are of equal status. This form of organisation yields a clear definition of responsibilities and spheres of action and is thus conducive to good control, with the way clear to efficient action unhampered by ambiguity. On the other hand, however, it tends to impede communications between departments and, according to the chart, they need to pass through departmental heads. This red tape is less serious, and more easily ignored, in a smaller rather than in a larger organisation. Larger organisations tend to be more formalised and bureaucratic than do smaller ones. Whilst an agreed and commonly understood structure and procedure are necessary, however, the formal structure becomes subject to informal amendment as time goes on and new situations arise: a Nelson eye can be a useful tool of management.

Line management involves a chain of command from top to bottom, and is a typical way of organising the central activities of a firm, e.g. the manufacturing and selling of a firm's product. There are, however, some functions which are common to several or all departments, e.g. personnel management, data processing, or running the firm's vehicles. Whilst it is possible in principle for each line department to carry out such functions for itself, there are advantages in centralising them into specialist departments. In this way greater expertise is placed at the disposal of line management and economies are achieved in the total cost of the services to the firm. Thus, some firms have a typing pool managed by a staff department instead of each line department employing its own typists. These functional departments are hierarchical within themselves but not

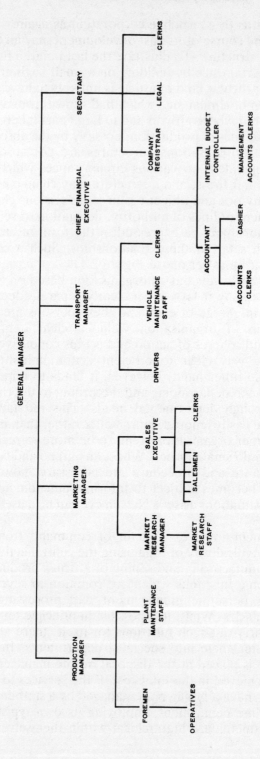

Figure 2.1

within the company as a whole. That is, they have responsibility for carrying out a service to line departments but no authority beyond their own staff. Some functional departments have a role which is designated as 'staff' in contrast to 'line', and in this case their function is in principle advisory rather than executive, and they obtain their success by persuading their line colleagues in discussion in which their specialist knowledge is brought to bear. Examples are personnel, organisation and methods itself, legal and corporate planning departments. There are inherent dangers of conflict between staff and line managers in such arrangements, and of employees being subject to instructions from more than one source. The functions of a personnel department are both advisory and executive, as it will be responsible for the fulfilment of the firm's obligations as an employer and ultimately, for the conduct of industrial relations; its other functions, like recruitment, career development, the fitting of round pegs into round holes, and the morale of the company's employees, are advisory.

A simplified representation of part of a functional form of organisation is as shown in Figure 2.2. Such a form of organisation has a degree of flexibility beyond what is possible when all functions are the responsibility solely of line departments themselves. Better quality and therefore more expensive expertise can be afforded when it is applied across the whole of the firm, and experience can be passed on to subordinates and colleagues.

Most organisations are a mixture of line and staff, and diagrammatic representation is more useful for illustrating principles than describing the total reality of the working of actual organisations. In practice an organisational chart is in any case usually supported by a manual, rule book or set of guidelines defining more precisely and in greater or lesser detail the delegation of responsibilities and limitations of authority in each of the various management functions. Such rules, rather than the organisation chart as such, may be an important factor in causing an organisation to work well. On the other hand, however, it may sometimes be the case that the existence of detailed organisation manuals and instructions about procedures is a sign that a particular structure is not working well. The degree of self-consciousness in organisations varies and is greatest, for better or worse, when manifested in the explicit existence of an Organisation and Methods Department. Many organisations have had little design effort applied to them but, like Topsy, have just 'growed'. The fact that the people concerned are used to a structure and a set of relationships may be a good reason for the structure to be allowed to persist. In the realm of organisation there is more than one way of skinning a rabbit, though there are also many ways which will not be satisfactory.

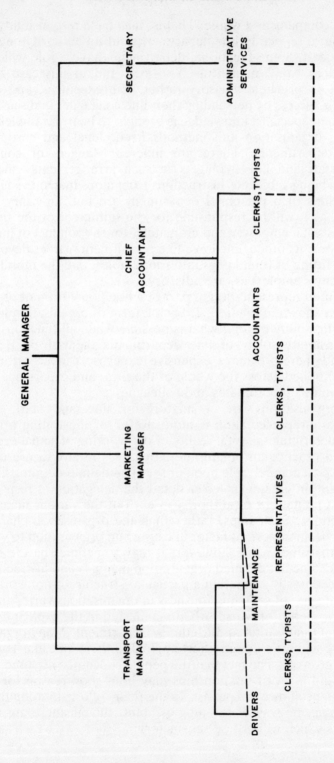

Figure 2.2

The personality of the chief executive will have much to do with the form of a company's organisation. Not only may a chief executive's personality affect markedly the actual organisation of a company but the idea of the centrality of the chief executive's role in the company's activities is sometimes given reflection in a form of organisation chart (see Figure 2.3)

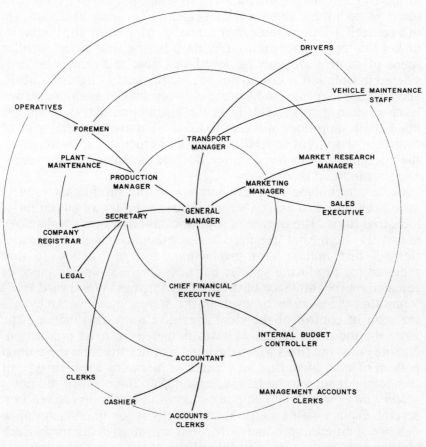

Figure 2.3

As can be seen, this chart consists of concentric circles and functionaries of equal status are on the same circumference. There are also other ways of setting out organisational relationships on paper, which some find more enlightening than others.

The number of subordinates supervised directly by any manager is known as his span of control. Obviously as this span becomes wider (i.e., as the number of his immediate subordinates becomes larger) the less attention can a manager pay to the activities of each of them. From this, it is often supposed that closer control is achieved by smaller spans. This is not really so. Consider the matter from the beginning, i.e. the number of employees on, say, the shop floor who are required for the basic task of producing the firm's planned output. With this number of employees, a narrowing of spans of control in the management tiers above them (culminating in the single manager ultimately responsible) results in a need to insert an additional layer of management. (Try some arithmetic on this yourself.) This increase in the number of levels in the hierarchy makes the top manager more remote from the shop floor. Smaller spans of control are only achieved at a cost and cannot be considered in isolation. They do not necessarily lead to tighter control, and a choice may have to be made between smaller spans and fewer levels of management. This is on the assumption that the required number of shop-floor workers is fixed. If narrowing the span of control of shop-floor supervisors increases efficiency so as to reduce the operative labour force required, then the balance of the argument is modified accordingly.

Certain technological characteristics of the production process have been found to exert a strong influence on the organisation of industrial firms. The degree of sophistication of a firm's technology may vary from that required for continuous mass production, through that required for production in large batches, to that required for producing smaller batches. One well-known piece of research on the influence of these characteristics (Woodward 1965) found that the number of levels in the management hierarchy and the span of control of the chief executive tended to increase the more the industrial technology was designed for mass production. Not only this, but firms which deviated significantly from the normal pattern of span of control and length of hierarchy for their type of technology tended to be less successful than those which did not.

Very large industrial companies, conglomerates diversified into several distinct fields of productive activity or manufacturing a number of different products, are often organised in divisions. Each division (which may be a subsidiary company) may be responsible for all the operations connected with its product. Alternatively, the total organisation or group may be divided by function and product, so that certain common functions like finance and personnel, and perhaps purchasing and marketing if the circumstances are suitable, are carried out centrally in functional departments. Then each product will have a division containing its line departments, such as production and sales, and there will be central departments dealing with accounts, personnel and so on. The variations in practice are legion.

Summary

Productivity activity takes place in firms. These vary in the form they take and the structure through which they are managed. There are advantages and disadvantages to the different forms an enterprise may take. The power to limit liability has had significant effects on the size of companies. Large size is accompanied by problems of organisation.

References and Further Reading

Berle, A. A. and Means, G. G. (1948) *The Modern Corporation and Private Property*, MacMillan.
Florence, P. S. (1961) *Ownership, Control and Success of Large Companies*, Sweet and Maxwell.
Woodward, Joan (1965) *Industrial Organisation: Theory and Practice*, Oxford University Press.

Review Questions

(1) Making your own assumptions about the number of employees required for certain tasks on the shop floor, and about the spans of control of supervisors and managers above those supervisors and so on, experiment with narrowing the spans of control and observe the results on the number of tiers of management.

(2) What, if anything, do you think should be done about the decline in personal shareholdings relative to those of financial institutions?

(3) Do you think that institutional shareholders should play a more active role in the affairs of industrial companies in which they are major shareholders?

(4) What distinctive contribution can part-time directors make to the policy decision making of a company?

To what extent do managerial objectives identify with those of the firm?

3
The Objectives and Performance of Industrial Firms

The Objectives of Firms

It was noticed in the previous chapter that the objects of a company are required to be set out in its Memorandum of Association. What is to be found there is a statement of objects in the sense of the kinds of productive activity in which the company is permitted to engage. The ultimate purpose of forming an industrial company, however, goes beyond the particular activities which it carries out, such as the manufacture of hand-tools, confectionery or whatever it may be: businesses are formed in the hope and with the expectation of making a profit from the particular activities in which they are engaged. Once a business is formed, profit is an essential condition for its remaining in existence, though there may be temporary periods of loss. The profit motive, however, is in practice supplemented and modified by other goals on the part of firms and groups which are constituent parts of firms.

Profit Maximisation

In economic theory it is convenient to make the assumption that firms set out not only to make a profit but to make that profit as large as is rendered possible by all the circumstances affecting the firm's costs of production and demand for its product. This is known as the assumption of **profit maximisation** as the objective of firms. This assumption has certain specific implications for the way firms are conceived to behave, and also for the way the economy as a whole is conceived to function. We shall not be pursuing these implications in their full rigour here, but we do need to notice some points about them.

One of these implications is that a firm will continue to increase its output as long as it adds more to its sales revenue than to its costs. The amount by which total sales revenue rises when a further unit of product is sold is the **marginal revenue**. (This may, but need not, be the same as the price for which the final unit is sold, and will not be the same – but less – if the larger output entails selling the whole output at a lower price per unit). The amount by which total cost rises when one further unit of output is produced is the **marginal cost**, an idea further explained in Chapter 6. The marginal cost is conceived as being bound to start rising after output reaches a certain point (and if this were not so, the whole world's output of that particular product could be produced by one plant alone). From this, there is some point at which marginal cost equals marginal revenue, i.e. some size of output below which to refrain from producing and selling an extra unit of output means missing the opportunity to add more to sales proceeds than to costs, and above which production and sale of the last unit of output causes more to be added to total costs than to total sales proceeds. At that output profit is maximised and the firm is in equilibrium. Being in equilibrium means that the firm will not alter its output nor its behaviour in any way, so long as the conditions determining demand for its product and the conditions determining the supply of its factors of production remain unchanged – so that their prices also remain unchanged.

The implications of the profit maximisation assumption extend beyond the traditional theory of the individual firm, and this basic assumption makes it possible to develop a coherent body of theory ramifying across a whole economy. This body of theory is a useful tool for dealing with questions of economic welfare and policy, not excluding policy relating to industry. However, empirical study of industrial firms, of which there has been a great deal, tends to show that the profit maximisation assumption, at least in any strict form, is not borne out in practice.

We have seen that in order to maximise profit it is necessary to produce that size of output at which marginal cost equals marginal revenue. These concepts have been found alien to most businessmen's way of thinking. They are also concepts which on the cost side are different from the information which cost accounts in practice reveal, and on the revenue side suppose businessmen to have more knowledge than they actually do have about the effect of a change in the price of their product on the demand for it and hence on changes in their total sales revenue. Beyond this inability to pursue strict profit maximisation, or to recognise whether or not it has been achieved, firms in practice wish to pursue other objectives, some of which may indeed be subservient to the profit motive in the long run, but none of which are compatible with seizing any and every opportunity to maximise profit in the short run.

Sales Maximisation

In the real world the objectives and behaviour of firms are greatly influenced by their nature and organisational structure, matters which were discussed in the previous chapter. The divorce of ownership from control, for example, has opened up the possibility of directors and managers pursuing objectives related to their own interests rather than those of shareholders. The personal remuneration of senior management tends to be related to the size of their companies so that they have a considerable interest in the growth of their firms. This observation has led to the suggestion that the objective of industrial firms is to be found in the maximisation of sales revenue, subject to some minimum profit level being attained. This minimum profit constraint is required in order to keep shareholders content and to maintain the stock exchange price of the company's shares. The reason for wishing the latter is that it makes it easier and cheaper for the company to raise further capital in the market if the price of its shares is relatively high.

There is, however, a difficulty in accepting the suggestion that firms pursue the objective of maximising sales revenue: its pursuit requires just as much knowledge of their marginal revenue on the part of managers as does the pursuit of profit maximisation, and we have seen that in fact usually very little is known about marginal revenue. It should be noted that this particular objective requires firms to maximise the value, not the quantity, of their sales. The theory behind it still requires firms to know exactly by how much the price of the product will fall following any given expansion of output and with the existing state of demand. That is, the marginal revenue would need to be known, just as for profit maximisation. Thus, although the observation that the objectives of firms are influenced by their organisational structure may be accepted as realistic, this particular theory stemming from it, that the objective of firms is sales revenue maximisation, is not so easily accepted. However, it is not the only suggestion that has been put forward about objectives in the light of the nature and organisational structure of firms.

Managerial Objectives

Building on the observations made about the passing of control from owners to directors, and then the ascendant position gained by managers, many have come to see the objectives of firms as being identified with the objectives of managers themselves. There are various insights as to what these objectives may be, each with its elements of truth: the incidence of various objectives will vary with the personalities involved and with the environmental constraints to which a firm is subject. One idea about managerial objectives is that managers are interested in the number of subordinates working under them and the total salary bill for which they are responsible, because these give a measure of their relative importance within the organisation; this importance is desired for its own sake and because their own salaries may be related to it. Other matters in which they are interested include their fringe benefits, such as a company car and executive pension scheme. On the other hand, fringe benefits in the form of share options or bonuses related to profit tend to exert an influence on managerial behaviour in the direction of increasing profit; and since many managers are-part of the shareholding community, and are sociologically similar to personal shareholders in many respects, the difference between their general interests may not be very great. Lastly, it is held that managers are interested in acquiring the power to make decisions about investment in new projects and to increase their department's share of the company funds budgeted for investment. Managers obtain satisfaction, or **utility**, from each of these things, and their objective is seen as the maximisation of their utility function, the best combination of utilities from the various sources which they can attain.

One consequence of managerialism has been seen as a lessening of the entrepreneurial spirit in the industrialised economies. The managers have secured control over key decisions in the enterprise, but the shareholders take the consequences of those decisions. This has altered the weights in the balance of risk and reward. The gains to a manager from, say, a successful investment decision are for him less than the penalty for failure. The preservation of his position, his personal survival as a manager, now carry more weight than the successful outcome of new ventures. For him, the 'down-side risk' is greater than its opposite. Management has therefore, on a perfectly rational calculation, become more timid and will not pursue profit maximisation even if that pursuit is possible; a business executive is not an entrepreneur. Such is the perception, and so runs the argument. The matter is eminently discussable.

There are variations on the general theme of managerial objectives. One such variation, applying to owner-managers rather than salaried executives, recognises leisure, which is obtained outside the firm rather than inside it, as part of the managerial utility function whose maximisation therefore requires a trade-off to be made between leisure and income. More of one implies less of the other; golf twice a week instead of once is at the cost of business activity conducing directly to profits. As with all maximising activity, this implies a marginal equality, but since the satisfaction of the leisure is subjective and the lost contribution to profits (the **opportunity cost** of a round of golf) is imponderable, the calculation cannot be made with any refinement. Difficulties may arise if management colleagues make different estimates of these matters! (It must not be assumed, however, that such differences necessarily contain an objection that a golfing manager is too often on the course; some may wish him there more, not less, frequently – for whatever reason!)

A similar, but not identical view, is that managers and workforce alike put a value on leading a quiet life rather than welcoming or tolerating the pressures on them which are associated with profit-maximising levels of activity. This perception may apply to two distinct aspects of the operations of firms. The first is called **organisational slack**. It is usually the case that a firm is not going 'all out' in the pursuit of profits and that it would be possible for it, under sufficient pressure, to increase profits by stepping up its effort. That this can usually be done is an indication that maximum profits are not usually being pursued, but rather some level considered satisfactory. The difference is the 'slack' existing between maximum and acceptable performance. The second aspect is called **X-inefficiency**, which refers particularly to the cost side of a firm's operations. Again, it is usually the case that actual costs are not pressed to their minimum level, so that here there is a difference between maximum and actual performance, and this difference is the measure of X-inefficiency.

Another variation on the theme of firms' objectives being heavily conditioned by their structure, and in particular by the relationships between the main constituents of shareholders, directors, managers, workforce and customers, recognises that there is no objective which is unequivocally shared by these constituents, who form a coalition rather than a unified entity, and whose several objectives are unlikely to be consistent. There is therefore, on this view, no single-minded and continuous attempt at maximisation of anything. According to one form of this view, firms fall back on the position of being satisfied with a reasonable return on their activities, which has been called '**satisficing**'.

According to another form, the satisficing takes place in a number of different directions at different times as a result of the bargaining or mutual pressures between the various members and groups comprising the firm. Pressures and bargaining demands are met by 'side payments' which keep the groups forming the firm together and which also keep individual managers whom it is desired to retain. Side payments are not always in money; they frequently take the form of policy commitments, allocation of authority and similar satisfaction of aspirations. These aspirations vary in intensity among the groups and individuals, in different ways at different times, so that cohesion of the organisation is maintained by dealing with them sequentially as pressure in any particular direction becomes acute. It is a matter of satisfying aspirations at an acceptable level rather than being a maximising activity, and is again a form of satisficing. It enables a firm to remain viable although containing contradictory aspirations on the part of groups and individuals within itself. The firm goes from one problem to another – which, in itself, is certainly true enough – and the fact that they are perceived to be dealt with in time serves to reduce conflict. It will be apparent that the existence of some degree of organisational slack is a condition for a behavioural model of this kind to operate. The utilisation of slack resources, which may result in an increase of efficiency, will often be required in order to implement a decision to move in the direction of satisfying a particular aspiration.

Survival

An overriding objective of any firm is to stay in existence. There may be a kind of exception to this fact if a company makes a bid to buy all the shares of another and so effect a takeover, provided it is a case of the latter company being willing that this should happen. Apart from that kind of situation, firms wish to survive, and in the ultimate analysis it is their paramount objective. It may be argued that the best means of ensuring survival is to aim at short-run profit maximisation since this offers the best way of building reserves to cushion the firm in times of bad trade and to meet capital expenditures required to adapt to changed technology or other circumstances in the industry, and since it offers the best way to thrive against competition. We have, however, noticed some of the difficulties of profit maximisation as a practical policy. Survival is desired above all because it means avoiding persistent loss. The emphasis on survival implies that the avoidance of loss carries more weight than taking risks which may, if successful, yield profit (as was noted above when discussing some managerial objectives). Survival is also desired by managers and directors because their personal positions, incomes and reputations depend on it.

In some firms it may be the case that the notion of survival means surviving in what is pretty much the firm's present form, for instance in an owner-managed company where the owner-managers wish to remain independent and in control. Their success in doing this will partly depend on the capacity of the firm to generate sufficient profits to allow it to finance any capital expansion required by technological developments in their industry. On the other hand, such a firm may not want to grow too much nor too fast for fear of dilution of control through having to add to the numbers of managers, or through having to borrow. For most firms, however, some growth is a concomitant of survival since contraction is a threat to it and remaining stable in size a difficult feat in a changing economic and commercial environment.

Growth

Growth is, indeed, sometimes seen as the actual objective of industrial companies, arising from managerial drives of the kind which we have noticed, and from a desire to increase profit even if the means of maximising it in an existing situation are not known with certainty. Growth may take place in various ways: by making efforts to sell more of the firm's products, by diversifying the firm's activities to include new products either by invading markets new to the firm or by innovation, or by merger with or takeover of other companies. However, there is a limit to the rate at which a firm can grow at any given time. This is set by two related factors: the finance of growth requires a certain level of existing profitability, because the required new investment is typically and at least partially financed from existing retained profits; and the ability to raise new finance on the new issue market or elsewhere is related to the company's existing profitability, and hence to the stock exchange valuation of its shares.

At the same time, progressive growth is likely to reduce this profitability because of the costs which are involved in increasing market share of existing products, fostering demand for new products and investing in innovation, and spreading management effort over larger and more numerous activities. Thus the greater difficulty of increasing profitability acts as a constraint on growth. It also acts on the company's stock market valuation, so that if the process of growth threatens to go too far, the valuation is reduced and the company may attract the attention of a large predator which sees an opportunity to buy up its shares cheaply and take the company over. The extent to which this may or may not be desirable from the shareholders' point of view varies very much with circumstances, but it is usually an outcome which directors and managers wish to avoid. The drive for growth, therefore, is constrained by profit levels and considerations of the company's security and survival in its present form.

Image and Social Responsibility

We noticed in the last chapter that since 1980 company law has required directors to have regard to the interests of the company's employees in deciding policy issues as well as those of its members (shareholders), though they owe this duty to the company alone.

How far this goes to establish any rights on the part of employees which they did not already have and derived from other sources may be doubtful and remains to be seen. On the other hand it would enable a board of directors to defend easily many actions favourable to employees which they might take by arguing that in their opinion such an action was in the company's interest. This legal change is a reflection of changing social attitudes to industry and changing attitudes on the part of those who run industry. Although it has received no very clear and precise formulation, there has grown up a widespread, if not evenly spread, feeling that industrial companies have a responsibility to society beyond their rôle of producing certain products and operating efficiently and profitably for their owners. Employees are seen as having a heavy stake in a company; customers and suppliers too may have more than a passing interest; and society in general is involved in many ways.

Both because of and as part of these changing attitudes a new kind of objective on the part of industrial companies is emerging. It is not wholly new in that there have always been firms which have acknowledged and pursued such objectives: what is new is their growing explicit recognition and their increasing pervasiveness. Especially for a company which is a household name, to have a good public image – or, at very least, not to have a bad one – has become a recognised objective. The desired image may be quite general in character, as of a company cherishing a responsible image in society; or it may be specifically related to the nature of the company's business, as an airline being associated with safety first, or a financial institution with soundness and solidity. The latter is often fostered by the architectural style of the buildings occupied by banks and insurance companies, though this is giving way, in part, to a desire for a more populist and friendly image in certain areas, with the aim of spreading the incidence of bank current accounts. It is not always possible to dissociate entirely the company image from that of its products, and both may serve the aim of maintaining or increasing the company's good will, which is recognised quite literally as a valuable asset (for a money value is sometimes put on it). Good will, however, relates strictly to a firm's customers and represents the value of the probability that their custom will continue in the future. Actions which are explained on the grounds of good will and which are at the expense of profit in the short run may, therefore, be seen as fostering profit in the long run.

A particular field in which questions of social responsibility arise is that of purchaser/supplier relationships. This simply means the continuing business relationship between a business which regularly buys materials, components, semi-finished products or finished goods, from another. Many questions and problems may arise from such a relationship, such as whether there is sufficient consultation between them about the possibility of making slight alterations to specifications, which might lead the supplier to produce in larger runs and supply, say, an export market at the same time and with consequent reduced costs of production to the benefit of all concerned. It is probable that there is considerable scope in British industry for improvements of this kind by suppliers and purchasers examining their problems more closely together. However, the particular point involving social responsibility in this area is that if the purchaser is a large company and the supplier is small, it can become fairly easy for the purchaser to secure a powerful position in bargaining over prices with the supplier, especially if the supplier has over a period come to devote most or all of his productive capacity to supplying the wants of this particular purchaser. He may have done this on the grounds that the large customer could be relied on for regular orders and, having put himself in this position, might find it more than difficult to attract back former and smaller customers should he wish to do so. (A market situation in which there is a sole buyer is known as **monopsony**). The large buyer is now in a position where he can exert powerful downward pressure on the price he pays, and the supplier's profits will be squeezed and may disappear. It is commonly recognised that there is a social responsibility element in such situations, and that it behoves large buyers to develop close relations with small suppliers heavily dependent on them, and to discuss frankly flows of orders, design, costs and prices in order to ensure some stability and a reasonable profit level for firms which have sacrificed their freedom of action by confining their market to one outlet. It is well known that Marks and Spencer plc, for example, now takes great pains in this direction with the companies which manufacture this retailer's stock lines. It is done as a matter of social responsibility but again, as with actions conducive to good will, it is possible to discern an element of self-interest.

Some matters of social responsibility on the part of industry are the subject of legislation, referred to further in the last section of Chapter 8. Such matters include safety at work, noise abatement, and the control of the disposal of noxious effluents and other by-products of some industrial processes. These legislative measures impose costs on industrial firms. The justification in principle for this is that some processes impose a detriment or cost (e.g., higher laundry bills, double glazing, impaired health) on society as a whole or that part of it in the locality of the operation, whereas a proper allocation of resources in society as a whole requires that costs shall lie where they are incurred. Furthermore, one effect of legislation is to protect companies with high standards of responsibility from the (anti-social) cost-cutting competition of others.

The objective of a responsible image in society is by no means something clearcut. Some of it is enlightened self-interest, some is enforced by an increasing volume of legislation designed to ensure socially acceptable practices. Some arises spontaneously or in keeping with evolving social attitudes on the part of people in general, irrespective of their specific role in or relationship with an industrial company. It is becoming more common than it used to be for chairmen and directors of companies to underline these responsibilities on the part of their companies to the various sections of society. Changing attitudes of this kind have related to demands that companies ought to be subject to a **social audit**. We have seen that the Companies Acts require publication of accounts and financial information about a company's affairs. Information of a kind relevant to their interests also has to be provided for employees. The demand for a 'social audit' takes these matters considerably further and would require an assessment of a firm's performance in the light of the criteria of its social responsibility.

We can but conjecture whether such an audit will ever be instituted. The general idea of the social responsibilities of companies is certainly gaining ground, not least within companies themselves. The idea that there is a responsibility only to the shareholding owners of the company might now find few defenders, and the reasons why even directors are not always to be found among its defenders may be various. All that is one thing, however. It is something completely different to have agreement within society about what the social objectives of a particular company ought to be. That takes us into a world of moral and ethical judgements, and there is no evidence that there is a single set of such judgements relevant to these matters on which society is agreed. The social audit bristles with difficulties and some would say that it is a non-operational concept. It seems likely that emphasis on socially responsible behaviour according to the lights of those in effective control of particular companies will continue to grow, with more or less debate about the desirability and morality of this in itself. Its content will vary with the character and predilections of those concerned, their value judgements and fashionable movements in the objects of 'caring' concern; and its extent will vary with the pressures to which firms are subject, their profitability and the degree of discretion which the external environment of firms will permit them to exercise. An important constituent of the latter is the structure of the market in which they are operating and how much leeway they have in the matter of prices and profits. Some kinds of social responsibility have a better chance when firms are prosperous: others conduce to prosperity.

Objectives Reconsidered

It is obvious that no firm could at the same time hold all the objectives which have been considered above. Moreover, there are other possible objectives which have not been mentioned at all: for example, it is conceivable that a firm could set itself the explicit objective of maintaining its workforce during the coming year. It might do this for reasons of social responsibility if it could achieve this without undermining the firm's liquidity or solvency; or it might do it because it foresaw a revival of, or a temporary fall in, demand for its products, and wished to hold together its organisation and skilled workforce to meet that demand. Thus the kind of objectives of which it is possible to speak can vary.

It is clear, too, that they can vary in precision. Profit maximising is at once a very general (in the sense of all-pervading) objective, and an extremely precise one. Yet its very precision renders it incapable of constant practical application. There are valuable and practical insights in all the kinds of objectives which have been noted, but they do not make a tidy system. We may say that firms certainly wish to make profits as the basic reason for their existence and their only guarantee of continued existence. Frequently they also desire growth, although this may be tempered by the concern to remain owner-managed; even without that concern, we have noticed that there are profit and security constraints to growth as an objective.

It is possible to regard the desire to increase profits, to survive and to grow, as compatible bedfellows if we modify the sales-maximisation hypothesis which was noticed above. It will be recalled that this was in terms of maximising sales revenue and hence contained all the difficulties of uncertain knowledge and lack of correspondence with reality which beset the profit-maximisation hypothesis. If we consider that a firm knows from experience that it can sell a certain size of output from its existing plant at a profit, and if we consider that the firm's costs are the fixed costs of its plant and establishment together with the direct costs of the raw materials and labour expended on producing the present size of output, we begin to see things rather as industrialists themselves see them.

To make a profit, the fixed and the direct costs of production must be covered. The direct cost of a unit of output can be calculated by knowing how much of the variable factors of production is required to produce a unit of the product. Let the overhead costs then be divided by, say, the latest accounting year's production (or a normal year's production); it is then known how much must be added to the direct cost per unit in order to cover overhead costs at last year's (or a normal year's) output. Let a percentage margin then be added for net profit, either separately or by incorporation in the calculation of overheads. This sum yields a costing price to be quoted to customers. If the firm is confident about the efficiency of its productive process, it knows that at this price it will not be undercut by competitors. It also knows that it can accept any order at this price and make a positive contribution to its overheads and, when they are covered, to its profit. It will therefore have as its object to sell as much of its product as it can at the price which it has costed. This is not the same as the sales maximisation which was noticed above: that was a matter of maximising sales revenue. The construct now outlined is a matter of maximising physical sales, and does not contain the same operational difficulty as the earlier formulation.

Some readers may not feel able to make up their minds about the rival merits of these various approaches to firms' objectives. There is no real need for them to do so. These are in some respects matters of dispute. The useful thing is to use any of these approaches in a particular situation when it seems relevant to do so.

Accounting and the Performance of Firms

Whatever overall objective a firm may have adopted, it is common for this to be broken down into constituent parts to form the objectives or, as they are usually called in this context, the targets of the relevant sections and departments of the firm. These targets will typically be in concrete and measurable terms even when the overall objective itself is rather general or not in precise quantitative terms. Appraisal at regular intervals throughout the year of the degree of achievement of targets at this level is a necessary part of the management of industrial firms, and is facilitated by the quantitative terms in which targets or budgets are laid down.

Quantitative concepts can also be brought to bear on the performance of a firm as a whole by use of information available from the firm's accounting system. Appraisal can thus become rather precise, depending on how such information is used in relation to the firm's objectives and how those basic objectives are translated into aims for the coming year. Since, as we have seen, profit is always at least an element in basic objectives, the absolute amount of profit made in a year is an initial indication of performance. In itself, however, it is not a very satisfactory indication. There are two reasons for this. First, a given profit target may in the first place simply have been what the firm thought it could achieve having regard to the previous year's profit adjusted upwards or downwards according to the firm's expectations of changes in the demand for its products and changes in other commercial conditions. Second, a given absolute amount of profit only means anything really significant when it is set against measurements of other characteristics of a business, in particular the capital employed to earn that profit. It makes an important difference whether a given amount of profit has been earned by using a small as compared with a large amount of capital. The setting of one figure against another in this way is known as a business ratio. A fairly large number of such ratios can be identified and used to throw light on various aspects of the position and performance of a business. Some of these are of greatest use and interest to the firm's management, some to its shareholders and some to its creditors, actual or potential. We shall look at firms' performance and position from these different points of view, and then from the general social or public policy viewpoint.

Profitability

From most points of view, performance in the efficiency with which a firm uses its assets is of prime importance, and the ratio which measures this is the **rate of return on capital employed**, or

$$\left(\frac{\text{Profit}}{\text{Capital employed}} \right) \%$$

The figure of profit taken for this purpose is before deduction of tax, so that the ratio does not fluctuate erratically for taxation reasons which do not arise directly out of a particular year's business operations. Interest paid on money borrowed by the firm is added back into the profit figure for this purpose so that the profitability of capital used will be indicated irrespective of how that capital has been financed. The figure of capital employed equals total assets (fixed and current) minus current liabilities (the latter being obligations to pay debts incurred in the day-to-day running of the business, such as trade and other creditors, and tax and dividends payable). This ratio is useful to firms in comparing their profitability with that of their competitors, and their own performance over time.

From the shareholders' point of view, an alternative measure of profitability may be more significant. They certainly do have an interest in a measure including the company's profit, for although this is not normally all paid out in dividends, the amounts retained in the company serve to increase shareholders' funds, or to provide funds for growth of the company and hence the value of their shares and future dividends. But as well as relating profit to capital employed, they will wish to relate profit to the company's equity, which is what they have a share in. The equity is the shareholders' funds, or the issued ordinary shares, reserves and undistributed profits. The profit of direct significance to shareholders is after tax, rather than before tax, and without adding back interest paid on borrowings, as it is only this net amount which is available to them. Thus a measure of profitability of prime interest to shareholders is the ratio:

$$\left(\frac{\text{Profit after tax}}{\text{Equity}} \right) \% = \text{Return on equity ratio}$$

They are even more interested in the ratio of dividend per share to that share's market price – the yield – on the stock exchange, but since it is possible to take a view that the market is at a particular time under- or over-valuing a share, an actual or potential shareholder may well wish to consider both ratios. He may also consider the firm's total earnings per share.

The rate of return on capital employed reflects the interaction of two further ratios: (a) the profit margin on sales, or markup, and (b) the total value of sales in relation to capital. Thus:

$$\left(\frac{\text{Profit}}{\text{Sales}} \right) \% = \text{Markup ratio}$$

and

$$\left(\frac{\text{Sales}}{\text{Capital employed}} \right) \% = \text{Turnover ratio}$$

The sales are the end result of the employment of the capital, and the purpose to which it has been directed. Movements in either of these two ratios will affect the rate of return, and movements in both may either reinforce each other, for good or ill, or offset each other, depending on the direction they move in. Some firms may have a realistic choice of policy whether to go for a low profit margin on sales coupled with a high turnover in relation to capital, or a high profit margin on a lower turnover. One of these choices is illustrated by the early history of Boot's the chemist in a verse by D.H. Lawrence who lived nearby:

> Little I thought, when I was a lad
> and turned my modest penny
> over on Boots Cash Chemist's counter,

> that Jesse, by turning many
> millions of similar honest pence
> over, would make a pile ...

Scrutiny by management of these two ratios assists in identifying directions in which efficiency and therefore the rate of return may be improved.

The total value of sales in relation to capital measures the frequency or rate at which capital assets are turned into sales. One way of obtaining increased efficiency is to economise on capital, if possible, when there appears to be no conceivable prospect of increasing sales. On the other hand, if growth takes place and capital employed is increased, it is important to see that sales rise at least in keeping or this ratio will deteriorate and the growth will simply be accompanied by lower profitability. More detailed analysis is made possible by breaking down the sales to capital employed ratio into the underlying ratios of sales to particular kinds of asset, as in the following related examples:

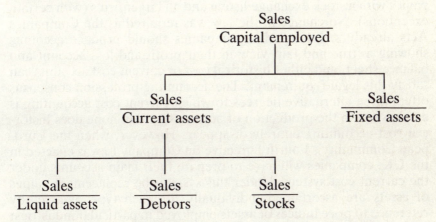

Each of these throws light on a detailed aspect of the running of the enterprise. They reveal changes in the efficiency of the company's operation of its fixed assets, its stock control procedures, its extension of credit to customers and debt collection, and so on. There are further quantitative measurements which can be undertaken to supplement such ratios, but it is not our purpose to follow them here.

Performance ratios relating to profitability can be seriously misleading if they refer to periods of time during which there has been a change in the general level of prices, or of relative prices, and if the figures recording the value of a firm's assets are not revised accordingly. According to the traditional historic costs method of keeping a firm's accounts, the value of assets remains based on what was actually paid for them, yet their value to the firm in its production process and commercial operations changes, rising in money terms in a period of inflation. This applies both to stocks and to fixed assets. Stocks **appreciate** while they are held, but then have to be replaced at the new higher price level; if no allowance is made for this in calculating profit for the period in question, then that profit will be overstated to the extent of the appreciation of the stocks held at the beginning of the year and used in the production and sale of output during the year. Similarly with fixed assets which last for a period of years, the annual depreciation charges put by on the basis of their original cost will at the end of the asset's life be insufficient to replace it; and profits over this period of years will have been overstated accordingly.

Inflation accounting has been introduced to deal with these problems. After much debate about the desirability of inflation accounting at all and about which of two main versions should be introduced, if any, the accounting profession reached a decision that from 1980 'current cost accounting' would be adopted for all companies with a stock exchange listing and all larger firms (with certain exceptions). No change in the law was required as the Companies Acts already stipulated that companies should produce accounts showing a 'true and fair' view in their profit and loss account and balance sheet, and either historical cost or current cost accounts can satisfy this legal requirement. The accounting profession consensus offers three alternative degrees to which current cost accounting is emphasised in the production of accounts, and in none does historical cost accounting entirely disappear. However, when the European Community's Fourth Directive on Company Law is enacted in the UK, companies will have to prepare their main accounts under the current cost system. Under this system the replacement values of assets are ascertained individually for each type of asset by reference to price indices of assets employed in particular industries; thus changes in the relative prices of productive assets (and of such assets in relation to other goods) are taken into consideration as well as changes arising from inflation. The other main version of inflation accounting referred to at the beginning of this paragraph would have taken account of inflation or the current purchasing power of money alone, by applying a general price index to the values of assets and liabilities. It is known as current purchasing power accounting.

Although an effective consensus on this matter appeared to have been achieved, debate continues, and, according to a proposal of March 1984, a form of inflation accounting would apply to all public limited companies, but it would take the form merely of a note appended to the accounts. In some quarters there is still a belief that historic costs represent the only objective, precise and unambiguous basis of accounting, and that to adjust these figures in any way introduces something arbitrary and suspect. The standpoint taken here is that a rate of return on this basis of, say, 15 per cent when the rate of inflation is, say, 10 per cent, is spurious; and that while any method of inflation accounting may only be approximate, it is better to be approximately correct than precisely wrong. Many industrial enterprises have in recent years shown profits in their accounts based on historical cost accounting when inflation meant that in real terms they were making losses.

Financial Stability

(i) Liquidity It is possible for a firm to be performing well as to profitability and yet at the same time be performing badly in that it is in danger of being unable to pay its way. For this, cash and money in a bank acccount are required. A proportion of assets must be sufficiently liquid – liquidity being the ease with which an asset can be turned into cash (some assets automatically do so on a due date, as when a debt is paid) – to ensure that the firm can continue its operations by paying wages and salaries, paying suppliers and continuing to be supplied with materials and services on credit. A shortage of liquidity may force even a profitable enterprise to cease trading. Consequently, a company's liquidity is a matter of concern to its employees, creditors and shareholders. In contrast, a company may well continue in business during a period of loss-making, or negative return on capital, so long as an adequate degree of liquidity is maintained even at the expense of borrowing and there is a prospect of eventual resumption of profitable conditions.

Whilst a firm needs cash to meet its obligations as they arise, it is also receiving cash in settlement of obligations due to it – payment by debtors for sales made to them, for example. To enable this process to continue smoothly through time, a certain prudent relationship between current assets and current liabilities needs to be maintained. This relationship is called the **liquidity or current ratio**. There is no suggestion that this relationship ought to be one of equality, and the possibility of unexpected requirements for cash or unexpected difficulties in obtaining payments due to the company, requires that current assets exceed current liabilities by an appreciable margin. There is in fact no hard and fast rule of general application as to what constitutes a prudent ratio, although rules of thumb are sometimes suggested for it. It must vary from one business to another, and will be affected by, for example, a company's ability to borrow for short periods in case of need, say by an overdraft facility at its bank. The liquidity ratio relates total current assets, which include stocks and work in progress, to total current liabilities. This being so, it is a weakness of this ratio that there may be considerable differences between the degrees of liquidity of some of the items included, although they are all technically current. These differences tend to overstate the liquidity of current assets: stocks of finished goods may be high precisely because demand for the product has unexpectedly fallen away, which reduces the liquidity of those stocks. Work in progress will usually, by its nature, be even more difficult to dispose of at its normal value. Thus, although the current ratio is in very frequent use, it becomes evident that caution is required in applying it at any particular time.

To overcome the weakness just noted, a further ratio may be employed to gauge a firm's performance in respect of liquidity. It is similar to the liquidity or current ratio itself, but measures those liabilities which have to be met in the near future (again, current liabilities) against only those current assets which have a high degree of liquidity; these are cash, debtors and any other highly liquid assets. This ratio excludes stocks and work in progress from the assets in the denominator thus:

$$\frac{\text{Current assets} - (\text{Stocks} + \text{Work in progress})}{\text{Current liabilities}}$$

and is known as the acid test. As with the current ratio its interpretation may be further supported by borrowing facilities if the firm has them. It is a more secure way of indicating liquidity than is the broader current ratio, and in this case there is significance in a generalisation about what its desirable magnitude ought to be. Subject to circumstances an acid test ratio of 1:1 appears desirable.

However, acceptance of the ratio at its face value may ignore the fact that current assets and liabilities, particularly debtors and creditors, are not moving together. Regular and frequent checks on the ratio will show if this is the case. The average length of time taken by debtors to pay may change. This may arise from poor credit control on the company's part, or from a change in its pattern of trading to, say, a greater emphasis on exports with larger credit periods. On the other hand, a shortening of the average credit period may indicate a tightening up on collection by the accounts department, seen as desirable in itself, but which if continued could lose the company business in favour of competitors who had not altered their credit practice. The number of possible causes of such changes in credit given and credit received is legion, but they will all have some effect on the company's liquidity and ultimate profitability performance.

The average number of days taken by debtors to pay, or the credit period, is calculated by dividing the average level of debtors during a year by the year's sales and multiplying by 365. Credit taken by the company may be similarly expressed, using average creditors and purchases. These ratios may be used to help in explaining changes in liquidity ratios and in determining remedial action if required.

Changes in price levels are relevant when considering liquidity. Receipts from sales and disbursements on items of cost form a sequential process. If costs rise during this process, the firm will be paying out for its factors of production at a higher general price level than prevailed when the sales revenue with which to make the payments was received. In this way inflation strains firms' liquidity and working capital.

(ii) Solvency   A firm is solvent when, irrespective of its liquidity position, its total assets exceed its total liabilities except its share capital: shareholders, as the owners of the business, are not creditors even though their share capital is a liability of the company. A company may be solvent although suffering from illiquidity and hence difficulty in meeting in cash the current and short-term claims on it. **Solvency** is a broader concept than liquidity and is longer term in the sense that the ability to repay its long-term liabilities (such as money borrowed by issuing debentures, or by raising a mortgage on its premises, for example) is brought into consideration, as is the saleable value of its fixed assets, as well as its current assets and liabilities.

Insolvency of a company does not necessarily lead to immediate collapse and cessation of trading. Directors, having perceived insolvency, may nevertheless form the opinion that a bad situation can be made less bad from the shareholders' point of view, and creditors such as the company's bankers may take the same view from their standpoint. Nevertheless, insolvency must lead to difficulty in raising further finance for remedial measures and for carrying the firm over a period of losses which may or may not turn out to be temporary. In such a situation a firm is heavily dependent on the view taken by its creditors in general, and a state of insolvency may therefore persist for a longer or a shorter period. Insolvency is not necessarily irremediable. To take a dramatic example, the question of whether Laker Airways could have survived given time is still disputed by some: at least one large creditor reached the conclusion that it could not, and a Receiver was hence appointed. Sometimes a Receiver will continue the operations of a company, or part of them, in pursuit of his duty to obtain the best outcome available for the company's creditors, whose several and relative rights in the matter of the order of their repayment are regulated by law.

(iii) Gearing   A company may raise further capital either by issuing more shares or by borrowing. The latter gives rise to debt, and the ratio between debt and equity capital is the **gearing ratio**. Thus:

$$\frac{\text{Debt}}{\text{Equity capital}} = \text{Gearing ratio}$$

A highly-geared company has a high ratio of debt to equity capital. With debt, the company pays a fixed annual rate of interest on the loan which may be in the form of a debenture or similar security; if borrowing from a bank or other financial institution, the rate of interest may vary at agreed intervals with changes in market rates of interest. Dividends on ordinary share capital vary with the company's profitability and the amount of profit retained in the business but added to shareholders' funds. A shareholder is interested in the gearing ratio as a guide to an aspect of company performance, because a high ratio offers him the opportunity to, in effect, benefit from the company's use of the borrowed capital if that use yields profits more than sufficient to pay interest on what has been borrowed. It also exposes him to the risk of a share of profits which may be reduced if the new investment for which the funds are being borrowed does not earn sufficient in all years to pay the interest on the debt. The shareholder has to consider the probabilities of these opposite outcomes alongside the gearing ratio.

A banker or other lender will consider the gearing ratio, as the higher it is the higher is the risk that a company will not be able to pay its total interest charges out of profits. Such a lender will also consider for this purpose the ratio between the company's profit before deducting tax and interest payments to the interest payments themselves. Thus:

$$\frac{\text{Profit (including tax and interest)}}{\text{Interest}}$$

This ratio gives a measure of the risk to which a lender is exposed in respect of the interest payments that would be due to him, having regard to the company's gearing ratio.

As with other ratios, the existence of inflation makes a difference to the way any given gearing ratio may be regarded. Continued inflation means that the real burden to a borrower of eventual repayment and of interest payments becomes less than it would otherwise have been. Thus a higher gearing ratio may be more acceptable in such a period than it would be in different circumstances.

Some Broader Considerations of Performance

Performance ratios may be obtained for an industry as a whole by aggregating the published accounting information for the individual firms in the industry. A particular firm may then compare its own performance with the average for the industry. It may also, so far as published information is concerned, compare itself with an individual competitor. The aggregated information for an industry may be used in addition by those interested in the effective use of society's resources. Ideas about an industry's performance from the social point of view are usually fundamentally based on the theorem of maximised welfare resulting from a regime of perfect competition. The latter is a matter of the structure of an industry. It is a structure in which the competing sellers are so many that a change in the output of any one of them does not perceptibly affect the total supply from the industry, and so does not affect the price of the industry's product, which is considered to be homogeneous. In an industrial context this is a rather artificial construct, though not without its uses. One of the implications of perfect competition is that the price is competed down to the point at which every firm is producing at the lowest average cost of production possible with its existing plant, and this in its turn means that unless he is favoured by some element such as a superior source of supply of a raw material, or superior organising ability, no producer can make any profit over and above the minimum amount necessary to persuade him to continue in the industry. This would mean low profitability ratios more or less all round. It would also mean, if such conditions prevailed in the economy as a whole, an ideal allocation of society's resources from the point of view of satisfying consumers' wants to the maximum extent made possible by those resources.

It is evident that a low profitability ratio may indicate, on the one hand, either poor efficiency or a period of low demand or the like, or, on the other, all the efficiency that competition can enforce. In order to tell which is operating we need to know the structure of the industry. However, as already stated, perfect competition is usually an artificial – a merely imaginary – construct in an industrial context. Nevertheless, it retains persuasive influence as a criterion by which to judge performance from the social point of view. The reasons for perfect competition being an unrealisable ideal in industry are various and include the fact that very many industrial products are not homogeneous and perfect substitutes for each other in the eyes of consumers – manufacturers try to differentiate their products and then to persuade customers that theirs are preferable to those of their competitors. Then, the assumption of many sellers, each of whom can only imperceptibly affect total supply, is often falsified by the technological facts about an industry's production process: production on a large scale usually leads to lower average cost per unit of output than on a smaller scale, so that the number of producers is reduced – sometimes to a very small number. Changes in one producer's output then become capable of affecting the price of the product and a producer is in the position of having an independent pricing and output policy, which is a luxury a producer in a perfectly competitive situation cannot afford. Prices are no longer equal to the minimum attainable average cost as in perfect competition, but are kept above it; but the minimum attainable average is now lower than could be obtained in perfect competition, because of the economies of scale. The economies of scale offset the lost advantages of perfect competition.

The recognition of this goes far to explain the acceptance of non-perfectly competitive conditions in industry. In its place as a criterion of performance from the social point of view there is sometimes applied the idea of **workable competition**; this is taken to be a situation in an industry where rates of return are not so high in relation to those prevailing elsewhere as to suggest the abuse of a relatively non-competitive position, and where there are no arrangements between the firms in the industry to maintain prices, restrict output or prevent potential new producers from entering the industry. Another approach is to say that an industry is workably competitive if no conceivable and practicable measures of public policy could improve its performance from the viewpoint of the benefits of competition to the consumer.

Businessmen are sometimes astonished and offended at the suggestion that their industry may be operating in imperfectly competitive conditions. This is understandable because they may be conscious of fierce rivalry between their firms. It only takes the existence of two firms for such rivalry to exist, and they may be doing everything they possibly can to woo customers from each other and to find new markets. The success which rewards the strenuous efforts of such a firm is at the identifiable expense of its rivals and may carry no benefit to consumers; it is the seeking of a position or the maintenance of a position which is impossible for both or all to hold. It may, indeed, lead to improvements in products or technological advances in methods of production, though this result is not certain. For the most part it is non-price competition with an emphasis on persuasive advertising. It may at times be characterised by bursts of price competition in which a firm may cut its prices below the full cost of production so that for a while overhead costs may not be fully recovered: examples of reasons for this are a desire to clear stocks of finished products to make way for a new version with the ultimate advantage that this can bring over rivals, and a simple desire to put a financially weaker rival out of business. It is not the case that rivalry can necessarily carry no advantages to customers, but the fiercest rivalry is something distinct from perfect competition.

Summary

Firms come into being because of the prospect of profit, and profit is necessary if they are to stay in existence. Industrial firms may also have other objectives, however, and some of these may arise from the nature of their organisation. Assessing a firm's degree of success in the pursuit of its objectives – its performance – is assisted by considering the ratios between certain entities whose measurements can be found from the firm's accounts.

Review Questions

(1) It is sometimes said that a firm must grow or die. What do you think?

(2) How may accounting ratios be used to appraise the performance of an industrial firm?

(3) What is meant by a minimum profit constraint?

(4) What circumstances would help a firm to decide between a policy of achieving a high turnover with a low profit margin, and a higher profit margin on a lower turnover?

Knocking off: Ford workers leaving the Dagenham Plant

4

The Human Assets of Industry

The end purpose of productive activity is consumption, or the satisfaction of human wants. Human beings supply labour, or work effort of all kinds, manual or mental, to firms undertaking productive activities.

It is not possible to distinguish the labour supplied by a person from that person himself in quite the same way as other factors of production can be dissociated from those who supply them. This fact, together with the close connection between the supply of work and the supply of output for consumption, makes labour different from other factors of production. If a firm borrows from a financial institution, it does not care about the personal characteristics of the ultimate supplier of capital, who cannot be identified anyway; and so with other factors of production, the firm is concerned with their attributes but not those of their suppliers. Furthermore, suppliers of even the same kind of labour vary even to the extent that no two are alike. In the organisation of an industrial process, infinite pains are taken to ensure that units of output do not unintentionally vary from each other. This entails trying to ensure that units of input of raw materials are as uniform as possible. Initial parts of the production process may be devoted to this purpose. The pressure towards uniformity in an industrial organisation and an industrial society is felt by individuals. Furthermore, although the ultimate aim of productive activity is consumption – and, indeed, because the productive activity is not being undertaken as its own reward and for its own sake – there is a clear break between the two. The working week becomes a much more distinct part of life as contrasted with the situation in a society where productive activity takes place more as part of custom, ritual or immediate necessity. All this raises human problems for management to deal with, for labour is a factor of production with social and human needs: the pay packet is not everything.

Jobs and work effort vary enormously but there is a common central element: manual workers, managers, operatives, foremen, engineers and salesmen are all supplying labour. Its remuneration is

67

wages and may include non-wage benefits such as free coal, accommodation, the use of a car, sports facilities, a pension scheme or other benefits. No distinction will usually be made here between wages and salaries, the difference being merely the intervals at which payment is made.

Productive activity results in output, the sales revenue from which represents the value of the output; some of this value has been contributed by factors of production bought in or hired by the firm from other firms outside itself, and the remainder is what has been contributed by the firm's own productive organisation, including the firm's own labour force. This latter part is called the **value added** by the firm, and is what is available for payments to the employees and owners of the firm.

We may take it as an objective of labour to maximise its share of the added value to which it contributes. From what we have already observed about the objectives of employing firms in relation to profits and growth, we may say that they are concerned to increase their value added. This is also a way in which the earnings of labour may rise. One aspect of the matter is a tug of war over sharing a given added value: the other is co-operation between management and labour to increase the added value to which both contribute. We hear more of the former.

Questions of a little more or little less in the size of a slice of the cake can certainly be of crucial importance to an industry at specific times, but in the long run the size of the cake itself dominates the general standard of living; this is so whether we are considering an individual firm, industry or the whole economy. We therefore begin by considering the human assets of industry from this point of view.

The Quality of the Labour Force

The inherent aptitudes and abilities, and their variety, of the working population of any country must count for much in determining the quality of the labour force, along with the particular social conditioning which occurs through being brought up in an advanced industrial society. The latter influence may even operate locally, where a particular industry is concentrated in a particular geographical area. It is one reason why the level of skill of the working population as a whole rises with the passage of time, another being that more is learned and passed on about jobs; this is not inconsistent with the disappearance of particular traditional skills or the fact that some become rarer, which is sometimes noted and lamented. We shall need to return to the matter of skill shortages; the point here is that in general the average level of skill rises. It is partly as though society itself were more experienced. This is quite independent of the age structure of the working population; individual members of the work force become more experienced with age and, up to a point, their skills increase, but we are not pointing to a situation where the average level rises because a particular age group is increasing as a proportion of the whole.

More specific causes of this improvement in the quality of the labour force over a fairly recent historical period in the UK and elsewhere have been improved public health measures, more widespread availability of medical services and a shorter working week. Union claims for the latter give rise to much controversy, especially when no reduction in actual hours worked is really intended, but rather higher payment for each hour worked beyond a new lower number paid at the standard rate. This raises employers' labour costs for a given output, and is resisted by them. They argue that increased productivity must first occur, which can then enable hours to be shortened. There seems no doubt that as living standards rise over a period, working weeks will continue to shorten, if only because leisure is required in order to enjoy the higher standards. There also seems no doubt that the progressive shortening of the working week which has historically occurred has improved the quality of the labour force. In any given set of conditions, however, there must be a limit to which this could apply.

The description of the workforce as human assets in the heading to this chapter is figurative: nevertheless, it has a literal element, for a skilled worker embodies some capital through his education and training which is a form of investment, either on his own or his parents' part, or that of an employer or the State. Investment of this kind is an important ingredient in the quality of the labour force, whether it be general education or specific training directed towards a particular trade or profession.

One form of such training is apprenticeship. This has its origin in the medieval guilds when it was a superbly effective means of training; at the same time it was, as part of the highly regulated society of the time, a means of restricting entry to occupations, for none might practise them without membership of the guild concerned. That it has survived is in some ways a testimony to its effectiveness through all the changes in society and technology which have occurred since its origins. Practical training on the job is a large part of the process of apprenticeship, and with a craftsman as instructor it combines at its best an all-round experience and training in a trade, keeps up to date with the actual practices and techniques employed in the trade, and maintains the motivation of the pupil more readily than might be the case in a training institution. However, in modern industry the place of apprenticeship is not always what it used to be. New processes, materials, technology and mass production have rendered apprenticeship at once both too little training and too much in comparison with the position it has held. Traditionally the craftsman who had served an apprenticeship acquired the whole breadth of skills of his trade and could turn with equal facility to any task or situation falling within it. Mechanisation, the increase in the division of labour and the spread of general education have meant that a worker may satisfactorily perform a given task without such a full training; apprenticeships have come to be unnecessarily long, and their original undesirable aspect of being used as a means to restrict entry to crafts has come to the fore again. Thus in recent times there has been pressure to shorten the period of apprenticeship. At the same time, a traditional apprentice type of training has become inadequate for some of the higher technical occupations which have emerged as industrial development has entered successive and rapidly changing higher stages. Some jobs become simpler and more routine, others have become more complex; the latter call for versatility not simply within a given range – which was a great strength of the traditional craftsman – but within new and expanded technological possibilities.

At a different level, but in some ways comparable, there is the question of whether the pattern of education in this country, and some others, is the most suited to the needs of an economy of which industry is such a significant part. There is some evidence to suggest that it is not, and that if adjustments were made in the numbers of students proceeding to different kinds of courses, the economic benefits would be considerable. The kinds of adjustment suggested by the evidence as being required would be, for example, more students on Higher National Certificate courses and fewer working for higher degrees. Such adjustments would be a move in the direction of a more vocation-orientated pattern of the educational system. There are two difficulties about this, apart from the fact that the evidence is not necessarily conclusive. The first is that whilst education is an investment in human capital, and thus a producer good, it is also a consumer good desired for its own sake as leading to welfare and the enrichment of life, and the basis of the discussion is the very point that there may be differences between the content of education for these two purposes. The opportunity cost of what are conceived to be good states of mind may be a lower material standard of life, and not all may agree on the choice to be made. The second difficulty lies in the extent to which it is wise to concentrate the educational system on the specialist skills and knowledge currently in demand at any time during a period of very rapid technological and social change. Today's specialists can be old-fashioned or obsolete tomorrow. A growing proportion of people in mid-career are in jobs of a kind that did not exist at all when they entered the labour force. There will, therefore, be an increasing premium on adaptability in the future. One line of argument is to the effect that highly specialised components of the labour force are less adaptable than those with a broader education when it comes to innovation based on new scientific discovery and to meeting the challenges in industry of unprecedented social situations.

To revert to the discussion on training, as distinct from education, industrial employers have always provided training to a greater or lesser extent and up to twenty years ago they were, in one way or another, responsible in total for most of the training taking place. Trade unions take an interest in the matter in consultation with employers, since the skills of their members have an obvious influence on their earning power; at the same time there is the other element which has existed since the time of the guilds, that of restriction of the numbers of those with particular skills, so as to maintain artificially their earnings through the mechanism of supply and demand. A problem in the sixties arising from the high levels of employment then being experienced was that growing shortages of skills in relation to the rising demands for them made it easy for those trained by one employer to move to another on the rising spiral of money wages. Employers with good training schemes became reluctant to incur the costs of expanding them, since they lost too many of those they had trained to others who were spending relatively little on training. Thus the total training provision by industry became inadequate. To meet this situation the Industrial Training Act of 1964 provided for setting up Industrial Training Boards (ITBs), of which a considerable number were created, each serving a particular industry for which it carried out training in the relevant skills and provided training advice to firms. Government contributed grants to help meet the costs, and the Boards were empowered to impose a training levy related to the wage bill on all but the smaller firms in their industry. Firms could continue training programmes of their own if they chose, and if these were approved by the ITB a payment was made back to the firm, which might be more or less than the levy paid.

Thus an attempt was made to ensure that all substantial employers of skilled labour shared proportionately the cost of training it. The boards fulfilled a need in the circumstances in which they were set up, and the general level of training was improved. In engineering the apprenticeship system was made more flexible and an overlap of training for the electrical and mechanical trades was combined with a shortening of the apprenticeship period. This should facilitate retraining later as engineering technology changes.

However, with the passing away of the era of full employment, the particular call for Training Boards was not the same, and their costs to government and to industry became an object of criticism, as did the bureaucratic procedures entailed. In 1982 most of the ITBs were wound up and firms in their industries became responsible for their own training again, though seven Training Boards remain.

At the present time the Government operates a Youth Training Scheme for 300,000 unemployed school-leavers, offering a training year in firms at low cost to employers. It should perhaps be regarded as a special employment measure rather than a training scheme as such.

The adequacy of the total amount of industrial training available, the extent of willingness to undergo training, and the difficulty of forecasting the types of skill which will be in greatest demand in the future are matters for concern. There is sometimes a reluctance to provide training and to undergo it until a need and a job prospect have been specifically revealed, yet by then it may be too late to begin. Even so, skill shortages are reported by many employers as a constraint on their output even in the present time of high unemployment.

Lastly, its mobility affects the quality of a labour force, for labour is all the more productive when the various kinds of it are available in the places where they are most demanded. Labour is less mobile than other factors of production, capital or most raw materials for example, though the extent of its mobility depends on various social considerations which may change from time to time. Financial capital is free to be moved anywhere at any time, subject to the possible existence of exchange controls where international movement is concerned and subject to the lender's feeling that there are some countries where he would rather not risk his capital even at prospective high rates of return. Labour is frequently more inert, as was referred to in Chapter 1. Ties of family, friends and familiar surroundings may be reinforced by reluctance to move children from their existing schools, particularly if public examinations are approaching. Housing in the private sector may very well be more expensive in a prosperous area offering employment opportunities, and if a family is renting a council house, they may be reluctant to give it up and face a lengthy delay, as newcomers, in obtaining another in a different area. The United Kingdom has a high proportion of owner-occupied housing by international comparison; the USA, by contrast, has a much larger proportion of private sector housing available to rent and this is believed to be a reason for greater labour mobility there. In the UK the most mobile section of the population is the 18–25 age group; this makes for flexibility in the distribution of relatively new entrants to the labour force; on the other hand, it also makes for problems in the areas which they leave; these then have a population whose average age rises faster than that for the country as a whole.

The Organisation of the Labour Force within Firms

The inherent and acquired characteristics of a firm's labour force require effort on the part of management for its productive capability to be realised to the full; management is itself part of the labour force, whose function is organising. In the first place employees have to be recruited and selected, and care has to be taken to see that they are chosen carefully for the particular tasks to be carried out, according to the aptitudes and inclinations of those available. Also, in some work situations it is important that those selected shall be capable of working together harmoniously as a team.

The organisation of the various and successive work processes comprising the firm's total productive activity, including the physical lay-out of a factory and the methods adopted for performing individual processes, affect the productivity of the labour force very markedly. In particular, it is necessary to take full advantage of the scope for the division of labour if the output of a given labour force is to be maximised, or an output of a given size is to be produced at minimal cost. However, great refinement of the division of labour, which is typical of large-scale mass production, is not without its problems. Constant repetition by an operative of a single simplified task in an allocated time, determined perhaps by the intervals at which a conveyor-belt presents a partly-assembled product or component at his or her work station, can be boring and stultifying. At some point it can become counter-productive. For this reason there have been some recent instances of firms reverting to a system of production whereby a small workgroup produces a whole unit of the product in one work sequence. The Volvo company has tried this with motor-car assembly in Sweden, and radio receivers are assembled from parts by single individuals in at least one plant in the UK. The Volvo experiment appears not to have yielded a positive result. Clearly there will be some cases where a labour force would prefer the elimination of unremitting repetition of a boring task and the satisfaction of building a whole product, even with a resulting reduction of their productivity and earnings. Workers' reaction to such a change depends on a number of variables in each situation, including the strength of the distaste on the part of the workers concerned for the highly divided tasks in the first place, and the possible reduction in their accustomed earnings occasioned by a lesser extent of division of labour. The latter factor means that it is easier to establish a plant on whole product lines than to adapt an existing factory, for no drop in experienced earnings from that employment is apparent.

The organisation of work processes is ultimately a task of management. Nevertheless, experienced and intelligent workers form ideas for the improvement of processes and products. It can be a source of frustration, a source of 'them and us' attitudes, and consequently of disaffection and lower productivity if there is no outlet by which such ideas can be received and considered. The very minimum is a suggestion box, which is not uncommon. A much more positive and creative device is widespread in Japanese industry and is slowly beginning to be adopted in Britain; it is the establishment of **quality circles**. These are regular meetings, during working-hours, of groups of workers engaged in a common task or process for the discussion of their work and its end-products, and the experience suggests that they have a marked positive effect on productivity. Some of this is psychological and motivational, whilst some arises from practical ideas first discussed in the quality circles and ultimately adopted by the company.

To the extent that the benefits of quality circles lie in the area of motivation, they tie in with the conclusions of the main management theorists who have emphasised the psychological needs in relation to the financial needs of workers. The price offered, compared where appropriate to the risks attached, may be taken to be the sole attraction for other factors of production and once attracted, their use within the firm is subject to management decision making in a less complicated way than is the case with labour. Equipment has to be maintained, the quality of a batch of a raw material may modify the use which is made of it, but workers have human needs at the workplace and these are not always obvious; and workers will, as has just been seen, have views on the organisation of the work itself. The degree of satisfaction or otherwise of these needs has profound effects on the performance of workers, and the needs become more sophisticated with the rise in material rewards. When living standards are near subsistence level, people's dominant consideration is with the amount received in return for their work, and their strongest motivation is the satisfaction of their basic needs for adequate food, clothing and shelter. Once achieved, the satisfaction of these needs ceases to have primary motivational force and is replaced by some higher need. This may still be dependent on higher income, so that financial reward continues to be a motivator, but as an individual's standards rise further and existing wants are met, new wants emerge to take their place and some of these are no longer to be bought with money. To that extent, financial rewards are partly replaced as the springs of motivation in the workplace;

the necessity to work continues, since the earlier and more basic needs continue to require to be met, but motivation at the place of work comes to have a more social character and to depend upon working conditions, the esteem accorded to the kind of work, the satisfaction derived from performing it and performing it well, and power and authority. Financial rewards may accompany any or all of these things but become relatively weaker as a prime motivator for their own sake, except as a sign of success and a source of esteem.

In short, the labour force is neither a lump nor an abstraction responding solely to financial inducement, but consists of human beings with human needs, some of which arise, willy-nilly, in an industrial context. Their psychological charateristics are part of the quality of the labour force, and able managers harness these characteristics to mutual productive benefit.

Communication, Consultation and Employee Involvement

Some of the areas of action for ensuring that the productiveness of labour reaches its potential are those of communication, consultation and employee involvement. Quality circles, which have already been mentioned, are an institution containing elements of all three. We cannot go into detail with these special topics here, but briefly they constitute measures to promote flows of information between management and workers in both directions, and between different departments of the firm. Information about the content and purpose of jobs, their inter-relationship with other jobs in the productive activity, and the way in which they contribute to the firm's objectives, leads to those jobs being done more intelligently and effectively. Management decisions taken after consultation, if appropriate, and with all the appropriate employees or their representatives for the purpose, are better decisions because they are better-informed and are more readily accepted than if reached and announced without consultation. Communicating the reasons for major decisions further increases their acceptability. The provision of information about senior management's thinking on plans and objectives for the future, where these are not of a kind which could benefit a competitor, is a help to good relations within the firm and makes plans easier to implement. Some decisions need no consultation and it is in the interest of the credibility of effective consultation that in such cases none take place. In other cases the scope for consultation is limited to a particular level or group within the firm. Equally, consultation and employee involvement are not a substitute for, or abdication of, management; managers retain their responsibility for decisions reached and hence also their authority to make them.

The kinds of subject on which consultation and employee involvement takes place are the working environment and health and safety (which, as might be expected, are the most common topics of consultation), production and work methods, training, pensions, layoffs and redundancies, changes in industrial relations policy and manning levels. Such consultations are separate from negotiations with trade unions, which take place on some of the same subjects; and questions about pay typically form only a small proportion of consultations within companies. A study by the Confederation of British Industry (CBI) of employee involvement practice suggests that the most common involvement method is face-to-face meetings between employees and the most senior manager, and that in only one-tenth of operating units do such meetings not take place. It also suggests that works councils or other joint consultative committees are to be found in something approaching two-thirds of the operating units in business, and that they are more common in larger than in smaller businesses. These methods of involvement do not, as is apparent from the figures, preclude each other, nor do they imply that further methods are not also in existence in the same units. Informal arrangements giving employees the right to regular information and consultation were found to exist in over two-thirds of cases. These results cannot necessarily be taken as representing the position in British industry as a whole and they do include some operating units in distribution and finance, as distinct from industry, but they may be taken as being fairly representative of the situation in large companies at least.

Some years ago there was a movement to extend participation to include a requirement whereby a substantial proportion of worker members was to be admitted to the boards of directors of companies. In 1977 the majority of a Committee of Inquiry on Industrial Democracy under the chairmanship of Lord Bullock reported in favour of representation of employees through trade unions on the boards of companies with over 2,000 employees in the UK; boards would consist of three groups, namely an equal number (x) of shareholder and worker representatives, and a smaller number (y) of independent members co-opted by agreement between the first two groups. This was known as the $2x + y$ formula. The number of independents (y) was to be odd and the Chairman would be nominated by the shareholder representatives. A minority report objected that the terms of reference given to the Committee precluded them from considering the prior question, whether employee representative directors should be appointed, and confined them to the question of how such appointment should be made. The minority stressed the importance of effective involvement of employees below board level and considered that if employee directors were appointed, the three groups should be of equal numbers, that the employee directors should include one each from the shop floor, salaried staff and management employees, and that they should be elected by secret ballot and have considerable experience of the company and its existing participation procedures. A board so constituted would be a Supervisory Board not responsible for the day-to-day running of the company. Supervisory Boards, however, are a feature of West German industry where the institutional background of their existence differs sharply from that of the UK, and where the effectiveness of employee participation lies in the works councils.

Opposition to the majority proposals of the Bullock Committee centred largely around the place they accorded to the trade unions and did not all come from one side. Many thought it inappropriate that unions would nominate employee directors, who might then be union officials rather than company employees; further, not all employees are trade union members and they would be discriminated against by not being represented. Another objection was that the proposals carried a danger of entangling negotiation with the making of company policy and decisions, which were seen as different kinds of activity. Another was that trade unions should not be seen in the role of supporting the capitalist system; while, in contrast, a further objection was that the proposals would facilitate the fight against capitalist management and its eventual replacement. No action was taken by government on the report.

Financial Participation

There are various forms of financial participation or profit sharing which are adopted to give employees a greater involvement in the profitable operation of the firm. They can be an incentive to increased output; they may foster a good atmosphere generally between a firm and its employees; and it is sometimes thought that they reduce the costs of supervision and replacement of equipment because of the greater assiduity and care which they impart to the workforce. They tend to work well in firms where the connection between individual effort and profitability is seen relatively easily, and this is more readily the case in small firms than in large. However, whatever their form, the annual or six-monthly intervals at which profit is usually calculated for purposes of distribution are long compared with a weekly pay interval, and some of the incentive effect can be lost through this separation in time of effort and its reward.

Financial participation schemes, strictly speaking, are not directly related to an individual's effort. When they are, they take the form of a bonus on wages or salary. We are considering here, however, schemes of a collective character relating a share of profits to each individual's wage or salary, so that the result for the individual depends on the profits of the firm or unit as a whole and hence on the efforts of all the workforce and the other influences affecting profits. The principle is most easily seen when a financial participation scheme takes the form of employee shareholding. Such a scheme may work under the Finance Acts of 1978 and 1979 whereby shares may be allotted to an employees' trust, which enjoys certain tax concessions, and the number of such schemes – which operated under less favourable taxation arrangements before the recent Acts – is increasing. Here the participation of employees is basically in the form of dividends. The allotment of shares to directors and senior management individually is another form of profit sharing.

Trade Unions

The protection and fostering of the interests of employees in all matters relating to their employment forms the primary purpose of trade unions. Pay is the item which appears most prominently in their activities, but hours and conditions of work are also important subjects with which they deal, including safety and welfare at work, and management methods of enforcing discipline.

About half the working population are union members, and the proportion in the industrial sector is considerably larger than that. The proportion within particular industries varies widely, with the mining and railway industries virtually completely unionised and the textile industry having about a quarter of its employees in union membership. The total number of unions in the UK is about 450, but some of them are very small. The scene is dominated by about a dozen very large unions with memberships ranging from something approaching a quarter of a million to something over two million members. They constitute fewer than 3 per cent of unions by number, but have 70 per cent of total union membership in the economy.

The union representative within an industrial firm is the **shop steward**. He is elected by his fellow workers, remains an employee of the firm and is unpaid for his part in union affairs. He collects subscriptions for union membership, so that the union can finance its day-to-day running and build reserves which may be required as a strike fund. He is the point of contact for the individual worker with his union, and for the union with the firm's management, at least in the first instance. He deals on the one side with a local branch official of the union, and on the other with the firm's managers as may be appropriate. The position of shop steward contains problems arising from the fact that he is elected and that those whom he represents sometimes wish to follow a path different from official union policy. This sometimes finds expression in unofficial strikes, for a shop steward has no power to call an official strike, yet finds it difficult to resist local feeling.

In a **closed shop** it is one of the steward's functions to check that each new worker employed is already a member of the union or, in the case of a 'post-entry' closed shop, that he becomes a member. A closed shop comes about by the union securing an agreement with the management that only members of the union will be taken on to the labour force. This matter is highly controversial and raises issues of individual freedom and the possibility of victimisation by a union. The arrangement also weakens the influence of individual members on the union because they lose the power of resignation without losing their job. On the other hand, it strengthens the union's collective power in relation to an employer. Some employers favour closed shops out of regard for the stability and discipline which they are said to bring.

Broadly speaking, there are four main types of union. The earliest kind to be formed were **craft unions**, whose members all practised the same trade. The National Graphical Association is an example which has a prominent position in the present day, but many craft unions dwindled as industrial processes changed with the growth of machine production and the consequent relative decline of crafts. It is of some importance for subsequent industrial relations in this country that the next kind of union to appear on the scene, from the 1880s, was the **general union**, whose members were not catered for by the craft unions and not confined to a particular industry. It helped to overcome their usually weak bargaining power if they organised with others in a similar situation in other industries. A present-day example is the Transport and General Workers' Union; it is the largest union in the country and reached this size partly by the nature of its membership and partly by amalgamations of previously existing unions. The general type of union organisation assisted the spread of the notion of **the rate for the job** (see the section on Bargaining Power later in this chapter) irrespective of the commercial situation of a particular industry or employer.

By contrast to the general union, the **industrial** type of union is based on the employer's business. Examples are the National Union of Mineworkers and the Iron and Steel Federation. With this type of union organisation, the economic conditions of a particular industry are more easily recognised as a factor in negotiations, as compared with cases where there is a general union, and differentials may be less apt to lead to leapfrogging.

Lastly, there are **white collar unions**, such as the National Association of Local Government Officers (which has something of the character of an industrial union) and the Association of Scientific, Technical and Managerial Staffs (which is, however, also a general union). This type of union is growing fairly rapidly and membership is sometimes attractive to the lower and middle levels of management in industry.

Wage Levels and the Quality of the Labour Force

In conditions where wages remain around subsistence level, as was frequently the case in the early period of the rise of British industry, the quality of the workforce is low because the workers are inadequately fed, clothed and sheltered. They are therefore a prey to sickness, not fully active and alert, and their standard of education is likely to be low. They are likely to have hardly any leisure and even that not worth much as recreation. In such circumstances successful pressure for higher wages has the effect of raising the quality of the workforce; the pre-existing productivity of labour may be below the level of the wage being sought, but will rise as a result of the higher wage obtained, so justifying the latter from the employers' point of view.

The scope for that particular kind of 'economy of high wages' is now for the most part a thing of the past. There is, however, another form of it. We have already met 'organisational slack'. Pressure for higher wages may justify itself in terms of productivity if, as a result, management is able to find ways (and the forms of consultation referred to above may be relevant) of improving the use made of the firm's plant, the suitability of its products for its markets, its search for new markets or any of the factors which affect its performance. The limit to this process is the extent to which increased efficiency can, in fact, be achieved. One possibility is that it can indeed be achieved, but only by installing new capital equipment which can produce the present output with fewer workers; the capital cost is higher but becomes worthwhile with a new higher wage rate for the size of workforce it requires. Unless it is possible to increase the market or raise prices without loss of sales, those pressing for higher wage rates may be confronted by a choice of objectives: to maximise the wage rate for the existing labour force, to maximise the total wage bill, or to maximise the wage rate irrespective of the number who may continue to receive it.

The Determination of Wages

Four different kinds of force may be found exerting an influence on the determination of wages: convention, the market forces of supply and demand, bargaining power as between employers and employed, and state intervention. Their relative strengths may vary from time to time, place to place, and from industry to industry; and so may the persistence of any wage rate determined predominantly by any one of these sets of forces at a particular time.

(i) Convention

The idea of conventional or customary rates of pay is deep-seated and rooted partly in medieval times, when the status in society of those in various occupations determined the rewards of the different kinds of work. There was a settled hierarchical order of society which commanded general acceptance, and payment both reflected this order and helped to maintain it. The criterion for rates of pay was that they should be right and fair in this light. They reflected qualities seen socially as inherent in the recipient. The hierarchical view still persists to some extent, with some tendency for pay and status to vary with each other, while the emphasis on customary differentials is probably as strong as ever. The notion of fairness manifests itself strongly today in a further way – the esteem accorded to the intrinsic requirements of effort and ability demanded by one job as compared with another.

The measurement of the intrinsic requirements for carrying out a job as compared with those for another is an attempt at something which cannot be measured objectively at all, and depends on conventional or consensus views about the qualities required and conventional assumptions that they 'ought' to be rewarded accordingly. It is attempted by **job evaluation**, which analyses each job by identifying the qualities required to carry it out – skill, training, experience, responsibility, intelligence, physique, together with the degree of stress or unpleasantness associated with the job. These broad headings are then broken down further into the detailed features of the job and the requirements to fulfil them. Points on a scale are allotted to each feature, relative to the rewards for that feature in other comparable jobs with which comparison is to be made. The total of points, set alongside those arrived at for other jobs in the same way and by the same assessors, represents that job's evaluation. Relative rates of pay for jobs embraced by the exercise follow the relative evaluations.

Individuals in particular jobs are required at least to match up to the job evaluations, but some will be found to surpass the minimum standard and it is felt fair that they should be rewarded for it and, indeed, they may actually be more productive. This is taken care of by a supplementary exercise of **merit rating**, which has similar procedures but is based on the qualities of individual workers rather than the characteristics of the jobs themselves.

All this is highly subjective and particular assessors or teams of assessors might vary in their assessments. It would be easy, but a mistake, to dismiss it as mumbo-jumbo. Its conventions are accepted because it fulfils a felt need for fairness, which is a concept very frequently brought into discussions about pay.

Finally, convention has ruled for a very long time in the matter of women's pay. The attention now paid to this issue through the Equal Opportunities Commission is a tribute to the power of convention, and of changing convention, and to that of State intervention on wages.

(ii) Market Forces

Market forces are those of the total supply and the total demand of anything which has exchange value. They interact to determine prices – in this case the wage rates of the various kinds of labour – which settle at a point at which they are stable until some change takes place in the supply or demand for the particular commodity or kind of labour concerned. For each amount of supply that might be considered there is a supply price below which not the whole of that amount will be offered, and for each amount there is a demand price above which not the whole of that amount will be bought. The price moves up or down, as the case may be, until the amounts for which there are willing sellers and buyers are equal. This is a very powerful and, in the long run, an inexorable mechanism so long as people are motivated by pecuniary advantage. Its results may be modified for very long periods by the forces of custom, convention and ideas of fairness which we have noticed, and for probably shorter periods by relative bargaining strengths and government intervention; and in the case of the supply of labour, the net advantages of a particular employment will be considered by those who might potentially form part of the supply – its relative pleasantness or unpleasantness, its location, whether the cost of higher training for a better-paid position and the loss of earnings during training are felt to be worthwhile, and so on.

If an industry or firm wishes to expand or start up a further plant in another location, it may be able to recruit labour of the kinds and in the numbers it requires at existing rates of pay because, if the area is sufficiently populous, enough people are willing to come forward to try a change of employment for all kinds of reasons. The firm may also find it possible because of high general unemployment: expansion may not be very likely during such a period, but could well take place for new productive industries arising on the ashes of old at a time when the structure of industry is changing. Many hope that the present will turn out to be such a time. However, our concern in this chapter is not with the level of rates of pay in general in relation to the level of total unemployment, but with relative rates of pay in different employments. If our expanding firm is not at first able to recruit all the labour it requires, it will offer higher wages. This step is required in order to expand the labour supply available to the particular firm or industry. Those who would have a longer journey to work (with its extra cost and inconvenience), those who are already in higher-paid jobs than those who moved without financial inducement, those who need a period of training with allowances less than their existing pay, and those who are reluctant to leave existing workmates or take the risks of going to a new employer, will all move if, and only if, adequately recompensed. There may be any number of reasons, any number and height of hurdles to be surmounted in individual cases. They mean that the more labour the employer considers recruiting, the more he must pay the last, the least eager, recruit.

There is a supply schedule of labour, such that as the number of units of labour required rises, so too does the supply price at some particular rate. The relation between a proportionate increase in the wage rate and the resulting proportionate extension of supply is called the **elasticity of supply**, and gives us an idea of the degree of responsiveness of supply (labour) to price (wage rate). This elasticity is considerably greater in the long run than in the short run for some occupations; it would not be possible, for example, to extend the number of heart surgeons in the short run; some doctors in mid-training might switch their proposed speciality, which would take several years, whilst the full effects would not materialise for longer still.

The supply of labour consists of not only numbers of people, but also the hours they will work and the effort applied. We have seen that when living standards rise, some people have a preference for a shorter working week at a new higher hourly rate of wages. A rise in the wage rate is, in effect, an increase in the price of leisure, and to that extent contains an incentive to substitute some more work for correspondingly less leisure, supposing that an individual is free to vary his hours. Even if he is not so free, he still harbours the preference. At the same time, his income rises for a given supply of labour; now, different people have different strengths of desire for additional income, depending on the extent of their family commitments, their ambitions and the lifestyle they desire. The balance of these contrary influences on the responsiveness of the supply of labour to a change in the wage rate works out differently for different people. For some, the supply schedule of labour is not positive at all points. At any one time, for a given change in rates of pay, some will, on balance, want to work more, some less. This is of great practical importance when hours or intensity of effort can be varied.

There is also a relationship between a series of wage rates that might be considered for a particular employment and the number of workers an employer will be willing to engage at each of those rates. This relationship expresses itself in a demand schedule for labour. The firm's demand for labour is derived from the demand for its products which have a price relative to the prices of other products competing for a share of the consumer's purse. In a given state of technology and with a given collection of other factors of production successive equal increments of a factor yield successively diminishing contributions to the physical product. This is the celebrated principle of diminishing returns; it is only a partial statement of a fuller principle but it is the part we need to use. That it is a valid generalisation may be seen by contemplating the results of trying to produce the country's output of wheat from one farm. There is an extent to which a firm's or an industry's input of labour can be varied, with a diminishing physical contribution coming from each successive input. This tendency to diminishing returns is more marked if the additional output can only be sold at lower prices, and if more has to be paid for the additional units of input. In fact we have seen that more does have to be paid for an increased input of labour itself. The marginal value product of labour falls as more of it is used. It should be remembered that all this is in the context of a given state of technology: it does not preclude – what would be manifestly absurd – the possibility of raising standards through time by invention and discovery.

Employers will not be willing to pay more for an extra unit of labour than its use will add to their sales proceeds. Thus the demand schedule is negatively inclined – the larger the quantity of labour of a particular type under consideration, the lower its demand price. Since the supply schedule of labour has been seen to be, in general, positively inclined, the two have a common point at which, for that amount of labour, less wages will not be accepted by workers and more will not be paid by employers. In other words, it is the wage rate (*OW* in Figure 4.1) at which the supply of and demand for that labour are equal.

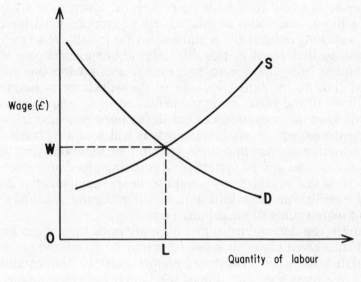

Figure 4.1

It is a general conclusion of this kind of analysis that the marginal revenue products of all factors are proportionate to their prices.

(iii) *Bargaining Power*

Bargaining over wages in industry is conducted by the trade unions on the one side and employers' federations or individual employers on the other. Before the growth of trade unions, workers were in a weak bargaining position for lack of the practical possibility of collective action, for lack of resources to provide strike pay in the last resort, and for lack of professional leadership which could be a match for the abilities of employers. In these circumstances exploitation of labour was not uncommon: we may unemotively define exploitation as the payment to a factor of production of less than its marginal product.

Each side enters a negotiation with a certain objective or objectives, for although wage rates are our focus of attention in this section, they are far from being the only subject of negotiations between unions and employers. Hours and conditions of work, manning levels, negotiating procedures themselves, individual grievances and many other matters are dealt with by negotiation at all levels. Some of these matters, such as hours and manning levels, have implications for pay through the influence of market forces. Given that the stated objectives of the parties conflict, the art of negotiation is to reach agreement on the best achievable terms.

Each side is likely to have a point beyond which it really is not willing to go, and skilful negotiators try to estimate what the other party's sticking point really is and endeavour to achieve an outcome as close to that point as possible. The ultimate sanctions, whose recognition brings power to bargaining, are, on the one hand a strike; and, on the other, lockout of the workforce, a permanent closedown of the plant, or implementation of an employer's offer regardless of the consequences but in the hope or expectation that sufficient numbers of individual workers will accept it. It has to be emphasised, however, that these are ultimate sanctions, and that in a developed and agreed system of negotiating procedures there are many stages of negotiation brought to bear, supplemented if need be by conciliation and arbitration, before resorting to actual use of the ultimate source of bargaining power.

If there is a demand price and a supply price for a given kind of labour in a given place, then surely, it may be asked, the result of a negotiation between skilful negotiators must be the equilibrium price? We have seen that one of the benefits of trade unions is to ensure that labour receives its full marginal product, by and large. But the economic model of the labour market is not a description of the real world, though a powerful element in helping to explain it. If a bargain is struck which is above the marginal product of labour, one or more of several consequences may ensue. Employers may shed labour if they can do so without renewing the dispute; this may take time if accomplished by failing to replace workers who leave in the normal course of events, or 'natural wastage'; in the meantime, their profit margins will be squeezed. Their profits may be permanently reduced and this tolerated because their level was the result of a monopoly position in the market for their products. They may, as has already been noticed, find that under the stimulus of higher wages they can find ways of improving the efficiency of their organisation by improving methods of production, making economies elsewhere, or finding new markets. Alternatively, they may raise the prices of their products, either immediately (and customers have some readiness to accept increased prices when it is shown that they result from increased costs), or at a later stage when seasonal or other price adjustments are in any case expected; price rises, however, are particularly dangerous in exporting and import-competing industries. If their market is expected to grow, they may carry on in the expectation of installing new and more efficient equipment to be operated by the existing labour force. Possible adjustments of this kind give play for the operation of bargaining power.

A notable effect of the impingement of trade union power on relative wages has been the notion of the rate for the job. Bargaining at national level has assisted in fostering the implementation of this principle. Rates of pay for a given job used at one time to vary quite markedly from one place to another, and sometimes within the same plant. This is now much less so because of union pressure, based partly on ideas of fairness and partly on the fact that union bargaining power was thought to be weaker where rates could vary. This principle has been very effective in changing the circumstances in which it was introduced. There has recently been some movement towards plant bargaining on the basis of national agreements, and to some extent this goes against the idea of the rate for the job.

(iv) State Intervention

State intervention in the determination of wages may take the form of regulation, or of the provision of arbitration as the last resort in the settlement of disputes by orderly process. Regulation may be a matter of laying down minimum legal wages in certain occupations, or a minimum wage payable in any occupation; or it may be part of a macroeconomic incomes policy having the intention of restraining increases in money wages.

Decisions imposed by state intervention and those reached by the mutual exercise of bargaining power evoke similar responses on the part of employers and workers, and their effectiveness is alike constrained by market forces and by those of convention. Arising from this, it is sometimes argued that the enforcement of a legal minimum wage higher than the current market level must result in some of the workers affected losing their jobs. Such is not so in all cases, however. We have seen already that there may be ways in which employers can respond to a higher wage rate reached by collective bargaining without causing unemployment, and the same considerations apply if the increased wage comes about by government action. Demand for labour in a particular industry will be relatively inelastic if wages are only a small part of the total cost of production. Demand for the product by the ultimate consumer will be less affected by the manufacturer's selling price if there is a long chain of distribution whose costs amount to a very substantial proportion of the final selling price. Demand for the product, and hence for the labour employed in its manufacture, will also tend to be inelastic if buyers cannot readily find an alternative source of acceptable supply. Conditions such as these are, however, by no means always present. In particular, if a product is competing in export markets or faces competition from imports, and the international trade is fairly free from restrictions, then buyers' possible sources of supply are widened and their demand is more responsive to the price of the product.

State intervention in the form of minimum wage legislation is relatively easy to enforce, partly because in some cases it may stimulate the kinds of reaction we have been noticing and which will make the minimum economically viable, and partly because there is a general desire to comply, at least on the workers' side. Maximum wage legislation, on the other hand, faces a desire by both employers and employees to escape from control. The conditions in which legislation which seeks to restrain pay rises is introduced are precisely those of 'over-full' employment and concomitant inflation of prices and incomes. Labour of all kinds finds itself in a seller's market, whilst employers suffer labour shortages and wish to overcome them. The incidence of the law is avoided by making adjustments to overtime, by promoting staff to higher grades which may even be invented for the purpose, and by the proliferation of fringe benefits.

Arbitration may result not only from government intervention but from being built into negotiating procedures agreed by the parties, as a final stage when agreement has not been reached. This poses a dilemma. On the one hand, arbitration is necessary when all else fails; on the other, the knowledge that there is provision for it to be invoked may lead negotiators to 'stick' at some point short of their true sticking point, so that the negotiations do not really run their full course and what was intended as a last resort comes to be used more as the final stage. This may not matter greatly in itself. However, a further consideration has to be noted, and that is that it seems likely that arbitration contains some bias towards raising rates of pay. There are two reasons for this possibility. Firstly, arbitration awards are more difficult to enforce against trade unions than against employers. Secondly, it is usually the case that some rise somewhere has occurred in the recent past, and it preserves differentials to follow suit and take part in a general rise. The more this happens, the more the rise is likely to be in fact general, and the easier will employers find it to raise the prices of their products to meet their even higher wage bills.

Summary

Labour differs from other factors of production because of the intensely personal element which it entails. The management of labour is much more complex than the management of inanimate resources and requires specific attention to be paid to the human element. Trade unions exist to protect and foster the interests of workers; there are four main types of union, organised on different bases. Collective bargaining power affects the level of remuneration of labour and so do the forces of custom or convention, and sometimes it is affected by state intervention, as well as by the forces of supply and demand.

Review Questions

(1) How far is participation of the workforce in company affairs distinct from negotiation with management, and how far do they overlap? Is the distinction important?

(2) Suggest ways in which employee involvement can make a positive contribution to productivity.

(3) Why does the Government provide industrial training facilities?

(4) Try to obtain information, perhaps in the form of a copy of a pay agreement, about wage rates in an industrial firm in your area; and try to assess, with the aid of supplementary information, the relative parts which different forces played in determining them.

Buying and selling on the stock exchange

5

The Financing of Business

In order to start producing and selling, an industrial firm has to pay for plant and equipment, materials and the services of its workforce in advance of receiving any revenue from the sale of its products. These payments have to be financed. Payments from customers, once they start to flow in, represent a source from which some of the firm's shorter-term cycle of payments can be financed, but they cannot be expected to cover anything like the firm's initial outlays within any reasonable period of time. The firm requires finance over different periods of time depending on the various and changing purposes for which it is required, and there is a corresponding pattern of different sources from which finance may be obtained. These sources are, broadly, the owners of the firm themselves, lenders outside the firm and, after a period of successful trading, sources internal to the firm.

(1) Long-Term Finance

Share Capital

Firms need money to embark on productive activity and if the enterprise is successful, they are likely to need more from time to time in order to finance the investment required for expansion. In Chapter 2 we saw how finance is provided in the first instance by those who become ordinary shareholders in a company, and we looked at the relationship between them and the company. **Ordinary shares**, or equities, are not the only kind of share which may be issued, but they form by far the greater part of the total of industry's issued capital. The other main kind of share is the **preference share**. When a company is formed it will certainly issue ordinary shares, and perhaps also preference shares. In any later issue of share capital either or both kinds of share may be involved. The amount of share capital of each kind which has been issued may not exceed the amount authorised by the company's Memorandum of Association, and if the directors think that they may wish to expand the company beyond this they will seek an amendment to the authorised capital laid down in the Memorandum.

When shares of any kind are issued, they may be either fully paid or partly paid, which means that the holder may be required to meet a further call or calls (which may or may not be on dates stipulated beforehand). However, the liability of holders of shares, whether the latter be fully or partly paid, is always limited to the nominal value of the shares; thus the owners of fully paid shares have no further liability for the debts of the company. The **dividend**, or part of the company's profits distributed to shareholders, is expressed as a percentage of the nominal share value, or as an amount of money (say 4.3p) per share. The **nominal value** is not really an essential concept and is not used in, for example, the USA. If shares are fully paid it has no meaning in relation to liability, and dividends may be expressed in absolute amounts of money per share rather than as percentages of an arbitrary nominal value which may be very different from the current market value of the share. The price at which shares are actually issued by the company may not even be the same as their nominal value, and is quite commonly higher. Suppose a company to have initially issued shares of £1 nominal value for £1, and to have traded successfully so that the shares are now £3 each; any new issue of shares is likely to be at a price below £3 but nearer to that figure than to £1.

There is no particular rate of dividend to which an ordinary shareholder has a right, and if profits are low or losses are made over a period then it may be that no dividend at all is paid until business improves. On the other hand, there is no upper limit to the amount which may be paid to ordinary shareholders other than what is actually available for the purpose. Thus the income to be derived from the ownership of ordinary shares is not contractual: furthermore, it is residual in that it may only be paid after the other kinds of subscribers of capital have been paid what is due to them. Ordinary shareholders are uncertainty bearers.

By contrast, the holders of preference shares are entitled to an income which is fixed, usually as a percentage of the nominal amount of capital represented by the shares, and this is allocated before the distribution to the other shareholders is determined but after the payment to debenture holders. One variation is the participating preference share, which becomes entitled to a further part of the profit alongside the ordinary share up to a maximum amount and after the ordinary shares have been allocated a minimum amount. Preference shares may be cumulative or noncumulative: in the case of a company not even paying the dividend on its preference shares in a particular year, holders of the latter kind forgo their right to that payment, whereas the right to payment in respect of cumulative preference shares is carried forward to the next or a later year and continues to rank ahead of the ordinary shares. There may also be first and second preference shares, indicating an order of priority of the claim to dividends between them; thus a company might have, for example, First Preference 6 per cent shares and Second Preference 6½ per cent. Sometimes preference shares are redeemable, and some carry a right to be converted at a future date into ordinary shares. The order of priority followed by the various kinds of shares and other instruments with regard to dividend and interest payments is followed for claims for repayment in the case of winding up the company. The Articles of Association usually lay down that preference shareholders may vote at shareholders' meetings on matters directly affecting their interests, and on any other matter if their dividend has not been paid or has not been paid in full. There are many variations of the standard types of ordinary and preference shares, both as to participation in profits and as to voting rights and such variations may, indeed, be invented at will and to meet particular needs so long as they are consistent with the law and so long as their terms are made plain.

Debentures and Loan Stock

Debentures represent loans to a company, and a debenture holder is therefore a creditor of the company and not a shareholder member of that company, though he is a supplier of capital. Debentures carry the right to interest at a fixed rate and rank in priority of payment before all kinds of share, both as to income payments and in case of liquidation of the company. The conditions which attach to them may vary: some have a stated date for redemption (repayment); others do not. Some – called mortgage debentures – are backed by a particular fixed asset belonging to the company, so that in the event of the company being wound up or redemption of the debenture falling due, the proceeds of sale of that asset are to be made available first of all for the repayment of those particular debenture holders ahead of other creditors; others are secured by a floating charge, i.e. they are backed by the company's assets in general, any of which might be sold if necessary to meet repayment on the redemption date. Others, often known as loan stock (which is sometimes convertible to equities), are unsecured, and their holders are in the same position as trade creditors and rank with them, but ahead of shareholders, in the event of non-payment of interest or capital.

Mortgage debentures may be first, second or other mortgage debentures, as with preference shares. Debentures may be issued singly to, say, a financial institution making a large loan, or in large numbers to the subscribing public, as with a share issue. In the latter case trustees are appointed to safeguard the interests of the debenture holders, and a trust deed transfers secured assets to them for use in case of default. The trustees would then either sell the assets concerned or require the appointment of a receiver to administer the company's affairs.

New Issues and the Secondary Capital Market

When a firm is raising finance either for the first time or in order to increase its capital, and it wishes its shares or other securities to be dealt in on the stock exchange, it has to seek what is known as a **listing** or **quotation** from the Stock Exchange Council. In applying for this, a great deal of detailed information about the company's history, profit record, financial situation, trading prospects, management and similar matters has to be supplied. Some of this information will be in the prospectus, a document required by the Companies Act to be published when the public is invited to subscribe for shares, but the rules of the stock exchange require further information if a listing is to be granted. On passing this stringent test, the company may proceed to issue the securities, and there are various methods by which this may be done. The choice of method (and the choice of the type of securities to be issued) is partly a matter of the size of the issue and conditions in the capital market at the time the issue takes place, though an element of fashion creeps in, based on observed experience of recent use of the various methods.

(i) Public Issue This method consists of an offer based on the prospectus, made by the industrial or other company to the general public, of a stated number of shares or other securities at a stated price. Such offers and prospectuses may be found in the business pages of newspapers from time to time. A company adopting this method will normally employ professional advisers, such as an issuing house or merchant bank, who will probably also handle the large volume of paper work generated by the issue. It is also likely that arrangements will be made for an issuing house to underwrite the issue, which means that in return for a commission they guarantee the success of the issue by agreeing to take up any shortfall in the number of shares applied for by the public. Part of this risk may be passed to other institutions as sub-underwriters. Obviously much skill and knowledge of the market is required to enable this function to be carried out, but even so occasionally 'fingers are burned'.

(ii) Offer for Sale This is a variation of the public issue method,

and is at present the method most frequently adopted. Under it, the new issue is bought by an issuing house and perhaps other merchant banks at a certain price. These purchasers then offer the securities for sale to the public at a certain higher price. This method requires just as much information about the company and the issue as does a public issue. It is used particularly when a new company is approaching the market for the first time, and is rather cheaper for the company, even allowing for the lower price it receives, than the total expenses of a full public issue. Even so, the expenses can readily amount to £¼ million for quite a moderately sized offer for sale.

(iii) Placing This is the process of negotiating with financial institutions and, through members of the stock exchange, with private or institutional investors for them to take up parcels of new or existing securities. The shares may initially be bought by an issuing house for onward placing. This method is suitable when the total issue is too small to warrant the high cost of a public issue or offer for sale, and the individual placings will be relatively large. At this stage the method is a private placing. A prospectus is still required, and if the securities are previously unquoted and are subsequently to be dealt in on the stock exchange, an 'introduction' is required. This means obtaining the quotation in the normal way, and in this case arranging for some securities to be made available at an agreed price so that jobbers may be in a position to begin trading and the public to buy shares. The method then becomes a stock exchange placing. The introduction alone may be used as a means of starting to use the stock exchange as the market for securities in previously unquoted public companies, ownership of whose shares is already fairly widespread; the object in doing this may be to pave the way for a future public issue.

(iv) Tender Instead of shares being offered to the public at a price stated by the issuing company or its merchant bankers, as with the public issue or offer for sale, they may be offered to the public for sale by tender. Potential subscribers bid for whatever number of shares they decide on, at a price named by them subject to a minimum price laid down by the issuer. All shares are allotted at the same price – the **striking price** – after examination of the tenders. In principle the applicants with the highest bids have their applications accepted until, working down the applications in rank order of bid, the number of shares on offer is allocated; the lowest successful bid price becomes the striking price. In practice this simplicity sometimes has to be modified. The stock exchange rules require that whatever issue method is adopted, at least 25 per cent of an issue

must end up in the hands of the public, in order to ensure an efficient market. If there are a few high bids for very large amounts, adherence to the simple procedure could break this rule, and it may also be wished to have a wider spread of shareholders than the minimum insisted on by the Stock Exchange Council. In such cases applications at the highest bids are scaled down and only a proportion of the number of shares applied for is allotted to those bidders. Smaller successful applications may be allotted in full; sometimes a ballot is used to decide between smaller applications if their number is very large and the total applied for greatly exceeds the number being issued. This situation is known as 'over-subscription'. The normal tender method implies that if the striking price is much above the minimum price, the company may attract more capital than it intends or requires; to meet this situation a little-used variation is to seek tenders for an unspecified number of shares to provide a stated amount of capital at the striking price.

(v) Rights Issue   This is an offer by a company of shares or other securities to existing holders, and so in the nature of things can only be employed when the company is already in existence. The company states the purposes for which the new capital is required, and the offer is for a number of new shares proportionate to existing holdings, say one for eight or three for five, at a price appreciably below the current market price of the shares; this price is below any likely level to which the existing shares might fall during the period of the rights offer. Thus the rights have a value, and a shareholder who does not wish to exercise them may sell them on the stock exchange; in this way all the rights will eventually be in the possession of individuals or institutions who 'take them up', i.e. subscribe to the new issue. From the company's point of view, a rights issue is an inexpensive way of raising further capital, for the administration and other costs are much lower than those for a public issue or an offer for sale. From the shareholder's point of view, the opportunity to subscribe to a rights issue is part of the total reward hoped for from shareholding, which also includes capital gains on disposal as well as dividends while the shares are held.

(vi) Unlisted Securities Market   Since 1980 the Stock Exchange Council has allowed dealings on the stock exchange in the securities of certain companies without a full official listing, but satisfying certain modified requirements as to size of capital, length of trading record and extent of public participation in ownership. The costs of obtaining an unlisted quotation are much lower than those of obtaining an official listing. A full prospectus does not need to be advertised except where the shares are the subject of an offer of sale

to the public, and then only in one newspaper; a prospectus still has to be filed with the Registrar of Companies. The minimum proportion of the equity required to be held by the public is 10 per cent as against the 25 per cent for a full listing. Entry to the market is obtained by offer for sale, placing or, provided 10 per cent of the equity is already held by the public, by introduction. It must be handled by a sponsoring stockbroker member of the exchange. An offer for sale is normally required to be underwritten. For what are sometimes fairly new and not very large companies, a market for their shares developed in this way can be a preliminary to the raising of further capital by one of the methods already outlined. Industrial companies are one of three sectors to be found in the unlisted market, the others being oil exploration and new technology.

The Queue

Mention has been made of two watchdogs who have to be appeased when making a public issue – the Registrar of Companies and, if the securities are to be traded on the stock exchange, the Council of the Stock Exchange. There is a third – the Bank of England. In the general interest of maintaining an orderly capital market, the Bank does not wish to see a situation in which it would be possible for the market to be overwhelmed by invitations to subscribe large sums within days of each other, followed by fallow periods during which new savings accumulate with no new outlets to absorb them directly or indirectly. It therefore operates a queuing system for new issues including rights, and dates are allocated for such issues in the light of the Bank's estimate of the market's capacity to absorb them.

Equity for Small Firms

Part of the Government's policy of encouraging small and new firms is concerned with making it easier for them to raise equity capital. Since 1980 a succession of measures giving certain tax reliefs to outside investors in such companies have been introduced. They are the Venture Capital, Business Start-Up and Business Expansion Schemes, and are concerned respectively with losses incurred on capital invested, with the investment itself in a new company, and with already existing unquoted UK companies.

The Issue Price

Companies making a new issue do so because they wish to raise a certain amount of capital for the purpose either of starting up, which will usually be by buying a business that already exists in some form, or of expanding their operations. An attempt to raise capital simply because the company was short of cash would be very unlikely to succeed. At any event the purpose of the issue and hence the amount required is known. We have seen above that a way of aiming to raise a specific sum is to seek tenders for an unspecified number of shares and to accept tenders down to the price which yields this sum. However, this is done but rarely. There is a sense in which, with the normal tender method, an issue may be over-subscribed or under-subscribed. In this case under-subscription may mean that the minimum price has been set too high.

With a public issue or offer for sale the price at which applications are invited is set and the decision about its level is a critical factor in the success or otherwise of the issue. When either of these methods is used, a fixed number of shares is put on offer and the aim of the company and its financial advisers will be to set the price at the highest level compatible with all the shares in the issue being taken up at that price. Prudence will dictate a margin of safety so that the issue may be seen to be a success. If the issue is heavily over-subscribed at the issue price, some applications, usually those above a certain size, will be accepted only for a certain proportion of the number applied for; alternatively, or additionally, applications may be the subject of a ballot. If the issue is under-subscribed, the underwriters will be left with the shortfall on their hands, to be disposed of as and when they can.

Speculators are always alert for opportunities to apply for new issues if they think that the price of the shares, when trading begins in them on the stock exchange, will be higher than the issue price. Those seeking a quick profit in this way are known as '**stags**'. Such profits act as a 'sweetener' to the market and enhance the view of a company taken by the investing community; this, in turn, may make it easier for the company to come to the market for fresh capital in the future, and is a further reason for setting the issue price lower than the maximum which the company and its advisers estimate that an issue might fetch.

The Secondary Market

When a company's shares have been issued they will then be dealt in on the stock exchange if the company has obtained a listing. This secondary market in securities performs important functions. Those who have capital available are more willing to invest it in an indus-trial company if they know that in case of need, say because of a change in their personal circumstances, they can liquidate some or the whole of their capital. An industrial company cannot pro-vide this facility because funds are locked up in buildings, machinery, stocks and other assets. The stock exchange provides a mechanism for obtaining immediate liquidity of a shareholder's investment, albeit at the market price, and whatever that price may be – either showing the shareholder a profit or a loss, but at any rate valuing his shares on a free market. The individual shareholder is also able to terminate the commitment of his capital to a particular company if his view of the company's prospects should change, or if he should perceive another investment opportunity which he considers preferable. He may spread the risks he undertakes by investing in a number of companies instead of only one, and in securities of different types and different levels of risk. The market also makes it possible for the savings of people of quite modest means to be channelled into productive use by commercial and industrial companies.

These functions of the secondary market are sometimes assisted by speculation, though they can also be hindered by it. The activity of speculation can ensure a fairly stable market price for a share, or it may cause undue fluctuations in the price. It depends partly on expectations based on the information available to the market. We saw above how stags feed on new issues. There are other speculative animals in the stock exchange menagerie. They are **bulls**, who buy existing shares in the expectation of a rise in their price; and **bears**, who sell because they expect the price to fall and they may then buy them back if it does. Some bears sell securities they do not at present own, in the expectation of being able to buy at a lower price before delivery is due; if the price does not in fact fall, they are caught in a 'bear squeeze'.

Retained Earnings

The secondary capital market and the new issues market are obviously closely interlinked. Essentially they form a part of the total economic mechanism of a system in which resources are directed into particular uses by the free play of the impersonal forces of supply and demand, reflecting ultimately the choices of consumers. To the extent that real investment in capital projects is financed by new issues, they also provide a means whereby the directions in which new investment takes place are powerfully influenced by those who provide and risk the finance. New issues, however, are not the sole source of long-term finance for industrial and commercial companies. The profits which companies earn are partly distributed to shareholders as dividends and partly retained in the business for 'ploughing back'. Such retained earnings remain as part of the shareholders' funds, or the equity which they own in proportion to their shareholding, and in the UK they have traditionally formed a significantly larger part of the supply of company finance than is the case in other countries. Indeed, for the aggregate of industrial and commercial companies in the UK, retained earnings during the five years from 1978 to 1982 have averaged over 64 per cent of the total sources of capital funds, whilst net new issues (allowing for repayment of matured debentures) accounted for merely 4 per cent of the total. The remainder was made up of bank borrowing and other sources. In considering figures of this kind it must be remembered that they are those for companies as a whole and that the experience of individual companies may vary markedly from the average. It should also be noted that the experience of the last five years is not necessarily to be considered as normal from now on; in the 1960s new issues formed a much higher proportion of the sources of capital funds (e.g. nearly 15 per cent in 1966), and the relative proportions represented by the various sources change a good deal from time to time. It remains true, however, that the reliance on retained earnings in British industry is relatively heavy.

At times in recent years the tendency for profits to be retained has been reinforced by periods of dividend control and of the treatment of profits by the Government for taxation purposes in a way which encouraged retention rather than the paying out of profits. These, however, have been temporary influences, and the relatively heavy reliance on retained earnings for the financing of British industry is a persistent feature. The underlying reasons for this are various. We have seen that the costs to a company of making a new issue are high, and these are avoided if the company has built up reserves sufficient to finance new projects. It is also easier for directors to do this in pursuit of their objective of growth, up to the point where it is constrained by the need to increase dividends, as was seen when discussing the objectives of firms in Chapter 3. This constraint, in its turn, is not rigid: shareholders who wish to reinvest dividends are spared the brokerage and other dealing costs of doing so to the extent that profits are retained for reinvestment within the company; in addition, they do not incur income tax on dividends they do not immediately receive, whilst the increase in shareholders' funds will tend to raise the market value of their shares. Furthermore, the retention of profits for use in potential productive opportunities ensures that the funds are available when required at a particular time, even if the financial market conditions at the time are not propitious for a new issue. There are thus substantial reasons favouring the financing of industry by profit retention even though it may be argued that the practice to some extent removes decisions about the allocation of capital from investors and the market to directors and managers whose motivation and objectives may result in a different pattern of resource use.

Amalgamations

New issues and retained profits are means of providing long-term finance for the growth of a business. Growth may also be achieved by two businesses amalgamating, and since this process also involves the share capital of the two businesses, we shall here make a short detour in order to examine it.

Amalgamation takes two principal forms: (a) merger, and (b) takeover. Of the two, **merger** is the more complete. In order to merge, the two or more existing companies set up one new company which issues shares to the shareholders of each of the old companies in agreed proportions and in exchange for the old shareholdings. These proportions will reflect the relative value of assets, profitability, share price and other factors of the old companies. Thus the new amalgamated company is set up by means of share exchange, and so the new company acquires the assets and liabilities of the previously separate companies. It is thus a cheap means of expansion, which avoids the costs of a new issue and preserves existing retained profits by avoiding such costs of growth as the penetration of a new market or the expansion of an existing market share, or the development of new products.

A **takeover** occurs when an existing company acquires all the equity shares of another. It may wish to do this out of a belief that it could use the physical assets of the other company more productively than they are being used at present. Such acquisition may be financed either by cash, or by the issue of shares in the 'predator' company in exchange for those in the 'victim', or by a mixture of these. To the extent that takeover is carried out by share exchange it is, like merger, a cheap and quick means of expansion. The price offered for the 'victim's' shares is likely to be rather higher than their current stock exchange price in order to induce acceptance of the offer by shareholders and, if possible, a declaration by the Board that the directors consider acceptance to be in their shareholders' interest. The takeover bid is in the form of a letter addressed to shareholders by the company which is trying to effect the takeover, embodying an offer to purchase the shares. If sufficient shareholders accept, the takeover proceeds. However, the Board also writes to its shareholders giving its view of the offer and its recommendation whether to accept or not. Not all attempted takeovers are contested, and some are actually sought. A so-called 'victim' may itself see, in being taken over, a route to expansion, a way out of liquidity problems or a way for the active directors of a small or family firm to retire while continuing to receive an income and ensuring the continuation of the business. The resistance to bids is sometimes a matter of bargaining in order to secure a better price. However, where well-known companies are concerned, the resistance is sometimes so fierce as to give rise to newspaper headlines, heated public exchanges between rival chairmen, and communication with shareholders by means of conspicuous press advertisements. It seems possible that there may be occasions when the motivation for either making or resisting a bid is something other than a solicitude for the shareholders. However, the shareholders of a 'victim' company may be fortunate indeed if they are pursued by two predators rather than one.

Takeover bids are monitored by the Panel on Takeovers and Mergers, which is a non-official and voluntary body set up as a 'watchdog' to see that the City Code on Takeovers and Mergers is observed. It has no legislative backing but has *de facto* sanctions since its powers to request the Stock Exchange Council to suspend dealing in a company's shares during a contested takeover bid, or to refuse a quotation for any new shares which might be issued as part of a takeover, are a strong deterrent to breach of the rules by those concerned in a takeover bid. These rules are designed to protect shareholders, and they stipulate certain information to be given in letters of offer, such as the length of time a bid must remain open; in addition, they require independent professional reports to be provided on profit forecasts, asset valuations and the resources available to cover an offer of cash. The rules also deal with the concealed and concerted buying of large numbers of shares by groups of purchasers, whether companies or individuals, and they require that if the holding of any individual, company or group reaches 30 per cent of the total voting shares, then a public bid for the remainder of the voting share capital must be made.

Amalgamations take place between firms of varying relative sizes. Sometimes they may be about the same size, sometimes one will be large and the other small- or medium-sized. In the latter case, the amalgamation is likely to take the form of a takeover. It is most common for amalgamating companies to be in the same industry, though the proportion of such amalgamations to the total has been declining, at least until recently.

Amalgamations resulting in diversification have been increasing as a proportion of all amalgamations. Table 5.1 illustrates these tendencies.

Amalgamations between firms in the same industry constitute what is called horizontal integration. In this context it is most usual to consider an industry in terms of its product; however, the processes a firm uses, and the market it serves, may provide a rationale for

Table 5.1 *Percentage of Proposed Mergers, by Number and by Value of Assets to be Acquired, Classified by Type of Integration*

| | Number of assets as % of total | | | | | |
| | Horizontal | | Vertical | | Diversified | |
	by no.	by value	by no.	by value	by no.	by value
1965–69	82	88	5	5	13	7
1970–74	72	65	5	4	23	31
1975–79	62	67	9	7	29	26
1980–82	64	68	5	2	31	30

Source: Office of Fair Trading.
Note: The figures for 1980 onwards are not strictly comparable with those of previous years (apart from the fact that 1980–82 is only a three-year period), but the difference is slight.

its amalgamation with another firm. The reductions thus obtained in production and distribution costs per unit of output may be very great and enable prices to the consumer to be brought down. (These economies of scale will be discussed further in the next chapter.) At the same time, however, amalgamations of this kind reduce the number of producers in an industry and so reduce the extent of competition and increase the possibilities of collusion or other monopolistic action to raise prices above what they would otherwise be.

When amalgamation takes place between firms undertaking successive stages of the production or distribution of a product, then vertical integration is said to occur. For example, a footwear manufacturer may take over shoe shops in order to ensure and control retail outlets for its products; economies in this case may also arise from the centralised management of the chain of shops by one management team containing specialists whose employment would not be warranted by one shop or a small group of shops alone. The iron and steel industry – now for the most part operated by a single public corporation in the UK – provides a number of technical ways in which costs are saved by carrying out successive processes in a single plant and therefore by a single firm. An example is that fuel costs are reduced if the metal does not have time to cool between one process to the next, say between the production of pig-iron and of steel ingots. Vertical integration is now, however, by far the least common sort. As with horizontal integration, the economies in costs of production which it may achieve can be accompanied or offset from the consumer's point of view by a strengthening of producer power in the market, though the scope for this is much less than in the case of horizontal integration. From the point of view of the amalgamating companies themselves, of course, an increase of their market power does not offset any economies achieved in production or distribution, but acts as a supplement to them because of the greater influence over the price of the product which it may bring.

Amalgamations are increasingly occurring between companies which are neither in the same industry nor engaged in successive stages of the production and distribution of the particular product. Indeed, their rationale is precisely that they are not connected in any of these ways, and that they become diversified. The entities which emerge from such amalgamations are known as conglomerates. An example is Granada Group, which operates in TV and video rental, television broadcasting, bingo social clubs, cinemas, motorway services, property, insurance and book publishing. Another is Trafalgar House plc, whose activities include contracting, engineering, housebuilding, shipping, aviation, hotels and the ownership and management of property (and which also included newspapers until recently when they were separately floated). Such enterprises are diversified rather than linked to a particular product, process of production, or market. The object of this diversification is to reduce the degree of risk to which the enterprise is exposed, by spreading the risk over varied commercial activities which, it is hoped, will not all suffer from the same adverse circumstances if such should arise. An aim which may be partly associated with this is to achieve greater stability in the generation of profits over time. And a third aim may be to preserve the possibility of long-term growth on the part of an enterprise which finds that the industry it is in has started to decline.

A Company's Long-Term Liabilities

In the foregoing part of this chapter we have been looking at sources of finance for business which are long term. With the exception of debentures and loan stock, but including retained profits, they also comprise the shareholders' funds of a particular business. In other words, they represent what would be available for distribution to the shareholders, or owners, of the company in conformity with their relative rights if the company were to be wound up. They are what the company would be able and liable to pay out in that event, so that after these payments had been made there would be nothing left and the company would cease to exist as a financial entity. Thus – and although this idea may at first sight appear paradoxical – such capital is a liability of the company. It is something which the company owes (to its shareholders, who are distinct from the company itself). If there is any feeling of paradox on the reader's part, it should disappear on considering debentures and loan stock, whose holders are clearly creditors of the company rather than part owners of it; yet they do have something in common with sharehol-ders – both are suppliers of capital to the company, and the company has a corresponding liability to them both. The accounting notions of liabilities and assets will be further considered later in this chapter.

(2) Medium-Term Finance

Term Loans

The main characteristic of **term loans** is that they are money which is lent to a company for a fixed period of, say, two or three to seven years, which is usually considered to constitute the medium term. Another feature of term loans is that they are usually made for a specific purpose, such as buying a particular asset (e.g, a machine or other piece of equipment), but they may sometimes be arranged for the purpose of increasing the working capital of a firm which is growing. When they are for the purpose of buying an asset, the term agreed will not be longer than the expected life of the piece of equipment in question, and in any case repayment is due on an agreed date or dates either in a lump sum or by instalments. The rate of interest on a term loan may be fixed at the outset, more specifically if the term is at the shorter end of the medium range; but usually it varies with financial market conditions as reflected in a bank's **base rate**, which is a notional rate of interest set to form a reference point on which a bank's various lending and borrowing rates to the public are based. In the case of a fixed rate loan repayment of the principal and payment of interest may be made by equal amounts each month or other period; this is like the mortgage payments to a Building Society, in that the interest component in successive equal payments diminishes while the repayment compo-nent increases by a like amount. Term loans are made by the commercial (or High Street) banks, merchant banks, pension funds, insurance companies and other banks and financial institutions.

Hire Purchase

Just as a consumer may acquire a TV set by **hire purchase**, so may an industrial firm acquire vehicles and plant and equipment required in its productive processes. A deposit is paid at the outset, followed by a series of payments at regular intervals, until the final payment is made which will transfer ownership to the firm which has hitherto been paying for the use of the piece of equipment. The advantages are that payment is spread, and made out of cash flow to which use of the equipment has contributed; and that if the equipment proves unsatisfactory or unnecessary, or becomes obsolete, the contract may be terminated, albeit with the loss of the capital repayments already made. Interest is at a fixed rate, but hire purchase contracts for equipment with a long life may extend for a fairly long period, in which case the interest rate will be variable. Just as with contracts for consumer durables, the rate of interest is likely to be expressed as a flat rate on the total sum, whereas the true rate is greater than this because part of the regular payments is repayment of capital advanced and is therefore not in fact lent for the whole period of the contract. Calculation of the true rate is necessary in order to compare the cost of financing by this method with that of others. Hire purchase is provided by finance houses, many of which are subsidiaries of banks and other large financial institutions.

Leasing

Leasing is to some extent similar to hire purchase, with the principal difference that ownership of the equipment being leased does not revert at any stage to the industrial company which is using it. Leasing agreements are of two kinds, of which the first is the *operating lease*. This is suitable where the equipment is to be used, or may be used, for a fairly short time only relative to its normal life. Such agreements are thus made for relatively short periods but may be renewed. Thus the risk of obsolescence lies with the lessor and the lessee is more highly protected against it than with hire purchase. The lessor, as owner, usually remains responsible for maintenance, and the cost of such a lease reflects the advantages which it has for the lessee. At its simplest, such an arrangement is akin to the more homely plant hire.

The second kind of leasing agreement is the *financial lease*. This is longer term than an operating lease and is related to the likely life of the equipment being leased, so that in contrast to the operating lease, the leasing company is not in the position of having to find further lessees for a piece of equipment during its lifetime. Indeed, a financial lease may not be cancelled by either party. Its use is therefore particularly indicated in the case of specialised equipment, though not confined to such items. An industrial company wishing to acquire the use of certain plant or equipment in this way arranges an agreement with the leasing company which then buys the equipment and leases it to the industrial firm for a recurring rental charge after an initial deposit. The lessee then uses it as though it were his own and maintains and insures it according to his own judgement.

On expiry of the lease the leasing company has recouped its capital and interest and may be willing to extend the hire for shorter periods at a reduced rental if the lessee still finds it serviceable; but the leasing company always retains ownership.

Apart from the advantage of spreading the capital cost, leasing is useful to an industrial company which has exhausted its capital allowances for corporation tax purposes. Until the 1984 Budget companies could charge the whole of their capital investment in a particular year against that year's profits for tax purposes. (The present allowance is 75 per cent of the investment; in 1985 it will be 50 per cent; and the allowance will be phased out in 1986.) Companies receive no benefit from the allowances to the extent that the latter exceed their profits. This situation can arise if a company is carrying out a heavy investment plan or experiencing a period of low profitability. A shipping company renewing its fleet to take advantage of low building costs during a slump in trade would exemplify both possibilities. A profitable financial institution with little real capital investment of its own can attract the capital allowances and pass on at least part of the benefit to the lessee in the form of rental charges lower than they would otherwise be. These charges are costs which the industrial company can set against taxable profits when they re-emerge in future years.

Sale and Leaseback

Sale and leaseback is a long-term matter but is dealt with here for convenience. A company which owns the freehold or leasehold of its industrial property may sell it to a financial institution on condition that the property is then leased back to the company. In this way a capital sum is made available to it now, and rent is paid to the financial institution for the duration of the lease, its level being subject to review probably every five or seven years. The property has to be suitable in the sense of being lettable to some other firm in case of need arising from the failure of the company which is selling and leasing back to meet its rental obligations. A modern office block or factory shell would be considered suitable subject to their location.

Leasing arrangements may be made with banks, their finance house subsidiarises and leasing companies.

All leasing arrangements, whether operating, financial or leaseback, set up a liability to make a series of payments over future years. Since these payments are regarded as recurrent rather than capital transactions it is possible for the company's balance sheet to reveal nothing about them, which may be misleading to a potential lender, who needs to consider the company's existing gearing ratio.

(3) Shorter-Term Financing

Some needs for finance are temporary and if it is necessary to
borrow in order to meet them, it is economical to do so for the
duration of the need only. Facilities for obtaining short-term finance
are provided in a number of ways and by a variety of institutions.

A common form of such finance, and one which is quick and
simple to arrange, is the **overdraft**. It consists of the permission of a
commercial bank for a firm (or individual) to write cheques totalling
more than the amount by which its current account with the bank is
standing in credit. This then causes the current account to be 'over-
drawn', and the firm may increase the amount by which it is over-
drawn at any time up to a limit which has been agreed with the
bank. As the firm receives payment for sales of its products or in
settlement of any other debts to it, so the amount of the actual
overdraft is reduced; but the facility to increase it again remains, up
to the agreed limit and until an agreed time. Thus the overdraft is a
very flexible form of finance, particularly useful where needs vary
from time to time. Interest is paid on the amount actually outstanding and for the length of time it is outstanding, at a rate of interest
which varies with the bank's base rate and is likely to be between
two and four percentage points above the rate; in addition to the
interest charge there will probably also be an arrangement fee
payable to the bank. In principle an overdraft may be called in by
the bank at any time and without notice, but banks are of course
aware that not all borrowers on overdraft would be able to comply
at any particular time with a notice to repay. The potential requirement to repay on demand is part of the traditional nature of the
overdraft as a form of short-term borrowing and lending. On the
other hand, however, it is possible, when the originally agreed time
for repayment arrives, for the overdraft facility to be renewed or
'rolled over' provided the borrower remains creditworthy, and in
this way the overdraft has now frequently become in effect a form of
long-term finance. This may be a suitable arrangement when, for
example, the amount required is not large enough to warrant a
capital issue by the particular company, having regard to the company's size; or, again, when it is hoped to reduce the debt out of
future profits. In the meantime, the interest payments rank as a cost
for the purpose of assessing the company's liability to pay Corporation Tax.

Short-term finance is in effect provided to a business by its trade
and other creditors. Those who provide raw materials to a manufacturer, or who supply the firm with any kind of goods or services, do
not usually receive payment on delivery. In many trades from which
industrial firms are purchasers, a customary period of credit is

extended to customers, usually one or two months, sometimes more. Basically, the purchaser is in effect borrowing from the supplier for this period. For a firm with only a short cycle of purchase, production and sale, this may be an important source of finance. Sometimes a supplier allows a percentage discount on the amount due if payment is made immediately. In such a case the debtor can readily calculate the cost to him of deferring payment, and can express it as a rate of interest per annum. It is most likely that such credit will appear cheap in relation to other forms of borrowing, and obviously the supplier in his turn has to finance the extension of credit by some means or another, none of which can be without cost to him. The granting of credit can be an element of competition between suppliers, to be considered in relation to price, quality, service and speed of delivery. On the other hand, where a certain period of credit is traditional in a particular trade, buyers may be expected automatically to take advantage of the short-term financing which it offers.

Finance by means of **trade credit** is a double-edged sword, however. It cuts both ways. An industrial firm will almost certainly have opportunities of using it as a source of short-term finance, but it is likely also not to receive immediate payment for its products when they are sold to its own customers. At any given moment, therefore, it has money owing to it by some of its customers who are debtors of the firm . The total sum of money involved is an asset to the firm – a short-term or current asset, for it is expected that it will shortly be turned into cash – but, like any other asset, it has to be financed in some way: a firm needs working capital for this and other purposes, such as paying for raw materials if they are not obtained on credit, paying wages, and so on. Devoting resources to working capital is not free of cost to a firm and it will therefore try to reduce it as far as possible. As far as its debtors are concerned, it may be subject to customary or competitive pressures similar to those affecting its suppliers, but within these constraints it will try to reduce the total of current debts due to it by collecting payment promptly.

In the case of export sales there is often a long gap between the time a consignment leaves the factory and the time it arrives on the overseas buyer's premises. The **bill of exchange** is a means of bridging this gap so that the seller receives payment without this delay and yet the buyer does not pay until such time as it is expected the goods will be in his hands, or even used in a product which will have been sold by him. The bill – which in essence works like a post-dated cheque – is drawn up by the seller of the goods in a form which requires the buyer to pay the sum of money arising from the transaction to the drawer or to a third party at a particular future time (its maturity date), which is often 60 or 90 days ahead. He sends it to the buyer for him to accept by so endorsing the bill and adding his signature. The bill is then returned to the seller of the goods who is then able, if he wishes, to obtain cash from his bank in exchange for it provided the bank is satisfied as to the acceptor's financial standing. The payment received is less than the face value of the bill, the difference being interest for the remaining tenor of the bill (the length of time it has to run before maturity) at a rate which will vary with the creditworthiness of the acceptor. The bill is thus said to be discounted. There are two kinds of specialist financial 'houses' which may become concerned in a particular bill of exchange; they are the *acceptance houses* which for a commission will add their acceptance to a bill in order to improve its class or standing, and the *discount houses* which buy bills of exchange which they may either hold until maturity or resell at some stage depending on financial market conditions. They form part of the short-term money market. The kind of bill of exchange discussed here, and based on the sale of goods, is known as a trade bill and its use is now almost, but not entirely, confined to foreign trade.

A second kind of bill of exchange is the bank bill; a company draws a bill on a bank which acccepts it, and the drawer then sells the bill at a discounted amount for cash but on finer terms than could be obtained for a trade bill; in this way the drawer obtains short-term finance immediately, but rather than providing the actual present funds the bank guarantees ultimate payment. A third kind of bill of exchange is the Treasury Bill, issued by the Government as a means of obtaining short-term finance.

For an industrial firm the trade bill of exchange is a means of turning certain of the firm's debtors (a current asset) into cash (the perfectly liquid asset). The reduction of debtors by efficient debt collection short of loss of good will and future custom is another; the aim here is to maintain a ratio between debtors and sales which experience and attentive insight show to be optimal for any particular company, though this is likely to be similar for companies producing competing products in the same markets. A third means of turning debtors into immediate cash is by factoring, or its variant of invoice discounting.

A **factoring company** will buy the debts due to an industrial firm, advancing 70 to 80 per cent of their values immediately sales invoices are sent out, and the remaining 20 to 30 per cent less a discounting fee when the payments are due by the firm's customers. This balance is paid whether or not the customer has actually settled his account by the due date, and it may be arranged that bad debts are covered by the factor. Factoring a company's trade debtors not only improves its cash flow position but ensures that increasing turnover is matched by the increasing short-term finance which is necessary to support it. The cost of factoring is a few percentage points above the base rates of the principal banks. In addition to the pure factoring service, factoring companies may also provide, for a separate fee based on the amount of work involved in each particular case, an administrative service in connection with sales and their analysis and credit control. Invoice discounting is a variation of factoring in which the factor's original advance is really a loan; the industrial company collects payment from its customers itself and repays the factor's advance on the date the purchaser of the goods is due to settle, whether he actually does settle or not. Under this variation the possibility of bad debts must necessarily remain the responsibility of the industrial firm itself.

(4) Government Sources of Finance

The foregoing parts of this chapter have been about the ways private sector companies finance themselves through market machinery. We now need to notice briefly that sometimes private enterprises are able to obtain finance in the form of grants or loans from the government, from their local authority or from European Community sources.

Firms with an establishment in an Assisted Area may be eligible for one or more of a number of forms of finance from all these sources. Some of these relate to capital expenditure on new buildings, plant and machinery, and some to the employment which the expenditure is expected to create or maintain. Not all finance from government sources is on a regional basis, however. Some finance in the form of grants is provided by the government for projects in manufacturing industry which are judged to be in the national interest but which would not be undertaken without this assistance. The government, through the Department of Trade and Industry, provides some finance for investment in the development of industrial products and processes, including microprocessor applications and support for the microelectronics industry. In the field of research and development (R & D), and apart from direct expenditure in its own laboratories, the government bears part of the costs incurred in some firms and industries.

Finance from European Community sources includes loans from the European Investment Bank (EIB), the European Coal and Steel Community (ECSC), and the European Commission itself. Such loans are made for investment which fits in with European Economic Community (EEC) regional, employment and economic policies, and they are on rather favourable terms because the EIB, say, is able to borrow in its turn on the national and international capital markets at the best rates of interest because its credit is backed by the EEC and its member states. In addition, ECSC loans may carry a subsidised rate of interest; they are made for reconstruction of the coal and steel industries and for employment-creating projects in areas where labour displaced from these industries may find jobs.

Grants from European Community sources, which may constitute finance for industrial firms, derive mainly from the European Social Fund (for employment and training purposes) and the European Regional Development Fund (for projects conforming to regional policy). In each case a firm must also be receiving a grant from its own government.

(5) Annual Accounts

The ways a business is financed for the long, medium and short terms is shown in its annual accounts. These give a picture of the whole financial position of the business on a particular date and of what happened, to lead to that position, during the year ending on that date.

The Balance Sheet

A **balance sheet** is a statement of a firm's assets and liabilities at a particular moment of time, and it is so called because it is a logical necessity, or at least a necessity deriving from the meaning of the words 'assets' and 'liabilities', that the two must balance, i.e. be equal. Suppose a firm starts up by issuing ordinary shares, as described earlier, in exchange for finance in the form of cheques from the subscribers, which it pays into a bank account which it opens. Its bank account is an asset: the amount in it is something which it owns. At the same time the share certificates which it has issued indicate that the company has a liability to repay. Actual repayment would not take place unless and until the company were wound up; and in the case of ordinary shares the amount payable will not be a fixed sum but the relevant share of the proceeds of winding up the business. All the same, if we want to show the company's financial position at the moment when it has issued shares and put the shareholders' subscriptions in the bank, we have the following simple balance sheet of the company's assets and liabilities:

LIABILITIES (£)		ASSETS (£)	
Issued share capital		Cash at bank	100,000
Ordinary shares	100,000		
	100,000		100,000

By convention, the liabilities are set out on the left-hand side (mnemonic: letter 'l') and assets on the right. Alternatively, they are sometimes set out in a single column, one below the other. The two-sided method of presentation will be useful to us because it emphasises the two-sided nature of every transaction and the double entry in the set of accounts recording those transactions; for this company so far, shares have been issued in exchange for money in the bank.

The company needs the finance in order to start producing, the first steps toward which may be the purchase of a factory building, plant and raw materials. These purchases will reduce its cash at the bank, and the new assets will replace the finance which has been expended on them. At this stage the assets side of the balance sheet has changed, for the company has changed the form in which it is holding its total assets, which are still financed by the funds provided by the shareholders. The balance sheet is now:

LIABILITIES (£)		ASSETS (£)	
Issued share capital		Building and plant	75,000
Ordinary shares	100,000	Raw materials	10,000
		Cash at bank	15,000
	100,000		100,000

The company is now in a position to start its operations of producing and selling its product. It pays wages and salaries, makes sales, receives payment for them from time to time, pays for electricity consumed as power to drive its machinery and heating and lighting its premises, buys further materials which it pays for at various intervals, pays for advertising, transport and so on. Its transactions are multifarious. They are all recorded in its accounts which therefore embrace the whole range of the company's activities in all their detail. These transactions take place over time, and it is conventional as well as being required by the Companies Acts to present their results for periods of one year in the form of a Profit and Loss Account which summarises their outcome in convenient form. The mass of detailed accounts of all transactions is necessary for record purposes, and is used (has Bucket Shops plc paid for all goods delivered to them up to two weeks ago? How much have we spent on vehicle repairs and maintenance so far this year?), but it is indigestible in the mass. The balances of groups of accounts are therefore aggregated so that the aggregates can be seen in relation to each other in a way which shows the results of the company's activities over the period. This information is gathered together in the **Profit and Loss Account** for the period in question. As we shall see, this account culminates in a figure for the net profit (or loss) made by the company in that particular year. We shall show such an account further on, but meantime let us suppose that during its first year of operations our company made a profit of £10,000 and let us return first to the balance sheet and see how it stands on the last day of the year. It would be something like the following:

LIABILITIES (£)			ASSETS (£)	
Issued share capital			Building and plant	75,000
Ordinary shares	100,000		Stocks	10,000
Profit	10,000		Cash at bank	25,000
	110,000			110,000

One result of the year's operations is that the profit of £10,000 is being held so far in the firm's bank account, which has increased by that amount as compared with the beginning of the year. The total assets have risen also by that same amount. The corresponding increase in the company's liabilities is simply a reflection of the fact that the profit which has been made belongs ultimately to the shareholders. The shareholders' funds have increased by that amount. Another name for shareholders' funds is owners' equity. The profits might have been distributed to the shareholders; indeed, they may yet be, either in whole or in part. The directors, on examining the profit and loss account at the end of the year may decide, for example, to pay a dividend of 4 per cent and this may be approved at a meeting of shareholders. The company then sends cheques totalling £4,000 to its shareholders, thereby depleting its bank balance to £21,000. The corresponding revision to the liabilities side of the balance sheet is that the item which we have so far called 'profit' becomes 'retained profit' or 'reserve' and is £6,000. The balance sheet still balances.

Once the fundamental idea of assets, liabilities and their equality is perceived, it will be seen that changes in a balance sheet imply that if an asset is increased or acquired, then either another asset is correspondingly diminished (a change in the form in which assets are held) or a liability is correspondingly increased or a new and corresponding liability emerges. The acquisition of assets has to be financed by some means or other; and that can only be the forgoing of another asset or the incurring of a liability. There are no other ways and means, bar theft which we rule out. We should now be in a position to examine a more realistic balance sheet as it might apply, after some years of trading, to the company whose early days we have been considering.

It can be seen that the company has grown. It will also be observed that the liabilities are set out to show the longest term first and the shortest term last, and that similarly on the assets side we have fixed assets first, ranging down to current assets last. On the liabilities side, the authorised share capital is simply a note of what it is and the figures do not enter into the balance; it simply indicates, by comparison with the issued capital, to what extent the company at present has power to issue further shares. The issued share capital is the initial constituent of shareholders' funds, and should be considered in relation to what has already been said about shares and shareholders earlier in this chapter and Chapter 2.

The next item, the General Reserve, is an example of what is called a revenue reserve which means that it has been created out of profits from the normal trading activities of the company. Together with the total of any other revenue reserves created by the company – such as reserves for particular purposes – it represents that part of profits which has not been distributed to shareholders; it is part of shareholders' funds. The balance sheet shows that it stood at £45,000, to which has been added £10,000 at the end of the year out of the year's profits. There is a further sum of £1,000 of undistributed profits which has not been explicitly allocated to any reserve, at least so far, but is being kept simply as a balance in the profit and loss account.

A capital reserve – one is not shown on this balance sheet – arises from transactions affecting the company's capital rather than from its industrial and trading activities. A capital reserve is also part of shareholders' funds but may not by law be paid out in the form of dividends. An example is the reserve created when a company issues shares at a price higher than their nominal value.

Under long-term liabilities we have examples of financing which have been discussed earlier in this chapter. This is also the case, under current liabilities, with creditors and bank overdraft. There may seem something paradoxical in the next item, provision for taxation, appearing in the guise of a source of finance for the business; however, it is a liability represented by a counterpart which is somewhere in the assets, and which may not necessarily be directly assignable to it. As it happens, the company seems to have taken the precaution of holding enough cash to pay its tax bill and its

The Firm and its Environment

Balance Sheet as at 31 December 19XX

Authorised share capital (£)

200,000 ordinary shares of £1 each	200,000	
100,000 5% preference shares of £1 each	100,000	
		300,000

FIXED ASSETS (£)

Freehold property		150,000	
Plant and equipment	80,000		
less depreciation	15,000	65,000	
			215,000

SHAREHOLDERS' FUNDS

Issued share capital		
100,000 ordinary shares of £1 each	100,000	
50,000 5% preference shares of £1 each	50,000	
		150,000

OTHER ASSETS

200,000 £1 shares in Rum Show Ltd, at cost	30,000

CURRENT ASSETS

Stocks – raw materials	45,000	
– finished goods and work in progress	10,000	
		55,000

Reserves

General reserve	14,000	
add Transfer from Profit and Loss Account	16,000	
		30,000

Profit and Loss Account balance	1,000
	206,000

Debtors	5,000	
Cash	17,000	52,000
		297,000

LONG-TERM LIABILITIES		
Secured mortgage	50,000	
Term loan	20,000	70,000

CURRENT LIABILITIES		
Creditors	6,000	
Bank overdraft	1,000	
Provision for taxation	8,000	
Proposed dividends		
Ordinary	4,000	
Preference	2,000	21,000
		297,000

dividends. Had this not been the case and the payments were due immediately, the bank overdraft would have to rise by £14,000, assuming that to be within its present limit or that it could be arranged.

On the assets side of the balance sheet the plant and equipment has been written down by an amount for **depreciation**. The deduction on the assets side is eqivalent to a positive item on the liabilities side, where it might equally well appear as a revenue reserve. The depreciation arises from the fact that equipment has a finite life in spite of money spent on it for current maintenance. By the end of the equipment's allotted span, and even, in fact, if it is still going strong at that time, the company must be able to replace the equipment if required. Furthermore, plant, machinery and equipment are liable to become economically useless even though in the prime of life and in good technical condition; this may arise either from technical progress in the production process or in the product, or by a reduction in the demand for the product. Being overtaken in any of these ways is known as **obsolescence**, and any of these causes will reduce the secondhand value of the asset in question. Obsolescence cannot be so readily nor so accurately foreseen as can the effects of wear and tear and the sheer passage of time on the life of an asset. The amount set aside for possible depreciation arising from obsolescence therefore cannot be determined with certainty and is a matter for judgement. The loss of an asset's value through wear and tear can be foreseen more clearly, and it is prudent to make adequate provision for this at least in the annual amounts allocated to depreciation.

There is quite a variety of different methods of calculating an appropriate annual depreciation charge, and no single one of them may be said to be the best in all circumstances. The simplest is **straight line depreciation**, which means an equal annual amount over the expected life of the asset. Another fairly simple procedure is the **declining balance method**, which makes the annual charge an equal proportion of the value of the asset after deducting all the previous depreciation allowances; the allocations thus diminish progressively year by year. These two are the most common, if least sophisticated, methods in use, and it may be that great refinement is out of place in many situations because of the uncertainties surrounding estimates of expected life, possible obsolescence and residual value of the asset on the secondhand market or as scrap. The straight line method deals with these uncertainties by simply spreading the cost evenly over the years of assumed life of the asset, for want of any better indication. The declining balance method is suitable if it is thought that the asset will be most productive early in its life, or that it will lose re-sale value more quickly in its earlier years (as e.g., does a motor car). Some methods of depreciation link the annual charge to production: thus the production unit method uses a fixed rate per unit of output during the year, the rate being determined by dividing the value of the asset by the expected number of units of output over its life-time; whilst the production hour method uses a fixed rate per hour of operation during the year, using the value of the asset and the expected number of working hours of its life. Other methods are of various kinds, and are usually more complex.

One of them, the **sinking fund method**, is like straight line depreciation except that the equal annual deductions are slightly smaller, and compound interest is added to the depreciation reserve so that the total of allocations and interest by the end of the asset's life equals its cost. The interest comes from investing the allocations in fixed interest securities maturing at the required date. Alternatively, the fixed annual charges may be used to pay premiums on an endowment policy for an amount which, by the required time, will equal the asset's cost. Apart from methods such as these, making provision for depreciation in the accounts does not of itself guarantee that liquid funds will be available to pay for replacement of the asset when that has to occur. Making allocations to a depreciation reserve sets up a liability which is automatically a source from which assets are financed, and these are not necessarily left in liquid form all the time. Apart from a method like the sinking fund or endowment policy, the assets being financed by the depreciation reserve are not attributable to it in particular. When depreciation is charged, the amount of profit available for distribution to shareholders is reduced, and the funds retained may be held in the form of cash, debtors, raw materials or any other asset. In the case of the two self-liquidating methods just described, the asset is identifiable in the form of securities or an insurance policy.

With any method of depreciation, the cost of replacement of the asset will not all be provided for, and annual profits will be overstated if there is inflation in the economy and if allocations are based on the original or historical cost of the asset. This has been referred to in Chapter 3.

The essence of the idea of accounting for depreciation is that the cost of an asset is not all charged to the Profit and Loss Account for the year in which a durable asset is purchased. The depreciation provision shown in our company's balance sheet consists of past accumulations plus the allowance charged in the Profit and Loss Account for the year just elapsed.

The 'other assets' item in our company's balance sheet is an investment in another company. Since Rum Show is 'Ltd', it is a private limited company and possibly a subsidiary. Our firm may have hived off part of its activities in this way in the interests of completely devolved management, or it may have bought another company as a way of diversifying its activities or of vertical or horizontal integration, or as an investment of spare funds accumulated into reserves by the retention of past profits. The investment may be temporary and notionally earmarked against depreciation, but in that case Rum Show is more likely to be a public limited company so that the shares may be readily sold on the market when liquid funds are required.

The last group of assets shown, the current assets, will now be readily understood in the light of what has gone before. They constitute the resources used in the daily round of production and selling. Raw materials are acquired for cash (which is thereby diminished) or by an increase of creditors on the liabilities side. Production takes place, thereby increasing stocks of finished goods and work-in-progress, and decreasing stocks of raw materials. Sales of the product are made, thereby increasing debtors or cash, and diminishing stocks of finished goods. And so it goes on.

It will be observed from the balance sheet that our company's current assets, at £52,000, exceed its current liabilities which are £21,000. This means that £31,000 of the current assets are being financed by long-term liabilities rather than short-term liabilities. This amount is known as the firm's **net current assets** or **working capital**. The reader will immediately notice a paradox: is not capital a liability, rather than an asset? The answer is 'yes', but the £31,000, as it is in this case, can be looked at from opposite directions. That it represents the firm's net current assets is fairly obvious. But these assets are being financed somehow, and financed other than by current liabilities (which are financing the other £21,000 of current assets). They are therefore being financed by long-term liabilities, which enables us to use the term 'working capital'.

The Profit and Loss Account

The Profit and Loss Account summarises all the firm's transactions which have taken place during the year, and thus shows what profit or loss has been made as a result of the year's operations. It also shows what has been done (or is proposed to be done subject to the passing of the necessary resolutions at the Annual General Meeting of the company) with the profit, or how the loss is to be met or accounted for. The part showing the disposal of the profit or financing of the loss may be shown either in an extended Profit and Loss and Appropriation Account or by a separate Appropriation Account, the difference lying merely in the way things are set out. It is common to refer to the final accounts as simply the Balance Sheet and Profit and Loss Account.

The Profit and Loss Account shows how shareholders' funds have changed between the balance sheet at the end of one year and that at the end of the next. It does this by showing how much of the profit has been retained in the business, so increasing the revenue reserves; and how much has been charged to depreciation of fixed assets during the year. The figure of net profit available for allocation is arrived at by stages, as illustrated in the accompanying skeleton account. The Profit and Loss Account itself only opens at the stage when the gross profit has been ascertained, which is done in the Trading Account (which in turn may be preceded by a Manufacturing Account). Gross profit is the company's sales revenue for the year, less the direct costs of the goods sold. Direct costs are those which vary directly with output, such as the cost of the materials embodied in the product and the cost of the labour applied in the production process. The indirect costs are those which do not vary in this way, and are fixed or overhead costs; they are charged in the Profit and Loss Account, except that certain overheads relate to the industrial production process only and these may be charged to a Manufacturing Account so that the cost of production up to this stage may be readily seen. The figures may be arranged as required if it is desired to separate out the direct and indirect factory costs. In all accounts debit items are entered on the left hand side, credit items on the right: expenses are debits, revenue is a credit.

In order to throw them into clear relief the only figures entered into the skeleton account(s) are those which are also to be found in the balance sheet; this should assist the reader to see the relations between the relevant transactions during the year and the state of affairs at the end of the year compared with that at the beginning. Some of the items could quite well have been entered differently: for example, depreciation of plant and equipment might have appeared in the manufacturing account to the extent that it relates to assets used in the industrial process itself (e.g. not vehicles for delivering finished goods to customers); much might depend here on the method of depreciation adopted, and how closely it is related to production. Again, indirect factory labour is an overhead cost since it does not vary with output; examples are maintenance and security staff; whilst some fuel consumption varies directly with output, some does not. If it is possible to identify the separate cost components, then they may be grouped together to show the total of factory overheads separately. There may be many difficulties of estimation and allocation of which these are but examples. Others arise from the valuation of fixed assets and stock. Their existence

Manufacturing, Trading, Profit & Loss and Appropriation Account for the year ended 31 December 19XX

Manufacturing Account

Stock of raw materials at 1 January	~		Factory production consigned to warehouse and carried down to Trading Account		A
add purchases	~				
less stock at 31 December	~				
Cost of raw materials used		~			
Direct labour		~			
Indirect labour		~			
Heat, light and power		~			
Factory cost of goods produced		≈			≈

Trading Account

Stock of finished goods at 1 January		~	Sales		~
Factory production brought down from Manufacturing Account	A				
less Stock at 31 December	~				
		~			
Cost of goods sold		~			
Gross profit carried down to Profit & Loss Account		B			
		≈			≈

Profit & Loss Account

Salaries	~	Gross profit brought down from Trading Account	B	~
Advertising	~	Dividend received from Rum Show Ltd		~
Heating and lighting offices	~			
Depreciation of plant & equipment	15,000			
Interest on bank overdraft & term loan	~			~~
	~			
Total expenses	C			C
Net profit before taxation carried down	~~			

Provision for taxation	8,000	Net profit before taxation brought down		C
Net profit carried down to Appropriate Account	D			
	~~			~~

Profit and Loss Appropriation Account

Transfer to General Reserve		10,000	Net profit brought down from Profit & Loss a/c	D
Proposed dividends —				
ordinary	4,000			
preference	2,000	6,000		
		16,000		
		1,000		
Balance carried forward		17,000		

implies a degree of arbitrariness, judgement and subjectivity in the presentation and content of final accounts, which may conceal rather than reveal.

It should be noted that sales revenue is recorded when goods are despatched and invoiced to a customer, and the sales figure in the Trading and Profit and Loss Account reflects this – not all the sales will actually have been paid for. We have already seen the relationships between stocks, debtors and cash when discussing the balance sheet. Similarly, costs relate to consumption of materials and services during the year, rather than to payments which happen to be made during the year on such items. Thus, raw materials and services used during the year but not paid for by the end of the year are costs; conversely, a contract to supply a service to the company and which has been paid for in advance with an unexpired period still to run at the end of the year is an asset at that time and may so appear in the balance sheet as a prepayment. Advertising expenditure, however, although its benefits may be reckoned to persist some time into the future, is normally charged to the year in which it is incurred because its future results are so difficult to measure and because it is in any case likely to be a recurrent item.

Final accounts are published in a form required by the Companies Acts mainly for the protection of the investing public. They are also useful to firms for management purposes, but are not adequate in detail for all such internal uses. **Management accounting** is therefore also commonly carried out, using the same basic data as for the summary accounts required by statute but preserving greater detail and providing analyses of the separate operations and processes of the firm as an aid to efficient performance. For example, particular costs are related to the firm's various processes in order to make comparisons between processes, products or departments within the firm. Ratios are calculated which are of the same general type as those referred to in Chapter 3 but at a more detailed level. Sometimes, if data are available for other firms or for the industry as a whole, external comparisons can be made. Thus cost and management accountants provide information which is used as a basis for management.

Summary

The ordinary shareholders of a company, as its owners, and its other subscribers of capital, provide the company with finance for the long term. What they receive in return varies with their position in relation to the company. Securities issued in exchange for subscribed capital are marketable and dealt in on the stock exchange.

which provides both a new issue and a secondary capital market. Apart from new issues of capital, long-term finance for growth may be provided by ploughing back profits, and growth may be achieved by amalgamation. Various other sources of finance are available for the medium term or a shorter period. The way a business is financed for the long, medium and short terms is shown in its annual accounts, and some relate closely to the operations of the business itself.

Review Questions

(1) What are the advantages and disadvantages of using retained earnings as compared with new capital issues for the financing of investment projects?

(2) Why is it that making provision for depreciation in a firm's accounts does not by itself ensure that cash is available to replace an asset when required?

(3) Compare the position of ordinary shareholders with that of other providers of capital to a firm.

(4) What are the advantages to firms and to the investing public of a secondary capital market (the stock exchange)?

(5) Deduce the amount of net profit before taxation in 19XX of the firm whose final accounts for that year are shown in skeleton form on pp. 116–117 and 122–123.

The Mini Metro production line: scale of production and costs in the long run are closely related

6
Producing the Goods

The Task of Production

Production may be either of goods or of services, as we saw in Chapter 1, and industrial production is a very important part of the total national production of goods and services in the UK. Industrial production consists of the conversion by altering their shape, form or physical or chemical characteristics, of raw materials and other physical inputs into material goods which may be finished consumer goods, intermediate products or capital goods. There is a wider sense in which these goods are not fully 'produced' until they are in the hands of the purchaser, as we have also seen, but for purposes of the present chapter, production has taken place when the goods come into being through a process of transformation. The part of the firm in which this activity is carried out, or the aspect of the firm which is considered when we look at this activity, is often called the **production function**[1] in a management context.

Production is pre-eminently a matter for line management. At its head is someone whose job title may vary but it will be something like Production, Works, Manufacturing or Process Manager or Director. He may be assisted by other managers or assistant managers; there will be a manager in charge of each shift and there will be foremen, skilled tradesmen, operatives and other workers. The labour force coming within his sphere is indeed likely to be the majority by far of a firm's total number of employees, and is probably about three-quarters for industry as a whole. His responsibility also embraces a similar proportion of his company's expenditure, the bulk of which is usually on labour and materials

---

1. This expression falls strangely upon the ears of economists. In economics the production function is a mathematical expression of the technological relationships between quantity of output and varying combinations of inputs or factors of production required to produce it. Thus $Q = f(M, K, L)$, or the size of output is a function of the quantity of materials, capital equipment and labour employed.

127

used in the production process. Likewise, he is in charge of the capital equipment and stocks of raw materials and these usually account for an approximately similar proportion of the company's assets.

The central production task is to carry out the production schedules agreed by the firm's management, probably at meetings of the executive directors. However, an extremely wide range of activities and subjects is subservient to this central aim, and these activities form part of the production manager's sphere. Production costs have to be controlled and waste of materials and labour kept to a minimum; in carrying out this task he may be acting partly on information in the form of analyses supplied by the company's cost accountants. Such data are derived from the same original sources as the final financial accounts drawn up for the shareholders, employees and Registrar of Companies, but are designed for detailed internal use in assessing the efficiency of the operations falling into the several constituent parts of the company's activity. Again, stocks of materials must be kept at levels which, in relation to expected production, are neither wastefully high nor dangerously low; and the quality of the product has to be tested and systematic faults diagnosed and eliminated. The production manager is also concerned, in consultation with the staff dealing with personnel matters, in training of the workforce, work study, safety regulations, negotiations over pay and conditions, and communications with the workforce – in a word, with the human side of production as well as the technological. A decision whether or not to automate one or more of the processes comprising the productive chain or network would require consideration of factors lying in all these diverse areas.

The function of planning, scheduling, co-ordinating and controlling production is best called **production management**. It is sometimes called **production engineering**, but this is an unfortunate use of words because it confuses two separate things. Production engineering, or engineering management, is also related to the industrial process but in a way which is different from production management. It is a matter of the technological design of the production process, the choice of the equipment to be used in the process and, where the equipment has to be specially made, its design in consultation with the equipment manufacturer; thereafter it embraces the installation and maintenance of the chosen plant and equipment, and of technological development of the process itself. Production engineering covers the design of technological resources: production management covers their deployment along with that of the other resources used in production. The two are conceptually distinct, even though responsibility for them is very often found to reside in one and the same manager. That this is so (and of course many industrial firms are not of a size which would warrant the separation of the two functions into the hands of different specialists) serves to underline the breadth and importance of the activities within the firm of the production manager.

All the stranger, then, is the fact that the criticism has sometimes had to be made that significant numbers of British industrial firms consistently underrate the qualifications and requirements for, and the relative importance of, production and engineering managers. It is argued that the prestige which is their due is also withheld from them by our society and that, whether this stems from the attitude within some firms or whether firms mimic the attitudes expressed by society, out-of-date social attitudes are of some consequence for the national material wellbeing. At the same time, however, a different criticism is sometimes made. This is that many firms are product orientated so that their prime attention is upon production, instead of being market orientated and dedicated to the discovery of what consumer wants really are and then producing what will satisfy them. These two criticisms are, unfortunately, not necessarily mutually incompatible. At any rate, it is clear from the second criticism that the production manager in a go-ahead company will be closely linked with the marketing department in his own forward planning, and this will be referred to again in the next chapter. In the meantime we may note that this is one further dimension in the activity of production management.

Costs of Production

The Short Run

Production brings together inputs which we may call by the general headings of **raw materials, labour** and **capital**, and then combines them in processes so as to result in a desired output. The use of these inputs represents **costs**.

There are two main ways of approaching the study of costs. One of them emphasises cases where the combination of inputs used in production may be changed by varying the quantity of one factor alone (labour, say, or one of the raw materials), and it is part of marginal analysis. The other approach emphasises cases where the combination of the direct inputs of labour and materials is fixed because the specification of the product determines proportions in which they must be used.

(i) Marginal Analysis We first follow the marginal analysis.

Marginal cost is the amount by which total cost varies when output is increased (or decreased) by one unit of product (see p. 44). This may be done by changing the input of one variable factor alone, so changing the proportions in which the inputs are being used. There is some proportion which gives the highest return to the last unit of input which is added. Short of this point, as units of the variable input are added, a technically more efficient combination of inputs is achieved and the marginal physical product of this factor rises; whilst beyond that point it falls. This is due to the operation of the celebrated and so-called **law of diminishing returns**. We can see that it is more correctly called the law of varying returns or principle of eventually diminishing marginal (and average) physical product. It implies that there is at first a stage of diminishing marginal cost as output is increased by taking on more of the variable input, that marginal cost reaches a minimum level and then rises again as output is further increased. This is shown in Figure 6.1.

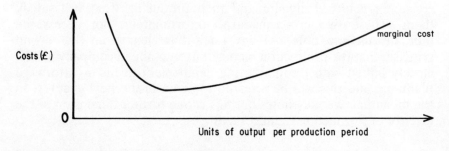

Figure 6.1

Since fixed costs do not change with output, the marginal cost is the same whether we are considering (a) the total of all costs or (b) just the total of the variable costs. If we divide (a) by the number of units of output, we obtain the **average total cost** per unit of output (which may be called simply the average cost); and dividing (b) in the same way gives us the **average variable cost** per unit of output. These two series of costs for different outputs may be added to the diagram as in Figure 6.2.

It will be observed that the marginal cost curve cuts the two average cost curves at the points where the latter are at their minimum. This must be so. When the marginal measurement is falling, it drags the two averages down; when it starts rising it tempers their fall; when it becomes equal to them the curves intersect; the averages have stopped falling but have not yet begun to rise; beyond those points the continued rise of the marginal measurement drags the averages up.

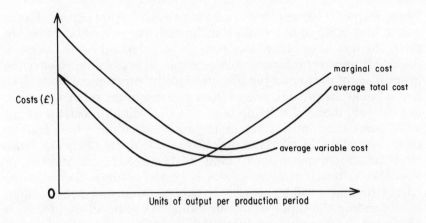

Figure 6.2

The average total cost curve reflects not only the changes in the proportions of the inputs but also the fact that as output rises the fixed costs are spread over a larger number of units of output. The effect of this on fixed cost per unit in the early stages is of course very dramatic.

A further kind of cost is variable overhead cost; an example is those maintenance costs which rise after a while in response to a sustained increase of output but do not vary with output directly and immediately. They will tend to move in steps and be reflected in irregular rises in the cost curves.

It should be noted that we have been assuming so far that the prices of a firm's inputs are constant and unaffected by the quantities of them which it purchases, for the modes of behaviour of costs that we have so far observed are based purely on physical or technological features. If the firm is buying its inputs in highly competitive markets, then the assumption that the prices remain the same apart from any outside influences is a reasonable one. However, it is possible that as the firm grows and its demand for a particular input increases to a point where it is a noticeable force in the market, then it may push the price up against itself. On the other hand, it is possible that its larger purchases may enable it to exact a discount for quantity from one or more suppliers, perhaps because their costs of handling and delivering larger orders are lower or perhaps simply because they do not want to lose such a large volume of business. Such movements in prices along with the quantity of output and hence the quantity of inputs bought will modify the level of costs at the various sizes of output.

The ability to vary the combinations in which the various inputs are used leads a firm to seek the least cost method of producing the

size of output it has decided upon for any production period. To the
extent that more of one input is technically capable of being substituted for less of another, this method will depend on the relative
prices of the several inputs. For example, it is possible to vary the
proportion of scrap and pig iron used in the production of steel, so
that a fall in the price of one of these relative to the other will result
in relatively more of it being used. This substitution can go on for
quite some time until it begins to cause difficulties which start to
raise costs again. Similarly, it may be possible to operate some kinds
of processes with more of one kind of labour and less of another, or
with less materials if more labour is bestowed upon them. In the
latter situation it will be possible to achieve some increase of output
by expanding the input of labour alone. As more of one factor is
employed, its marginal product falls. There is a rise in the marginal
productivity of the factor(s) of which less is employed or whose
quantity remains the same; the latter arises from the fact that the
same quantity is being combined with more of the input which is
being varied. Decisions about substituting one input for another will
depend on the behaviour of their marginal products as the quantity
of one or the other is increased, and on their prices. This is known as
the **principle of substitution**, and the least cost combination of inputs
is that which satisfies the following condition:

$$\frac{\text{Marginal product of factor } A}{\text{Price of factor } A} = \frac{\text{Marginal product of factor } B}{\text{Price of factor } B}$$

So long as these two expressions are not equal, it pays a producer to
achieve his desired production by increasing the input of the factor
whose marginal product relative to its price is the greater, and to
reduce the input of the other. This substitution reduces the marginal
product of the factor being increased, and increases that of the
factor whose quantity is decreased, until an equilibrium is established by the two marginal products becoming proportional to their
prices. It should be noticed that this principle is what underlies the
choice of the means by which a certain size of output shall be
produced once that size of output has been determined. The
determination of the size of output itself is, according to the marginalist and profit-maximising way of thinking and as noted in Chapter 3, a matter of achieving equality between marginal cost (with the
most favourable combination of factors as just outlined) and marginal revenue.

However, and as observed in Chapter 3, the fixing of the size of
output depends on the objectives of any particular firm and the
extent of the knowledge of marginal costs and, more particularly,
marginal revenue, which is available to it.

(ii) Direct and Indirect Cost Analysis   For the reasons just stated, an alternative approach to the examination of costs is required. It is one which accords more with the actual procedures of most industrial firms when examining their costs especially as a basis for determining their prices. It sees costs as being divided into **direct and indirect cost**, the latter being further divided into **fixed and variable overheads**. The direct costs are labour and materials and appear in the firm's manufacturing/trading account, as do the variable overheads associated with production. The fixed overheads appear in the profit and loss account (though if depreciation is charged by a method which relates it to output these divisions may begin to appear a little slippery).

We have already noticed above that as output rises, fixed costs are spread over a larger number of units of output; average indirect costs fall not only continuously, but proportionately, as output is increased. If such an increase continues, it will eventually begin to come up against the limits of what can be produced in the process performed by that piece of the firm's equipment which has the lowest capacity. This limitation is not rigid, however, and can be overcome at least initially by working overtime on that process or by installing extra units of machinery of the kind used in the process which is limiting production. If the continued increase of production is gained by overtime working, then the decline in average indirect costs per unit of output will continue smoothly, at least until the next bottleneck is reached; direct costs will also be affected (we shall return to them shortly). If, on the other hand, the continued increase of production is gained by installing an extra unit of similar equipment, then average indirect cost will jump to a higher level, from which it will then resume its decline in proportion to the increase of output. Figure 6.3 illustrates the behaviour of indirect costs in the short run.

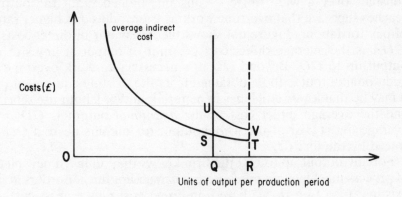

Figure 6.3

OQ is the output at which it is decided whether or not to invest in a new piece of equipment for the least-capacity process. *ST* is the continued path of declining average indirect cost if output is increased beyond *OQ* by working overtime, the extra cost of which is a direct labour cost. (Overtime may or may not have been worked before this point: it makes no difference to indirect cost.) *QU* is the average indirect cost per unit of total production immediately after a new piece of process equipment has been installed, and *UV* is the path of average indirect cost if output is increased beyond *OQ* by this method. *OR* is the output at which some new resistance to increased output appears, which may be either because the limits to the capacity of the further piece of equipment in the same process are now being reached, or because those in another process are being reached, or because the maximum output from the largest-capacity process machinery is being reached. In the latter case the problem is one of the scale of the total plant, which is by definition a long-term matter.

Limits to capacity are not normally reached all of a sudden and at some single, clearly defined point. This is recognised in practice by taking 'full' capacity working to be something of the order of 80 per cent of the theoretical maximum output from a plant. Beyond some such point further increasing of output from the same plant is possible but only by incurring extraordinary costs, of which one may be overtime working; others may be lower efficiency in materials used, and lower labour efficiency under pressure of larger through-put either with or without overtime working.

These latter considerations lead us to direct costs. They consist of labour and materials; and since the specification of the product requires a precise quantity of materials and this in its turn requires a certain amount of labour of different but definite kinds to be applied in processing the materials, the direct costs per unit of output are constant over a wide range – constant, indeed, until the output reaches such size that overtime working is introduced at higher rates of pay for labour. Figure 6.4 shows the behaviour of direct costs.

OA is the average direct cost per unit of output at any size of output up to *OQ*. Beyond *OQ* it is necessary to work overtime if additional output is to be obtained from the existing equipment (or it may be that lower efficiency in materials and/or labour use sets in) and the average direct cost of the *additional* output is *QD*; the average direct cost of the *whole* output for outputs beyond *OQ* is traced by the line *CD*.

For any output up to *OQ* the firm knows that, unless a new piece of process machinery is purchased, it can accept further orders at an existing price (see p. 54) based on direct cost plus a gross costing margin which spreads indirect costs over an assumed output and

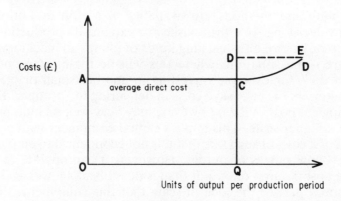

Figure 6.4

allows for a profit at that output. Accepting such orders covers its direct costs and makes a contribution (equal to the whole of the gross costing margin) to the firm's indirect costs if output in the production period is so far too small to have covered them; and it adds (again, the whole of the gross costing margin) to net profit thereafter. Orders which will push output to a rate beyond *OQ* but which can be fulfilled by overtime working are also very likely to be undertaken. Orders are not turned down lightly, for reasons of good will, and the firm may well be willing to absorb the short-run increase in its average direct cost in order to secure and maintain an expansion in its market in the face of actual or potential competition. If the high level of business comes to appear permanent, the firm will consider raising its scale of production in the long term.

This is a matter to which we shall now turn. Before doing so, however, we may note that the main difference between the two approaches outlined above is less in the cost analyses themselves than in the explanations put forward, partly on their bases, about the determination of price and output. The direct cost approach uses perceptions which are in fact widespread in industry and which affect the way firms act.

The Long Run

In the **short run** a firm's production is constrained by its existing plant. Of course, it may also be constrained by the market for the product, but the plant sets some limit to the firm producing more even it if wants to. The **long run** is defined as a period of time adequate for the firm to change its production facilities and methods to a different scale. At any given time all presently known technologies, plants and methods are available to a firm as options for long-run decisions. If a firm wishes to expand its production, one way is to buy more of its existing kinds of plant and machinery, and there are some situations where this will be the most economical thing to do – for example, investing in another small or medium-sized bakery in order to save costs in delivering the product. Known technological possibilities, however, may very well include production on a higher scale. This implies capital equipment with a capacity, and of a cost, of such size that it is not economical to employ it at relatively low ranges of output. However, it can operate at lower average cost per unit of output than is possible at a lower scale. It is an essential part of the idea of scale that this equipment is indivisible: if it is used at all, it is all used. It is not possible to operate a plant consisting of large-scale equipment in fractions if only part of its output is required. In a plant consisting of several smaller-scale pieces of equipment performing the same process in parallel, this can be done by 'mothballing' one or more of them. However, the larger units are often more efficient than the smaller because of technical **economies of scale**. The basic reasons are physical or technical and may be explained by means of examples. At the simplest level, a storage space of cubic shape increases in the progression 1, 8, 27..., while its floor space and surface materials increase by only 1, 4, 9... (This progression can continue until modified by the need to incur the cost of reinforcing the strength of the walls.) The relationship between square and cube underlies many instances of increasing returns to scale, with the costs varying with the area, and the output varying with volume. Large ships have a lower capital and operating cost per unit of usable carrying space than do small ones.

The long-run options in production scale open to a firm arise from the present state of technological knowledge. They have nothing to do with possible technological progress in the future: decisions cannot be taken now on the basis of what is not at present known – apart from a class of decisions dependent upon probabilities. The options are the possible choices now between a series of scales of production each of which, once and if adopted and installed, would have its own average cost curve which would then be short run. These options are illustrated in Figure 6.5.

In theory there may be an infinite number of production scales from which to choose, each with its short-run average cost curve of which only three are shown here. At first, the minimum average costs of successively larger scales of operation fall; they themselves reach a minimum level from which they then begin to rise. They rise because of the emergence of diseconomies of scale and because decreasing costs as output rises cannot, in a given state of technolog-

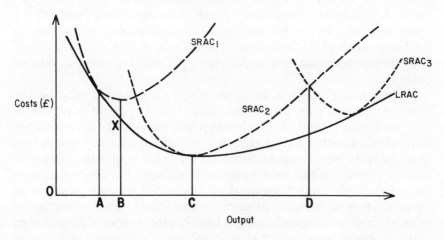

Figure 6.5

ical knowledge, go on for ever. The long-run average cost curve traces out the points, one on each short-run curve, which indicate the most economical scale of production to choose for each one of the whole series of sizes of output. It is thus tangential to each short-run curve. However, this point of tangency is not at the point of minimum short-run cost except in the case of one of the short-run options, and in that case the short- and long-run minimum costs coincide (at a point vertically above *C* in the diagram).

If the firm plans to produce *OA* units of output, it will choose to do so by the method which has $SRAC_1$. This method would be capable of producing the larger output *OB* at an average cost lower than for *OA*, so if the firm has once chosen the scale with $SRAC_1$, it will wish to try to increase its sales to *OB*. In the long run, however, there is a scale of production which may be chosen for output *AB* at the lower average cost of *BX*. That short-run average cost curve is not shown but is tangential to the *LRAC* at *X*. Similarly, there is in principle a scale of production which will in the long run produce output *OD* at a lower average cost than any other. If in practice that scale of production is a will-o'-the-wisp, then the choice will be between $SRAC_2$ and $SRAC_3$, each of which is capable of producing *OD* at the same average cost. In this case the choice may depend on whether the firm reckons its market is more likely to expand or to contract.

The technical sources of economies of scale may lie in enlarging the size and altering the nature of a total process and benefiting from the fact that the resulting proportionate increase of output is greater than the proportionate increase in costs; or they may lie in putting together in one continuous operation successive processes which had hitherto been carried out separately and probably by separate firms. In the former case, the expansion is horizontal; in the latter, vertical. In both cases[1] the returns to scale[2] are associated with units of output per production period, i.e. with a rate of output.

A further source of scale economies in production may be the total volume of a production run rather than the quantity produced in a particular period. There are two ways in which this may manifest itself. Firstly, the designs of durable consumer goods are changed from time to time in order to set or keep up with fashion, or to keep abreast of technical improvements, and the costs of designing new models and setting up the tools for their production can be very heavy as in the case of motor cars. The larger the number of units of each model produced the lower is the average of the design and re-tooling costs per unit, irrespective of the time period over which they are produced. The costs which have previously been examined do vary essentially with the rate of output, or the number of units produced in a given period. The second way in which the total or accumulated volume of production may be associated with economies is through the experience or learning built up by management and labour in operating new tools and equipment or assembling new models, or running plant on a new higher scale. The greater skill which they develop means an increased output from given inputs. The learning process begins all over again each time a new scale of production is adopted or a new design of product introduced, and the more capital intensive the production process, the more the learning economies are associated with management, and the more labour intensive, the more they derive from labour. The reductions in cost derived from learning effects are frequently very substantial and it has been suggested that they are typically 20 to 30 per cent of the value added (sales revenue less bought-in materials and services) for each doubling of accumulated production.

1. When production is made up of processes within a firm which run either successively (in series) or in parallel, it is unlikely that the various pieces of equipment will have the same capacity. If some piece of equipment, probably the largest-capacity piece, yields economies of scale, then the others have to be chosen on a 'least common multiple' principle, e.g. 1 machine of 100 capacity; 2 machines for the second process at 50 each; 5 machines for the third process at 20 each.
2. According to a purist view these alone may be called economies of scale. We take a more relaxed view here. Nor do we find it worthwhile to distinguish economies of scale from returns to scale.

Large-Firm Economies

The scale economies so far mentioned arise out of the size and technique of the production process and apply therefore to plants. There are also other advantages which arise from a firm itself being large. Large plants must be owned by correspondingly large firms which therefore reap both the technical economies of large-scale production and the benefits, if any, of being a large firm. A small plant may be owned by a correspondingly small firm or it may be one of several producing the same or different products and owned by a large firm which enjoys what may be called economies of scale, though they do not arise from the scale of the production process. There are several main kinds of such economies.

(i) Managerial Large firms spread fixed costs over large outputs and therefore find it worthwhile to employ teams of highly-paid managers and professionals to carry out specialist functions. This is an aspect of the division of labour. In smaller firms these functions are less clearly differentiated, so that the company secretary may also be the chief accountant, or the works manager may also be responsible for personnel matters. Furthermore, the process does not stop at the specialisation of tasks which on a smaller scale are carried out by people who combine them with other tasks. Some functions may not be present at all when a firm is on a small scale. There is some size of management organisation below which it is not worthwhile to employ a computer programmer, and reliance is placed instead on packaged programmes, if indeed the firm has a computer at all. An example worth noticing in particular is research and development (R&D) with its teams of highly qualified scientists and engineers; they are engaged full-time on the systematic search for improvements in the firm's products and in its processes of production, and for new products which the firm's knowledge of technology or markets would enable it to produce profitably. Some of the results of their work may extend the range of scale options open to the firm for the long term, and only a firm which is already in any case large could benefit from them. So there are cases where only a large-scale company can afford R&D, some of the results of which contribute to its going on to a still higher scale. This is, however, not a closed virtuous circle. In the first place, there is also at the present time an increasing number of small- and medium-sized firms not, at least as yet, working on a large scale of production, whose success is based on advanced technology and its application through their own R&D. In the second place, there is no clear evidence that most major industrial innovations are made by large firms; small firms, academic laboratories and individuals all

contribute to discovery and invention, though the resources for development are usually found in industrial firms.

Adding a specialist or a specialist function to the managerial organisation is not just like adding a further accounts clerk, say, because work on the debtors' ledger has fallen behind with a growth of output. That would be like adding a further piece of equipment of a kind already being used; it would be a matter of the proportions in which factors are used and not of the scale of the managerial organisation. Changing its scale requires it to take a new form, with changed techniques of business management. That happens when managers with a high level of expertise are introduced to the organisation.

Managerial economies are likely to be prominent when the firm is engaged in multi-plant production and those plants are not themselves necessarily on a large technical scale. The plants need not be in the same industry, and one of the *raisons d'être* of diversified conglomerates is the spreading of pure management and financial expertise of a high order over a large range of activity and output.

(ii) Financial   Large firms find it easier to obtain finance than do small ones and this is reflected in the fact that they pay less for it. A large well-known firm is usually accepted as a good risk and will need to pay a rate of interest on borrowed money lower than is required from a smaller firm. Often the difference is about 3 percentage points in the rate of interest. Part of the rationale behind this is that if the project for which a firm is borrowing turns out to be a failure, a large company has the earnings from all its other productive activity to fall back on in repaying the bank or other creditor, but a small firm would be brought down along with the project; outright failure aside, the firm with multiple projects will be reckoned to have a lower variation in profits. Another source of financial economy is that the costs to the company of an issue of shares or other securities do not rise in proportion to the amount of capital being raised. Furthermore, the financial institutions, which have emerged as the main channel for the provision of industrial capital, have a preference for buying the securities of large companies with a stock exchange quotation. In addition, their own dealing costs are lower for large transactions and these are only possible in the securities of large companies; and the amount of analysis done by stockbrokers and others feeding information into the financial markets is greater for large firms than for small. For their own part, smaller owner-managed firms are in any case reluctant to borrow from institutions seeking an equity share, for fear of loss of control.

(iii) Buying Economies   When a firm's purchases of raw materials

or services such as electricity, carriage of goods, or vehicle leasing from a particular supplier reach a certain size, it may be able to negotiate discounts for quantity on its bulk purchases. This possibility comes partly from the market power its large purchases give it, and this will be reinforced if the supplier's own average costs fall as the quantity supplied to a particular purchaser increases. On the other hand, a firm purchasing materials or components may prefer to forego part of this advantage when it has a choice of alternative sources of supply for the sake of the greater security of supplies in case of mechanical failure, natural hazard or a labour dispute suffered by a sole supplier. This practice is called dual sourcing. When the scale of purchases of a component reaches a certain size it sometimes pays a firm to set up the plant required to manufacture the component for itself. Thus originally the mass production of motor vehicles was essentially an assembly process with the parts being bought in; subsequently it was found that the output of some motor vehicle producers warranted installing a foundry and other plant to produce parts of the engines and bodies themselves; at the present time there is a tendency arising from a changed cost structure to close some of these installations such as the Ford foundry at Dagenham.

(iv) Marketing economies   These arise from marketing and distribution. There are scale economies in distribution when an industrial firm's output of a consumer good, such as footwear or ready-made clothing, is large enough to warrant it acquiring its own retail outlets; or again, simply when its sales and distribution organisation can handle an increase of sales volume with a less than proportional increase in its sales and distribution staff and facilities. The latter may not always be so. A firm may be extending its sales penetration to areas of the country to which it has not distributed hitherto. The required increase of sales effort and distribution facilities may be at least proportional to the resulting increase of sales, yet the exercise may be undertaken because the technical economies in production derived from the increased output make it profitable.

Often the largest source of scale economies derived from selling activities is advertising. Not only does a given expenditure on advertising represent a lower cost per unit of product when output is large than when it is small, but advertising campaigns of less than a certain intensity – and hence of less than a certain total cost – are much less effective in terms of consumer response for each £1,000 spent. An expenditure of £1,000 alone would probably be completely useless. Seeing or hearing an advertisement once may not induce any consumer to buy the product, or at any rate it will cause only a few to do so; and of those consumers who do respond, most will need several exposures to the advertisement before it registers and their behaviour is affected. Once some influence is achieved in this way there is often a fallout from it which comes from one consumer influencing another through conversation or emulation and 'keeping up with the Joneses'. The whole process has been likened to an epidemic: a small attack by a virus has little effect on society and recedes, but a sufficiently large attack takes hold and spreads by contagion or infection to a significant porportion of the population. By analogy, expenditure on advertising beyond a certain threshold level achieves a magnified response and there are increasing returns to scale. After a certain further level of expenditure has been reached, the rate of increase in the response declines until a saturation point is reached beyond which further advertising is ineffective and may even be counter-productive. Large and small firms each require the same amount of advertising to create the threshold level of awareness, to reach which costs the larger firm a lower amount per unit of output. Between that minimum effective level and the level at which consumers begin to be aware of resistance, the effect of increasing the level of advertising is cumulative, and the response increases faster than expenditure. This confers an advantage of scale on a large rival over a small one. This advantage may be compounded by interaction with production economies of scale as advertising boosts sales and the increased output eventually warrants a larger scale of production. It is also compounded by the discount which large advertisers are able to obtain on the cost of newspaper or hoarding space, radio or TV time.

There is no point in a firm advertising unless the product can be differentiated in the minds of consumers from those of its rivals. If this can be done, then the product can be branded and advertised, with the aim of creating a preference on the part of consumers for the advertiser's brand. Success in this aim does not entail that the benefits from the scale economies of advertising will necessarily be passed on in part to consumers in the form of lower prices. On the contrary, it may happen that if the preference is securely established, the firm will be in a position to raise its prices above those which a smaller rival may be charging.

The Optimum Size of Firm

Although large firms are able to benefit from economies of scale in the ways described, they do not have everything going their way. In fact, although studies which have been carried out on the matter are not altogether conclusive, it seems likely that large firms in general do not enjoy a higher profitability than smaller ones though their profitability is less variable. The reasons for the lower variability in the profits of larger firms are that they are spreading risks over their various products, that some of their products are likely to be at the most profitable stage of their life cycle while others are petering out, and that in the case of conglomerates the firm is in more than one industry and these industries may have different cyclical or seasonal patterns of trade which tend to balance out the fortunes of the company as a whole over a year or longer period.

The reason for their lower profitability in general could possibly be that they pass their economies on to consumers in lower prices, but it is likely that although they reap the benefits of technical economies of scale, these are offset by diseconomies elsewhere. The sources of organisational slack and the drive for growth at the expense of profitability to the shareholders have been explored in Chapter 3. Apart from these, there may be diseconomies of scale. They are not likely to be technical diseconomies, except for the possibility that a firm may find itself in the short run operating a larger-scale plant than it would now wish, the level of demand having dropped away. There may, however, be managerial disecono-mies. In the first place, although the large-scale firm can afford highly-skilled and highly-paid specialists and benefit positively from their expertise and from their cost being spread over a large output, some of the need for specialists comes from problems which arise in the firm's organisation itself as it increases in scale. Corporate communications executives appear when organisations become large and complex, while some of the work of personnel officers comes from motivational problems sometimes associated with work-ing in large, impersonal organisations. Secondly, as the firm grows to a larger scale of management, it becomes bureaucratic, the senior managers become more remote from the shop floor, their degree of control slackens, their capacity to organise and to take correct decisions becomes stretched and co-ordination between the range of departments becomes more difficult. At the same time, the manage-ment team, being larger, is joined by newcomers to the business and there is often a substantial lapse of time before they become com-pletely absorbed into the informal intimacy which marks the rela-tionships of colleagues of long standing and which can make an important contribution to the running of a company in the upper reaches of management.

Thus, economies of scale may be reaped in one direction, only to be accompanied by diseconomies in another. On the other hand, it is also possible that economies in more than one direction may go together and even react with each other to compound their effect, as we noticed with marketing and production economies. The tech-nical economies of scale are prominent because they are probably larger than the scale economies or diseconomies from other sources in an industrial firm, and they are much easier to observe and measure. The results of an increase of technical scale can be, and are, calculated beforehand; and it is possible to regard any abnormal divergence from these results as basically attributable to management, though they may not represent a diseconomy of management scale as such. The existence of diseconomies of management scale may be suggested by the results of company operations, but they are not readily identified or quantified.

The exploitation of potential economies of scale depends on there being a market for large numbers of a standardised product in a restricted range of variations. Even when this condition is fulfilled, small firms may survive and flourish in an industry alongside the large-scale ones. Small firms have not disappeared in a world of industrial giants, in the first place, because new ventures do typically start small and if they are successful they grow and eventually become public companies either by flotation or by takeover. Some of today's small firms are tomorrow's large firms in the making. Secondly, not every owner-manager of a small firm wants his business to grow beyond the size at which he can continue to be the owner-manager, because he values his independence highly. Thirdly, smaller firms and plants are often more flexible and responsive to the changing wants of customers than are large ones, and they are well-adapted to serving specialist markets and the tastes and (it may be) the pockets of a minority. For this reason bespoke tailors, brewers of distinctive local beer and bakers of quality bread are able to stay in existence, as are many small specialist firms supplying components or equipment to other industrial firms. However, the existence of economies of scale sometimes reduces the level of competition by acting as a barrier to entry to a particular industry; established firms producing on a large scale are able if need be to reduce their prices to below the level charged, or which would have to be charged, by new firms with a small output.

From this it would appear that the optimum size of a firm may depend on a number of different factors and the viewpoint from which they are regarded, e.g. that of the producer or of the consumer. From one point of view we may say that a firm is of optimum size when it is operating at the minimum cost per unit which it can attain with known technology and organisational methods. That would be at output OC in Figure 6.5. However, much empirical evidence suggests that in practice long-run average production cost curves in industry are not approximately U-shaped as in Figure 6.5, at least for any practical part of their length. Instead, such evidence suggests that the long-run average cost curve is roughly L-shaped, that it does not reach a minimum at a single point of output from which it then rises, but that it descends sharply to a level from which it continues to fall more slowly and then more or less flattens out. This refers to technical economies of scale. There must, of course, still be some conceivable, if unbuilt, size of plant beyond which costs will rise; the extreme case would be one so large that with present technical knowledge it would collapse under its own weight. To this must be added the inevitability of managerial diseconomies at some scale with present knowledge of managerial techniques. For these reasons long-run average cost must be taken to rise eventually at some large scale. This is illustrated in Figure 6.6.

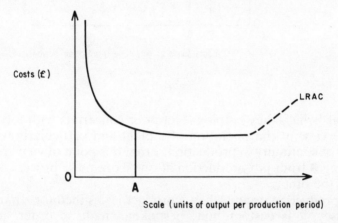

Figure 6.6

Beyond a certain scale, further scale increases do not result in any appreciably lower average unit cost, and the latter does not vary appreciably over a further wide range of increased scales. Two implications of this are (a) that there is a **minimum efficient scale** of production (MES) at the point where average cost ceases to fall much further, at scale *OA*; and (b) that there cannot be said to be any particular optimum scale of operations, only that the optimum is not less than *OA*.

The extent of the cost disadvantage suffered by a firm of, say, two-thirds the MES depends on how fast costs fall between that scale and *OA*. In Industry 1 (Figure 6.7) operating at scale *OB*, whose output is two-thirds that of the MES, causes average cost to be double that of the MES. In Industry 2 the difference in costs is much less.

Scale and Production Process

Production processes can be classified in several ways depending on the standpoint from which they are being viewed; for instance, they can be sorted according to the technology or according to the

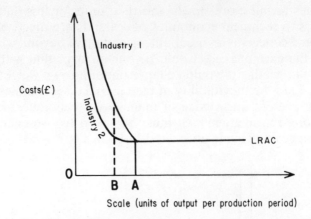

Figure 6.7

materials which they employ. Here our concern is with a comprehensive view of the operation of a plant and particularly with the
degree of continuity in production. From this point of view, production ranges from job production at one extreme to process production at the other.

Job production occurs when a product is destined for a particular
purchaser; it is custom-built, bespoken, made to order, unique,
one-off. Examples are building a house to plans drawn to meet the
client's individual requirements, and printing a handbill. The producer of the latter is called a jobbing printer. Characteristics of this
type of production are that the producer is free of commercial risk
of the product remaining unsold, that stocks of the finished product
are not held, and that adjustments of the production layout and
changes of tooling may be required from one job to another.
Machinery and equipment used in the production process are not
used continuously and fixed costs are therefore not spread over a
very large output in a given period of time. Scope for division of
labour in such a production process and in its associated management is apt to be very limited. Management of all the firm's functions is often retained in one person's hands. Production and management organisation are on a small scale. Production is apt to be
labour intensive and skilled, and detailed production decisions are
highly decentralised, devolving on those actually producing the
product.

Products which are not unique are **standardised**, either wholly or
partly. Standardisation of the product facilitates the adoption of
modes of production which are less and less intermittent as the need
for re-arrangement and re-tooling of the equipment, or the use of
different materials, is less and less. Some products are basically

standard but have variations to suit particular large customers or particular export markets, or to add variety to what is available to purchasers. They are often produced by the mode of production known as batch production. The batch is produced in an uninterrupted run which needs to be of some minimum size to make it feasible to incur the special costs it imposes and recoup them in a price which the customer will pay. Batch production may be undertaken to special order or for stock. It requires the application of skills when re-jigging and re-tooling is taking place but during the batch run production is relatively routine, which means both that more supervision is required and that some functions which would be carried out by top management in a jobbing firm are delegated to an emerging class of middle managers.

Mass (or flow) production takes place when the product is completely standardised and required in large numbers. It is characterised by large-scale production and the fullest exploitation of the possibilities of the division of labour. Branded breakfast cereals and motor cars are examples. Mass production can also be undertaken for a product which is not itself completely standardised but which consists of components which are and which may be arranged in assembly to form a product with a degree of variety. The products, being machine-made, are of high quality in the sense of not varying unintentionally; yet little skill may be required to operate the machinery which produces them, and the labour required can be monotonous. It is a prime task of management to seek and adopt techniques of enriching and enlarging the contents of such jobs in the interest both of human satisfaction and the profitability of the company. Mass production requires a great deal of attention to the co-ordination of production, sales, marketing, design and in fact all the aspects of the company's activity. Because of this and because of the large scale upon which it is conducted, the number of tiers of management associated with it tends to be larger than with small-scale and intermittent production, so that management also tends to be on a large scale. The production activity itself is reduced so far as possible to routine, with tasks clearly and minutely defined and with unusual occurrences being reported upwards until they are dealt with at what is now laid down to be the appropriate level in the organisation.

Continuous (or **process**) **production** takes us to the end of the range of modes of production. It is almost as though production of a commodity had been set in perpetual motion, as though a highly elaborate technical and managerial apparatus had been set up where the chief executive rings a bell, whereupon in turn the production manager presses a button (on his desk) and the whole thing starts up and works like a charm. Real life examples do not match such a picture in perfection, but examples may be taken to be oil refineries and chemical plants; the products are in continuous demand at some level, and the outputs may be varied in grade within a range given by the natural properties of the inputs. Such a process will tend to be highly capital intensive, as far as possible automated and automatically controlled, on the largest scale commercially and technically feasible, and operating twenty-four hours a day.

Although the range from jobbing to continuous production has been set out in four discrete modes for sake of convenience, it is really more like a continuum, with a particular plant being quite like its neighbour on its left in some respects, and like its neighbour on the right in others. As we move along the range away from job production, technical and managerial scale both tend to increase. The mode and technique of production affect the social relationships of the workplace and the whole structure of management. The more production becomes routine the more managers are required to lay down the rules of routine working; check that they are being observed; make decisions on how to deal with deviations from the norm of occurrences, which on a smaller scale and more intermittent mode of production would be dealt with nearer to or at the workplace; ensure that production and other phases of the firm's activity are highly, and in detail, co-ordinated – a task that requires more co-ordinators the larger is the scale on which these phases are conducted; ensure the continued motivation, health and safety of the workforce; and so on.

A firm faced with an enhanced order book of large batches or embarking on flow production may have the option of deciding, for the long run, to increase the scale of its production process or to go over to working its existing plant in two or three shifts each day or for part of the week. The first option will reduce average cost per unit of output, but give a hostage to fortune should the enhanced demand prove temporary or cyclical. The second option will increase the direct labour cost per unit of output, but will reduce average fixed costs per unit; this option is the more flexible for making future adjustments to output should they be required. Such adjustments can fairly readily be made in a downward direction; upward adjustments will depend on whether three shifts are already being fully worked.

Summary

Production is defined more narrowly for the purposes of the present chapter than it was in Chapter 1. The production task within the firm is, however, very wide in its scope.

Ways of analysing production costs in the short run are examined. Costs in the long run are related to scale of production and production process. Technical economies arising from the size of plant are distinguished from economies arising from the scale of firm. The idea of the optimum size of firm is introduced.

Review Questions

(1) Explain the ways in which economies of scale may be associated with (a) the size of plants, and (b) the size of firms.

(2) What is the principle of substitution? Show how it helps in deciding on the means by which a given size of output is produced.

(3) Why are some industrial firms large, and some small? What meanings can be attached to the idea of an optimum size for a firm?

(4) What range of tasks may a production manager be responsible for? Say how they relate to other functions within the firm.

Piccadilly Circus at night: if only one was unable to read!

7
The Firm and its Markets

The Market Orientation

Marketing is the Alpha and the Omega of the industrial firm's activity. Traditionally it has been seen only as coming at the end of a series of stages in that activity. On that view of things, first the product is designed and its specification laid down, then the equipment and materials to make it are assembled, it is made, put into stock and finally marketed. That is a view which mistakenly equates marketing with selling. Marketing includes selling, but is very much wider; the difference is fundamentally important.

In the early stages of the Industrial Revolution the innovations at first took the form mainly of capital goods, and they helped to make possible increases of output of existing consumer goods which became cheaper, of more reliable quality, and in many cases of better quality than those that had previously been available. These commodities were already well known, even if hitherto beyond the reach of many, except perhaps for infrequent purchases. There was already a demand for them, though much of it was not effective demand, i.e. it was not all backed up by money available for first-time or further puchases. Their lower prices following the introduction of machine production meant that many more people could now afford to buy some of them, and many who were already part of the market could now buy more. Producers and consumers became better off. As an addition to this process the new manufactured products found markets overseas, in countries from which Britain imported in return increasing quantities of raw materials to feed the expanding industries. At this stage the enhanced production found ready markets, and the industrialists tended to have their attention concentrated for the most part on the product and, even more, the production process. That is what was new and changing fast; that is what brought the economies that widened the market; that is what commanded attention.

The emphasis on product and production had its roots in the experience of products finding a ready market, which led to a

151

feeling that a good product would always sell. Technical excellence in product and process came sometimes to be sought as automatically desirable, and from this it was but a step to seek them for their own sake. Associated with this, the notion of **engineering efficiency** was rather pervasive at that time; the idea of economic efficiency had not yet been clearly formulated, though some economic writings had been feeling their way towards it. Engineering efficiency is a relationship between physical inputs and physical outputs, whereas economic efficiency has regard to the values put on those inputs and outputs by the market. To the extent that many industrialists tended to think in terms of engineering efficiency, they were production orientated. Furthermore, producers on a mechanical scale tended to be further removed from their newly extended markets than were most of their predecessors on a manual scale of production, and this too tended to keep their eyes on production and the product itself. In addition, the population of Britain was rising fast and approximately doubled in each fifty years of the nineteenth century, despite enormous effluxes by way of emigration; the emigrants remained part of the market in their oversea settlements and, indeed, because of their prosperity, a relatively larger part than if they had stayed at home.

The innovative changes which had taken place were the result of economic pressures: there *were* enlarged markets to be had if costs of production could but be reduced; and the means of reducing them while producing more were found. Gradually, over a very long period, the locus of economic pressure shifted. Industry expanded enormously and new industrial products also appeared, which meant a large rise in material standards of living. There had arisen a market in which consumers received higher real incomes on average than had ever been enjoyed in the past, and in which they were able to become more and more discriminating in their purchases, both as between the brands offered by rival producers of the same kind of article, where differentiation was possible, and between one kind of article and another kind – for example, the choice between a new-fangled wireless set and a bicycle. A growing number of producers had to face competition from abroad as other countries also developed their industries. The pressure was now on producers to be able to market their products. In many cases they experienced growing difficulty in expanding or even holding their share of the market. Increased selling pressure arose and many producers became aware that, especially if their product was distributed to the final consumer through intermediary wholesalers and retailers, they often had only an imperfect idea of what their market really was, and where and how it might be expanded; they knew little of the kinds of people who would be likely to buy their product, and how much of it at a time and in what size of packet they would find it convenient to make their purchases; they had little systematic information about the domestic backgrounds of their customers and potential customers, where they lived and what their incomes were, and even incomplete knowledge in the case of some products about all the uses to which the products were put and how they were used; and in general they knew little of the tastes and preferences of their actual and potential consumers, either as to the characteristics and design of the product itself or as to its packaging.

Market Research and Market Orientation

The pressure on producers was heaviest where they had reached the stage of mass production with the aid of expensive capital equipment, giving the business a high level of total fixed costs. Failure to expand or even to hold their share of the market might threaten the firm's very existence, yet any increase of selling effort might in substantial measure be wasted where it was undertaken in partial ignorance of the actual and potential market.

Industrial firms therefore turned to identifying the characteristics of their markets both actual and potential, usually by employing the services of one of the specialist firms of consultants or market research agencies which started to proliferate. (Some of the largest industrial companies now undertake this work themselves.) This process was further encouraged as technological development raised further the costs of investment in plant for the production of a new product or of an existing one on a larger scale; a mistaken investment was now more costly than ever. The chances of an investment project turning out badly are reduced if it is only undertaken in the light of the results of prior market research. This would assess the acceptability of the proposed product, the characteristics which different groups of consumers would demand of it, the incomes and possible purchases of those consumers, the other items in their expenditure budgets with which it would be in competition, the level of price at which the product would be expected to sell, and so on. The results of such research might lead to modifications in the proposed product and hence in the equipment ordered to produce it. Gradually the product — and production — orientation of industrial firms is modified and swings towards the market which has to be considered first. Not all producers change equally readily, nor to the same extent, and the process still goes on.

Knowledge of the characteristics of the markets and the demand for a company's products is one thing. Systematic effort to obtain it, even when supplemented by data about competitive products, consumers' attitudes to them and the selling tactics of rivals, does not amount to complete market orientation, however. It is possible for a firm to be energetically engaged in the acquisition of such information yet still be tied to the notion that it is inherently in the industry defined by its product. That notion is at present receding and being replaced by the idea that the industry in which a firm is based is to be defined by reference to the market(s) in which it sells. The Marketing Director of Bryant and May has been reported in the press as saying 'We asked ourselves what business we are in. At first we said matches. But we were not. We were in the 'lights' business. Until that realisation, we had looked at disposable lighters as the enemy' (*Financial Times*, May 31, 1984). The perspective is wider than that provided by the product alone, and looks rather at the kind of want which it is used to satisfy. Market orientation exists when a firm is primarily concerned with identifying and satisfying the effective demands in the market, with discerning future demands, and when this sensitivity to current and potential market changes is matched by a readiness to respond to them throughout the organisation. In this way decisions about what is to be produced, by what method and on what scale, for how long a production run, and about the details of design of the range of products and their packaging are all taken with the intention of meeting ascertained market demands, with a preparedness to modify the product range or the way it is presented and marketed, or to change to the production of different products if that is what is required.

The explicit notion of **market orientation** is of recent origin; it has a management context and may be seen as associated with the much older idea of consumers' sovereignty in economics (that in perfect competition the pattern of resource-use in society is that which satisfies consumers' wants to the fullest extent of which those limited resources are capable).

Although it is possible to see a clear contrast between production and market orientation, and although many industrial firms have suffered or even been forced out of existence through lack of adequate care for the market, it is not the case that industrial firms have ever totally neglected the marketing dimension of their activities. Orientation in relation to the market can in practice only be a matter of degree and emphasis. Market research, in the sense of deliberately gathering information about buyers and their wants, market trends and the activities of competitors, has always gone on, and increased in intensity under the pressures referred to earlier. At first, much of this was done by salesmen talking to customers who might be the wholesalers and retailers along the distributive chain. The statistical technique of sampling, and its application to social surveys, was being developed before the First World War, and these methods became applied to market research on behalf of industries fighting to maintain or expand their markets during the depression of the 1930s. Since that time, the methods have become increasingly sophisticated and some of this development has been due to market research itself, the use of which has grown throughout industry.

Value Analysis

Just as there has never been a widespread total disregard for the market, so an exclusively market-orientated approach is an exaggeration. A corrective is provided by **value analysis**, which is a formalised procedure within a firm for examining a proposed or existing product from the point of view of the function which purchasers expect it to perform, the features which might make it attractive or otherwise to them, and how these relate to the costs of production and to the prices which are being aimed at or which purchasers are believed to be willing to pay. The object of value analysis is to reach an optimal combination of characteristics in the product, including its price, taking into account the firm's knowledge of the market and the ways in which various possible features in the product would affect its costs of production. It depends to a large degree on the possibility of quantifying the various factors which it reviews, and this in turn depends on the effectiveness of the systems set up by the management accountant to identify costs in detail. It is a co-operative exercise by members of the firm representing marketing, design, production, cost accounting and other functions which may be affected or have something to contribute (such as procurement of material and parts), and it is a forum for the balancing of conflicting considerations so as to achieve the maximum benefit for the firm.

The Marketing Function

At least some of the functions for which a marketing director or manager is responsible will be evident from the previous section of this chapter. Clearly market research is one of them. Following directly from market research in a firm which is at all market orientated is product planning and development, and this therefore may well be located within the marketing sphere, though it may reside in the area of responsibility which includes production. In either case, to be successful it will need to be carried on in close association with market research.

When an idea for a new product or a modification of an existing one takes shape, it is common for specifications to be compiled and drawings made; perhaps some samples or a model, prototype or 'mock-up' are made. All these are subjected to analysis, examination or test as appropriate, and one of the things that may be looked for is the scope for using components or subassemblies which the firm's plant is already equipped to produce, with an eye on reducing the amount of new investment required. The major criteria by which a potential new product or modification will be judged arise either from marketing or production considerations. On the marketing side are questions of consumer acceptance; the quality required; the effectiveness of the product in the uses for which it has originally been designed, and in any other possible uses; and the price which such a product might command. On the production side are the size of the investment required in new productive equipment; patentability of the product, and whether it would infringe any existing patents; skilled and unskilled labour requirements; and the costing price of the product (see p. 54) at the likely scale of production. In the case of some entirely new products, the feasibiliity of developing a production process from the research stage would require investigation and development work in the production sphere.

The most obvious elements of marketing are advertising, sales, distribution methods and after-sales service of durable goods. These, together with pricing, sometimes enjoy the hideous sobriquet '**marketing mix**'. The idea of the marketing mix is that there is some combination of effort and expenditure on these which will conduce to maximising the share of the market gained by the firm. There are also choices to be made within these elements, such as the kinds of media through which to advertise, the age- and income-groups of the population to be aimed at, and the kind of image to convey. More is said of advertising below.

Within **sales and distribution policy** it has to be decided whether sales should be through wholesalers or to retailers, or direct to the final consumer, and, if the latter, whether by mail order, by door-to-door salesmen or by the firm having its own shops. This may be indicated for consumer goods in certain circumstances, e.g. if the firm has a sufficient range of products, or if it produces goods which have a certain degree of durability in use by the consumer, and a purchase occupies a fairly significant fraction of consumers' budgets so that they are willing to go – perhaps out of the way of their weekly shopping round – to a particular shop for this item. To illustrate further, a sales and distribution policy may take the form of conveying a chi-chi up-market image by advertising, and selling through a restricted number of high-class shops or the manufacturer's own departments within large stores, at a price deliberately higher than the general level for fairly similar articles sold elsewhere; such a policy requires appropriate and more expensive packaging and, at the production stage, a high standard of quality control; in such a policy, also, price is being used as a means of suggesting quality rather than being a result of a preference for perceived quality.

When considering distribution policy an industrial firm requires to take account of trends in economic organisation which may affect its marketing arrangements. For instance, the growth of multiple re-tailing including supermarkets has shifted the balance of bargaining power away from the manufacturer. This growth, which was taking place in any case, has been assisted by the abolition of resale price maintenance (except for books, maps and pharmaceutical products) which has hastened the trend of elimination of high-cost small retailing businesses to the advantage of the multiples with their lower unit costs. The existence of this trend could well affect the sales and distribution policies of some manufacturers, for example by going with the trend and concentrating their sales on large buyers and setting the saving in distribution costs against lower prices received. The determination of some of the choices to be made, and also of modifications to the product, and even whether to finally adopt a new product, is sometimes only settled after a period of test marketing, usually in a particular region of the country. The settling of these matters is never final, however; and firms need to keep the effectiveness of their marketing policies, and the proportions in which the marketing budget is expended on its various elements, under continuous review in order to remain attuned to changing consumer tastes and preferences and changing tactics by competitors.

After-sales service applies to durable goods, usually of a technical kind, and it is part of their marketing to decide whether to offer guarantees and, if so, of what, bearing in mind that the law in any case offers consumers some amount of protection. Electrical and mechanical goods require periodic attention in the normal course of events and a policy decision is required about whether purchasers are to be left to deal with this according to their own devices, perhaps with the aid of a leaflet giving information, advice and instructions; or whether the firm is to offer service, and at what charges, at depôts or by sending the article back to the works; or whether it is to train mechanics who are employees of other firms which become authorised service centres (e.g. motor cars and some electric shavers). Arrangements of the latter kind are usually part of the firm's distribution policy, the authorised service centres being also retail outlets or, sometimes, wholesalers. A particular aspect of after sales service is handling enquiries and complaints from puzzled or dissatisfied customers, and this is sometimes made a specialised activity under the name of customer, or consumer relations.

It is evident from the scope of **marketing activity** that its conduct requires a great deal of liaison with those responsible for other activities within the firm. This is, indeed, one of the important truths behind the idea of market orientation. Production schedules cannot rationally be laid down without sales targets based on market intelligence, and the sales targets are unlikely to be reached without the appropriate marketing policies. Co-operation with research and development is required so that the firm's technical and scientific research on product design and the quest for new products are guided by the actual and emergent requirements of the market. Financial budgeting and management accounting are concerned because of the financial implications of setting prices and setting targets for sales, production, the procurement of materials and labour supply, and laying down an advertising budget. Questions about the feasibility of obtaining the required supplies of labour and materials need liaison with the personnel and purchasing departments. In short there can hardly be an aspect of the firm's activity which is untouched by considerations of marketing. The achievement of the general objectives of the firm requires concerted action by all its departments, with marketing playing a central part.

Sometimes there is conflict between departments arising from the different roles which they play. The following example from a real firm is probably fairly general. When the price of one or more of the raw materials rises, this raises the firm's costed price. At first, if the rises are moderate and the effect on the costed price is within certain limits, the firm absorbs them in its profit margin. If the process continues, it is found that the chief accountant is always the first to bring up the question of raising prices, and to argue for it; the sales manager invariably resists this because his salesmen do not like any change of price, especially one in an upward direction, as they have the task of informing customers and explaining its necessity to them. Even a downward change of price is not welcomed by salesmen because new price lists have to be prepared and if there is a large product range, they can be hard to get used to and a nuisance to salesman and buyer alike. Although it has been suggested above that marketing plays a central part in the firm's range of activities a conflict of view like this cannot be settled by the marketing manager alone. It either has to be argued out to reach a rational consensus, or settled by someone like the managing director, making a decision.

As well as trying to impinge in a direct way by sales promotion on the motivation of potential puchasers so that they become actual purchasers, companies like to have a good corporate image in the community at large. A good general reputation is sought to be maintained by **public relations**, and staff or a department of this name are often found within the responsibilities of a marketing director. The means by which the department may pursue its aim include making press releases on general matters affecting the company or on company events or plans which are of national or local interest, for example decisions to build a new factory or to close one. Sometimes a press release will be made at a conference at which managers talk to journalists and then answer their questions. It may be a matter of the firm blowing its own trumpet – preferably without appearing to do so – or of putting an incident or a decision in the best light to which it is susceptible. Staff doing this work are sometimes called information officers. Other public relations activities include making representations to government departments and members of Parliament about proposed legislation or regulations affecting the company in any way, or seeking the abolition or amendment of existing provisions; and securing publicity, understanding and, at best, support for points of view, arguments and policies which are favourable to the company's interests. Since those with opposed interests can be relied upon to be doing the same, it can be said that such activities are necessary in self-defence and are often cancelled out. Other public relations activities may include the sponsorship of sporting and artistic events; at some of these there is an element of direct advertising where the name of the firm appears on tee shirts, hoardings and, more discreetly, on programmes, but the principal object is prestige and the cultivation of a good image through commendable associations.

Advertising

'To advertise' originally meant 'to inform' and it was used in connection with any kind of matter. The most common use of the word nowadays stems from the practice of informing the public of the existence of a product and of its characteristics including its price. Modern **advertising** of the products of industrial firms has gone much beyond this stage, though the classified advertisements in newspapers usually confine themselves to an informative content. Beyond being informative, advertising may be persuasive. It may also be defensive in the sense that it would not be undertaken on such a scale were it not for the fact that competitors are advertising extensively and it is believed to be necessary in order not to yield market ground to them – in order merely to keep one's place in the sun. The defensive or competitive element in some advertising has in the past few years become more and more combative and adversarial to the point of consisting sometimes of denigration of a rival product – the 'knocking' element.

Because of its competitive character, modern advertising of consumer products is sometimes claimed to be wasteful of resources, not necessarily from the point of view of an individual industrial firm but from that of society as a whole. If one advertisement is put out, a rival has to put one out. The campaigns become mutually countervailing. Consumers gain nothing, nor do the advertisers except to the extent that between them they have advertised a class of commodity of which their brands are members. New consumers may be glad of the informative content which has drawn their attention to the commodity, but in general consumers gain nothing except the apprehension that they are footing a handsome bill for advertising. So the argument runs. However, there are other arguments running in the opposite direction.

Before following on the opposite tack let us notice certain relevant matters. Firstly, it is well-nigh impossible in practice to distinguish the informative element on the one hand, and the persuasive and other elements on the other hand. The running down of rivals' products is obvious enough, but even such advertisements convey some modicum of information about what the advertiser himself is offering. Still, the major difficulty lies in distinguishing information and persuasion. Secondly, the value of the informative element to consumers is not to be gainsaid, and it is quite possible that many producers do not offer as much information in their publicity as consumers would like. Many consumers do in fact undertake search costs for such information and one of the most obvious manifestations of this is that the Consumers' Association's periodical *Which?* is well known and widely used, and that several commercial publications with a similar object for particular groups of commodity also exist, although in these cases allowance has to be made for the fact that some of these interests are hobbies. Thirdly, advertising is only possible when a product can be differentiated, at least in the minds of consumers, from the similar offerings of rival producers. This differentiation is either followed or created by branding the product with a trademark. This means that competition in the industry is not perfect, that one producer's product is not a perfect substitute for that of another, and that each producer has a measure of market power greater than he would otherwise have. He has a monopoly of his own brand. It is not, however, a perfect monopoly because there are other similar products which can act as substitutes to some degree.

Let us now return to the effects of advertising. If a producer succeeds by advertising in enlarging the market for his product the effect on his production activity may be that if he feels he can maintain the position, and after a period long enough to make the adjustment, production is moved on to a larger scale. The economies which this brings are profitable to the firm, and they may also make it possible to reduce the price of the product to the consumer. In fact, this may be the firm's strategy all along, and the new larger scale of production may be adopted sooner rather than later in order to add lower prices to advertising in the firm's competitive armoury. In this way the firm will be ready to fulfil the stronger demand for its product and expand its market share. In this way advertising may pay for itself from the producer's point of view, and confer the benefit of lower prices on the consumer.

There is no guarantee that this must always be a successful strategy. Not all advertising is successful, and it cannot save a product which consumers will not accept. It has been found that over three-quarters of new products fail even though some of them have been extensively – and expensively – advertised. Furthermore, the 'epidemic effect' which was noticed earlier when discussing economies of scale can work in reverse: if some consumers recoil from a product as from the plague, others will avoid it too. Advertising is at its most effective when it is pushing at a door ajar. It is the function of market research to discover such doors. From market research is to be learned who have what needs or incipient wants, what is their income and social standing, what magazines and newspapers they read, when they watch TV and whether they watch the commercials – everything about them, in fact, which builds an Identikit of them as bundles of wants and the degree of affluence at their disposal to indulge them. From this, advertising can be steered in the most cost-effective direction as to its content and the image of the product it conveys, the media through which its messages should be conveyed, and the target group or groups of the population at which they are aimed. Rather than artificially creating or shaping people's wants, it is more a matter of playing on latent wants which have been discovered to be already there. In these ways some argue that advertising is not wasteful and assists the forces for progress and higher living standards in the economy.

Although advertising may be part of a process which includes economies of scale in production (and economies of scale in advertising itself), and which leads to lower prices and higher sales, the lower prices relative to the prices of other goods may sometimes turn out to be temporary. They are a competitive weapon and rival firms may be permanently damaged by them and the greater differentiation and preference which the advertising has achieved. Some may be forced out of existence. At all events, advertising has helped to lead to greater market power. This position is then reinforced by the existence of the heavy advertising expenditures and the high level of investment required to produce on the large scale which the firm has reached. A newcomer to the industry must match this investment in order to produce at as low a cost, and would have to undertake similarly heavy advertising to break into the market at all. These two high investments constitute what are called **barriers to entry** to the industry. They can be made more formidable by the practice of **limit pricing**, which is setting price at a level low enough to deter new entrants to the industry; existing producers have the cost advantage of their large scale of production, while an outsider thinking of coming in would realise that any new entrant on a smaller scale would have higher costs and that if he entered on the same large scale as existing producers, the price could well collapse. The use of limit pricing is, however, an example of prices being kept lower than they might otherwise be by the threat of potential competition. At the same time industries can, partly through advertising and partly for reasons of the technology of production (see Chapter 6 above), become concentrated, i.e. have an overwhelmingly large proportion of their output produced by a small handful of firms. The measure of this is an industry's **concentration ratio**; thus 3CR=80% means that in a particular industry 80 per cent of the output is produced by the three largest firms.

Even in the case of a highly concentrated industry, however, advertising can assist a new entrant to break in. If he can produce a differentiated product for a particular kind of demand which he has identified within the market, then he may choose to specialise in it and gain a profitable place in the industry as a whole. In other cases advertising may be able to break old buying habits by conveying the information that a new product exists, and the cost of advertising will not always constitute a barrier to entry.

The extent of advertising by firms in different industries varies greatly. Of course, this must be so because some firms and industries are larger than others, so to make comparisons we use the **ratio of advertising expenditure to sales revenue**. In order to maximise the contribution made by advertising to the firm's profit, it will continue to increase its advertising expenditure for so long as the increase in advertising cost is less than the resulting increase in profit. The latter depends on how responsive sales volume is to the increase in advertising, and what contribution is made to profit by the increase in volume of sales. The maximun contribution is being made when the marginal cost of advertising equals the marginal revenue product of advertising.

In practice, while such an abstract rule of behaviour has some background influence, advertising budgets are usually set according to criteria which are more easily measured. Sometimes the previous year's sales, or the coming year's forecast sales, are taken as a basis;

this still does not give us an explanation of what percentage is normally applied to these amounts in arriving at the budget other than the firm's past experience, nor of any changes in that percentage which may occur from time to time. However, last year's sales may not be a good guide to the desirable level of advertising this year: if sales are falling, it may be right to reduce certain kinds of advertising depending on the reasons for the fall, but there may be a good case for increasing advertising rather than reducing it; and if sales are rising and plant working at near its capacity, in the short run there may be no call to increase advertising expenditure. Next year's forecast sales may be no better as a base for applying some customary percentage. If the forecast is downwards, the most reasonable response may be to increase expenditure on selling and advertising, even though the firm's accountants may argue that with falling sales revenue this cost should be cut according to formula. In an industry characterised by defensive advertising, a firm's advertising budget is set according to the amount which it thinks its rivals will spend. According to the marginalist profit-maximising rule, changes in advertising expenditure are seen as leading to changes in profits. But some ways of setting advertising budgets seem more consistent with the opposite of this, with changes in profits (resulting from changes in sales) leading to changes in advertising expenditure.

Between industries the advertising to sales ratio is affected to a very large extent by the kinds of goods being produced, and particularly by whether they are of a kind where experiment by consumers between one brand and another is cheap or costly. With some products, information about their attributes and how well they serve the buyer's purpose is obtained by actually using them; what can be learned by looking at or touching them, or their packets, beforehand is rather limited and the proof of the pudding is in the eating. Such products have been called **experience goods**; they contrast with **search goods**, whose relevant attributes are apparent before buying as, for example, in the case of ready-made clothing. Expenditure on persuasive advertising of search goods tends to be less than on experience goods because the buyer is in any case in a position to judge for himself, before buying, how well a product will serve his purpose. Experience goods are advertised more heavily as buyers are more dependent on information and susceptible to suggestion provided otherwise than by their own senses. Other kinds of products for which the advertising to sales ratio is usually high are those which are associated with personal sensitivities, e.g. with children and family, health, personal appearance and social esteem. Since sensitivities can be played upon, they are prime targets for advertisers.

Another distinction of importance in the context of the ratio of advertising to sales is that between durable and non-durable commodities. This distinction has something in common with a division of commodities into those for which a sale normally represents a relatively large proportion of a consumer's budget against those for which it is small. The lower the unit value of the product the higher is the advertising-sales ratio likely to be; the cost to the buyer of an 'experiment' is low, and another purchase of this or a rival product will be required soon; if advertising can affect the initial choice, it may have a chance to establish brand loyalty.

The possibilities of advertising normally depend, as we have seen, on being able to differentiate a firm's product and to brand it. When this condition is not fulfilled, advertising may still occur collectively as in the campaigns of the Marketing Boards with advertisements of the 'Go to Work on an Egg' variety. In industry, the producers may have differentiated their products and be in competition between themselves yet, because their commodity is in close competition with others, they may decide to advertise collectively. Brewers have done this, with the slogan 'Beer is Best'.

The Product Life Cycle

The **product life cycle** has interactions with advertising and with the other marketing weaponry. Manufactured products, particularly consumer goods both durable and non-durable, go through a series of market phases which together are likened to a life span. Some products come and go very quickly, perhaps enjoying a tremendous vogue for a short period. Others maintain a place on the market for many decades. The process may be represented in terms of the quantity sold each year or other period over the lifetime of the product until it is finally withdrawn from the market.

Following on the birth or launch of the product on an astonished world, there is a period of introduction which may be gradual and perhaps on a test market at first; this gives an opportunity to judge whether the product is likely to be successful and whether modifications to it are required. The mortality rate is very high as has already been mentioned, with over 75 per cent of new products failing to survive the initial stages. Survival is followed by a period of growth during which sales rise, partly as the result of the cumulative effects of advertising, and the product is established on the market. From then onwards the product's sales are at around their peak level and the market is saturated. The inevitable decline sets in because of changing consumer tastes and the emergence of new products, and is followed by eventual demise. This chain (shown in Figure 7.1) is

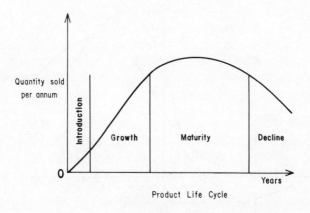

Product Life Cycle

Figure 7.1

merely representational of the general idea of the succession of stages, and the relative lengths of the different periods and rates of growth and decline vary widely from one product to another. Skateboards disappeared as quickly as they came: the Bisto Kids have been around for 65 years.

There is a stage before those outlined in Figure 7.1. To begin with one must conceive the idea of the product, and a gestation period must follow during which development of the product and its eventual production process takes place; this might occupy anything from a year or two, perhaps less, to a few decades or so. During this stage research and development costs are incurred – and they may be very heavy – and when the product is finally launched on the market, further heavy expenditure on advertising is probable. During this stage there is an outward flow of cash from the firm. When sales commence there is still a net outward flow of cash because of the high initial costs of penetrating the market, coupled with the low initial sales volume. Eventually the negative net cash flow is reversed. Then at a later stage still the net inflow has recouped the past net outflows, and the product is in profit. The accumulated output at which this is achieved is the breakeven point; and the number of years taken to reach it is the payback period. The totals represented by the two shaded areas in Figure 7.2 are equal.

One reason that firms like to be engaged in multi-product rather than single product activity is that their various lines are then likely to be at different stages of the product life cycle at any given time. Products at their mature stage can be generating cash flow, part of which can be used to finance the development of new products to replace those at present in decline. However, these things cannot be matched exactly as the various stages are not under close control, though their length and rate of change can be affected by marketing

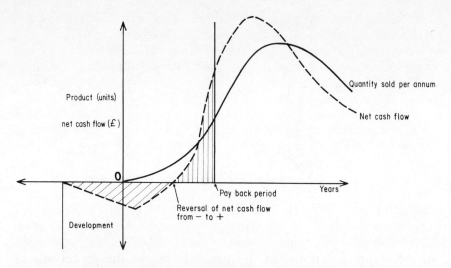

Figure 7.2

strategies as well as by the attributes of the product itself and consumer attitudes to them. The market strategies are likely to change as successive stages of the cycle are reached; at one stage the amount and type of advertising may be of prime importance, at another the price, and at yet another the effort of salesmen. Knowledge of the probable course of the cycle for a particular product in the absence of a change in marketing policy is useful in devising that policy. It is impossible to carry out such forecasting precisely. Furthermore, it is not even possible at all times to tell exactly where a product is in its life cycle. The curve which has been drawn in Figure 7.1 is artificially smooth. In practice it will have an irregular course with short-term ups and downs from year to year or over irregular periods of years. Statistical techniques enable a trend to be fitted, but its extrapolation is subject to some margin of error. Furthermore, the record of a product's sales in the past does not give information about all the things which may affect them in the future, such as the introduction of rival products by other producers. Such matters, and their likely effects, have to be estimated as well as may be.

At the introductory stage the speed at which new products are absorbed by the market can be affected by advertisement; its effect is probably greatest at that stage, especially if it is conducted in ways indicated by preliminary and current market research. For this reason innovation is encouraged by advertising and the knowledge of what it can do to shorten payback periods. The question of price policy as a marketing weapon at the introductory stage is less clearcut. A high initial price may be adopted in order to reap temporary monopoly profits from the section of the market which is willing to pay a high price and is perhaps eager to have the cachet of owning – and no doubt displaying – the product while it is new. Such a policy is a form of what is called **price discrimination**, or charging different prices in markets that can be separated. On the other hand, a lower initial price may be set in order to encourage quicker growth of sales and to develop brand loyalty at an early stage before competition appears on the scene. Which of these policies gives the quicker payback depends on how responsive sales are to different prices.

During the growth phase of the cycle, if a relatively high price has been established at the introduction stage, it may be continued in order to help recoup the development costs as quickly as possible. However, it is at this stage that new competitive products are most likely to appear, and the firm has to assess this possibility against the speed at which it can break even with a lower price as against the initial price. For its part, a potential new entrant has to weigh the price at present set by the existing seller against the possibility of devising cost-reducing improvements to its planned production process, and market-appealing improvements to the existing product. Because of actual or potential competition, advertising in the growth phase will become more brand conscious than it had been in the introduction stage, when the emphasis could have been on conveying information about a new product as such. This tendency becomes even more marked in the mature phase of the product cycle.

In a product's declining phase there is usually a reluctance to continue spending on advertising and sales promotion on the scale on which they were conducted when the product was increasing its sales, and the emphasis in sales policy may shift to price competition. If the volume of sales still has some momentum of its own, a reduction of selling and marketing costs can be accomplished and yet the product remain profitable largely because of the saving; however, much also depends on the level of fixed costs and the extent of the decline in sales. There can be no fixed rule and all the circumstances of a particular case have to be considered. There is also a trap that a firm has to be careful not to fall into: if the conclusion is drawn that a product is declining and resources are therefore withdrawn from marketing it, the conclusion may be merely self-fulfilling. If the marketing effort had not been reduced, the product might have continued at an acceptable level for some time longer. What constitutes an acceptable level is related to the profitability of the alternative uses to which the firm could put those resources which at present are devoted to the production and marketing of the product in question.

In addition to avoiding action which causes a product's further decline, a firm may at a relatively early stage of the declining phase examine the possibility of what are called **extension strategies**. Total decline can sometimes be profitably postponed by making alterations to the product so that a new line is added to the range, which will gain entry to new markets. The markets may be new in the sense of places where the unmodified product did not sell (because of the voltage, for example, if it is a piece of electrical equipment), or in the sense of sections of the population for whose use it has not hitherto been suitable. It may be that new uses for a product, modified perhaps, can be thought of and be the subject of informative advertising. Perhaps the extension to the market consists of use of the product in different circumstances from those which have been usual, or simply in use more frequently or in larger quantities. Other expedients include adding to the variety of shapes, sizes, colours, textures and the like in which the product is available in order to make repeat purchases more attractive. They also include redesigning so as to keep up with changing tastes in matters of style; so as to introduce genuine improvements in the product's fitness for its purpose; or so as to render existing items of the product in the hands of users obsolescent.

Industrial Products

The meaning of the expression **industrial products** may not be clear at first sight. It means **producer goods**. They may be capital equipment, components or raw materials – for example, lathes, printing presses, steel in sheets or bars or other forms, chemicals and paint (which is also a consumer good). Such things are produced by one industry for sale to another for use in its productive process. The buying industry itself may also turn out industrial products, though somewhere along the line final consumer goods must appear. The proportion of the total output of all UK industrial firms which is of this kind is over 40 per cent, so industrial products have a very important place in the scheme of things. The markets for them also have certain features which are different from the typical markets for consumer goods. Four such features may be identified.

Firstly, purchasing is done by specialists in a large firm, and even in a small firm it is done by people with technical knowledge of what is required, and a greater degree of expertise in assessing the quality of the product than final consumers normally have. The buyers have a close appreciation of the price/quality relationships of rival products. However, they do not necessarily decide to buy the product for which this ratio is lowest; that depends largely on the buyer's marketing strategy in his product market and how far it rests on quality. At one extreme, if the quality of the final product is more important than its price, the industrial buyer may opt for quality absolutely, especially if the industrial good accounts for only a small proportion of his costs. At the other extreme, if the price of the consumer good is the major consideration, then the buyer may decide in favour of the producer good with the lowest absolute price, especially if it forms a large part of his costs. This extreme of low price preference is not common, and very often the seller of industrial products must reckon with the buyer's expert knowledge of quality, and compete according to the requirements of the buying firm's market.

Secondly, the industrial good, if it is an intermediate product like a component or raw material, or the service provided by it if it is a piece of capital equipment, is only a part of the cost of the final product. It may be a large or a small part, and one kind of implication of this has just been mentioned in the previous paragraph. The proportion of the cost of the final product represented by a particular industrial product is not necessarily similar for all buyers, for the industrial product may be one which is used in the production of a number of different products at the next stage, whether final or not. The demand for industrial products is called 'derived demand' because they are not wanted for their own sake but have a demand which derives from that for ultimate consumer goods. The marketing of a producer good can depend on different market conditions for different consumer goods, as well as on the proportions of their final costs which the producer good represents. This can be particularly important in making decisions about price.

Thirdly, the customers of industrial producers often have special requirements which are peculiar to them. The producer is marketing a product differentiated by his customers rather than by himself, and is either supplying the same thing to a particular group of buyers, or producing a basic product with special modifications as specified by each buyer. He is, in short, a specialist producer. Some of his equipment has been installed to meet the requirements of buyers. A tailor also makes a suit for a particular person, but the transaction does not involve the same commitment of capital equipment, nor knowledge of a production process employed by the buyer. Industrial producers are likely to have direct contact with their customers and to sell direct to them. The buyers are few, as compared to a mass-produced consumer good, and this, together with their individual needs, makes it cheaper and more effective to visit them than to deploy marketing effort in intensive advertising. It is not the case that producer goods are not advertised at all, but there is an emphasis on direct contact with buyers and direct selling

to them. For all these reasons industrial producers are often working in a market for their general kind of product which is segmented,
so that each producer has its own market or part of the wider
market. This kind of situation is reached through non-price competition, particularly the ability and willingness to meet a customer's
special requirements, and producers have some added degree of
freedom in deciding on their prices; this is strictly limited, however,
by the threat of potential competition.

Fourthly, in the markets for producer goods assurance of continued supply is in many cases a decisive consideration for buyers.
This applies particularly to components and raw materials, without
which a buyer's whole production process would be halted. A study
of this topic found that a difference in price of up to 10 per cent was
not sufficient to persuade many industrial buyers to switch to the
cheaper source from a supplier whom they had found reliable; this
was so even in the case of basic materials and standard undifferent-
iated components. A buyer may even regard a low price as a sign
that continued supply from that source is questionable and that the
ability of the supplier to remain in business is in doubt. It may even
be taken as a sign that he is already in financial difficulty. Again the
main thrust of competition is away from price and towards regular-
ity, promptness and continuation of supply. Considerations of this
kind count for much less in the markets for consumer goods, and are
usually not present at all. The supply of spare parts for consumer
durables has some similarity; however, in this case, when weighing
price against the probability of spares being readily available when
required, the consumer considers the prices (and other attributes) of
rival durables rather than the prices of their spares.

There are some other fairly common features about transactions
in industrial products which call for mention. Prices are sometimes
quoted by tendering for a contract to supply certain goods or carry
out certain engineering or construction work. Normally the lowest
tender is successful, especially if tenders are confined to those who
have been invited to submit them. The specification of the goods
required or the work to be carried out will be laid down by the buyer
in the appropriate technical detail together with the delivery or
completion dates. In such cases price competition acquires
increased significance relative to non-price competition. However,
one of the features of contracting for the supply of large items of
capital equipment or civil engineering works, whether by tender or
by negotiation, is that the buyer may be swayed by the offer of
credit terms; he may even require them, in which case the terms
which a contractor can offer are an important element of non-price
competition. This is often an important consideration for export
orders. Obviously, however, credit cannot be offered without cost

to the contractor; he suffers either the opportunity cost of having his funds tied up and not available for productive use, or he has to obtain the funds on the financial markets.

Another feature concerns the development of close relations between customer and supplier. These may sometimes become so close, and sales to a particular buyer such a large proportion of the supplier's total output, that the supplier agrees to confine production to the buyer's requirements only. This is only likely to happen if the buyer's market share is growing. A great deal of confidence between the two firms is required, but it has the advantages of greater assurance of a market to the seller, and of secure supplies to his own specification for the buyer. An example is Marks and Spencer plc and the knitwear manufacturer Corah plc. Another aspect of customer–supplier relations is that if they are close, they enable the seller to explore with a home market buyer the scope for modifying a product to fit a specification called for in an export market; this may make the difference between being able to compete in the export market or not.

It has been noted above that there are reasons why industrial producers are likely to have personal contact with their customers and to sell direct to them. Since they know their buyers at first hand, they are able to gather from them a good deal of information about their needs, the performance of the product, the impact on them of any advertising that may take place, and their attitudes in relation to price, sales promotion and after-sales service. From this there is sometimes a tendency for industrial producers to assume that with complete coverage of their market in this way they have no need of market research. Such an assumption ignores some important considerations. An industrial producer's prospects depend not only on the more immediate attitudes and reactions of those who buy from him, but on what is going to happen in his present customers' consumer markets and in other markets to which he might potentially be an indirect supplier. Some of this is apparent when an industrial product is recognisable by the consumer, such as the make of speedometer and other gauges in a car. In such cases industrial producers sometimes advertise direct to the consuming public to try to set up a preference on their part, and sometimes join with a customer in advertisements which mention both products. Advertising and sales promotion, however, tackle only a part of the marketing problem; and advertising with consumers as its target is pointless when the industrial product is not recognisable by the consumer, as with the make of the material used for covering the seats in a motor car.

Research in consumer markets, consumer tastes, aspirations, habits, incomes and their trends is no less important to industrial producers than it is to producers of consumption goods. The need is for information independent of that provided by the immediate buyers, and wider in scope. The destiny of an industrial producer is not necessarily uniquely and indissolubly linked to those of his present customers. The information required from market research certainly includes information about present final markets and about the intermediate market, and all that affects likely trends in their conditions of supply and demand, and their likely size and character in the future; but it also includes the search for and assessment of potential markets, new applications, and new products. Orientation towards the product and its process of production is particularly tempting in the case of industrial goods, but the need to look to consumer markets is no less great than it is for those who would serve those markets direct.

Consumers' Sovereignty

Consumers' sovereignty is the economic theory that the pattern of resource use in the economy is dictated by the preferences of consumers as expressed through the relative strengths of their demands for the various final goods. For this to hold sway absolutely there has to be a state of perfect competition in all industries throughout the economy, and all firms must have profit maximisation as their object. These two conditions are not fulfilled in practice, and the sovereignty of the consumer is impaired accordingly. Some of the conditions for perfect competition and for profit maximisation to exist are unattainable, and we have also seen that if economies of scale are to be achieved, then the extent of competition is reduced. Nevertheless, if all producers are thoroughly market oriented and apply value analysis on the basis of thorough market research together with up-to-date knowledge of technical possibilities in their production processes and product designs, and if they go on to compete by offering consumers the best combination of product attributes – quality, reliability, design, delivery and price – then the preferences of consumers can be said to determine the pattern of resource use to all practical intents and purposes. The extent to which this is so in an advanced industrial society is a matter of dispute.

One writer who believes that consumers' sovereignty has been seriously impaired is Professor J. K. Galbraith. He has America primarily in mind, but his arguments are applicable to the UK. In *The Affluent Society* and *The New Industrial State* he focuses attention on the largest industrial producers. They are controlled by managers whose paramount goal is management success. This breaks down into three aims. The primary aim is self-preservation and the survival of the organisation. Aiming at maximum profits means taking large risks, so that is not their object: maximum profits are not essential to their primary aim, and losses may militate against it. Next, they wish to preserve their autonomy, or power of decision making. This is done, according to Galbraith, by fostering social attitudes favourable to the beliefs that large size brings efficiency and that interference with the market mechanism and the institutions of the market are damaging to the best uses of resources; this latter belief is fostered despite the fact that the actions of the largest industrial firms themselves reduce the power of markets. Thirdly, the firms aim at growth of their production and sales; they plan for this, and try to eliminate uncertainties or things which would interfere with their plans. They therefore try to control as much of the firm's environment as they can, and one of the avenues along which they do this is the manipulation of consumer demand to conform with present and planned production.

Social approval of the growth objective is available through the attention paid to the gross national product as an indicator of national welfare. It is the nature of an ideology that its aims are seen as having a social purpose. The dominant management group, or technostructure, is primarily concerned with producing goods and with managing and developing the demand for those goods, because of the greatly increased capital in the form of large-scale technology that has been committed to their production. They are assisted in this for some products by their increasingly technical character, of which most consumers are imperfect judges. There is no longer a one-way flow of instructions from consumers to producers: the largest producers reach out to control the prices of what they sell, and of what they buy, and to influence the quantities of what they sell by persuasive advertising; and the design, quality and variety of their products are under their close control.

Thus for a group of the largest firms – which Galbraith calls the industrial system – consumers' sovereignty undergoes considerable modifications, and its effective strength has diminished. This group, however, is one that has been growing faster than the rest of industry and occupying a larger share of the total market for manufactured products. For the remainder of firms, which is the vast majority by number, traditional elements of ownership, management and technical structure are still strong enough for them to retain objectives which make their behaviour more responsive to their perception of consumer preferences.

Summary

The distinction is drawn between market orientation and product orientation on the part of firms. Market-orientated firms are likely to be the more successful and their advertising will also be more effective.

The total scope of the marketing function is described. The concept of the product life cycle is introduced and its relevance to marketing explored. The features of the markets for industrial products (as distinct from consumer goods) are examined, and the implications drawn for the marketing of such products.

The behaviour of market-orientated firms matches the criterion of consumers' sovereignty, by which an enterprise system is judged; the extent to which consumers' sovereignty in practice holds sway is briefly looked at in the light of the ideas of J. K. Galbraith.

Review Questions

(1) (a) What are the different kinds of advertising?

    (b) Say what the effects of advertising are, using your classification and considering the uses of market research.

(2) In what ways and in what circumstances may price be used as a marketing weapon?

(3) (a) What is the difference between a firm being market orientated and being product or production orientated?

    (b) Why is it considered necessary for industrial firms to be market orientated?

(4) What differences are there between the marketing of a consumer good and that of a producer good, and what similarities?

The Albert Dock was in a state of decay before the Merseyside Development Corporation stepped in

8

Industry and Government

Background

In all the time since the emergence of the centralised nation state there has never been any supposedly golden age in which economic activity was free of the attentions of government. The reigns of the Tudors and Stuarts were a tangle of regulation from which emanated the Mercantilist system, lasting into the second half of the eighteenth century. It was based on the belief that increased national power and wealth rested on the development of trade, especially foreign trade and the accumulation of gold and silver in exchange for exports. We cannot explore here the fascinating rationale behind this apparently fruitless objective, but it was sufficiently valid in its time to hold sway for three hundred years. The system manifested itself in a labyrinth of legislation, the detailed parts of which, to be sure, changed from time to time though the whole retained its essential nature. Some well-known examples of the legislation are the Statute of Artificers (1563), providing for the direction of labour; the Navigation Acts of the seventeenth century, with many predecessors from the fourteenth century onwards designed to encourage English shipping; and the many Acts and Charters regulating trade by the grant of monopoly.

The economic policies and measures comprising Mercantilism were attacked by Adam Smith (*The Wealth of Nations*, 1776) and he, and the classical economists who followed him, argued for a *laissez-faire* or free market system to take its place. Such a system would provide the most profitable environment for trade and industry and, by the same token, the highest levels of satisfaction for consumers. Man's self-interest – the profit motive – in serving consumers' wants required no regulation to produce a pattern of production and exchange yielding the greatest mutual benefits. Interference by government could only produce a less desirable situation. These ideas commanded much attention and were greatly influential. They suited the circumstances of the early Industrial Revolution. Under pressure of the new economic theory and of the needs of the new thrust in economic progress, much of the structure of the old interventionism was dismantled.

The classical economists' view of the proper scope of state functions has been dubbed a 'policeman' theory of the state. It was the government's responsibility to provide the environment within which business activity takes place, to hold the ring and lay down the rules of fair play under which transactions of all kinds to do with producing and exchanging might take place. It was not for government, with some exceptions, to enter the arena and take part in or alter the course of transactions. Its scope was indicated by needs such as the maintenance of law and order within the country, including the definition of property rights, the laying down of standard weights and measures, and the protection of the citizens against external attack. These things are still basic government functions, bringing important benefits in the form of greater stability and certainty to private economic activity. To them Adam Smith added institutions and public works of a kind whose provision is accomplished to better advantage by the state than by a private organisation; they should not necessarily be provided free of charge, but even with a charge they might be unprofitable. Things of this kind included some roads, education and the currency. Other areas considered by later writers as stemming from the classical position and therefore legitimate from that point of view are those where what is provided is indivisible and its consumption is collective, such as public health measures, and measures to deal with things which might frustrate the free working of markets. The restriction of the power of monopolies would come into the latter category.

Politicians came under the influence of the new economic doctrine, which was also seen to be consistent with what was needed by the rising new industries if they were to prosper. Much of the legislation restricting and distorting business behaviour was, over a period stretching well into the nineteenth century, done away with. The Statute of Artificers was repealed in 1813–14, the Combination Acts in 1824, the Corn Laws (which had featherbedded agriculture, not for the last time in our history) in 1846 and the Navigation Acts in 1849; by 1861 the customs tariff had practically been dismantled and a regime of free trade established, to last until modified during and after the First World War and abandoned in 1932 after the crisis which broke in the previous year.

However, whilst some kinds of intervention by government receded in this sort of way, another kind began to emerge. The new industries brought new economic and social problems of their own, with appalling conditions which cried out for action by government. The classical economic writers who followed Adam Smith were quite pragmatic about interpreting the central doctrine about the boundaries of government action, and Adam Smith himself had been highly practical in outlook and knowledge of the world. Nevertheless, unscrupulous or shortsighted employers were able to use the tenets of the new economic system of free markets in opposition to calls for legislation affecting their factories. The upshot, however, was a flow of legislation of which a notable example, though not the first, was the Factory Act of 1833, limiting the hours of work of child employees. Subsequent legislation affected the employment of women, employment in what were designated as dangerous trades such as mining and the merchant marine, and a range of other employment matters.

Another set of new problems centred around monopoly. The dislike of monopoly in the classical economic doctrine was tempered by the recognition of 'natural' monopolies such as railways, gas and (later) electricity; large amounts of capital were required for these utilities and it was clearly wasteful for them to compete in the same areas, and inconvenient to duplicate tracks and pipes. Their local monopolies were therefore protected but their fares and tariffs were regulated, with one eye on their levels of profit.

Such changes – and those cited are merely representative illustrations rather than an account – amounted in sum to quite a considerable degree of government intervention in industry. They were adopted as a series of pragmatic responses to particular problems where unbridled market behaviour failed to yield the beneficent results predicated of it. The contrary movements of freeing industry yet checking it were not inconsistent.

One reason for an important market (that for labour) not performing perfectly is that workers who are offering labour and employers who have a demand for it often have imperfect knowledge – the one of opportunities available, and the other of suitable labour available. It was to improve the working of the market that government intervened in 1909 by an Act to establish local employment exchanges (then called labour exchanges), where information is brought together for the benefit of both workers and employers.

The twentieth century has witnessed a very much enlarged area of government intervention in industry and in the economy generally, and ideas about the role of government have shifted to accord it a much more prominent place. The spread of social justice as a criterion of economic conditions and the emergence of modern macroeconomic theory both place government in a position central to the whole system, while as regards individual industries we now have a mixed economy in which productive activity is divided between private and public enterprise. The deep and prolonged depression of the thirties, with its mass unemployment and waste of resources, caused the government to enforce policies of rationalisation on various industries so as to reduce surplus capacity and leave a structure which would be profitable. The Bank of England was instrumental in arranging some of the schemes. The process had in fact started in the twenties, with the organisation of the very large number of (then privately owned) railway companies into four, and with attempts to put the coal mining industry on a sound footing. Both industries had been under government control during the First World War, and neither had a structure making for efficiency. During the thirties the cotton, iron and steel, and shipbuilding industries were the subjects of rationalisation schemes, which had various degrees of success. Free trade was eroded during the twenties and abandoned in 1932 in favour of tariff protection for industry. No judgement is being made here about the effectiveness of any of the particular measures which were adopted: the point is that because the period between the two world wars was one of widespread unemployment and deep malaise in many industries arising from their structure, the changed situations in world markets and other factors, the belief that unaided market forces would correct all economic imbalances ceased to be anything like so widely held as it had been in the past; and government involvement with industry increased and ceased to be regarded as an aberration from a ringholding norm.

At the level of the economy as a whole rather than that of individual industries, the Great Depression of the 1930s stimulated economic thought about the causes and cure of mass unemployment and the workings of the economic system as a set of relationships between overall entities such as employment, income, savings, investment, the balance of payments and the level of prices. Keynes's *General Theory of Employment, Interest and Money* was published in 1936; it started from the theorem that whilst free markets might eventually achieve equilibrium in the economy, there was nothing to guarantee that the equilibrium would be at a level of activity giving full employment – to maintain *that* required government intervention. Unemployment receded somewhat in the late thirties as a result of the Government's rearmament programme and the stimulation of the building industry following low interest rates; but there were searing memories of what the depression had meant to millions of people, and the experience of having to fight the Second World War, along with the spectacle that full employment was possible in support of war purposes, brought a determination that after the war economic policies should place full employment for full lives in peacetime at the forefront of their aims. The tight control over the economy exercised by the government in order to conduct total war, and the new economic analysis of Keynes, together contributed to a more intimate relationship between government and the economic environment within which firms work than previously. The achievement of full employment was accompanied by inflation, with subsequent modification to the objectives of macroeconomic policy; but government responsibilities in this field have remained more explicit and continuous than was once the case, warranting intervention as something normal.

Other Aspects of Industry–Government Relations

So far the national government of Britain has been the subject of this sketch of the background to relations between industry and government. Since 1973, however, the UK has been a member of the European Community[1] whose purpose is to secure greater unity among its members, thus reducing the possibility of armed conflict between them. The European Economic Community aims at increased productive efficiency through free trade and free movement of labour and capital between the Member States, and a common external tariff of customs duties. To this end it seeks to secure unified policies towards industry and the lifting of restrictions on the movement of products and of restrictive behaviour in their markets, including monopolistic practices. Part of the idea of creating one single and large European market was to derive the benefits of the economies of scale which it would offer.

The organs of the Community constitute in effect another layer of government. Community policy decisions are made by a Council of Ministers consisting of one minister from each country, the particular individual varying according to the subject matter, e.g. industry, agriculture, finance, etc. Decisions are carried out by the Commission, which can and does make proposals to the Council of Ministers for directives to be issued subject to the Council's agreement. Before any decision is made to adopt what is, in reality, a new law, the opinion must be sought of two other Community bodies: the Economic and Social Committee, and the European Parliament. The former consists of representatives of such bodies as trade unions, employers' organisations and consumer groups in the member countries, and industry is therefore represented on it. The Parliament contains 81 elected UK members out of a total of 434

---

1. This expression is convenient for its brevity, but is inaccurate. There are three distinct European Communities: the European Coal and Steel Community (ECSC) set up under the Treaty of Paris, 1951; the European Economic Community (EEC) set up under the Treaty of Rome, 1957; and the European Atomic Energy Community (Euratom) set up under a separate treaty also signed in Rome in 1957. Each has its own finances.

members; it has certain powers in connection with the Community's budget and may initiate certain kinds of legislation which may affect industry, but the adoption of such legislation is subject to the veto of any member of the Council of Ministers. It can be seen that the Governments of the individual member countries remain at present, through the Council of Ministers, in a very strong position in relation to proposals for Community legislation which they do not like, or which they are persuaded to oppose by pressure groups in their own countries.

Relations between government and industry are not all one way. Intervention is preceded by consultation, and sometimes occurs because representatives of industry ask that it should. Sometimes the government, represented probably by the Department of Trade and Industry, will consult with representatives of particular companies. On more general matters there exist organisations called representational bodies, but more often called pressure groups, which are available for consultation and which in any case make representations to government at all levels and to the European Commission, whether they are asked for or not. The main body of this kind is the Confederation of British Industry (CBI), whose 11,000 or so direct members include companies, employers' organisations, trade associations and most of the nationalised industries. The total number of firms represented, including those represented through these Employers' Organisations (EOs) and Trade Associations (TAs), is about 300,000. The CBI acts as an advisory and consultative body (it does not itself undertake wage negotiations), as a source of information including statistical data to its members, and as a forum for ascertaining the views of its members and forming collective policies. This work is done in a series of committees culminating in a council of 200 members. The policies are then pursued by representing them to the appropriate governmental authorities and by seeking to influence public and parliamentary opinion. The CBI is represented on public bodies such as the National Economic Development Council, the Manpower Services Commission, and the Advisory, Conciliation and Arbitration Service. In particular industries there are trade associations, which make representations on matters peculiar to, or particularly affecting, their individual industry, and which may provide common services for their members and may regulate trading practices. Individual industries also sometimes have employers' organisations for the collective negotiation of rates of pay and conditions of work.

The Trades Union Congress (TUC) is also an important part of the representational and consultative machinery, and it has members on the same public bodies concerned with general economic and industrial policy, and labour matters, as does the CBI. Its membership consists of affiliated unions, which number over 100 and have a total membership in the order of 10 million. It is not itself normally involved in particular negotiations about wages and conditions of work, though it sometimes plays a part in difficult and important cases of dispute. It is not able to enter into agreements on these or on other matters (say, with government) which bind its members, though it may have a persuasive influence on them. It is normally consulted by government on matters of industrial and employment policy, and in any case makes representations on them and on general economic policy.

The Objects of Government Economic Policy

Successive governments in the period since the Second World War have set out to affect certain salient features of the economy, viz.: (a) the level of employment; (b) the rate of inflation, or the rate at which the general level of prices is changing (upwards); (c) the rate of economic growth, i.e. growth in real terms of the gross domestic product; (d) the balance of payments to and from other countries for imports, exports and other transactions; (e) the distribution of income between different sections of the population; and (f) the efficiency with which the economy's resources are being used. Different governments have not placed the same relative importance on their aims in these various areas, and these differences of emphasis are partly what have distinguished one political party from another while in office. A high level of employment and rate of growth, a more equal distribution of income, and efficient use of resources through publicly owned enterprise and government intervention in industry have tended to be stressed by Labour governments; whilst stability of the price level, a healthy balance of payments, and efficient use of resources through free market competition reflecting consumer choice have tended to be stressed by Conservative governments. Objectives in the several fields are not always compatible with each other: increasing employment may conflict with reducing the rate of inflation or reducing a balance of payments deficit; preserving existing jobs may conflict with securing a more efficient distribution of labour; a high rate of interest as part of monetary policy to reduce inflation may, by making it attractive for foreigners to hold funds in the form of sterling assets, keep the rate of exchange of sterling so high as to reduce price competitiveness of UK products in overseas markets; and reducing inflation may conflict with a desired direction of change in the distribution of income. Economic policy making very frequently requires that part of one objective be traded off against part of another, and this gives rise to differences of opinion about how much of one objective to sacrifice for the sake of a greater achievement elsewhere.

Policies to promote greater efficiency in the use of the economy's resources are microeconomic and are the subject of the latter sections of this chapter. They are related to macroeconomic objectives, and may be used in support of them, as when subsidies are paid to firms which move to Development Areas or grants are paid to assist the mobility of unemployed labour. Equally, there may again be conflicts: for example, mergers may be encouraged in order to assist the balance of payments through the increased international competitiveness flowing from economies of scale, and this may run counter to domestic competition policy. When policies at the microeconomic level are not devised in pursuit of macroeconomic objectives, one reason they are brought in is failure of the market to work as it is supposed to. Intervention of a kind which in the nineteenth century was seen as exceptional and pragmatic is now seen as being justified by market imperfections, such as incomplete information available to buyers or sellers, or inequality in their bargaining power or the like. Employment exchanges, measures against monopoly and restrictive practices, and Wages Councils rest on this basis. Another reason for such purely microeconomic policies is the existence of externalities, which are costs or benefits imposed by an industrial activity on third parties and which are not paid for. The contamination of rivers by factory effluent, and the benefit derived by ships from a lighthouse are examples.

Macroeconomic Policy

It is not possible within the scope of this book to deal in detail with macroeconomic theory and the causes of the various situations in which macroeconomic policies are applied as presumptive remedies. Our task is to try to see something of how macroeconomic situations and the use of macroeconomic policy instruments form part of the economic environment in which industrial firms must operate.

The two principal means by which macroeconomic objectives are pursued are fiscal policy and monetary policy. Each of these means aims to influence the level of aggregate demand or total spending on goods and services in the economy. It was a deficiency of aggregate demand which was identified by Keynes as being the source of mass unemployment and of the *laissez-faire* system bringing about an equilibrium at a lower level than that which would use all the labour available for employment. Where does the demand come from? Aggregate demand is made up of consumer spending, plus investment spending on capital equipment and stocks, plus government spending on wages, salaries, materials and public investment, plus exports (spending from outside the country on part of the country's production). One person's spending from any of these sources sets another person to work and gives him income.

The level of aggregate spending can be influenced by monetary policy in the form of changes in the rate of interest and the money supply, which affect investment and consumption; and it can be influenced by fiscal policies including changes in taxation to affect consumption, and changes in government spending, which contribute to changes in aggregate demand directly. There is also an additional, indirect, effect which follows from any injection of spending into the system. The first recipient of an increase of expenditure from any source will spend some proportion of it (and save the rest), thus increasing his contribution to total demand; and this is so with the recipients of additional income at this second stage, who add an amount to total demand but less than their increase in income; and so it goes on, by the operation of what is called the **multiplier**, the addition to aggregate demand being a multiple of the original injection.

Immediately, however, we come across conflicts between policy objectives, or unwanted side-effects from the use of policy instruments. Measures may be taken to boost demand in the pursuit of a higher level of employment. If, then, the supply of some goods and services, materials and equipment, and labour of particular kinds cannot respond immediately to the enhanced demand, their prices will rise. Some of the prices that rise are consumer prices and some are costs of factors of production. The rises of consumer prices may excite fears of inflation and hence stimulate behaviour which helps to bring inflation about. The rise of some costs may cause some producers to raise prices if the cost rises are not outweighed by productivity gains from their increased output. Yet price stability is also an object of policy: inflation brings bottlenecks and the economy works more smoothly when prices are fairly stable than when the price level is changing sharply.

Not only may price instability be a result of boosting demand, but the increased demand may also suck in imports to the detriment of the balance of payments, though increased imports would help to moderate the domestic inflation by adding to aggregate supply. Particular industrial producers would be exposed to increased competition from abroad in both the domestic and export markets. Again, the rises of prices and wages may affect the distribution of real incomes in the economy, probably in ways which, at least in part, would be considered undesirable, e.g. some members of the community have fixed money incomes and suffer when prices rise.

The box containing macroeconomic policy instruments has a label warning that their use may have side-effects. For simplicity, what follows is largely concerned with their main effects. It should not be forgotten, however, that the existence of these other effects is one of the things which makes macroeconomic policy difficult and contentious. The present is a time when some individuals have begun to question whether the disease is worse than the cure.

Fiscal policy

Fiscal policy is the use of the government's taxation, borrowing and expenditure for macroeconomic purposes. There are three occasions when explicit changes are made in these: the Chancellor of the Exchequer's annual **budget** presented to Parliament in the spring, a statement which has come to be made of recent years in the autumn and which is sometimes called a mini-budget, and spasmodic use of the regulator. The **regulator** is power to alter indirect taxes (taxes on goods and services, as distinct from those like income tax and corporation tax, which are direct levies on taxpayers) by up to 10 per cent upwards or downwards between budgets; it has been little used recently.

Originally the budget was a statement of the Government's estimated expenditure in carrying out its functions in the coming year, and of how it proposed to meet that cost. At a time when government activity was little more than carrying out its classical functions, its transactions represented only a small proportion of the total economic activity of the country. A balanced budget was considered the normal and proper thing, perhaps wisely at the time as a check on extravagance. As the scope of state activity widened, so did the budget increase in size, both absolutely and even as a proportion of the country's total economic activity, until now it approaches half of the total spending in the economy. This means that a relatively small change in public expenditure, revenues or borrowing can have considerable effects on what happens elsewhere in the economy. With this widened range of the public finances, it has also come to be realised that not only is the budget a massive engine for driving the economy and influencing the speed and direction at which it operates, but that the idea of balancing it is inappropriate. No private individual or business can survive repeated annual deficits, but the borrowing represented by government deficit financing is (except for borrowing from abroad) the incurring of a debt by the community to itself. Government debt in the hands of private holders of its bonds and bills is serviced as to interest and redemption by the taxpayers as a whole. There is a flow of payments from taxpayers to bondholders with the government as an intermediary. The two groups – taxpayers and bondholders – overlap; but to the extent that they do not, the redistribution of income brought about by the transactions may be considered undesirable in itself and so may conflict with a distributional policy objective. In addition, the transactions may affect the levels of private consumption and investment expenditures, and it can matter greatly whether borrowing is from the banking system or from the non-bank private sector. But the government's debt itself is not a direct 'burden' on the community and a budget deficit does not of itself reduce the wealth of the community. Furthermore, and in contrast again to private borrowing, no part of the real cost to the community of a project financed by internal borrowing is transferred to the future – it can only be met now.

Apart from the appropriateness of the notion of a balanced government budget, its very meaning is arbitrary and dependent on merely conventional ways of accounting for some items of expenditure. It is possible to argue, and some do, that if government borrows to finance a nationalised trading or industrial project which is expected to be profitable, it is only doing what a private enterprise firm would do in the same circumstances, and that such borrowing ought not to be considered part of the current deficit. If that is accepted, then a difficult question of where to draw the line arises. It is only a short step to say that borrowing to finance a project which is equally beneficial but which will not return an income in the form of payments for its use, say a road or a hospital, ought not to be included either. Again, it is sometimes questioned whether the sale of existing assets can rightly be thought to affect the budget balance. Since the notion of budget balance is both inappropriate and arbitrary, it is better to confine attention to the effects of changes in government receipts and expenditures.

Changes in the total amount levied in taxation or in the amount of government expenditure, or both together, can be used to control the level of aggregate demand, encouraging it at times when it is inadequate to take up the current level of output or the output that could be produced if the community's productive resources were more fully employed; and discouraging it in the opposite situation, when the economy is 'overheating', the signs of which are lengthening order books of industrial firms, bottlenecks in the supply of components and materials, labour shortages, falling stocks, rising costs and prices and a high level of imports. Changes in the government's current revenue and in its expenditure can be used to influence the composition of aggregate demand as well as its level. The behaviour of aggregate savings is important in this connection: income not consumed is saved and releases resources for investment in new productive equipment, but the resources are not automatically put to work in this way; if consumption is lagging behind final output and investment is lagging behind what people wish to save, the government can, by using fiscal means, encourage investment to keep up with savings and at the same time cause incomes and hence consumption to rise.

Incentives to invest exist in the form of initial allowances, which mean that although a firm makes provision for depreciation of an asset over a number of years, it is permitted for corporation tax purposes to charge a higher proportion to the asset's first year. At present the whole cost of plant and machinery in manufacturing is allowable in the first year (though special first-year allowances are now to be phased out), and by the operation of this rule many industrial firms with continuous investment programmes do not actually pay any corporation tax. Changes in the rate of corporation tax may affect investment, and so may charging different rates on distributed and undistributed profits. Another means of encouraging investment lies on the expenditure side of the government's budget and consists of subsidies or grants towards investment, and these may be confined to investment in particular areas of the country or to particular industries. It is a disadvantage of attempting to influence investment through the rate of corporation tax or depreciation allowances that only firms which are making good profits and paying the tax are affected; among such firms are those whose good profits are due to a monopoly position. On the other hand, the alternative of paying investment grants to firms means that grants will go to some which are not only at present unprofitable but are, for one reason or another, doomed to remain so.

Consumption can be influenced by changes in the rates of income tax, changes in the personal allowances which are deducted from assessable income in calculating taxable income, and in the rates of employees' national insurance contributions, which are in reality a direct tax. Income tax rates are progressive, i.e. the rates payable increase with bands of increased income. This fact adds to their characteristic of being a discouragement to the various kinds of effort which an individual has to exert in order to increase his standard of living through his working career, though it is not clear how strong this theoretical feature is in practice. A reduction in personal allowances, which increases a person's total tax payable without increasing his marginal rate of tax, may in some circumstances (if an increase in direct taxation is required) be preferable. Consumption can also be influenced by changes in indirect taxes such as the specific duties on alcoholic drinks and tobacco and on petroleum products, and these obviously impinge on particular industries. To the extent that products subject to such taxes have a low price elasticity of demand, i.e. demand contracts less than in proportion to a rise in price, they are from a revenue-raising point of view attractive to a Chancellor of the Exchequer and the reduction in consumers' purchasing power which they accomplish is general and not concentrated on their purchases of the commodity forming the tax base. However, there is always a possibility that a further increase in (the real level of) such a tax will cause a contraction in demand and producers in such industries are not comforted by the thought of collecting taxes as a byproduct. Incidentally, it may be noted that a tax intended to discourage the consumption of a particular commodity will not be very effective in that aim if the demand is not very responsive to price: revenue raising and discouragement of consumption are not entirely compatible, except on the cynical view that so far as the Chancellor cannot have the one, he will be pleased with some of the other.

Some features of the government's finances have a beneficial effect on a changing economic situation without the government taking any decision to alter its revenue and expenditure. They are known as built-in stabilisers. When incomes and aggregate demand are falling, unemployment rises and so does the government's expenditure on unemployment benefit; and, again, when incomes are falling, because of progressive rates of income tax, the tax yield falls more than in proportion to income (and savings are also likely to fall[1]). In these ways the fall in consumption demand is moderated. The reverse things occur when incomes and aggregate demand are rising.

On the expenditure side of the government's budget, changes in the level of unemployment benefit, supplementary benefits, state pension, student grants and other transfer payments (payments not in exchange for current goods or services) are reflected in consumption demand very quickly. Some of the government's other expenditure, however, is not easily changed. Public works, nationalised industry investment projects and local authority capital spending take time to plan, and although priorities may already exist, the planning and design of the top priorities is not always at a stage at which they can be implemented quickly. A top priority whose planning is completed is likely to be pressed for commencement on completion of the plans. Public capital expenditure cannot always be turned on like a tap. Nor is it always easy to turn off. Roads, hospitals and schools at various stages of construction are being built under contract, and there is always social and political resistance to cutting projects in the fields of health and education. Some

---

1. They may, however, rise as the proverbial rainy day is thought to be closer, and if the existing level of consumption allows it.

current expenditure is inescapable because certain capital expenditure has already taken place. Public expenditures vary in the ease with which they are adjustable, and it is in recognition of this that the method of restraining expenditure through the use of cash limits has been introduced.

The difficulty of adjusting the level of public capital expenditure does not mean that work on public projects proceeds at an even level irrespective of changes in the level of activity and in government policy. It means merely that the response to decisions to change them may take longer than decisions to influence consumption directly. Indeed, the construction and defence industries, for example, are notoriously dependent upon the level of government contracts in progress. The response of consumption to changes in the level of transfer payments and rates of tax is more or less immediate, but some industries may be more affected by them than others. Social security benefits tend to affect the lower income groups, whilst the groups affected by direct tax changes depend on exactly what the changes are. The effects of these changes on particular industries depend on how responsive the demand for the various products is to changes in income, i.e. on their income elasticity of demand.

In the period following the mid-1970s the economy suffered a new phenomenon which came to be called '**stagflation**'. After a prolonged period of inflation prices continued to rise even though the level of activity and employment dropped. It used to be the case that prices would fall in a slump. The new kind of situation made the task of macroeconomic policy more difficult than it would have been in past slumps if present knowledge of economic analysis and techniques of economic management had then been available. The fall in demand and output meant that the unit costs of industrial products rose and added an impetus on the cost side to a movement of rising prices that was in any case continuing. The objective of price stability thus assumed a higher priority than it might otherwise have done, and monetary policy came to the fore once more after its partial eclipse by fiscal policy since the thirties.

Monetary Policy

There are two main aspects of **monetary policy**. It can influence the general level of spending through the total supply of money, and it can do so through changes in the rate of interest. The most immediate ways in which industrial firms become aware of these are, respectively, in the availability of credit in the form of loans and overdrafts from their banks, and in the price they have to pay for that credit.

Money is that which is universally acceptable within a country in exchange for anything else, or in payment of a debt. The supply, or stock, of money at any time is, however, far from easy to measure. There are several definitions in official use, each being serviceable from the point of view of a particular set of problems. The deposits held in banks by their customers figure prominently in these definitions, and one of the most commonly used, sterling M3 (£M3), consists of notes and coin in circulation plus all sterling deposits held by UK private and public depositors. When it is a matter of controlling the money supply, monetary policy works on the fact that its main constituent is bank deposits. Banks earn their living by lending. When a bank makes a loan or grants an overdraft, the customer acquires a deposit which he can draw on.

Deposits are liabilities of a bank. They can come into existence either by the customer paying into his account or by the bank making him a loan. In each case the bank incurs a liability, but in the case of making a loan the bank creates the deposit.

Prudence dictates limits to which the banks can incur liabilities in this way, and those limits are related to the amount of their cash and liquid assets. The banks' main liquid assets are cash, balances at the Bank of England, money at call lent to discount houses, Treasury and commercial bills, and short-dated government securities. Their other main assets are longer-dated government securities and other investments, and the advances which customers will become due to repay to them. The limits to lending dictated by prudence are based on the likelihood of customers wanting to turn their deposits into cash.

Apart from the banks' own prudence, it has at times been part of monetary policy for the government and the Bank of England (the monetary authorities) to lay down rules giving a minimum ratio of cash and liquid assets to deposits. Another device has been to put upper limits on bank lending so as to moderate the increase of the money supply in inflation. Yet another device which has been used in the past has been to require the banks to make special deposits with the Bank of England of a certain proportion of their total deposits; the special deposits were not liquid assets and could not be used as a basis for advancing credit to customers, so that by increasing the proportion required the Bank of England could reduce the ability of the banks to increase deposits. Conversely, by releasing special deposits the Bank of England enabled the banks to make credit more readily available. Methods such as these have at times been reinforced by informal requests by the Bank of England to the banks to reduce the rate at which they were making loans and overdrafts, or to moderate their lending in certain directions, e.g. personal loans or property transactions, and give preference to lending for purposes considered desirable in the national economic interest at the particular time, e.g. fixed investment and stocks for industry, or the finance of export transactions. Large borrowers have often been able to avoid restrictions operating through the banks because of their ability to borrow from other sources such as insurance companies and pension funds.

In 1981 new arrangements were brought in. Since 1981 the principal banks have been required, along with all other banks recognised as such and all deposit-takers licensed as such under the Banking Act 1979, to hold with the Bank of England in non-interest-bearing deposits a proportion of their 'eligible liabilities', which are defined in a particular way. The proportion (originally and at present 0.5 per cent) is fixed for several months at a time. These deposits with the Bank of England are non-operational and have a purpose which is not in itself part of the substance of monetary policy; their purpose is to provide the Bank of England with the resources necessary to earn the income required to keep it in being. They replace previous arrangements, and are accompanied for some banks by a requirement to keep funds with the discount houses, money brokers and gilt-edged jobbers in the interests of an efficient market in government bills and stock. These compulsory, non-operational and non-interest-bearing accounts are mentioned here solely so that the reader will not confuse the situation since 1981 with what preceded it. Previously, compulsory accounts at the Bank of England were an intrinsic part of monetary management. They may at some time be thought so again, and the arrangements introduced in 1981 allow for the reintroduction of special deposits for monetary control purposes if required.

The major commercial banks, including the five London clearing banks (National Westminster, Barclays, Midland, Lloyds and Williams and Glyn's, in order of size), the Scottish clearing banks (the Bank of Scotland, the Clydesdale Bank and the Royal Bank of Scotland) and the Northern Ireland banks, keep voluntary deposits with the Bank of England, which are accounts held for clearing and other operational purposes as well as constituting a liquid reserve. **Clearing** is the settlement of the indebtedness between banks arising from customers of one paying customers of another by cheque. It is upon the balances in these voluntary and operational accounts that the Bank of England now relies in influencing the money supply. It does so by open market operations which are, indeed, a very old technique of the central bank. If it wishes to expand the availability of credit in the economy, it buys government stocks on the stock exchange and pays for them by cheques which the sellers pay into their bank accounts; or it buys Treasury and other bills in the money market, i.e. from the discount houses and the commercial banks, and pays for them by increasing their deposits with the Bank of England itself. In each case, directly or indirectly, the liquid assets which the banks held in their accounts with the Bank of England are increased, and on the basis of this they can expand the amount of credit (deposits) which they make available to their customers. They do so within the limits of prudence, but this still means they are able to expand deposits by some multiple of the increase in their liquid assets.

Sales of government stock and bills by the Bank lead to a tightening of monetary conditions. Customers of the banks draw on their accounts to pay for the securities they purchase, and the banks' deposits with the Bank of England are reduced. However, the banks always have money at call with the discount houses and some of this may be recalled in order to offset the drain on their deposits. The discount houses may then need to seek assistance from the Bank of England, which provides it by acting as '**lender of last resort**'. It either lends to them or buys bills from them. In either case a short-term interest rate for first-class, practically riskless, paper is applied – in the case of borrowing, as a rate of interest; and in the case of buying bills, as a rate of discount – and this rate then rises, so reinforcing the open market operations. This is the rate which in the past used to be called **Bank Rate**, was announced weekly by the Bank, and was by strong convention the standard by which other interest rates in the economy were set. Then in 1972 it became **Minimum Lending Rate**, also published, but determined by formula in relation to the rate for Treasury Bills (save that in exceptional circumstances the government could step in and fix the rate notwithstanding the formula, a power which was used in the oil crisis of 1973). In 1981 the Bank ceased publication of a rate at which it would discount first-class bills, in order to make interest rates less subject to administrative decision and more sensitive to market conditions. The Bank now tries by its operations to keep very short-term interest rates within an undisclosed band which is movable, and the rates at which it has transacted business are then published. This change is in line with the increased emphasis on the money supply and on market forces which has characterised recent policy. However, the Bank is still a powerful agent in the market and still the lender of last resort, and changes in short-term money rates are still a market fact when they occur and, like any other change, they still percolate through the markets to have an effect on other interest rates.

Influencing rates of interest for domestic economic reasons is constrained by international considerations and the degree of control which can be exercised over unwanted incidental results. A rise in interest rates may be desired domestically for monetary restraint, but it would tend to attract funds from abroad which might penetrate the monetary system and tend to undo the measures of domestic restraint. They would also put upward pressure on the exchange rate, something which might not be considered desirable; at all events, exporting firms would suffer, and importers would gain, including those importing industrial raw materials.

Open market operations influence the supply of money by the banks and hence the availability of credit to industrial firms and other borrowers. The rate of interest charged by the banks affects the demand for credit advanced by them. The smooth working of this mechanism presupposes that industrial borrowers have investment projects which they might undertake and which have various expected rates of return. Those with an expected rate of return in excess of the rate of interest on the funds which would need to be borrowed in order to finance them are worthwhile, and the funds are borrowed and the investment goes ahead. Other ideas for projects constantly emerge and the rate of interest rations finance among them, causing investment to increase when the rate falls and to decrease when the rate rises. The reality is not quite so simple. The high proportion of industry's investment which is financed by retained earnings has been remarked upon in an earlier chapter. Rationality requires that an imputed cost for these funds equal to the market rate of interest should be introduced into any investment decision involving their use. It is not clear that this is always done in practice, and consideration of some of the objectives of firms discussed in Chapter 3 may suggest part of the explanation. Self-financing tends to thwart control through interest rates. It ought not to, but it sometimes does.

There are more respectable reasons for investment not responding sensitively to changes in interest rates. Large investment projects take a long time to complete and can neither be cut off nor accelerated when interest rates change. Projects in manufacturing industry typically have quite a short payback period, which implies a high annual depreciation charge before the asset is written off; this renders the difference between one amount of interest and another rather a small proportion of all the capital charges. The impact of a change in interest rates is also reduced by the fact that interest is a cost which is set against tax (provided the company is in the position of paying corporation tax). The rate of return which a project will earn cannot be known exactly in advance, in the face of all the uncertainties to which business is a prey; instead, a range of estimates of possible rates of return is considered, and given this range, an alteration to the rate of interest is not of great significance. Expectations about rates of return have been shown by empirical studies to figure more largely in investment decisions in industry than does the rate of interest. This means, in particular, that in a slump low rates of interest do not induce widespread borrowing for investment. Some kinds of activity are, however, sensitive to interest rates, and among them are the sections of the construction industry engaged in building houses, offices and shops, in which investment is long term with a long payback period, and the returns are not subject to a wide range of uncertainty. Among them also are those distributors who borrow to finance stocks and for whom interest payments are a significant proportion of total costs.

In considering the rate of interest as the cost of borrowing funds it has to be borne in mind that when the general level of prices is changing the real rate of interest is different from the nominal rate, which is the one quoted and paid, because a given sum of money becomes worth less (more) in real terms through time as prices rise (fall). Some real rates of interest have on occasions even been negative, when the rate of inflation has been higher than the rate of interest. The capital sum repaid is also worth less in real terms to the borrower than when he borrowed it.

In addition to monetary and fiscal policy, another class of macroeconomic measures which have been used in the past is **direct controls**. Prices and incomes policy, including control of dividends, and hire purchase controls come under this heading. Efforts to control prices and incomes through a succession of ill-fated quangos punctuate the economic history of the 1950s, sixties and seventies and by and large were disliked by industrial firms and by trade unions, though the latter usually favoured price controls. The difficulty with such measures was that although they could be quite effective and useful for a short while, it was not long before strains appeared with which they could not cope. The patterns of demand for different products and different kinds of labour are not static. Relative prices and relative wage rates need to be able to change (though the sacred cow of 'differentials' inhibits this at the best of times) in order to induce the required changes in the supply of different products and labour. Furthermore, the conditions of supply of different commodities and raw materials are constantly changing. Administrative control inhibits the free working of the allocative machinery of the market, and makes for bottlenecks, black markets and artificial wage and salary payments, promotion and job titles. Restriction of dividends probably kept investment down somewhat. Nevertheless, controls can and did moderate for a while strong upward movements in prices and wage costs, but the experience was that when control was relaxed, the surge took over again and the previous benefits were lost.

Hire purchase controls affect spending on consumer durables particularly, by regulating the proportion of the price that must be paid as the initial deposit in any hire purchase transaction, and the period over which the remaining payments may be spread. When they existed they were altered on many occasions in order to manipulate the level of demand for consumer durables. Consequently, the manufacturers of such products were particularly affected by them.

Since increased emphasis came to be placed on monetary policy in the mid-1970s, one feature has been the adoption of targets for growth of the money supply. A decline in the rate of growth of the money supply would lead to a fall in inflation, and the announcement of targets would in itself assist that process by setting up expectations that inflation would become more moderate, and general economic behaviour based on this expectation would help to bring it about. The advantage in buying now in anticipation of higher prices later would be reduced, wage expectations would not be so high, and there would be greater caution about raising prices. Targets for the money supply were adopted in 1976. In the 1980 Budget the Conservative Government (elected 1979) reduced the target and introduced a medium-term financial strategy incorporating a target range for growth of the money supply into future years, and this has subsequently been updated and expressed in three alternative statistical measures of the money supply. In the years since 1979 to the present (1984) monetary policy in the UK has been much infuenced by the doctrine called **monetarism**, whose various tenets include the article of faith that increases in the money supply are the cause of inflation. This belief is derived from the quantity theory of money, first expounded by scholastic writers of the sixteenth century and in its modern form expressed by the equation, or rather the identity, $MV=PT$. In this identity, M is the money stock; V is the velocity of circulation of money, or the average number of times a unit of money is used in transactions in a given time; P is the price level; and T is the physical volume of transactions in the given time period, or in other words the real output. Monetarism regards V as being determined by institutional arrangements and social habits, such as whether working people are paid weekly or monthly and the speed at which money can be transmitted through the banking system; such things do not change rapidly and V is therefore thought to be relatively stable according to the monetarist view. So is T; the level of activity in the long run depends on real factors such as population and resource endowment, and in the short run is self-correcting. This leaves M and P, so that changes in the money supply are reflected in changes in the price level. Now, the evidence that the index of retail prices (to take one measure of changes in the level of prices) moves in a somewhat similar manner to, say, Stg. M3 (to take one measure of changes in the money supply) is rather strong. Many take it that this, however, is not of itself sufficient to establish that changes in *M* cause the changes in *P*, and certainly not in any direct and simple manner. The statement of an identity does not state, still less explain, whatever causal relationships may be at work. It is far from clear that changes in *M* are not at any time accompanied by changes in *V* and *T*, and changes in the latter are held by some to be a cause of changes in the money supply.

These are matters of much dispute, as are most aspects of monetarism. Whatever the truth of them, the money supply and the inflation of prices were seen as being primarily influenced by high government spending and the high level of the public sector borrowing requirment (PSBR) which accompanied it, especially to the extent that the latter was financed by the banking system holding increased quantities of government securities. The government therefore set about reducing the targets for each. The rate of inflation, after an interval, was certainly reduced. At its height in 1975 it had been about 27 per cent per annum: in early 1984 it was just over 5 per cent. Monetary restriction and the fall in demand, however, caused liquidity problems for many firms, especially as their costs continued to rise for a while. The number of bankruptcies rose and so did the level of unemployment, to an alarming height.

Regional Policy

Fiscal instruments are also used to deal with microeconomic problems, one of which is the disparate levels of income and unemployment in the various regions of the country. Unemployment can be of various types according to its underlying cause.

(a) **Cyclical unemployment** results from a deficiency of aggregate demand in periods of depression, which alternate with periods of high economic activity to form the trade cycle. It is the kind of unemployment with which macroeconomic policy is mainly concerned.

(b) **Voluntary unemployment** arises on the part of those who do not accept employment at the going wage rate even if it is available. There may be various reasons for this, including the level of social benefits to which a person may be entitled, considered in relation to the relevant wage.

(c) **Seasonal employment** arises from the effects of the seasons on either the production process, as in agriculture and the construction industry, or the demand for the product, as in the service trades comprising the tourist 'industry' or the manufacture of ice cream.

(d) **Frictional unemployment** is a consequence of the ever-changing pattern of demand for different commodities, and of their changing conditions of supply. These shifts cause some industries to expand and others to contract, and labour is temporarily displaced in the process until it is reabsorbed elsewhere. The length of time for which an individual may remain unemployed through this process depends on the speed with which new employment opportunities arise, the efficiency with which the labour market transmits information about jobs available and people available to fill them, and the extent to which some of those rendered unemployed are willing to extend their period of unemployment so as to spend their time seeking a better job than the first one offered to them. They are said to incur search costs, in the form of income foregone and money spent on fares and the like; the justification for such costs is related to the probability of obtaining better-paid work and the likely level of pay. Some frictional unemployment comes from important technological advances which cause widespread unemployment yet herald rises in the real income per head of the community. Some of the unemployment caused in this way may persist beyond a short period and so be considered as structural in character.

(e) **Structural unemployment** also arises from changes in the conditions of demand and supply for the products of particular industries. It is classified separately because of its persistence over long periods of time and the intractability of the problem of curing it. It is particularly associated with certain geographical regions of the country because certain industries have been localised there but, as we have just seen, a falling away in the demand for specific kinds of labour which are not highly concentrated regionally may also be a structural problem. In each case the unemployment in question could persist even at a time when the overall demand for labour in the economy was high, and the removal of the unemployment requires a structural change in the economy. The regional aspect of the problem is the more serious.

The basic industries of coal, iron and steel, heavy engineering, shipbuilding, and cotton and jute became located in their traditional areas in the nineteenth century for very good reasons. The coal industry must obviously be where the coal is found and the location of shipbuilding must also be constrained to some extent physically, but like the others its locations have been influenced by the kinds of economic considerations referred to in Chapter 1. These industries prospered in their time. From the fact that they derived their demand from outside their regions, whilst the latter depended heavily on them for their prosperity, they came to be called basic industries. Through the operation of what would now be called the local multiplier the development was advantageous to the areas concerned. This was so until demand for the output from these industries fell away, as it did sharply after the high levels of government demand during the First World War. These had masked the developing market tendencies for a while. Coal suffered in competition with overseas oil, both in its domestic and overseas market, and from discoveries of coal abroad. Although new industries manufacturing many new products arose in the course of the present century, the advent of electric power cut the cord tying industry to the coalfields and they tended to locate in areas like the West Midlands, with its labour force skilled in metal working, or the South East, with its large market. The other basic industries also suffered from rising foreign competition in their export markets and at home. It was thus that a regional problem came to be recognised in the 1920s and thirties.

The levels of unemployment in the north and northwest of England, and in parts of Scotland, Wales and Northern Ireland, were higher than in the rest of the country but the difference showed no sign of being corrected by market forces – certainly not within a humanly acceptable time scale. This is an example of market failure. For the market to work properly resources – in this case labour – should flow out of the areas where their price is low or they are unemployed to those where their price is higher or there is a demand for them. Very many people have in fact moved since the regional problem emerged more than half a century ago, but many have not. The imperfection of the market mechanism lies in the fact that there are resistances to this movement.

People do not have that perfect mobility which is required by perfect markets. In the first place they are likely to lack adequate knowledge of suitable employment oppurtunities in other parts of the country. In the second place, even with such knowledge and even if alternative opportunities are in fact available, there is very frequently a reluctance to move: housing is likely to be more expensive in a more prosperous area; if a worker has a council house he will not lightly give it up; children may be at a stage in their education when moving school seems undesirable; and people are often reluctant to leave the accustomed warmth of parents, friends and in-laws for the presumed chill of a strange environment. The absence of a fully self-correcting mechanism is a market failure. This, together with the resulting social costs, consisting of the damage to community life in the hardest hit areas and costs of congestion in the ever-growing southeast of the country (which are called 'externalities', because they are not borne by those whose actions give rise to them), has justified government intervention to try to improve the situation. Two prongs of attack were possible: the first, to reduce the supply of labour in the hardest hit areas by measures to encourage mobility of labour from these areas to other areas; the second, to increase the demand for labour in those areas, mainly encouraging the movement of firms into them and the setting up of new establishments in them.

The earliest measures taken, starting in the late twenties, were of the first of these two kinds. Unemployed workers in the depressed areas were given financial help to move, usually to a known vacancy, and sometimes retraining was given. There are disadvantages in tackling the problem in this way. Reliance on moving population means that extremely large numbers of people would have to be moved under administrative schemes, rather than spontaneously. The movement of people out of a depressed area, whether spontaneous or organised, inevitably means that the exodus is led by those with skills, youth and enterprise on their side, with relatively few of the others in fact following. The area becomes even more depressed and less likely to attract new industry, and the problem for those who remain becomes more severe. On the other hand, there is much advantage in assisting those who are willing to move if there are unfilled vacancies for their kind of labour in another area. Although sole reliance on this kind of measure lasted no more than half a dozen years, it still has a place in current policies in the form of assistance for job search, and for removal and rehousing costs.

In 1934 the Special Areas (Development and Inprovement) Act was passed, to be followed by further legislation in later years providing for financial assistance of various kinds to firms which would locate establishments in those areas. The emphasis had swung from the movement of labour to a policy of taking industry to the workers. Success was not conspicuous. In the early years there was severe general depression, and few industrial firms were prepared to open new factories or relocate existing ones; unemployment, though worst in the Special Areas, was general. Later, there was full employment during the war and munitions and other factories were built in the Special Areas. The Barlow Royal Commission on the Distribution of the Industrial Population had been appointed in 1937 and its report was published in early 1940, recommending that steps be taken to secure a better balance in the distribution of industry between regions, and greater diversification within them. This influenced policy in the period after the war, when the Distribution of Industry Acts of 1945 and subsequent years again offered assistance to firms locating in certain areas particularly prone to

principle of efficient resource use whose application has many difficulties in practice, though it is reflected in off-peak fares and electricity charges. The White Papers of 1961 and 1967 in general favoured a more commercial approach to prices and investment than had previously prevailed. The present guidelines for pricing and investment were put forward in a White Paper of 1978 on the nationalised industries in which marginal cost pricing is again referred to, but which recognises as key factors in setting prices the market circumstances of the various products and the financial target set by government for each corporation. The financial target for each corporation takes into account among other factors the earning power of the whole of its assets and the non-commercial or social objectives which it is required to pursue. The criterion for undertaking new investment is a real (not nominal) rate of return (RRR) set for three to five years at a time and at present standing at 5 per cent. 'Real' means after taking out the effect of inflation from the nominal rate of return (see p. 59). The RRR is intended to reflect the real rate of return in the private sector. By this means it is intended to ensure that capital is not used by the industries of the public sector when it could be used more effectively by those of the private sector.

There exists a broad consensus that the UK economy ought to be mixed, i.e. contain elements both of private and of public enterprise. There is less wide agreement, and some sharp disagreement, about where the dividing line ought to lie. For the last few years the Conservative Government has been denationalising some parts of public sector industry for a mixture of reasons: to increase efficiency by removing shelters from market forces; to reduce the area of industrial operations subject to political influence; and to use the funds received through the sale of shares in the enterprises to replace government borrowing as part of an overriding anti-inflation policy. The problem of marking out the boundary between the sectors remains unsettled, but the question of ownership may be less important than the competitive conditions in which an enterprise operates. The problem of accountability and of the relations between the public corporations on the one hand and the sponsoring ministries and the Treasury on the other hand, also remains unsettled. Lastly, there is a fairly widespread belief that the nationalised industries ought to be more exposed to market forces and operate more as commercial enterprises in the interest of their operating efficiency, and this remains to be reconciled both with the tendency of government to require them to lower their prices (to reduce inflation) or raise their prices (to reduce the public sector borrowing requirement) and with the provision by nationalised industries of social benefits as a spin-off for which no payment is received.

Other Forms of Intervention

The factory legislation referred to in the first section of this chapter
has continued to develop, partly in response to the introduction of
new industrial processes, materials and technology. In 1974 there
existed 30 Acts of Parliament and about 500 sets of regulations
under these statutes affecting the operation of industry and designed
to protect the safety, health and welfare of industrial workers. In
that year much of this legislation was codified in the Health and
Safety at Work Act. The Act also established the Health and Safety
Commission, a body containing representatives of employers,
unions and local authorities with the function of developing policy in
this field and the protection of the general public from industrial
hazards. The Commission has a Health and Safety Executive responsible to it, which took over the administrative work in this field
previously carried out by six separate government departments and
the enforcement work of seven central Inspectorates and the local
authorities. The Act requires employers to ensure health, safety and
welfare at work, and places an obligation on employees to exercise
reasonable care for their own and other people's health, safety and
welfare. It entitles trade unions to appoint safety representatives at
places of work, and obliges employers to consult them. Legislation
of this kind imposes the same costs on all competing firms in an
industry in ensuring that standards are everywhere up to a socially
acceptable minimum or norm. Provided the regulations are sensibly
devised, therefore, they are in the interest of the best employers
who would wish to reach the standards in any case.

A newer and separate line of development has been legislation to
protect the environment. Public intervention in location decisions
takes place under the Town and Country Planning Acts on environmental grounds (as against the use of Industrial Development Certificates for locational reasons). The discharge of industrial effluent
into public sewers is controlled by the Public Health Acts, and into
rivers by the Rivers (Prevention of Pollution) Acts; the former also
control the creation of noise and dust by industrial activity. Pollution of the atmosphere is controlled by the Clean Air Acts. The
latter three are strengthened and extended by the Control of Pollution Act. The theoretical justification for this kind of measure is
distinct from that of the long line of factory legislation. It rests on
the existence of externalities in the situations with which it deals;
that is to say, on the existence of a difference between social and
private costs or, more simply, on undesirable side-effects of an
industrial process. These side-effects are a detriment to those outside the firm who suffer them, so that part of the cost of the
industrial process is being borne by people other than the firm.

There are two ways, in principle, of dealing with such situations. One is to tax the activity which it is wished to discourage and to set the tax at a level at which it is, for example, cheaper to reduce output or install equipment to muffle noise than to pay the tax. This leaves firms free to make their own decision within the framework laid down, and is a use of the price mechanism. The method generally adopted, however, is to lay down a desired standard by legislation – the desired standard may be zero, i.e. the offensive activity may be completely forbidden – and to enforce it by the use of heavy fines. This method is more certain in its effect than is a tax and is therefore preferred when risk to health is at stake.

Externalities need not be detrimental. They may be beneficial to sections of the public from whom the producer receives no payment. Thus a rural bus service may not cover an operator's costs, yet its total benefits to the villages served – whose very existence may hang on it – may exceed those costs. In such cases the social benefits may be recognised by the payment of a subsidy to induce continuance of the service.

Summary

This chapter ranges widely, covering the main areas of relations between industry and government. Different ideas about the basic nature and proper extent of such relationships are held in different historical periods. The emergence of industrial society and, later, of macroeconomic policy, have seen a great increase in the extent of government intervention in relation to industry, though in some respects it has diminished. The main kinds of present-day policies are introduced.

Review Questions

(1) Why does government intervene in industry?

(2) Can you suggest reasons why conflicts between the objectives of a government may be more common than conflicts between those of a firm?

(3) What are the advantages and disadvantages of selective assistance to industry, as against general assistance?

(4) Explain the possibility of conflict between competition policy and some other policies in relation to industry. Can you give examples of this occurring?

(5) How does the approach to competition policy differ between the UK and the USA?

(6) Why is there a regional problem in the UK? What are the merits and demerits of the policies which have aimed to encourage the movement of firms into high unemployment areas?

(7) What are the differences between public and private enterprises? What changes have taken place in the financial objectives laid down for public corporations?

(8) Describe how the use of various macroeconomic policy instruments may impinge on industrial firms.

Suggestions for Further Reading

Harbury, C. (1981) *Descriptive Economics*, Pitman Books.
Harbury, C. and Lipsey, R. G. (1983) *An Introduction to the UK Economy*, Pitman Books.

G. C. Allen, (1966) *The Structure of Industry in Britain*, Longman.
G. C. Allen, (1970) *British Industries and their Organization*, Longman.
Baddeley, J. M. (1983) *Understanding Industry*, Butterworth.
Beacham, A. (1970) *The Economics of Industrial Organization*, Pitman Books.
Florence, P. Sargent (1964) *Economics and Sociology of Industry*, Watts.
Jarrett, H. R. (1977) *A Geography of Manufacturing*, Macdonald and Evans.
Jones, T. T. and Cockerill, T. A. J. (1984) *Structure and Performance of Industries*, Philip Allan.
Turner, G. (1971) *Business in Britain*, Penguin Books.

Allen, G. C. (1968) *Monopoly and Restrictive Practices*, Allen and Unwin.
Hare, P. and Kirby, M. (1984) *An Introduction to British Economic Policy*, Wheatsheaf.
Lee, D. (1980) *Regional Planning and Location of Industry*, Heinemann.
Pass, C. and Sparkes, J. (1980) *Monopoly*, Heinemann.
Skuse, A. (1972) *Government Intervention and Industrial Policy*, Heinemann.

Bates, J. and Parkinson J. R. (1982) *Business Economics*, Basil Blackwell.
Cairncross, A. and Sinclair, P. (1982) *Introduction to Economics*, Butterworth.
Livesey, F. (1983) *Economics for Business Decisions*, Macdonald and Evans.

Handy, C. B. (1976) *Understanding Organizations*, Penguin Books.
Pugh, D. S. (ed.) (1984) *Organization Theory*, Penguin Books.
Pugh, D. S., Hickson D. J. and Hinings, C. R. (1983) *Writers on Organizations*, Penguin Books.
Stewart, Rosemary (1970) *The Reality of Organizations*, Macmillan.
Stewart, Rosemary (1979) *The Reality of Management*, Pan Books.

Goodman, J. (1984) *Employment Relations in Industrial Society*, Philip Allan.

Johnston, T. L. (1981) *Introduction to Industrial Relations*, Macdonald and Evans.
Palmer, Gill (1983) *British Industrial Relations*, Allen and Unwin.
Williamson, H. (1981) *The Trade Unions*, Heinemann.
Worrall, N. (1980) *People and Decisions*, Longman.

Leonard, R. and Clews, G. (1984) *Technology and Production*, Philip Allan.
Powell, J. (1978) *Production Decisions*, Longman.
Wild, R. (1980) *Management and Production*, Penguin Books.

Frain, J. (1983) *Introduction to Marketing*, Macdonald and Evans.
Kotler, P. (1976) *Marketing Management*, Prentice-Hall.
Littler, D. (1984) *Marketing and Product Development*, Philip Allan.
Tinniswood, P. (1981) *Marketing Decisions*, Longman.

Corbett, P. (1978) *Accounting and Decision Making*, Longman.
Couldery, F. A. J. (1982) *Understanding Accounts*, Gee.
Farmer, E. R. (1983) *Understanding and Interpreting Company Reports and Accounts*, Gee.
Mott, G. (1984) *Accounting for Non-accountants*, Pan Books.
Sizer, J. (1979) *An Insight into Management Accounting*, Penguin Books.

Index

Index

WHALES

BLANDFORD MAMMAL SERIES
Advisory editor: Ernest G. Neal M.B.E., M.Sc., Ph.D., F.I. Biol.

DEER
Raymond E. Chaplin

BADGERS
Ernest G. Neal

WHALES

W. NIGEL BONNER
B.Sc., F.I. Biol.

BLANDFORD PRESS
POOLE   DORSET

First published 1980 Blandford Press Ltd,
Link House, West Street,
Poole, Dorset, BH15 1LL

Text Copyright © 1980 W. Nigel Bonner

British Library Cataloguing in Publication Data

Bonner, William Nigel
  Whales (Blandford mammal series).
  1. Whales
  I. Title
  599'.51   QL737.C4

ISBN 0 7137 0887 5

Printed in Great Britain by
Butler & Tanner Ltd., Frome and London
Colour plates by Tonbridge Printers Ltd

Contents

Illustrations

The black and white photographs and two colour plates were provided by the author. Other sources, which the author and publisher gratefully acknowledge, are listed below.

Colour plates

Bryan and Cherry Alexander: 13
Heather Angel: 2, 3 and 4
Jen and Des Bartlett/Survival Anglia: 10
Fred Bruemmer: 11 and 14
Michael Bryden: 1
Derek Gipps: 5
Institute of Oceanographic Sciences: 8
Ken Lucas/Seaphot: 12
Robert Pratt: 6

The line drawings, sketches and scraper-board illustrations were specially prepared by Michael Clark.

Acknowledgements

I should like to express my gratitude and indebtedness to the many whale researchers from whose published works I have drawn in preparing this book. They are too many to name here, but they are acknowledged in the text in the usual way. However, I must acknowledge a special debt to two of them. The late Dr Francis Fraser C.B.E., F.R.S., who is so sadly missed by his friends in the world of cetology, made contributions to the study of whales that have been a model for all who came after him. His support and encouragement sustained me during my early years with the whalers and sealers in South Georgia. I owe him a great deal. His colleague and predecessor in the 'Discovery' Investigations in South Georgia in the 1920s, Dr L. Harrison Matthews F.R.S., has likewise been an inspiration to me. His common sense and clarity of exposition have done much for science generally and marine mammals in particular.

I am grateful to Dr Ray Gambell, Secretary of the International Whaling Commission, who was kind enough to read and criticise part of the book; to Professor R. J. Harrison and Mr D. A. McBrearty, who helped with some of the references. Michael Clark showed his customary care and skill in preparing the illustrations. Mr Derek Gipps and Professor Michael Bryden very kindly allowed me to reproduce photographs of a Minke Whale and a Humpbacked Dolphin respectively.

My thanks are due also to Dr Ernest Neal, who suggested this book to me in the first place, and to the staff at Blandford Press, particularly Beth Young and Maggie O'Hanlon for their help in preparing the final manuscript. Carol Romm and Gill Tew did the typing and I am grateful to them both for coping so well with my handwriting.

I am particularly grateful to my wife, who has shared my interest in whales and whaling from the time she spent with me at the whaling station at Grytviken—though never quite to the extent of taking a trip out on a whale-catcher! She checked through the manuscript, collated references, prepared the index and was a continual source of encouragement and support during the book's preparation.

Preface

My interest in whales was first kindled when some thirty-five years ago I watched a group of Risso's Dolphins from the cliffs of Cornwall. This interest was greatly intensified when for no very good reason I found myself in South Georgia in 1953, in the middle of the reek and clangour of a whaling station. I came to spend nine whaling seasons at South Georgia, most of them at the station set up by the father of Antarctic whaling, C. A. Larsen, in 1904. The great majority of the whales I saw during that period were lying dead on the flensing plan, but their great corpses were a challenge and an inspiration to me.

In this book I have tried to convey some of the basic facts and theories about those features of whales that serve to distinguish them from the rest of the mammals and fit them for a life in the sea. To keep the book to a reasonable size, I have had to be selective in what I presented. I apologise to those readers who find that their particular interest has received too little attention. I am myself very conscious of the omission of any adequate treatment of the behaviour of whales in the wild. Unfortunately, we have little but anecdotal evidence on this important subject and I fear it will be a long time before we can progress much further in that field, so that we might eventually be able to understand the circumstances that lead a school of False Killer Whales to drive themselves ashore, or a Humpback to breach clear of the water.

The great whales have all suffered grievously at the hand of Man. In recent years an increasing interest in these fascinating animals has led many people to question an exploitive philosophy whose only concern has often been to get as large a share of the whales as possible, regardless of the status of the stock or the ecosystem at large. Some people have reacted with public demonstrations for the total abolition of all whaling. Others would not go so far as this but feel that better safeguards should be sought and more humane methods developed. An interest in the plight of whales has led in many cases to an interest in the animals themselves, and the history of their contact with man. It is to these people that this book is offered.

W. Nigel Bonner
Godmanchester

FOR
Jennifer
and to the memory of
Francis C. Fraser C.B.E., F.R.S.
1903–1978

1 *The cetacea and their environment*

Of all the orders of mammals, none is more distinct or more instantly recognisable than the Cetacea, or whales. But, although whales are easily distinguished from other mammals, it by no means follows that their mammalian nature has always been recognised. Aristotle, who, in the fourth century B.C., had made a careful study of many of the marine creatures of the Mediterranean Sea, was aware that the possession of warm blood, and the habit of breathing air and producing their young alive, distinguished whales from fish. However, this piece of information, like a good many other astute zoological observations by Aristotle, was soon forgotten and whales were generally regarded as fish because they lived in the sea and possessed fins but no fur. Burton (1973) drew attention to a practical value of such a classification—in an age governed by an authoritarian church it meant that porpoise flesh could be eaten in Lent.

As Fraser (1977) has pointed out, John Ray, in 1693, recognised the true nature of cetaceans:

'For except as to the place on which they live, the external form of the body, the hairless skin and progressive swimming motion, they have almost nothing in common with fishes, but the remaining characters agree with the viviparous quadrupeds.'

Linnaeus, who was the first to produce a comprehensive classification of the animal kingdom, placed the Cetacea with the fishes in the 1735 edition of *Systema Naturae*, but, by the tenth edition, generally regarded as the authoritative one, he had recognised the mammalian nature of whales (a warm four-chambered heart, lungs, movable eyelids, ears with an external opening, penis and mammary glands) and separated them from the fishes. Linnaeus' classification did not find instant acceptance, at least amongst those who hunted whales. Herman Melville, who, while lacking Linnaeus' scientific insight had at least given much thought to the matter, concluded that the whale was a fish, albeit different from all other fish in being 'a spouting fish with a horizontal tail'.

There is room for confusion for whales superficially resemble fish (and some fish-like reptiles) to a marked degree (Fig. 1.1). The reason for their similarity, and their distinctiveness from other mammals, is not coincidence but the result of an evolutionary response to the aquatic environment in which they live. This same factor, which led to the evolution of the body shape of sharks and of the extinct ichthyosaurs that flourished in the Jurassic, determined the contours of the whale.

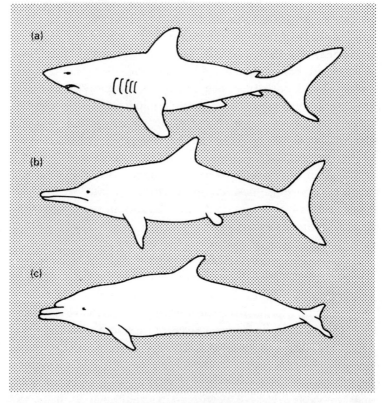

Fig. 1.1 The body forms of whales resemble those of fish and some extinct reptiles—an example of convergent evolution to adapt to the aquatic environment: (a) shark, (b) ichthyosaur, (c) dolphin. (After Howell, 1930.)

Probably all mammals are able to swim to some extent, even such unlikely candidates as a few bats being capable of limited progression in water. No less than eleven mammalian orders contain members which are definitely, although not necessarily exclusively, aquatic (Howell, 1930). These range from the Platypus of the rivers of Australia, through the familiar Musk Rats and Beavers, a couple of Swamp Rabbits in the southern USA, to the exclusively aquatic Sirenia (the Sea-cows and Dugongs) and the Cetacea (Fig. 1.2).

From the time of their initial evolutionary radiation in the latter part of the Cretaceous period, mammals probably always found advantages, associated either with feeding or protection from enemies or pests, in water. For the most part, the modification involved was minor and did not greatly affect the basic mammalian plan. The provision of webbing between the toes is an obvious modification to facilitate swimming by paddling with the feet, but it still leaves the legs fully available for orthodox locomotion on land. The coat might develop denser and finer fur fibres, as in the Sea Otter, so as to maintain body heat in a colder environment, or the nostrils and eyes might migrate to a more dorsal position, as in the Hippopotamus, so as to provide better sensory reception when lying nearly submerged, but animals modified in this way remain recognisably mammals. Indeed, some of the most aquatic differ scarcely at all from their much more terrestrial relations. The Polar Bear, which has often been reported swimming as much as 320 km from land (Burton, 1965), anatomically closely resembles the larger brown bears, such as the Grizzly.

It is clear, therefore, that the basic mammalian plan is easily adapted to the requirements of aquatic life. However, with the exception of the Sirenia and the Cetacea, all the aquatic mammals are compelled to resort to dry land (or ice) to produce their young, which has necessitated the retention of those features, such as limbs, needed for locomotion on land. Whales and Sea-cows, however, have severed this final link with *terra firma* and have been able to devote themselves, at least from Eocene times, to an exclusively aquatic existence.

What are the characteristics of a watery environment that

3

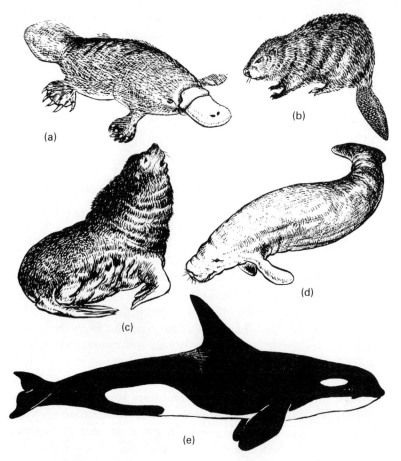

Fig. 1.2 Aquatic mammals: (a) Platypus, (b) Beaver, (c) Southern Fur Seal, (d) Manatee, (e) Killer Whale.

have so altered the body shape and way of life of whales from that of their originally terrestrial ancestors? The comparison we need to make is not between water and dry land but between water and air, for a whale lives *in* water as a terrestrial mammal lives *in* air. Whales only by chance come into contact with a substratum, the sea-floor or more often a beach, and then often with fatal consequences.

Both air and water are fluids, but water is a much denser and more viscous fluid than air. It has a much greater thermal con-

Table 1.1 Various Properties of Air and Water Compared. Values Are for Pure Water, except for the Density Value, Which Is for Sea Water

	Property	Units	Air	Water
1.	Density	$kg.m^{-3}$	1.22	1,025
2.	Viscosity	$10^6.kg.m^{-1}.s^{-1}$	18	1,708
3.	Thermal conductivity	$10^{-3}.W.m^{-1}.K^{-1}$	1.3	16.4
4.	Specific heat	$J.K^{-1}.kg^{-1}$	720	4,200
5.	Heat capacity per unit volume	$J.K^{-1}.m^{-3}$	880	4,300,000
6.	Refractive index	—	(1)	1.33
7.	Speed of sound	$m.s^{-1}$	332	1,531

* From Weast, 1976–77

ductivity and a very much greater specific heat. It absorbs light more readily than air and has a higher refractive index. It transmits sound faster than air and with less attenuation. Finally, naturally occurring water, unlike air, can support, floating freely within it, a community of plants and herbivorous and carnivorous animals, which, together, make up a highly productive ecosystem.

All these features (summarised in Table 1.1) have, in one way or another, affected the evolution of whales and left their mark on the form of the whale's body or its way of life; they will crop up again and again as we consider various aspects of whale biology.

Certainly the most striking feature of whales is their size. No other members of the animal kingdom, living or extinct, even nearly approach the size of the large rorquals. The largest whale ever reliably measured was a female Blue Whale, *Balaenoptera musculus*, taken near the South Shetland Islands in April 1926, which measured 32.3 m from snout to the notch in the flukes. Accurate weights are, of course, much more difficult to obtain, but a 29.5 m female Blue Whale, shot at South Georgia in 1930, was calculated to weigh 177 tonnes, on the basis of the number of cookers filled with its blubber, meat and bone, and making some allowance for losses in the form of blood and guts, and

Fig. 1.3 The largest mammal in the sea, the Blue Whale, and the largest ter-restrial mammal, the Elephant.

another 27.6 m female, recorded on the Soviet factory ship *Slava* in 1947, weighed 193 tonnes.

The largest living land animal, on the other hand, is the African Elephant, of which the average adult bull weighs 5.8 tonnes, although a record-sized bull was estimated to weigh 10.8 tonnes, still greatly below the whale's enormous mass (Fig. 1.3).

Not all whales are as large as Blue Whales, of course. Indeed, the majority of cetaceans are the much smaller dolphins and porpoises, but, nevertheless, whales as a group are large mammals and include no very small species, such as those found among the insectivores, rodents or carnivores.

Large size offers a biological advantage in a number of ways. It confers protection from many enemies, which may be limited in the size of prey that they can tackle, and it gives a direct sexual advantage in those species where the males fight with each other for possession of the females, but, perhaps most importantly in the case of whales, it offers a metabolic advantage to a warm-blooded animal living in an environment colder than itself. This last property needs a little explanation. Obviously a warm animal in cold surroundings will lose heat; in air this will be by both conduction and radiation, but in water nearly all the heat will be lost by conduction from the body surface. The amount of heat an animal produces will depend on its activity and absolute mass of metabolising tissue, but the rate at which the heat will be lost will depend on the area of the surface over which it is lost. If the animal remains the same shape, the mass

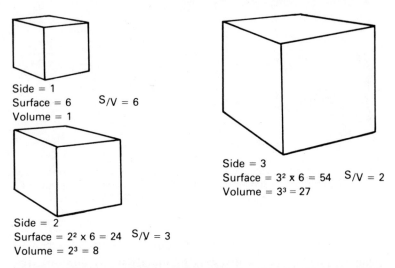

Side = 1
Surface = 6   S/V = 6
Volume = 1

Side = 3
Surface = 3² x 6 = 54   S/V = 2
Volume = 3³ = 27

Side = 2
Surface = 2² x 6 = 24   S/V = 3
Volume = 2³ = 8

Fig. 1.4   As the linear dimensions of similarly shaped bodies increase, so their surface increases as the square, and their volume as the cube, of the linear dimension. This means that the surface-to-volume ratio declines.

(or volume) will increase as the cube of the linear dimensions, while the surface area will increase only as the square of the linear dimensions. It is difficult to visualise this in the case of a whale, but the same principle applies to any solid object. Consider a cube of side one unit: its volume is 1 and its surface area 6. If the length of the side (the linear dimension) is doubled, the volume becomes $2^3 = 8$ while the surface area increases to $6 \times 2^2 = 24$; for a cube of side 3, the equivalent values are 27 and 54. We can see that the ratio of surface area to volume declines 6/1, 24/8, 54/27, or 6, 3, 2 and so on (Fig. 1.4) so that the potential rate of heat loss is proportionally reduced as the animal increases in size, thus effecting important economies in the amount of energy required for the simple maintenance of life.

This relationship between surface area and volume has profound biological implications, concerning not only heat transfer, but also the absorption of food from the gut, the excretion of nitrogen by the kidney and innumerable other biological processes.

There are thus biological advantages in increasing size.

Fig. 1.5 In the terrestrial environment, increasing size throws a greater proportional strain on the supporting limbs, as weight increases faster than the
cross-sectional area of the limb. Hence the 'graviportal' limbs of large terrestrial
mammals compared with the slender limbs of smaller ones.

However, on dry land, there is a limit to the size that can be
reached. The weight of a terrestrial mammal has to be supported by
its limbs and here again the geometrical relationship of volume
and area play a part. The weight of the animal increases with its
volume (the cube of its linear dimensions), while the strength of
its limbs, as compression struts, increases only with their cross-
sectional area, which is related to the square of the linear dimension. Consequently, as the size of the animal increases, the body
weight tends to overtake the strength of the limbs available to
support it, so that, when one looks at a series of similarly
shaped terrestrial mammals of increasing size, one notices that,
proportionally, the size of the limbs increases faster than the
size of the body. The trunk-like limbs of the Elephant are an
extreme case in terrestrial mammals; other 'graviportal limbs',
as they are called, can be seen in other large mammals, such as
the Rhinoceros or the Hippopotamus (Fig. 1.5).

Not only do the limbs of a large terrestrial mammal have to
be specially stout, they have to be connected to the trunk in such
a way that the weight of the body is transmitted *via* the limbs
to the ground. In mammals there is no bony connection (or at
any rate, very little) between the vertebral column, with its
attached rib-cage, and the fore-limbs. Instead the shoulder-blades
are embedded in the trunk musculature and the weight of the
thorax and head transmitted through them to the fore-limb. The
hind-limbs, on the other hand, are articulated to the pelvic girdle,

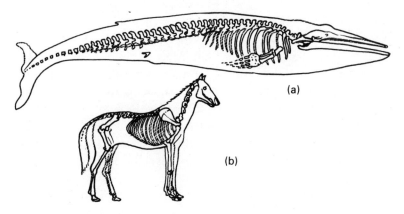

Fig. 1.6   The skeletons of: (a) a cetacean, the Blue Whale, (b) a terrestrial mammal, a horse.

which itself is rigidly connected to the specially modified sacral vertebrae.

The general effect, then, is of a weight-bearing girder, the vertebral column, with at one end the head, attached by powerful ligaments running to large neural processes on the thoracic vertebrae, and the whole supported on the four limbs (Fig. 1.6).

This process has probably, or nearly, reached its limit in the elephants. These are the largest of terrestrial mammals and the extinct elephants were not very much larger than those known today. *Parelephas trogontherii*, which lived about a million years ago in central Europe and North America, is the largest of the extinct forms and reached a shoulder height of about 4.5 m, which is not very much larger than the record African Elephant at 3.9 m.

Were elephants to get much larger they would have problems in accommodating the thicker legs which they would need to support their weight, while still retaining the necessary mobility. They would also be more vulnerable to injuries resulting from slips and falls because of the much greater energies developed when a large body falls to the ground.

Some extinct reptiles, such as *Brontosaurus* and *Diplodocus*, were over 24 m long and must have weighed nearly 50 tonnes. It was once believed that these forms were aquatic, but this view is less popular now. We know very little about how these dinosaurs lived, but we may suppose they were slow-moving animals that relied on their bulk for protection.

There are, then, practical limitations to the weight of a terrestrial mammal. In a dense medium, like water, these limitations are removed; the aquatic mammal, displacing its own weight of water, is, in accordance with Archimedes' Principle, weightless. A whale is supported on all sides by water. It needs no limbs to transmit its body weight to the substratum; its vertebral column no longer has to function as a weight-bearing girder; its huge head is supported by water and requires no specially strong ligaments to maintain its position at the end of the vertebral column.

Released from this limitation by the density of the medium in which they live, whales have increased their size far beyond the usual mammalian range and, indeed, beyond that of all other aquatic creatures, although the largest plesiosaurs (e.g. *Kronosaurus*) were about 15 m in length and the largest fish, the extant Whale-shark, *Rhincodon*, and an extinct shark (*Carcharodon megalodon*) may both have reached a maximum length of about 24 m.

The density of the medium in which whales live has facilitated their huge increase in size; it has not caused it. Once gravity was no longer a restraint, the process of selection was able to act on the whales, moulding the body to a shape best fitted to survive in its environment. This is the reason that not all the Cetacea are as large as the great whalebone whales. For some whales, which have evolved as predators on active prey, too great an increase in size would be disadvantageous and these (most porpoises and dolphins) have retained a size more typical of mammals.

The second property of water that has affected whales is its viscosity. Water resists the passage of an object through it and this feature provides whales (and all other aquatic mammals) with a means of locomotion, since, by applying a backward force to the water, the resistance of the water provides a forward thrust which drives the body ahead. This is by far the commonest method used by any vertebrate in moving through water. Fish, for example, use undulations of the caudal part of the body to propel themselves through the water; a penguin swims by backwardly directed beats of its flippers, as does a sea-lion, although here the hind-flippers also play a major part. The same principle, of course, is used by flying birds and bats, where the wings act against the resistance of the air. Because of the lower viscosity and density of air, the wings of a flying vertebrate have to be large in relation to its size, in contrast with the propulsive surfaces of whales.

In whales, the propulsive force is provided by the flukes, unique fibrous pads developed at the extreme end of the body and forming an expanded *horizontal* surface, unlike the tail of a fish, which is set in a vertical plane. The special nature of a horizontal tail was a feature recognised by both Aristotle and Melville, as was noted at the beginning of this chapter.

In terrestrial mammals, normal locomotion is effected by the action of the limbs against the ground. For whales, with the body floating freely in the water and remote from a solid substratum, this form of locomotion is neither available nor appropriate; far more efficient is the elegant and economical action of the flukes, as can be realised by anyone who has seen a dolphin swimming around its pool in an aquarium.

Relieved of their responsibility, both for supporting the body and propelling it, the limbs of the cetacean ancestor changed profoundly. The fore-limbs became changed into paddles. The limb bones, humerus in the upper arm and radius and ulna in the fore-arm, became shortened and flattened; the wrist bones, the carpals, assumed a mosaic-like appearance and the hand became elongated and flattened. The number of digits did not increase above the basic vertebrate five-fingered (pentadactyl) pattern—indeed in the Blue Whale, amongst others, the first digit is lacking (Fig. 1.7)—but extra bones were added to the extremities of the digits to produce the condition known as polyphalangy. The digits themselves are bound up in a common investment so that they are not separately distinguishable (although their outline can usually be seen in the flippers of the Sperm Whale, *Physeter catodon*) and little or no independent movement of the hand is possible. Whales use their fore-flippers as balancing planes; they have no direct locomotory function.

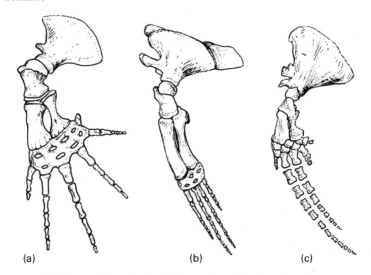

Fig. 1.7   Skeletons of fore-limbs of: (a) Right Whale, (b) Blue Whale, (c) Pilot Whale.

The hind-limbs have completely disappeared, as has the pelvic girdle, apart from two small rods of bone, which represent part of the ischial portion of the pelvis (Fig. 1.8). In some right whales and, exceptionally, Sperm Whales, a small nub of bone is found which represents the femur. Very occasionally a whale is found in which more extensive remnants of the hind-limbs persist. A Humpback Whale, *Megaptera novaeangliae*, has been taken with legs that stuck out a metre from its belly, with separate bones and cartilages compounding to the usual limb segments. As Scheffer (1969) remarked:

'How vanishingly small are the odds of a gene persisting through millions of years; inactive, yet suddenly able to quicken the embryo of a whale and to resurrect hind legs?'

Fig. 1.8   Pelvis of a Fin Whale. This rod of bone represents the ischial portion of the pelvis and to it are attached the corpora cavernosa of the penis (or clitoris).

The pelvic remnants normally present are usually held to be functionless, but the penis in males is anchored to them, as is the clitoris in females, and thus they play a small but highly significant part in the whale's anatomy.

The resistance which water offers to a body moving through it has consequences other than those concerned with swimming as a means of locomotion. Compression forces are set up in the body of a moving whale and these have left their mark on its structure. These forces will be most strongly felt at the head, which has to part the waters for the rest of the body to pass through, as the bow of a ship parts the waves. Surely no part of a whale's anatomy is more strangely constructed than the skull! Although mammalian skulls are very varied (indeed, all, or nearly all, mammalian species can be recognised from a study of their skulls alone), the whale's skull is far more modified than that of any other group.

The main bones of the skull of a terrestrial mammal do not vary greatly in their relative sizes; they fit together edge to edge, with little or no overlap, to form an elongated brain case with, usually, a recognisable snout or muzzle with the nares or openings of the nasal passages at the extreme end and the teeth-bearing jaws beneath (Fig. 1.9).

In whales, however, the skull has a completely different appearance. It is difficult to summarise the alterations simply and briefly but reference to Fig. 1.10 should help to make the situation

Fig. 1.9   Skull of a typical terrestrial mammal, a dog.

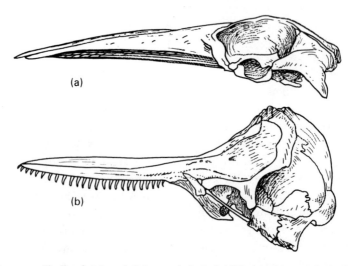

(a)

(b)

Fig. 1.10   Skulls of: (a) a whalebone whale (a Sei Whale), (b) a toothed whale (a Bottle-nosed Dolphin).

clearer. The anterior part of the skull, the rostrum, is formed, as in most terrestrial mammals, of the premaxillae and maxillae and is greatly elongated; the nasals, which usually contribute to the formation of the snout in terrestrial mammals, are withdrawn to the top of the cranium (this is clearly an adaptation to breathing at the surface and has little if anything to do with the compression forces we are discussing). The remainder of the skull presents a telescoped appearance. This differs in detail in the two sub-divisions of the Cetacea, the whalebone whales and the toothed whales, but we can take as an example the porpoise, one of the toothed whales. Here the maxillae and premaxillae spread backwards, so as to over-ride the frontals, and the parietals are crowded out to the sides. The occipital bone pushes forward over the top of the skull so that, in the words of Romer (1945):

'Apparently there is no top to the skull, it is all front and back.'

Even more strangely, the skull is asymmetrical—the right side of what may be termed the facial region is always larger than the left, a condition which is unique to the toothed whales. In some forms this asymmetry is less marked, but it reaches its extreme

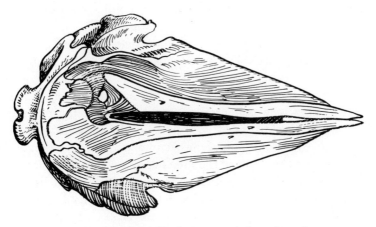

Fig. 1.11   Dorsal view of the skull of a Sperm Whale to show the assymmetry.

in the Sperm Whale (Fig. 1.11). Several theories have been advanced to account for this remarkable asymmetry; one view was that the action of swimming tended to turn the animal to the left, thus resulting in a thickening of the cranial bones on that side and a consequent broadening of the right side. Another theory held that the asymmetry of the laryngeal region of the Sperm Whale had caused a compounding asymmetry of the skull, but did not explain how. Really we know nothing of the reason for the unique condition of the skull. Like so many other aspects of whale biology it still awaits a logical explanation.

The manner in which the individual bones join with their neighbours is also peculiar. Instead of meeting edge to edge, as in most mammals, the bones of a whale's skull overlap one another in a sort of laminated, or squamous, suture. This may provide a stronger attachment, while allowing for growth, than would be possible with the ordinary type of suture.

In general, the jaws of whales are relatively weak. Howell (1930) has commented on the weakness of the attachment of the anterior part of the skull in the whalebone whales (but very properly noted that it was entirely adequate to the needs of the animal). It is characteristic of whales that there are no large bony developments on the cranium for the attachment of the jaw muscles, as one sees in the dog or the rat. However, the great enlargement of the occipital provides an anchorage for the main muscles of the back, which run along the thorax.

It would be over-simple to assume that all these peculiar features of the whale's skull are the consequence of the combined effects of the resistance encountered when swimming through the water and the support provided by the buoyancy of the water. Howell, after long deliberation, concluded that the external form of the cetacean head was modelled by these forces, but that the peculiar condition of the occipital and the telescoping of the skull were the result of the modification of the musculature, following from the relatively static position of the head vis à vis the vertebral column, a condition related to the feeding habits of whales.

At this stage it is appropriate to step back from the skull of our whale and take a general look at the form of its skeleton. No part of an animal can tell us more about its way of life than the enduring bones and, even without the evidence of living and recently dead whales to examine, we could tell much of their nature from an examination of the skeleton alone.

If we contrast the skeletons of a dog (a fairly typical mammal) and a porpoise (a conveniently sized cetacean), and the comparison will be made easy for us if we have the opportunity to examine the excellent exhibit at the Whale Gallery of the British Museum (Natural History) in London, we shall at once be struck by the simplicity of the skeleton of the whale (Fig. 1.12). The almost total absence of hind-limbs, pelvic girdle and sacrum contributes greatly to this impression and the reasons for the reduction of these elements have already been discussed. The reduction and modification of the fore-limb represents also a simpler condition than that found in the dog. A dog's fore-leg must be capable of complicated movements in its several segments in the various routines of walking, running, digging holes, etc. The porpoise's flipper, however, is limited to slight rotation and raising and lowering, while the opportunities for independent movements of the hand, wrist and fore-arm have completely disappeared in the adult. Hence, the intricate articulations and detailed patterns on the bones, which provide ridges and processes for the attachment of muscles and tendons and which

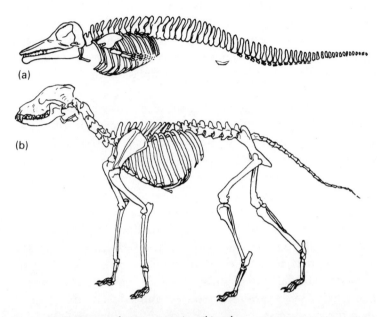

Fig. 1.12   Skeletons of: (a) a porpoise, (b) a dog.

are to be seen in the skeleton of the fore-leg of the dog, have been all but eliminated in the cetacean limb; the individual bones simply butt against one another, with no trace of the synovial capsules which ordinarily provide the friction-free bearings between bones, and are bound together with ligaments to form a relatively immovable whole.

The axial skeleton, too, is much simpler in the porpoise. Like all cetaceans, the porpoise possesses a negligible neck. The seven cervical vertebrae which are normally found in all mammals (some sloths excepted) are greatly compressed and form only a tiny proportion of the total length of the vertebral column. In the rorquals, some of the river dolphins, the White Whale, *Delphinapterus leucas*, and the Narwhal, *Monodon monoceros*, all seven cervicals are separate, but in all other whales some degree of fusion has occurred. Right whales and Bottlenosed Whales have all seven cervicals fused into a single mass, while in toothed whales (except those mentioned before) the first two cervicals (the atlas and the axis) are fused together and often some of the posterior cervicals are fused to them. In sperm whales, however, the atlas is separate and the other six are fused. All this implies that the whale has very little mobility between the head and the trunk; what movement there is occurs mostly in a vertical plane, the occipital condyles of the skull being elongated in this direction.

The thoracic vertebrae number thirteen in the porpoise, each bearing a pair of ribs. The number of ribs varies in cetaceans, from twelve to sixteen pairs in most to as few as eight pairs in the Southern Bottle-nosed Whale, *Hyperoodon planifrons*, which is unique in possessing fewer ribs than any other mammal. In the dog, as in other terrestrial mammals, the ribs each articulate with the vertebrae by a double head; in Cetacea, a double head is found only on the first three or four pairs of ribs (or, in some whalebone whales, on none at all). In toothed whales, the ribs connect to an ossified sternum by means of a varying number of sternal ribs (eight pairs in the porpoise). In whalebone whales, the sternum is reduced and only the first pair of ribs is attached to it.

The remaining vertebrae in the whale comprise the lumbars and the caudals as, lacking a pelvic girdle, no vertebrae are modified to form a sacrum. Lumbar vertebrae usually number five or seven in terrestrial mammals, but in whales there are many more (sixteen in the porpoise), each bearing wide transverse processes and a high neural spine (Fig. 1.13). These vertebrae, like the others making up the axial skeleton, are connected by large ossified intervertebral discs, rather than by articular facets (zygapophyses) on the neural arches, as in terrestrial mammals.

Posterior to the lumbar vertebrae are the caudal vertebrae.

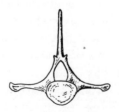

Fig. 1.13   The lumbar vertebra of a porpoise.

These are comparatively minor elements of the axial skeleton in the dog, having little to do but support the tail. The physical role of the tail in a terrestrial mammal is small; it may function as a flywhisk, or, to some extent, as a balancing organ, or even as a prehensile fifth limb in South American monkeys and the pangolins, (although these perhaps can scarcely be considered typically terrestrial because of their arboreal adaptations). In the dog, however, its chief function is to serve as a visual signal in social communication. The tail region of the porpoise and all other whales, however, is massively developed as the organ of locomotion and is where the bulk of the animal's muscle is concentrated. Apart from the last few, the caudal vertebrae are well formed with large neural spines and transverse processes; they are of the same order of size as the thoracics. Each caudal vertebra has associated with it, on the ventral side, a chevron bone, a V- or Y-shaped element faceted to the under-surface of neighbouring vertebrae in such a way that each chevron bone articulates simultaneously with the hind-end of one caudal and the front end of the next one following. Chevron bones occur in some other mammals, but, except in whales, they are fused to the caudal vertebrae themselves, rather than articulating with them.

We see, then, that the vertebrae of the porpoise present a very simple series compared with those of the dog. Articular surfaces are only slightly developed, or absent, and the structure of individual bones (except in the caudal region) is much simpler. As in the case of the fore-limb, the explanation is to be found in the far more restricted range of movement of which the cetacean vertebral column is capable. A dog curls up to sleep, can arch its back in preparation for a leap, or twist sideways to grasp a rabbit. The only part of a whale's body that has equivalent mobility is the caudal region and there the movement is almost entirely confined to a simple up-and-down beat. For restricted movements, fewer articulations are required and the complicated moulding of the dog's vertebrae has no equivalent in those of the porpoise. On the other hand, great power has to be developed in the movements that the cetacean does make with its body and, for this reason, the surfaces provided by the neural spines and transverse processes are expanded and supplemented in the caudal region by the chevron bones, so that a greater area is available for the attachment of muscle and tendon. Compression along the length of the strut formed by the vertebrae will take place as a result both of the resistance of the water when swimming, and of the stresses set up by the swimming movement itself (Chapter 3); hence the broad, but flattened, faces of the bodies of the vertebrae and the large intervertebral discs.

The resistance offered by the water when a whale swims has modified its internal anatomy as we have seen. But it has affected also the external surface of the whale. A frictional resistance is set up at the skin-water interface of a moving whale. Air resistance, in the form of an opposing force, affects fast-running terrestrial mammals to some extent, but frictional drag is scarcely a problem at all. Not so for the whale and, in order to overcome drag, the shape of the body has to be modified and unnecessary protrusions from the surface eliminated.

The general shape of a whale is 'stream-lined'. This is a rather vague term when applied to animals, as the variety of form in whales and fish amply demonstrates, but, basically, it implies a smooth body which tapers at both ends, but is typically blunter at the anterior end. All whales show the hind taper that is characteristic of the stream-lined form, but there is a bewildering array of different shapes for the head end. One might naturally suppose a slim, pointed head with a sharp snout would be an ideal form for cleaving the water with the least resistance and drag. The head of a Common Dolphin, *Delphinus delphis*, approaches such a shape, but other cetaceans, the Pilot Whale, *Globicephala melaena*, for example, have rounded foreheads, while the Sperm Whale has an enormous blunt head. This latter may be a special case, but the value of a blunt anterior end has been demonstrated in modern ship-building technology by the development of the 'bulbous bow' which is fitted to super-tankers and large cargo ships. In fact, different outlines of head (Fig. 1.14) may be an evolutionary response to different swimming attitudes and it is likely that the rounded forehead (it is really the creature's upper lip!) of the Pilot Whale is just as hydro-dynamically efficient for its way of life as is the sharper snout of the Common Dolphin.

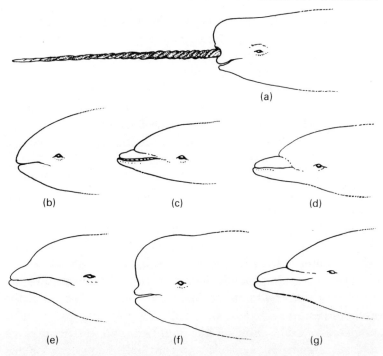

Fig. 1.14   Head shapes of various whales: (a) Narwhal, (b) Porpoise, (c) Fraser's Dolphin, (d) Spotted Dolphin, (e) Killer Whale, (f) Pilot Whale, (g) Common Dolphin.

Another essential for a smooth passage through the water is the elimination of all unnecessary protruding parts that would offer resistance to the water and cause turbulence in the flow over the skin. Thus we find that whales have eliminated external ear pinnae, protruding nipples or reproductive organs. In the female, the anal and vaginal openings are enclosed in a common furrow, with the recessed nipples close alongside. In the male, the penis is normally completely retracted within its sheath, so as to be invisible externally, while the testes lie within the abdominal cavity; no trace of a typical mammalian scrotum exists. The absence of a constricted neck region allows the head to 'fair' smoothly into the trunk and the development of the blubber layer beneath the skin smooths off the slight irregularities that would otherwise be associated with individual muscle groups.

Finally, the skin of cetaceans has developed a degree of smoothness unparalleled elsewhere amongst the mammals. The surface of the skin is completely smooth; no fold-lines or pores break the continuous surface of the epidermis. That characteristic and diagnostic feature of mammals, hair, has been all but completely eliminated in the whale. Not only the general body covering of hairs, but all traces of the follicles associated with them, and the sebaceous glands, have disappeared. Indeed, cutaneous glands are entirely absent from cetacean skin.

This statement needs qualifying. Hair follicles are a kind of gland and whales still show a scattering of hair follicles, with perhaps a few associated bristles, situated on the snout. These are best developed in rorquals, where small bristles occur in a cluster beneath the chin and along the sides of the upper jaw. These number about 100 in the Fin Whale and rather fewer in the Blue. The Humpback is said by Japha (1907, 1912) to be the hairiest of the whales, a hair being associated with each of the nodules that are scattered over the head, but Ling (1977), who prepared a table showing the numbers and distribution of whiskers in whales, was able to record only eighty-two for this species. Toothed whales have even fewer hairs (which are often represented only by their follicles) and these are confined to the upper jaw, except in the river dolphins, where, according to Norman and Fraser (1948), both upper and lower jaws have numerous well developed hairs. The Common Dolphin has about twenty follicles on its snout and the Porpoise about four. These hairs are not to be regarded only as the vestigial remains of a once luxuriant fur covering. They are functional sense organs which probably play an important role in feeding and, technically, are classified as sinus hairs (Ling, 1974).

Hairs serve several functions in terrestrial mammals, not least of which is the mechanical strength and protection that their horny shafts give to the hide. I have only to recall the last time I bumped my head against a sharp surface without breaking the skin, or think back to when I last saw a pair of Antarctic Fur Seal bulls slashing at each other's shaggy necks and shoulders, to appreciate the protection provided by hair. So it is not surprising that the hairless skin of the whale is very fragile. In a fresh state it can be slit with a knife as easily as rather soft cheese. Sea-birds have little difficulty in pecking through the skin of a stranded whale, in striking contrast with that of a dead seal, whose body contents are usually accessible only through the natural openings in the hide. Because of their fragile skins, whales have an added reason for avoiding contact with rocks and shoals, although there are many recorded instances of whales, particularly Humpbacks, deliberately seeking out ships in order to rub their backs against the hull, no doubt to ease the irritation set up by the Whale-lice (isopod crustaceans of the genus *Cyamus*—not insects) that infest these creatures.

So far I have discussed two of the properties of water, its density and viscosity, and how they have affected whales. Another property that whales have had to cope with is the much greater capacity of water to absorb heat (its specific heat) and the greater rate at which it will do this (its conductivity) when compared with air. All warm-blooded animals are liable to lose heat to their colder surroundings. Terrestrial mammals reduce their heat losses to a level within their range of physiological compensation (without too serious an energy expenditure) principally by insulating their bodies with hair, or by behavioural mechanisms which lead them to seek shelter in protected places, or to build nests, where heat loss can be minimised.

Some smaller mammals (and a few large ones) give up the battle completely at certain seasons and allow their body temperature to drop to rather near that of their surroundings. This is what happens when bats, dormice or hedgehogs hibernate. On the arrival of more favourable conditions, the hibernating mammals awaken and warm themselves by muscular activity until their body temperature is within the normal range. Hibernation seems generally to be related to seasonal feeding patterns, occurring when food would be scarce or otherwise difficult to find.

Whales, however, live in a very equable environment; seasonal temperatures in the ocean vary only a few degrees. A whale cannot avoid heat loss by seeking out a warm or protected part of the sea to sleep in—all the water available will be at more or less the same temperature. This is not quite true for all whales. Brodie (1975) has observed White Whales in the MacKenzie

Delta region of the western Canadian Arctic changing their environment in July from one of pack-ice and open water leads at about 0°C to a 12–18°C estuarine habitat. They can do this in a swimming time of less than an hour, from the ice-edge to the river mouths of the delta less than a mile away. For many species of whales, temperatures vary considerably over latitudinal ranges (although to nothing like the *seasonal* range in some terrestrial habitats) and whales do make major migrations to warmer waters to produce their young. This behaviour, however, does not provide a means of balancing the heat budget of the individual. No whale hibernates (which may be associated with the evenness of the environmental temperature and the necessity to move to breathe) and hair is not available to act as an insulator.

Heat exchange in water is about twenty-seven times greater than in still air at the same temperature (Ling, 1974) and hair alone would probably not be a very effective insulator in water. A hair layer acts as an insulator mainly because it traps a layer of still air next to the body surface of the animal. Because of the low specific heat and low conductivity of air, this layer is soon warmed and further heat loss reduced. In water, a hair coat can be effective, provided the air layer is preserved. Many aquatic animals, such as the Platypus, the Beavers, and the Musk Rats, possess deep soft layers of fur, but perhaps the finest coat of all is that of the Fur Seals. Here a layer of very fine fur fibres (some 40,000 per sq cm in the Antarctic Fur Seal) is supported by a much sparser layer of coarse guard hairs. The under-fur is relatively waterproof, for the fibres themselves are water-repellent so that they do not become wetted, while the guard hairs hold the under-fur fibres erect and maintain the insulating layer. Thus in air or shallow water the fur seal's coat provides good insulation. However, should the seal dive, the layer will be compressed by about half its thickness for each 10 m depth, greatly reducing the insulation provided. Fur seals are relatively shallow divers; other seals, which habitually dive deeper, such as the Walrus or the Elephant Seal, have reduced their hair covering and provided themselves, like the whale, with another form of insulation—blubber.

Blubber is the layer of fatty tissue which lies beneath the

dermis. It is often spoken of as lying beneath the skin, but it should properly be regarded as one of the layers, the hypodermis, which make up the skin. Its inner surface lies rather loosely connected to the sheet of skin musculature, the panniculus carnosus, so that the blubber of a whale can be peeled off as one would peel an orange.

Professor Slijper, the Dutch cetologist, gave measurements of the approximate blubber thickness of several species of whales (1962). Right whales develop the greatest thickness of blubber, an average of 23 cm, with a maximum of 50 cm in the Bowhead, *Balaena glacialis*. In the Sperm Whale, the blubber varies in thickness from 12–17 cm, in the Blue Whale it is about 12 cm and, in the Fin Whale, 7.5 cm. However, there is much variation in thickness between individuals and in the same individual at different seasons, as the blubber functions as an important food store, as well as insulation.

Blubber is about half as effective an insulator in air as an equal thickness of fur, but in water the insulation of a blubber layer is reduced to only about one quarter less than in air (Scholander *et al.*, 1950) and hence the whale's insulation is effective in water, its natural habitat.

There has been much discussion about the heat relations of whales. Not surprisingly, there are few measurements of their body temperature in anything remotely resembling natural conditions. Most recorded temperatures are between 35° and 37°C and the normal value probably lies nearer the lower end of this range. So it seems that the deep body temperature is fairly well in line with other larger mammals (e.g. man, body temperature = 37.0°C).

Nor is it easy to measure that other fundamental parameter of the heat budget, the basal metabolic rate, which is what maintains the body temperature. Extrapolation in terms of the weight of the whale from known values for land mammals leads to rather unreliable projection through these orders of size. On the basis of the known insulative properties of blubber, it had been calculated that, if a rorqual had a metabolic rate appropriate to its size, it would need a layer of blubber at least 15 cm thick to maintain the body temperature. In fact, the blubber is a good deal thinner than this in most of these whales, so it was argued that they would have to keep swimming in order to generate enough muscular heat to keep warm. The flaws in this argument were pointed out by Harrison Matthews, an English biologist who had begun his study of whales on the flensing plans of South Georgia more than half a century ago. Matthews (1952) drew attention to the arbitrary and unconfirmed nature of the figures on which the argument was based. He felt it basically unlikely that such a highly evolved creature as a whale would have evolved an insulating layer of blubber that was too thin, when, by adding to its thickness, it could become fully efficient.

Later investigations did, in fact, indicate that whales had a higher basal metabolic rate than might have been expected from their size in relation to other mammals. Most mammals average between 776–1,078 kcal per sq m of body surface per 24 hr, but whales seemed to have a much higher rate of around 9,600 kcal per sq m per 24 hr (Kanwisher and Sundnes, 1966). More recently it was appreciated that the ordinary rules for calculating basal metabolic rates really could not be applied to whales. The whale carried with it an enormous store of fat (up to 45% of its total weight) in the form of blubber. Besides acting as an insulator, this constitutes an inert store of food. If the metabolic rate of a Fin Whale were to be calculated by using the total weight of the animal relative to its food intake, then the corresponding approach with, say, a rodent, would be to weigh the animal along with a considerable part of its food cache (Brodie, 1975). And we have to consider carefully what is the metabolic surface of a whale. Brodie considered these matters and, by rejecting those parts of the whale's surface which did not surround metabolically active tissue, or were provided with special devices to conserve heat (the surface of the flukes and flippers and that of the head), came up with a metabolic rate of 984–1,032 kcal per sq m per 24 hr, which fits neatly within the standard mammalian range.

The subject, and the arguments about it, are complicated, but there is little doubt that blubber is an effective insulator and that whales are not normally severely thermally stressed by their environment. This is not to say, however, that rorquals do not find it advantageous to maintain a more or less constant forward motion (probably associated in these slightly negatively buoyant whales with planing to the surface to breathe) nor that a whale in cold Antarctic water does not need to use more food to maintain its body temperature against the steeper temperature gradient it experiences, compared with conditions in warmer waters. This is a field I shall discuss more fully when considering the energy relationships of feeding in whales.

The efficiency of blubber as an insulator may be accepted. Two questions arise from this: does a whale ever get overheated and embarrassed by its thick insulative coat and how does the living tissue (the dermis and epidermis) *outside* the blubber layer cope with its cold isolation?

During the hey-day of British whaling in the 1950s I often saw a whale drawn up on the flensing platform and stripped of its blubber to reveal the flesh falling in dark brown tatters from the bones; if I put my hand into the reeking meat it would be hot to the touch. Such a whale was one which, for some reason or other, had been delayed in the journey from its place of death on the open sea to the processing station. Perhaps the flagged carcase had been lost, perhaps bad weather had prevented the whale-catcher making headway. Maybe 48 hours had elapsed between the fatal harpoon and the whale's final surfacing up the ramp to the flensing platform. At all events, the heat generated by decomposition, unable to escape through the blubber, had cooked the meat, despite its being surrounded by icy water.

These whales were perfect demonstrations of the insulative properties of blubber. But how is it, then, that a whale does not get dangerously overheated if it engages in a sharp burst of muscular activity? The answer is to be found in the architecture of the circulatory system throughout the blubber. Blubber is a surprisingly vascular tissue, its fat cells and fibres being traversed by numberless fine blood vessels which break up into capillaries just beneath the surface of the skin. If blood is pumped into these capillaries, it is quickly cooled by the surrounding water and heat is lost from the body.

This system will work only in the living whale, for obviously it requires the blood to circulate for it to be effective; hence the dead whale rapidly heats up and putrefies. But, in the living whale, it is also clear that a system is required to direct the blood away from these superficial capillaries to avoid excessive loss of heat when there is no over-production, that is, to allow the blubber to do its work as an insulator.

This diversionary system is provided by a series of vessels which link the arteries and veins beneath the superficial layer of the skin and allow the blood to be returned rapidly to the warm core of the body before excessive cooling has taken place. These linking vessels, or arterio-venous anastomoses, as they are called, together with the superficial arteries, are provided with well developed smooth-muscle coats, so it seems likely that the autonomic nervous system, which regulates the body temperature of the animal, can control the flow of the blood, either through the capillary bed, or *via* the arterio-venous anastomoses, as appropriate, depending on whether the need is to dissipate or conserve heat.

A further device for minimising heat loss is found in those areas where a blubber layer is lacking: the flukes, flippers and parts of the surface of the head. This consists of another modification of the blood vessels. The arteries running to the skin in these regions are surrounded by complicated spirals of veins (Fig. 1.15). These structures, or peri-arterial venous retia, function as counter-current heat exchangers.

Counter-current exchangers are devices of considerable engineering importance which man has developed over the last couple of centuries. Nature has anticipated these developments by many millions of years and counter-current exchangers form the basis of several biological organ systems, notably the kidneys of birds and mammals. The system is simplest when one considers heat exchange. If a pipe carrying a hot liquid passes from an insulated area to one where it can lose heat and then back again, the greatest loss of heat will occur from the hottest part of the liquid, where it enters the cold surroundings (Fig. 1.16a). But, if the return pipe is run in close contact with the delivery pipe, *with the flow in the opposite direction* (counter-current), then there will be a transfer of heat from pipe to pipe, the coldest inflowing liquid absorbing heat from the coolest out-

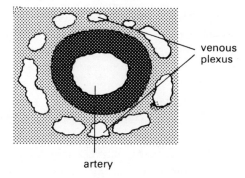

artery

Fig. 1.15   Peri-arterial venous retia in the skin of a porpoise. These structures transfer heat from the warm arterial blood to the colder venous blood returning from the skin.

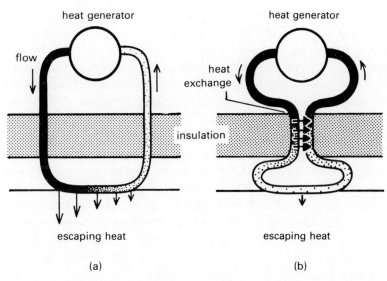

Fig. 1.16   The principle of the counter-current heat-exchanger. (a) Simple system with no counter-current. Warm liquid (blood) flowing from the heat generator (the body core) will lose heat to the exterior (the sea). (b) Counter-current system. The flow and return pipes (arteries and veins) run in close contact with each other. The coldest liquid (venous blood) entering the insulation (blubber) is warmed by extracting heat from the hot out-flowing liquid (arterial blood). Because the flow is in opposite directions (counter-current), the maximum temperature gradient is maintained between the two flows over the distance they are in contact with each other, thus the maximum amount of heat is exchanged.

flowing liquid, and an even temperature differential is maintained between the adjacent pipes. If the system is a closed one, there will be only a small escape of heat to the exterior as the out-flowing liquid will have given up most of its heat before leaving the insulated area (Fig. 1.16b).

In the whale, the delivery outflow pipe is represented by the superficial arteries of the skin of the flukes and flippers and the return pipe by complex anastomosing networks of veins surrounding the arteries. Such a branching network of blood vessels is known as a rete (plural: retia), and, since they are veins surrounding the arteries, they are collectively known as peri-arterial venous retia.

The action of the peri-arterial venous retia is controlled by an ingenious mechanism. If the arterial pressure is increased, the dilation of the arterial wall within the rete restricts the passage of blood through it, so that the counter-current exchanger is cut off and the blood must return by another route, thus causing heat to be lost from the system (Scholander and Scheville, 1955). Muscular activity will result in production of heat and also a rise in blood pressure, so the system tends to be self-regulating —an example of homeostasis by negative feedback, to use the technical jargon.

The arterio-venous anastomoses and the peri-arterial venous retia allow a safe flow of blood to the skin, either to dispose of surplus heat, or to provide the physiological requirements of the living tissue external to the insulating layer. Without such provision the insulation provided by the blubber would prove more of an encumbrance than an asset to the whale, for it might die of heat stroke if it exerted itself and its superficial skin cells, if once damaged, would regenerate too slowly to allow healing to take place.

We have not exhausted our list of the differing physical properties of air and water and the way the change from an aerial to an aquatic environment has affected the whale. Important differences exist in the behaviour of light and sound in water from that in air, and both these have modified the body, and behaviour, of the whale, but these subjects will be dealt with in the section on the sense organs.

2 The diversity of whales

Primitive whales: sub-order Archaeoceti

The origin of the Cetacea, like that of so many other orders of mammals, is shrouded in mystery. The earliest remains that can be recognised as derived from cetaceans appear in the Middle Eocene, some 40 million years ago. These animals, the archaeocetes, however, so differ from existing whales that it seems unlikely that they can be regarded as ancestral to either of the two surviving lines, the toothed whales (Odontoceti) and the whalebone, or baleen, whales (Mysticeti).

The earliest archaeocete specimens were found in northern Africa, suggesting that they may have originated there. They show some affinities with the now extinct Creodonta that flourished in the Eocene and are believed to have given rise to the present day Carnivora. *Protocetus*, from the Middle Eocene of Egypt, has been claimed as the intermediate between the creodonts and the Cetacea, but, since there are older archaeocetes than *Protocetus*, it is clear that divergence from a creodont stock (if it occurred at all) must have occurred at an earlier stage.

The first archaeocete fossils to be described were found in 1832 in Alabama and Louisiana, USA, and were believed to have been reptilian remains. On account of their size, the name *Basilosaurus* (= king-lizard) was given to them. Richard Owen, who examined a skull, used the name *Zeuglodon* (= yoke-toothed) to describe the way the roots of the posterior teeth are joined. Both names have been used subsequently.

Most archaeocetes were very elongate animals and, were any to have survived, would fit remarkably well the usual description of sea-serpents or lake-monsters. Some reached as much as 21 m in length and one, exhibited by its discoverer in North America,

Fig. 2.1   Skeleton of an archaeocete whale.

was about 34 m long. Unfortunately, it was later discovered that, in a fit of enthusiasm, Dr Albert Koch had included the vertebrae of at least two animals in his reconstruction (Harrison and King, 1965). The great length of these early whales was the result of an increase in the length of the centra of the vertebrae posterior to the middle of the thorax and also to an increase in the actual number of vertebrae behind the thorax (Fig. 2.1). The processes of the vertebrae are not greatly developed and Howell (1930) argued that these forms must have progressed with a wriggling eel-like motion, passing S-shaped waves down the body, so that the reaction of the lateral surfaces with the water drove the animal forward. *Basilosaurus* probably had little if anything in the way of tail-flukes, although it may have had a vertically flattened posterior part to its body. There were short, fin-like fore-flippers, with a movable elbow joint. By Upper Miocene times the hind-limbs had been reduced to vestiges which did not protrude beyond the body and were quite functionless in locomotion.

Although the skeleton of the body was already highly adapted to an aquatic life in the earliest archaeocetes known, the skull remained relatively primitive. The snout was elongate, but not excessively so for the size of the animal, and the nostrils had migrated backwards part of the way (Fig. 2.2), but the rest of the skull was still very similar to that of a creodont—a long, low braincase with no trace of the telescoping seen in the modern whales (Romer, 1945). The teeth did not exceed the basic number

Fig. 2.2   Skull of the archaeocete *Basilosaurus*. The snout is elongate, but the nostrils have migrated back part of the way (arrowed).

of forty-four, characteristic of placental mammals, and, in contrast to modern toothed whales, showed some division of function, the anterior teeth being simple cones or pegs, while those towards the back of the jaw were elongated in the anterior–posterior plane and many-cusped. These teeth have been compared with those of the Antarctic Crab-eater Seal, *Lobodon carcinophagus*, which feeds on the shrimp-like krill. But it seems unlikely that the archaeocetes fed in a similar manner—filter-feeding of this type would require a much larger filter bed than their posterior teeth could provide. More probably they were fish-eaters, using the teeth at the front of the mouth for seizing the prey and those further back to slice it up.

Besides the elongate archaeocetes, of which *Basilosaurus* is an example, and which disappeared about the end of the Eocene or a little later, there were others with more orthodox whale-like proportions—*Dorudon* was an example—which persisted through the Oligocene to the beginning of the Miocene, about 25 million years ago. These may have resembled modern dolphins, but were not ancestral to them.

It would be convenient to be able to arrange all the known cetaceans, both fossil and extant, in a neat evolutionary sequence, or family tree. Unfortunately this is quite impossible. We cannot say how the existing whales were derived from the archaeocetes, or indeed whether they were derived from them at all. Probably the best course is to recognise that all these cetacean sub-orders, the archaeocetes, the odontocetes and the mysticetes, are distinct, and had an origin near the beginning of the Eocene. It used to be believed that the Cetacea were derived from the creodonts, a now extinct group that gave rise to the modern Carnivora in the Palaeocene. Now it is more commonly believed that the whales shared a common ancestor with the Artiodactyla, or even-toed ungulates, the group which today contains the pigs, hippopotami, camels, deer and cattle. As will be seen later, there are similarities in parts of the reproductive system and serological typing has shown that the serum proteins of Cetacea have more in common with artiodactyls than with any other mammalian group (Boyden and Gemeroy, 1950).

Not only is the ancestral group unknown, it is still a matter for debate whether the whale sub-orders arose from a common ancestor or separately. Many of the common features shown by odontocete and mysticete whales can be explained in terms of response to the extreme environment to which the early whale had to adapt. The development of horizontal tail-flukes would be an example of such a character. On the other hand, the existence of a set of homodont teeth (or homodont tooth germs) in both the odontocetes and the mysticetes is less easy to explain in this way and might be regarded as evidence of common ancestry. Palaeontologists and comparative anatomists will argue about these questions for a good while to come. Less specialised biologists may prefer to keep an open mind on the question.

Other fossil whales

There are fossil remains of both extant groups of whales, including families that flourished in the Miocene but are now totally extinct. In the Upper Oligocene, several million years before the last of the archaeocetes became extinct, a new group of whales, the squalodonts, appeared. These were clearly recognisable as odontocetes but possessed a fairly typical mammalian set of teeth, divided into distinct incisors, canines and cheek teeth. Despite the primitive nature of their teeth, the squalodonts showed many advanced cetacean features. The telescoping of the skull was completed, the parietals had been eliminated from its top, the maxillae were in contact with the supra-occipitals and the blow-hole had reached its posterior position above and behind the eyes. A significant feature that links the squalodonts with the modern river dolphins (Platanistidae) is that the temporal opening is not roofed over with bone, as in other modern odontocetes. The squalodonts, which flourished in the Miocene and disappeared in the Pliocene, probably lived in much the same way as modern porpoises.

A fragmentary Upper Eocene fossil, and one or two Oligocene specimens, seem to show the beginning of the type of skull telescoping that occurs in modern whalebone whales. Also in the Oligocene, and a little earlier than the squalodonts, appeared a group of primitive whalebone whales, the cetotheres. These had lost their teeth and developed a baleen filter bed suspended from the maxillae to strain their food. The skull showed the typical telescoping, but it was not so extensive as in the modern whalebone whales, for there remained a considerable gap between the supra-occipitals and the posterior processes of the maxillae. The cetotheres were relatively small whales, often less than 7.5 m in length. In many ways they resembled the Grey Whale, the sole surviving member of the family Eschrictiidae. Cetotheres were most abundant in the Middle Miocene and were gradually replaced by the modern baleen whales, the Balaenopteridae and the Balaenidae, in the Pliocene.

Many other fossil whales are known, but all belong to families that have at least some living members today, and they will not be considered further here. However, a glance at Fig. 2.3 shows that most whale groups that we know today were at one time more diverse or abundant. The Upper Miocene was a great age for whales: what we see today is only a fraction of the forms that once inhabited the seas.

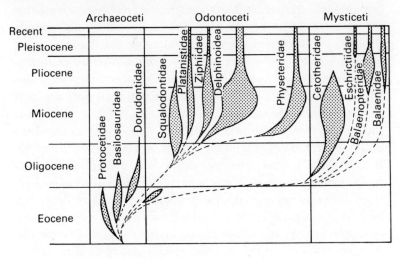

Fig. 2.3   A family tree for Cetacea.

The toothed whales: sub-order Odontoceti

The odontocete whales comprise seven families, more or less, depending on which systematist is followed. All odontocetes are characterised by the presence of teeth (although in some they do not emerge through the gum), an asymmetrical skull, a single external nasal opening, double-headed anterior ribs, sternal ribs present (cartilaginous in some families) and a sternum composed of three or more sternebrae, articulating with three or more pairs of ribs.

River dolphins: family Platanistidae

The river dolphins (Fig. 2.4) are generally accepted to be the most primitive cetaceans living today. The skull does not show the extreme telescoping characteristic of other whales and the individual bones are more clearly delineated. The temporal fossa is open, as noted earlier. There are numerous simple teeth in the elongated and very slender jaws; the two halves of the lower jaw are fused over about half their length. The cervical vertebrae are separate, a feature which allows the river dolphins to move their heads from side to side to a considerable extent and in consequence there is a discernible neck. The genus *Platanista* contains the Ganges Susu, *P. gangetica*, and another form from the Indus river, usually known as *P. indi*, but which may be only a variety or subspecies of the former. The Susus (they get their name from the sighing noise they make when they exhale) are strange little dolphins, the males reaching a length of about 210 cm and the female about 250 cm. The eyes of the Susu are practically non-functional, as they lack a lens. The animals can distinguish light from darkness but of course cannot form an image on the retina. Since the waters they live in are thick with suspended silt, a sense of sight would be of little use to them and many other examples of blind cave- or tunnel-dwelling vertebrates remind us of how necessary use is to maintain the complex apparatus of sight. However, the Susu manages to find its food, small fish and crustaceans, well enough without sight, using an additional sense that the odontocetes have refined to a remarkable extent. This, which

Ganges Susu
(Platanista gangetica)

Boutu
(Inia geoffrensis)

White-flag Dolphin
(Lipotes vexillifer)

Franciscana
(Pontoporia blainvillei)

Bottle-nosed Whale
(Hyperoodon ampullatus)

Cuvier's Beaked Whale
(Ziphius cavirostris)

Baird's Beaked Whale
(Berardius bairdii)

True's Beaked Whale
(Mesoplodon mirus)

Pygmy Sperm Whale
(Kogia breviceps)

Fig. 2.4 River dolphins, beaked whales and Pygmy Sperm Whale.

depends on the directional reflection of high-frequency sound waves, is discussed later.

In the many branches of the Amazon and Orinoco rivers in South America is found the Boutu, *Inia geoffrensis*. This river dolphin is similar to the susu, but not quite so blind—its eyes, though small, appear to be functional. Perhaps the waters of the Amazon and Orinoco are clearer than those of the Ganges and Indus, or perhaps the Boutu has found a role for its sight out of the water. There are tales of Boutus peering out of the water and even heaving themselves about on the forest floor, largely out of the water, in time of flood.

The White-flag Dolphin, *Lipotes vexillifer*, is one of the least-known cetaceans—only five specimens are in museums. It is found solely in the Tung Ting lake and the Yangtze Kiang river in China. The White-flag Dolphin grows to about 250 cm; its beak is curved upwards in a strange manner and its eyes are greatly reduced and almost non-functional. The remaining platanistid is the Fransiscana, *Pontoporia blainvillei*, a coastal species found from the Valdez Peninsula in Chubut, Argentina, north to central Brazil. Although technically a river dolphin, this species is really estuarine when it is not overtly marine. Its alternative name, the La Plata Dolphin, indicates its occurrence in that great body of fresh water. A female *Pontoporia*, 172 cm long, weighed 40 kg.

Beaked whales: family Ziphiidae
The beaked whales (Fig. 2.4) form another group of comparatively primitive whales. They are medium-sized toothed whales characterised by a snout drawn out into a beak from which they get their name. Existing forms (with one exception) all show a strong reduction in the dentition, usually with one–two pairs of visible teeth in the lower jaw. Between two and seven of the cervical vertebrae are fused. There are two diverging longitudinal grooves on the throat. The flippers of beaked whales are comparatively small and there is a small dorsal fin set well back on the body; there is no central notch between the flukes. All are oceanic.

The best known beaked whale is the Bottle-nosed Whale,

THE DIVERSITY OF WHALES

Hyperoodon. There are two very similar species, the Northern Bottle-nosed Whale, *H. ampullatus,* and the Southern, *H. planifrons.* The Northern Bottle-nosed Whale is often seen off British coasts. The male grows up to about 9 m in length, the female to 7.5 m. The head is very bulbous, due mainly to the presence of an oil reservoir in the 'forehead' (really the upper lip), but also, particularly in old males, to the growth of a pair of bony maxillary crests on the rostrum. The snout is short and a pair of large conical teeth is present on the tip of the lower jaw, but only in older animals do their tips protrude beyond the gum. The flippers are very pointed and there is a small dorsal fin. The Bottle-nosed Whale is dark grey to black above, a little lighter below. Old males assume a brownish colour. This species was important to the Arctic whalers in the late nineteenth century and, more recently, there has been an industry based on them working out of Norway.

Cuvier's Beaked Whale, *Ziphius cavirostris,* is a widely distributed ziphiid, occurring in all the oceans of the world, although it does not extend into high latitudes. It is known mainly from stranded animals, from as far south as Tierra del Fuego to the Bering Sea in the north. It differs from the Bottle-nosed Whale in lacking a bulbous forehead. Males mature at about 5.4 m and females at 6.1 m.

There are two species in the genus *Berardius*: Baird's Beaked Whale, *B. bairdii,* and Arnoux's Beaked Whale, *B. arnouxii.* Both are very similar but Baird's Whale inhabits the North Pacific, while Arnoux's lives in the southern oceans. *B. bairdii* is the largest ziphiid; a female measures 12.8 m in length and a male 11.8 m. The southern species probably reaches similar lengths, but few have been measured. *Berardius* resembles *Hyperoodon,* but there are four large triangular teeth in the lower jaw, of which the anterior pair project outside the mouth, since the lower jaw protrudes beyond the upper.

The genus *Mesoplodon* comprises a rather uncertain number of species. Twelve species are named by Edward Mitchell in the report of the Sub-Committee on Smaller Cetaceans of the International Whaling Commission (1975) but some are known from very few specimens. Probably a more careful study of a larger series would reduce the number recognised. Some species have a wide distribution, such as Blainville's Beaked Whale, *M. densirostris*, which is found in tropical and temperate seas throughout the world. Others, like Stejneger's Beaked Whale, *M. stejnegeri*, are restricted to a single ocean basin, in this case the North Pacific. Sowerby's Whale, *M. bidens*, is a species which is often stranded on coasts on both sides of the Atlantic. It has a slender beak with a single large triangular tooth on each side of the lower jaw in males. In females, the tooth is hidden in the gum. Sowerby's Whale is a slender fast-swimming form, coloured black above with a slightly paler belly. It reaches 4.9 m in length. A similar, but slightly larger (5.2 m) species is True's Beaked Whale, *M. mirus*. It is known from only six strandings, two on the North American coast and four in British waters.

An equally rare whale is Shepherd's Beaked Whale, *Tasmacetus shepherdii*. This is known from eight specimens stranded in New Zealand, Chile and Argentina. Unlike the other ziphiids, it has fifty-two teeth in the lower jaw (the pair at the apex being much the largest) and thirty-eight in the upper jaw.

Sperm whales: family Physeteridae
This family contains three species in two genera. The most familiar is the Sperm Whale, *Physeter catodon* (Fig. 2.7). The enormous head of the Sperm Whale makes it recognisable in almost any situation. The head makes up about a third of the bulk of the animal and its giant size is caused by the presence of the spermaceti organ, a specialised tissue that produces an animal wax, important in maintaining the hydrostatic balance of the animal. This subject is discussed more fully in Chapter 3 on diving. The skull which has to accommodate this strange and monstrous organ is of a peculiar shape, with a high transverse crest rising out of a concave basin and known as 'Neptune's chariot' to the old whalers. The lower jaw is armed with eighteen–twenty-eight pairs of large conical teeth (much blunted in old animals) which fit into sockets in the upper jaw, where a few small degenerate teeth may be found. The dorsal fin is ill-defined but is followed by a series of four or five low humps. The body surface of the Sperm Whale is irregularly corrugated, although this is less

apparent in fat animals taken on the feeding grounds. The general colour is a dark slaty-grey, paler on the belly, where white patches often occur. The inside of the mouth and the lips are white. Albino Sperm Whales are recorded but uncommon although Herman Melville's *Moby Dick* (1851) has, however, made them famous. Old Sperm Whales of normal colouration become paler with age as a result of scarring of the skin. Most of the scars seem to result from scratches from the horny suckers of the squid on which they feed, but males may be scarred in sexual fighting.

The Sperm Whale is by far the largest of the odontocetes. Unlike the ziphiids, where the females are the larger, the male Sperm Whale greatly exceeds its mate in size, reaching approximately 18.5 m in length, while females normally grow only to 11–12 m. This sexual difference is associated with the polygymous pattern (one male to many females) of their reproductive behaviour, as in so many other mammals.

Sperm Whales occur in the warmer parts of all the world's oceans, but only the larger males penetrate the cooler waters of high latitudes. Only male Sperm Whales have ever been stranded on British coasts.

The other genus of the Physeteridae, *Kogia** contains two species, the Pygmy Sperm Whale, *K. breviceps*, and the Dwarf Sperm Whale, *K. simus*. Little is known of either of them. They resemble the huge Sperm Whale only slightly, in particular the external appearance of the head being very different, though internally a spermaceti organ is present. There is a clearly defined dorsal fin (Fig. 2.4) and the flippers are bluntly pointed, not rounded as in the Sperm Whale. The nine–fourteen pairs of teeth are slender, pointed and strongly curved backwards and a significant point of similarity is that they occur only in the lower jaw, the tip of which does not extend to the end of the snout, just as in the Sperm Whale, although in contrast to most other odontocetes. Both species of *Kogia* are dark-coloured: *K. breviceps* grows to about 3.5 m and *K. simus* appears to be a little smaller, although there are very few measurements.

---

* This is one of the fortunately few barbarous and unmeaning generic names, although it has been suggested in its defence that it is derived from 'Cogia Effendi' who is said to have observed whales in the Mediterranean.

Narwhals and White Whales: family Monodontidae

There are two superficially very dissimilar whales in this family (Fig. 2.5), the Narwhal and the White Whale, or Beluga. The Narwhal, *Monodon monoceros*, is remarkable chiefly for its unicorn-like tusk. It is a localised high Arctic whale, absent from the north Siberian shelf and rare in the north Alaskan sector. It has a bulbous forehead but no beak or dorsal fin, only a slight crest just behind the middle of the back. The flipper is short and rounded. In colour, the Narwhal is mottled grey, lighter on the sides and belly. Fully grown adult males reach 4.7 m, females 4.0 m. Occasionally the Narwhal strays down from its cold Arctic seas and strands in European waters, the latest example being two which ended up in the Thames estuary in 1949.

The White Whale, *Delphinapterus leucas*, is a more normal-looking cetacean. It has a high swollen forehead, no beak and eight–ten pairs of teeth in both upper and lower jaws. The head has considerable mobility and there is a suggestion of a neck, a rare condition in whales. As the name suggests, the White Whale is very pale in colour, being white or cream, although this is attained only as the animal matures, the calves being grey. It reaches a length of between 3.7 m and 4.3 m. White Whales are found in shallow or estuarine waters in the Arctic or sub-Arctic. It is a rare visitor to British waters, the last recorded being in 1932, in the Firth of Forth.

The remaining odontocetes comprise three rather similar families which can be grouped together in a super-family, the Delphinoidea.

Rough-toothed and Humpbacked Dolphins: family Stenidae

The Rough-toothed Dolphin, *Steno bredanensis* (Fig. 2.5), is a small (2.2–2.75 m) dolphin found in tropical and sub-tropical waters of the Atlantic and Indo-Pacific. The teeth are peculiar in being furrowed on the crowns. *Steno* is dark grey on the back, lighter on the sides, and white beneath, the colour sharply delimited. It is truly pelagic species that occasionally strands in large numbers.

The genus *Sotalia* contains a single species, the Tucuxi,

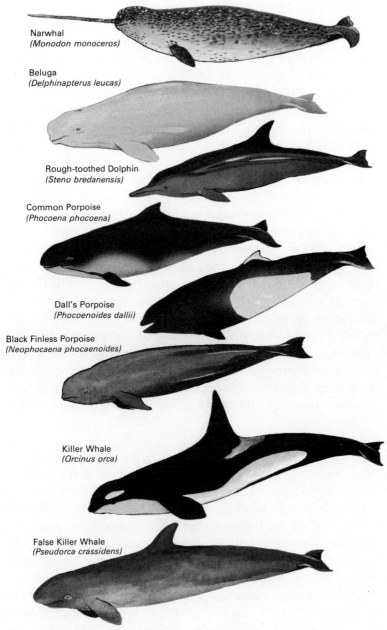

Narwhal
(Monodon monoceros)

Beluga
(Delphinapterus leucas)

Rough-toothed Dolphin
(Steno bredanensis)

Common Porpoise
(Phocoena phocoena)

Dall's Porpoise
(Phocoenoides dallii)

Black Finless Porpoise
(Neophocaena phocaenoides)

Killer Whale
(Orcinus orca)

False Killer Whale
(Pseudorca crassidens)

Fig. 2.5   Narwhal, White Whale, Rough-toothed Dolphin, porpoises and true
dolphins.

S. fluviatilis. This very small dolphin is found in the large rivers and along the Atlantic coasts of South America. It reaches about 1.6 m in length, although females from the Amazon can be sexually mature at a length of only 146 cm, which makes the Tucuxi the smallest of the Cetacea.

The Humpbacked Dolphins comprise two species—the Indo-Pacific Humpbacked Dolphin, *Sousa chinensis* and the Atlantic species, *S. tenszii.* They are warm-water dolphins with distributions indicated by their names. Like *Sotalia*, they have a well-developed beak with thirty-two pairs of teeth in both jaws. Their most characteristic feature is the marked hump on which the dorsal fin is borne. The stock of the tail is laterally compressed with high dorsal and ventral ridges. Plate 1 shows a specimen of *S. chinensis* from North Australia and its striking white colour can be well seen. However, not all populations of this species are so pale; the form along the East African coast is often spotted, while in muddy Indian waters they are grey. The Atlantic Humpbacked Dolphin is often stated to feed on vegetation. This statement appears to have arisen either because of accidentally included plant remains in the stomach of the specimen first discovered, or because of outright confusion with the Manatee, *Trichechus senegalensis*, which occurs in the same area. Like most other dolphins, this species feeds on fish. Humpbacked Dolphins grow to a little over 2 m, but few have been measured.

Porpoises: family Phocoenidae

There is little justification for separating the porpoises (Fig. 2.5) from the true dolphins on anatomical grounds at family level, but the distinction is a familiar one to Europeans—porpoises are those delphinoids which lack a beak and have spade-shaped teeth; dolphins are the remainder (the Stenidae being separated by rather obscure specialities of the air sinus system in the head). In America, however, the term 'porpoise' is freely applied to what in Europe is a dolphin, thus the Bottle-nosed Dolphin of the English (*Tursiops truncatus*) is the Bottle-nosed Porpoise of the Americans. (Neither side of the Atlantic would ever confuse it with the Bottle-nosed Whale, *Hyperoodon ampullatus*, of course.)

The family Phocoenidae, defined in the manner given, contains six rather similar species. The most familiar is the Common or Harbour Porpoise, *Phocoena phocoena*. This is often seen in the coastal waters of the North Atlantic, though sadly it seems a good deal less common than it was previously. It is one of the smallest of the Cetacea, females reaching a length of only 1.8 m and a weight of 90 kg, males being slightly smaller. There is no beak and the head slopes up to a low, receding forehead. There are twenty-two–twenty-seven pairs of charactistically spade-shaped teeth in both upper and lower jaws. The large dorsal fin is triangular and situated about in the middle of the back; the flippers are set back at about one third of the length of the body and are ovoid and relatively small. There is considerable variation in colour—the back is black, the belly white and there is a variable amount of grey on the sides. There is always a dark streak from the corner of the mouth to the insertion of the flipper. Harbour Porpoises are often caught accidentally in fishing nets; occasionally they are captured deliberately, as their meat is said to be very good eating. Because of their coastal habits in highly industrialised areas, Harbour Porpoises are liable to suffer from the effects of pollution, as well as from fishing activities, and some of the decline observed in European waters may be attributed to this.

There are three other species in the genus *Phocoena*: the Cochito, *P. sinus*, of the Gulf of California; Burmeister's Porpoise, *P. spinipinnis*, from the Atlantic and Pacific coasts of South America; and the Spectacled Porpoise, *P. dioptrica*, from the western South Atlantic. The Cochito is a localised species and the Spectacled Porpoise appears to be uncommon, but Burmeister's Porpoise is caught in great numbers in gill nets off the coasts of Peru and Uruguay. Like the Harbour Porpoise, they are coastal species. The Cochito is another very small cetacean, but the other two species are larger, probably around 2 m long when fully grown.

Dall's Porpoise, *Phocoenoides dalli*, is an oceanic porpoise of the clear blue water over the continental slope of the North Pacific. It is about 2.5 m long, black with conspicuous white flanks and belly. Several thousand are taken each year in the winter off the north-east coast of Japan for food, using hand-held harpoons, and about 10,000 are captured accidentally in the summer in Japanese gill-nets and discarded.

The Finless Porpoise, *Neophocaena phocaenoides*, is distributed along the coasts and rivers of Pakistan, India, and the whole of South-East Asia north to China, Japan and Korea. It grows up to 184 cm in length and the males are believed to be slightly larger than the females. As its name suggests, it lacks a fin, its place being taken by a low dorsal ridge. It is a widely distributed porpoise, but does not appear to be particularly common anywhere.

True dolphins: family Delphinidae

The true dolphins (Fig. 2.5 & 6) collectively form the last and largest family of the odontocetes. There are probably about twenty species, although many more have been described. There is a well developed beak (except in the Orcininae) and the jaws are neither exceedingly long nor narrow, with the tooth rows well separated and diverging posteriorly. They are the most abundant and varied of all the whales and are to be found in all the oceans of the world, from the tropics to the polar seas.

The family is divided into four sub-families, the first of which is the Orcininae. The most famous member of this group is undoubtedly the Killer Whale, *Orcinus orca*. Killer Whales, once seen, are unmistakable. They are startlingly black and white, with a grey saddle behind the dorsal fin. The white is mostly on the belly, but there is a lobe of white extending up over the flanks, between the dorsal fin and the flukes, and a lens-shaped white patch behind the eye. The rounded flippers are black all over and the flukes black above and white below. The dorsal fin is tall and sharply pointed; in old males it becomes disproportionately tall, reaching a height of up to 1.8 m. The height and slenderness of these fins has caused some authors to compare them with great swords but this is at best a fanciful simile. Likewise, in old males, the flippers also become greatly enlarged, increasing from an original length of about one ninth of total body length of the young male to about one fifth in the old male. Fins and flippers thus afford good examples of differential

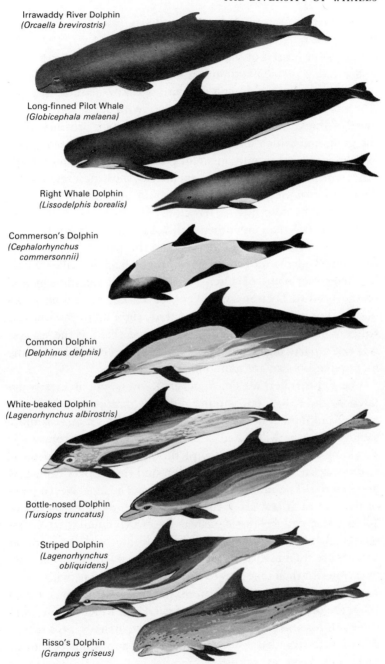

Irrawaddy River Dolphin
(Orcaella brevirostris)

Long-finned Pilot Whale
(Globicephala melaena)

Right Whale Dolphin
(Lissodelphis borealis)

Commerson's Dolphin
(Cephalorhynchus
commersonnii)

Common Dolphin
(Delphinus delphis)

White-beaked Dolphin
(Lagenorhynchus albirostris)

Bottle-nosed Dolphin
(Tursiops truncatus)

Striped Dolphin
(Lagenorhynchus
obliquidens)

Risso's Dolphin
(Grampus griseus)

Fig. 2.6   True dolphins.

or allometric growth and, seeing this is found in the males only, this is regarded as a secondary sexual character. The Killer Whale is the largest of the dolphins. Males attain a length of up to 8.2 m (a possible maximum is 9.4 m) and females 7.0 m (perhaps up to 8.2 m), although they are sexually mature at 4.9 m. The mouth of the Killer Whale is armed with about ten–thirteen pairs of thick, heavy teeth, up to 5 cm of which protrude from the gum, and which interlock when the mouth is closed. Killer Whales go about usually in small groups or packs, and include other warm-blooded animals in their food, showing a remarkable degree of group hunting co-ordination in obtaining it. This has led them to be described as ferocious. Of course, Killers are no more ferocious than any other carnivore and, when not feeding, can be remarkably gentle. Because of the pejorative sound of the name 'Killer' a movement has started to call the Killer Whale by the gentler name of 'Orca', a usage which has the sanction of the Oxford Dictionary. Killers, or Orcas, are found in all oceans, but mostly in the cooler waters, right up to the ice. The Killer Whale represents the top of the food chain in the sea, yet it is not a particularly abundant whale. The factors controlling its population size are quite unknown.

The False Killer Whale, *Pseudorca crassidens*, is clearly related to the Killer, but is quite different in appearance. It is a smaller dolphin, males reaching 5.6 m, females 5.0 m. It is more slender than the Killer and is black all over, apart from white speckling on the leading edge of the flipper. The dorsal fin is sickle-shaped, rather than triangular, and the flippers elongated and tapered. The snout is rather bulbous. The nine–eleven pairs of teeth in each jaw are similarly stout like those of the Killer Whale, but can be distinguished by being circular in cross-section, while those of the Killer Whale are oval. False Killer Whales are found worldwide except for the polar seas. They are notorious for their tendency to run aground *en masse*, with about 100–300 animals coming ashore in the bigger strandings. Up to 1927, the only British specimens of the False Killer Whale were three sub-fossil skeletons from the Fens, but, in that year, a school of 150 were stranded in the Dornoch Firth and, since that time, there have been several other strandings.

A third member of this group, the Pygmy Killer Whale, *Feresa attenuata*, was known only from a couple of skulls until 1950, when stranded specimens started to turn up. It is still not very well known, although several specimens have been maintained in captivity. It lives in tropical and warm temperate waters. Few specimens have been measured, but seven each of males and females measured in Japan were 214–244 cm and 208–227 cm in length respectively.

The only delphinid that regularly occurs in fresh water is the Irrawaddy Dolphin, *Orcaella brevirostris*. This is distributed from the Bay of Bengal to the waters around Indo-China, Indonesia and north Australia. Here it enters large rivers, and can live permanently in fresh water, but it is really a dolphin of the tropical seas. It is a relatively slow moving dolphin with a notably flexible neck, rather like the White Whale. The dorsal fin is small and rounded, the flippers long and paddle-shaped. There are twelve–nineteen pairs of teeth in both jaws. In colour it varies from slaty-grey to whitish.

The Electra Dolphin (or Melon-headed Whale), *Peponocephala electra*, is another warm-water dolphin in this sub-family. It was formerly regarded as very rare, but, like the Pygmy Killer Whale, there have been some large strandings, indicating that it is commoner than was once thought. However, very little is known of it. It seems to be darkly pigmented all over, with the exception of a white patch midway between the jaw and the flipper and an elongated white ventral area. The lower lip and around the eye may also be pale. The length seems to be in the region of 2.5–3.0 m.

The remaining genus of the Orcininae is *Globicephala*, the Pilot Whales. There are probably two species, *G. melaena*, the Long-finned Pilot Whale and *G. macrorhynchus*, the Short-finned Pilot Whale. The former occurs as two widely separated stocks in the cooler waters of both hemispheres. The southern form is sometimes referred to as *G. edwardii*. Pilot Whales are long slender dolphins with a spherical bulging 'forehead'. The dorsal fin is sickle-shaped and the flippers very long, up to one fifth of body length. The colour is black with a conspicuous white patch on the throat extending tailward a variable distance.

Males are considerably larger than females, which rarely reach more than 5 m, although males of up to 8.5 m are known. A 6 m pilot whale weighs about 2,900 kg. There are eight–ten pairs of teeth in both jaws with a diameter of less than 1.3 cm; the tooth rows are confined to the front of the jaws. Pilot Whales are very gregarious, occurring in huge schools of many hundreds. They are a migratory species, breeding in warm temperate waters and migrating polewards to feed. There have been many strandings on European and American coasts and a drive-fishery is still active in the Faroe Islands. Exploitation in the Southern Hemisphere appears to be very slight. The Short-finned Pilot Whale is found in the warmer waters between the two populations of its sister species. It is very similar, apart from its shorter flippers.

The sub-family Lissodelphininae contains the two species of Right Whale Dolphins, *Lissodelphis borealis*, the Northern Right Whale Dolphin, and *L. peronii*, the Southern form. The former occurs in the North Pacific Ocean while the latter is distributed circumpolarly in the sub-temperate waters just north of the Antarctic Convergence. They get their name from the absence of a dorsal fin, as in the right whales. These dolphins have a slender beak with about forty pairs of teeth in each jaw. The upper surface is black but there is a large white patch on the belly between the flippers and a long narrow streak of white extending from this around the vent to the root of the flukes. The under-surface of the flukes is white apart from a black basal part. There is a small white patch beneath the chin. The northern species grows to about 2.7 m; the southern is slightly smaller, about 1.8 m.

The next sub-family, the Cephalorhynchinae, contains four species, all in the same genus: Heaviside's Dolphin, *Cephalorhynchus heavisidii*, found off South Africa; the Black Dolphin, *C. eutropia*, along the coast of Chile; Hector's Dolphin, *C. hectori*, around New Zealand; and Commerson's Dolphin, *C. commersonii*, from the western South Atlantic and around some sub-Antarctic and Antarctic islands. These are all small dolphins, the largest of which reaches a length of about 1.8 m. There is a short and poorly defined beak and about thirty pairs of teeth in each jaw. All the *Cephalorhynchus* dolphins are patterned in black and white. Hector's Dolphin is dark above with a white ventral surface and a greyish zone between the two. A narrow belt of black connects the flippers ventrally. Commerson's Dolphin, a familiar and well-loved little dolphin to those using Stanley Harbour in the Falkland Islands, is more strikingly marked. The head and flippers are black although there is a triangular white patch on the chin. A broad belt of white encircles the trunk but the posterior part of the body is black, this colour extending forwards along the ridge of the back to include the rounded dorsal fin. There is also a small patch of black around the vent.

The remaining sub-family is the Delphininae which includes six genera. The genus *Delphinus* probably contains only one species, *D. delphis*, the Common Dolphin. This is found worldwide in temperate and tropical waters, both coastally and offshore. Although several morphologically distinct populations occur they can all be regarded as belonging to the same species. The Common Dolphin is one of the brightest of all the Cetacea. It is black above, or a very dark brown, with a white belly. There is a complicated pattern of alternating light and dark bands on the flanks and two waves of yellow and white intersect at the level of the dorsal fin. There is a dark circle around the eye and a tapering band from the base of the flipper to the side of the lower jaw. The beak is elongated and clearly separated from the rest of the head by a groove at its base. Males grow to 2.6 m and are a little larger than the females. This is one of the commonest, if not **the** commonest, of all marine mammals and is familiar to many on account of its habit of following ships at sea and swimming alongside or in front of them. It occurs in large schools (which may be mixed, or in some localities, age- and sex-segregated). The Common Dolphin has been the subject of an industry in the Black Sea, where as many as 120,000 were taken annually, but this has now ceased. Common Dolphins associate with Tuna and some thousands have been killed annually by being entangled in nets set to catch Tuna. Because they like to ride in ship's bow-waves, Common Dolphins are easily captured and have been maintained in oceanaria, but they cannot be trained as easily as some other dolphins.

The genus *Lagenorhynchus* contains at least six species, two of which occur in European waters. *L. albirostris*, the White-beaked Dolphin, is found throughout the North Atlantic from Greenland, south to France and Massachusetts, USA. It is a stoutish dolphin with a short beak. There are twenty-two–twenty-five pairs of teeth about 6 mm in diameter in both jaws. The beak, throat and belly are white while the 'forehead' and back to at least behind the fin are black or very dark brown: longitudinal white areas occur on the sides which may meet above the tail. The tail-stock, flukes and flippers are black. There is a black line from the base of the flippers to the corner of the mouth and a speckled area above and behind this. It grows to about 3.1 m. The White-beaked Dolphin is very gregarious and is often stranded on British coasts, usually on those bordering the North Sea.

The White-sided Dolphin, *L. acutus*, is another North Atlantic form, very common off the coast of Norway. There are thirty–forty pairs of slender teeth about 5 mm in diameter in both jaws. The snout, top of head and back are black, the belly white. The pigmentation on the sides does not extend ventrally so far as in the White-beaked Dolphin and the flippers are inserted in the white area. Flippers, flukes and chin are dark and there is a dark streak from the insertion of the flippers to the corner of the mouth. There is a broad oblique band of light brown on the flanks from the level of the dorsal fin to the end of the tail stock. It grows to about 3 m in length. This species is not so frequently stranded on British coasts as the White-beaked Dolphin.

The Dusky Dolphin, *L. obscurus*, is an inshore species with a circumpolar distribution around South America, South Africa, Kerguelen, southern Australia and New Zealand. The Hourglass Dolphin, *L. cruciger*, occurs in a similar range, but appears to be more pelagic. Peale's Dolphin, *L. australis*, is another coastal species found off South America and the Falkland Islands. *L. obliquidens* is the Pacific White-sided Dolphin, found only in the North Pacific ocean. It is easily captured alive and has been successfully maintained in oceanaria.

Fraser's Dolphin, *L.* (= *Lagenodelphis*) *hosei*, (named after Francis Fraser) was, until 1970, known only from a single skeleton from Sarawak. More recently it has been reported from the eastern and central tropical Pacific, Japan, Taiwan, eastern

Australia and South Africa. It is clearly another tropical dolphin and probably not very rare.

The Bottle-nosed Dolphin, *Tursiops truncatus*, is distributed in temperate to tropical waters everywhere. It is usually seen in small schools round the British coasts but in other localities can occur in large groups. There are twenty-two–twenty-five pairs of teeth in both jaws, each about 10–13 mm in diameter. There is a very distinct beak, from which it derives its name. It is coloured slate-grey and light brown above (although it appears darker when stranded). The throat and belly are white with a greyish zone above the insertion of the flippers and running back towards the vent. There is a streak of lighter colour from the base of the beak to the blow-hole. Flukes and flippers are dark. British specimens grow to about 3.7 m, but different populations reach different ultimate lengths. The Bottle-nosed Dolphin is the dolphin most commonly seen in captivity; it is easily captured and trained and even wild specimens have been known to associate with bathers and yachtsmen. Much of the research that has been done on cetacean physiology and behaviour has been done on this species.

The genus *Stenella* contains two clearly distinct species and a number of forms which are difficult to distinguish and together make up probably another two species. The Blue-white, Striped, or Euphrosyne Dolphin, *S. caeruleoalba*, occurs in most warm temperate and tropical seas around the world. It is uncommon around British coasts, with only three recorded strandings, all in the south-west, but is abundant in the Mediterranean. It is a small dolphin (to about 2.5 m) with a prominent beak. There are forty-three–fifty pairs of slender teeth (about 3 mm in diameter) in both jaws. It resembles the Common Dolphin but there is no yellow on the sides. There is a characteristic narrow stripe from the eye along the side to the vent, giving off two branches to the base of the flipper. The Striped Dolphin has been heavily exploited for human food in drive-fisheries in Japan.

The Spinner Dolphin, *S. longirostris*, is found in tropical waters of the Atlantic, Indian and Pacific Oceans, where there are separate well defined populations. These dolphins are called Spinners because of their habit of leaping from the water and spinning on their axis in mid-air before falling back—a very characteristic sight. Because they associate with Tuna schools, Tuna fishermen look out for Spinners and then set their purse-seine nets around the dolphins. The catch of Tuna is accompanied by a by-catch of Spinners, which become entangled in the nets and drown.

Spotted Dolphins (to which the names *S. dubia*, *S. frontalis*, *S. attenuata* and *S. plagiodon* have been applied) are found in nearly all coastal and offshore tropical seas and in some warm temperate areas of the North and South Atlantic also. They have long conspicuous beaks and the skin is patterned with many small, mostly elongated, pale spots on a darker ground. Like the Spinners, Spotted Dolphins are often associated with Tuna schools and suffer accordingly. In 1972, about 231,000 Spotted Dolphins and 55,000 Spinners perished in the Tuna fishery in the eastern tropical Pacific.

The last of the Delphininae is Risso's Dolphin, *Grampus griseus*. Unlike the other members of this sub-family, Risso's Dolphin lacks a beak. Indeed, it more nearly resembles a pilot whale, although the large dorsal fin is set further back. The head is bulbous and there are no teeth in the upper jaw but usually four on each side at the tip of the lower jaw. It is generally grey in colour but lighter on the head and belly. Usually the body is marked with long narrow white scratches, often in parallel rows of two or three. These may be caused by squid suckers. Risso's Dolphins are found in tropical and temperate waters everywhere and are not infrequently stranded on European and North American coasts. The most famous Risso's Dolphin was 'Pelorus Jack', who used to escort steam ships that crossed Cook Strait between the two main islands of New Zealand between 1888 and 1912. Anthony Alpers (1960) has written a charming account of this well loved (and legally protected) dolphin, but, apart from anecdote, little is known of this species.

The whalebone whales: sub-order Mysticeti

All mysticetes lack teeth (except as embryonic vestiges), possess baleen plates, have a symmetrical skull, paired external nasal openings, single-headed ribs, no sternal ribs, and a sternum composed of a single bone articulating with the first pair of ribs only.

There are three families with living representatives of the Mysticeti; the cetotheres formed a fourth family, but are now all extinct.

Right whales: family Balaenidae

This family comprises three species (Fig. 2.7). The Black Right Whale, *Balaena glacialis* (sometimes referred to as *Eubalaena glacialis*), is the most widely distributed, formerly being found in all the temperate waters of the world. Three sub-species have been described from the North Atlantic, North Pacific and Southern Oceans, but while these are effectively genetically isolated, since the whales do not enter tropical or north polar waters, it is not certain that they are distinct. These right whales are heavy-bodied creatures, growing to about 18.3 m in length (the female a little larger than the male). A specimen 17.1 m long weighed 67 tonnes. The head is enormous, making up about 25% of the length of the animal; there is a huge arched rostrum from which hang about 230 pairs of black baleen plates, usually about 2.5 m long. The top of the head carries the series of strange callosities known as the 'bonnet' and similar callosities may occur on the lower jaw and around the eye. Although basically black (or very dark grey) all over, there may be patches of white on the under-surface and these, like the callosities, vary individually, allowing individual right whales to be recognised by their pattern. Black Right Whales may be identified at sea by their lumbering progress, rarely exceeding 11 km per hour (6 knots) and often as little as 3.7 km per hour (2 knots) and by their characteristic V-shaped spout, separate plumes issuing from each nostril and rising obliquely to about 3–5 m above the surface. When the whale dives it 'flukes', showing its tail-flukes clear above the surface. Black Right Whales are migratory, moving to higher latitudes to feed but breeding in protected coastal waters. This has made them easy prey to whalers for many hundreds of years and the stocks are much reduced from what they once were.

The Greenland Right Whale, or Bowhead, *B. mysticetus*, is confined to the polar seas of the Northern Hemisphere. It resembles the Black Right Whale in many ways, but is perhaps a little larger (specimens of 20.6 m have been claimed). The baleen is larger, about 3 m or even up to 4.46 m, and more abundant, about 300 pairs. There are no callosities on the head, but there is a characteristic white patch beneath the chin. The Greenland Right Whale is one of the least known of the great whales. It has not been commercially hunted since the early years of this century but there is little if any evidence that its populations are recovering. Off Alaska the improvident natives are using modern equipment in what is claimed to be part of their cultural heritage to kill the last few remaining Bowheads.

The Pygmy Right Whale, *Caperea marginata*, is a very strange animal. It is found only in the Southern Hemisphere in waters north of the Antarctic Convergence but does not extend into the tropics. As its name implies, it is very small for a mysticete, growing to about 6.4 m. It has small narrow flippers and a small dorsal fin and possesses the distinction of being the cetacean with the greatest number of ribs—seventeen pairs. The 230–250 pairs of baleen plates are small, the largest reaching about 70 cm. Very little is known of Pygmy Right Whales. Sometimes they appear to associate with other whales, both whalebone and toothed. From the peculiar structure of its skeleton it has been suggested that it is a very deep diver and actually lies on the bottom (Davies and Guiler, 1957). What a filter-feeder like *Caperea* would do in such a situation, besides meditate, is not clear.

Grey Whales: family Eschrictiidae

This family contains only one species, the Grey Whale, *Eschrictius robustus* (also known as *E. gibbosus*, Fig. 2.7). This whale is in some respects intermediate between the right whales and the rorquals. It is also akin to the now extinct cetotheres. Its body is slender with a blunt but narrow snout. The rostrum is curved, but not arched to the same extent as in the right whales. There is no dorsal fin, but on the posterior part of the back is a series of up to ten low humps running towards the tail, something in the manner of a Sperm Whale. On its throat is a pair of short (about 1.5 m) grooves, rarely two pairs, which resemble the pleats of the rorquals. There are about 150 pairs of short (40 cm), thick

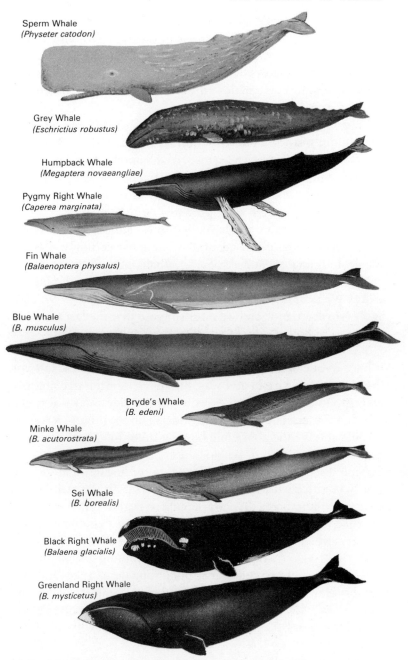

Sperm Whale
(Physeter catodon)

Grey Whale
(Eschrictius robustus)

Humpback Whale
(Megaptera novaeangliae)

Pygmy Right Whale
(Caperea marginata)

Fin Whale
(Balaenoptera physalus)

Blue Whale
(B. musculus)

Bryde's Whale
(B. edeni)

Minke Whale
(B. acutorostrata)

Sei Whale
(B. borealis)

Black Right Whale
(Balaena glacialis)

Greenland Right Whale
(B. mysticetus)

Fig. 2.7 Sperm Whale, Grey Whale, rorquals and right whales.

creamy-white baleen plates. The colour of the body, as its name suggests, is grey, but all adult specimens are mottled with white marks which may be the scars caused by the barnacles and whale-lice with which these whales are infested. Female Grey Whales grow to about 15 m, males to about 13 m. A 13.3 m female weighed 31.5 tonnes.

Grey Whales are now confined to the North Pacific Ocean, although in historic times they occurred in the North Atlantic. Sub-fossil skeletons have been recovered from the Low Countries and East Anglia and the sixty whales that were killed by Ohthere the Norwegian and his five companions in two days (or so he claimed to King Alfred) were probably Grey Whales. The 'Sand Loegja' referred to by the Icelander Jon Gudmundsson Laerde in the early seventeenth century was almost certainly a Grey Whale and, finally, Dudley's Scrag Whale, hunted on the coast of New England in the early eighteenth century was undoubtedly a Grey Whale. However, this is the last we hear of Grey Whales in the North Atlantic and we must suppose that the last few sur-vivors were boiled down for oil by the Yankee whalers.

The Grey Whale has fared a little better in the North Pacific. It once frequented the coasts of both the east and west sides of the North Pacific basin and was the subject of primitive hunting in Japan, Kamchatka and Siberia on one side, and down the North American coast to Baja California on the other. However, it could survive the aboriginal hunting quite well, but, when the right whale and sperm whale-hunters from New England and Europe discovered the Grey Whale's breeding grounds in the nearly land-locked Mexican lagoons in 1846, it seemed that its days were numbered. A vast slaughter began and the species declined rapidly. The hunt fell off around the beginning of this century, when a decline in the value of whale products, coupled with a shortage of available quarry made hunting uneconomical. There was a slight recrudescence of hunting in the 1920s and '30s but the Grey Whale has been protected from commercial hunting since 1947. This protection has resulted in a most encouraging recovery in numbers and the Grey Whale is one of conservation's success stories.

The Grey Whale has the convenient habit (convenient, that

is, to both hunters and whale-watchers) of making its regular migrations to and from the breeding lagoons very close in to shore. It was earlier known as *Rachianectes*, an appropriate name that signified, in Greek, 'the swimmer around the rocks'. (I recall deploring the abandoning of this beautiful name in favour of the guttural-sounding 'Eschrictius', and being sternly reproved for it by Francis Fraser, who pointed out that Eschrict's august status as a cetologist fully merited a whale being named for him.) '*Rachianectes*' has quite properly been abandoned on the grounds of the priority of *Eschrictius*, but Grey Whales still swim within a few hundred metres of the rocks of Point Loma above San Diego Bay where annually about 1 million visitors gather to watch the great whale migration. On the other side of the Pacific, things are less satisfactory for Grey Whales. The stock here was drastically overhunted, primarily by Japanese whalers, between 1899 and 1933 and this group is now considered extinct. The occasional Grey Whale that does show up in those waters is probably a straggler from the American side.

Rorquals: family Balaenopteridae

The remaining six species of mysticete whale are all grouped together in a single family, the Balaenopteridae, or rorquals. This name is derived from the old Norse 'rørhval', or 'grooved-whale', and refers to the pleats on the underside of the throat and chest. All these whales have a dorsal fin and pointed flippers, rather than the smooth backs and rounded flippers of the right whales. The lower jaw is conspicuously bowed outwards, and the upper jaw is flat, not arched upwards as in the right whales and, to a lesser extent, the Grey (Fig. 2.7).

There are two genera; the first, *Balaenoptera*, consists of five species of long, slender whales. The largest of these is the Blue Whale, or Sibbald's Rorqual, *B. musculus*. Although the length of these whales can exceed 30 m in the Southern Hemisphere, Blue Whales in the north tend to be smaller, females not usually exceeding 28 m or males about 24 m. Appropriately, the Blue Whale is a dark, slaty-blue in colour with a number of paler patches or mottlings on its flanks and belly. After a prolonged stay in cold water, the Blue Whale acquires a film of diatoms on its skin and, occasionally, these may be coloured a bright yellow, giving rise to the name 'Sulphur-bottomed Whale' which was once used, mostly by Americans. The dorsal fin is small (33 cm high) and set rather far back on the body. The throat grooves are about 5 cm deep and are separated by ridges about 5–7.5 cm wide; they number between fifty-five and eighty-eight and reach back almost to the umbilicus. The baleen plates are black all over, seldom more than 95–120 cm long and number 270–395 on each side. Blue Whales were formerly very common in the cooler and cold waters of both hemispheres (as with other rorquals, except Bryde's Whale, there are separate northern and southern stocks) and were often seen as migrants passing along the edge of the continental shelf off the Hebrides. Now, however, following the vast destruction of these stocks and the other large rorquals by the whaling industry (a story that will be told later in this book), Blue Whales are rare animals everywhere. Although now protected, no recovery has yet been detected and, in the North Atlantic, the only place where Blue Whales are seen at all regularly is in the western North Atlantic. Strandings seem always to have been rare, only four records on the British coast since 1913, all before 1923, but the model in the whale gallery at the British Museum (Natural History) in London is a plaster cast of a 25 m female Blue Whale that stranded at Wexford Bay in 1891.

A smaller kind of Blue Whale, known as the Pygmy Blue, and named *B. musculus brevicauda*, had been described from the waters around the Kerguelen Archipelago in the Indian Ocean. According to Harrison Matthews, it occurred also around South Georgia but had quite disappeared by the time I first visited there in 1953.

The next of the large rorquals is the Fin Whale, Common Rorqual or Razorback, *B. physalus*. Although smaller than the Blue Whale, Fin Whale females growing to 24 m and males a little less, the Fin Whale has a larger dorsal fin, which reaches a height of about 61 cm and is located slightly more than one third forward from the tail-flukes. The head is narrower than in the Blue Whale and more V-shaped, but has the same flat surface with the single head-ridge running forward from the blow-holes. The colouration of the Fin is characteristic and strangely asymmetrical. The body is dark grey to brownish-black, with none of the mottling shown by the Blue. Along the back, just behind the head, is a paler greyish-white chevron, the arms pointing down the back. The underside, including the ventral surface of the flukes and flippers, is white. On the head the dark colour reaches further down on the left than on the right side. The lower lip on the right, the mouth cavity and the anterior third to fifth of the baleen row on that side are yellowish white. The remainder of the baleen plates are striped with alternate bands of yellowish white and bluish grey. The largest are less than 92 cm long and they number 262–473 on each side. The ventral grooves (56–100 in number) extend to the navel or beyond. The hinder part of the body (anatomically the tail) has a marked acute ridge on the dorsal surface, hence the name Razorback. Like the Blue Whale, the Fin Whale has a worldwide distribution and several populations have been distinguished, all now much depleted. Nevertheless, it is a good deal commoner than the Blue and perhaps always was so. Certainly it was very much more frequently stranded on British coasts, mostly at the time of the migrations between the warm breeding grounds and the colder waters where they feed in the summer.

The Sei Whale, or Rudolphi's Rorqual, *B. borealis*, received its vernacular name (which is pronounced something between the English words 'sigh' and 'say') on account of its appearance off the Norwegian coast at the same time as the Coal-fish, called 'sei' in Norwegian. I have never heard anyone refer to it as Rudolphi's Rorqual, but the name goes on being repeated in the books, including this one. The Sei Whale is rather less slender than the Fin Whale, but has a similar sharply pointed snout. It grows to about 18.5 m, but usually averages about 15 m. The dorsal fin is relatively larger than in the Fin Whale and in fact may reach the actual dimensions of that of the larger whale. It is set at a greater angle (more than 40°) to the back and is more than one third forward from the flukes. The colour is dark grey on the back and sides and the posterior part of the ventral surface. The underside of both flipper and fluke is dark. The body often has an appearance that has been compared to that of a newly galvanised sheet of iron, because of the many scars that cover its surface. There is a region of greyish-white on the belly confined to the area of the ventral grooves. These are fewer than in the Blue or Fin, numbering about thirty-eight–fifty-six and end well before the navel. Sei Whale baleen is much finer than in any other rorqual—there are thirty-five–sixty fibres per cm in the fringe, all other rorquals having far fewer than this. The plates, which are up to 78 cm long, are uniformly black with a greyish fringe, though there may be a few small white plates at the front of the series. There are about 318–340 on each side. There is a single ridge on the top of the snout. The Sei Whale also has a cosmopolitan distribution, although it does not extend as far polewards as the Blue or the Fin, but may have a greater tendency to enter tropical waters. Although a relatively common whale in the North Atlantic it has only infrequently been stranded in the British Isles. Because of its relatively small size and low oil yield it was not so heavily persecuted in the early days of whaling. More recently, however, its excellent meat yield (Sei Whale meat is delicious) established a high demand in Japan, with consequent ill effects for the whales.

Bryde's Whale (pronounced 'Breuders'), *B. edeni*, was recognised as a separate species only in 1913. Unlike the other rorquals it is confined to warmer seas. In general appearance it is very similar to the Sei. It reaches about 14 m, is dark grey all over, although there may be a small area of lighter pigment on each side just forward of the dorsal fin. This is up to 45.7 cm tall, and often appears notched or frayed on the trailing edge. There are forty–fifty ventral grooves which are larger than those of the Sei, reaching at least to the navel. The baleen plates are very much shorter, only up to 42 cm long, and are slate-grey with coarse dark bristles. Bryde's Whale has the habit of approaching ships closely, so it is often possible to see the surface of the head, when a clear distinguishing feature becomes apparent—there are three ridges extending forward from the blow-holes, the central one, as in other rorquals, and two flanking it, one on each side of the nostrils. Bryde's Whale is distributed throughout tropical and sub-tropical waters of the world. Unlike the other rorquals it does not appear to undertake regular migrations between breeding and feeding grounds. However, its distribution may be greater than realised at present, as it is extremely difficult to distinguish from a Sei Whale at sea.

The final member of the genus is *Balaenoptera acutorostrata*, the Minke Whale, or Lesser or Piked Rorqual. Although the terms Lesser and Piked Rorqual were well established, they have now been virtually abandoned in favour of the Norwegian name 'Minke' (pronounced 'minkeh'). And this too is a replacement name—the old name in Norway was 'Vågehval'—the 'Bay Whale', but the whalers from the Antarctic renamed it after a whale-gunner named Meincke, who misidentified these tiny whales as Blues! Or so the story goes. Minkes are by far the smallest of the rorquals, reaching maximum lengths of about 9.1 m. They have an extremely pointed snout, triangular when viewed from above. They are generally black above and pure white below from the chin to the tail-flukes, including the flippers. There is a conspicuous diagonal white band across the middle third of the upper surface of each flipper. This distinguishing mark is very characteristic, but unfortunately it is often lacking in Southern Hemisphere specimens. The baleen plates, which reach only 21 cm in length, are all white, or yellowish white; they number 300–325 on each side. There are fifty–seventy ventral grooves which end short of the navel, often just behind the flippers. Minke Whales are the commonest of the rorquals and, although extensively hunted for their meat in recent years, it seems possible that, in the Antarctic at least, their numbers have increased as a result of the reduction of the larger rorquals, and the consequent lessened competition for food. Minke Whales often strand on British coasts and the pattern of stranding seems to indicate that they enter the North Sea round the north of Scotland. They are frequently seen in the voes of the Shetland Isles, where they are known as 'herring hogs'.

The remaining rorqual is sufficiently distinct from the other five to be placed in a separate genus. This is the Humpback Whale, *Megaptera novaeangliae*. This is a stout, thick-bodied whale with enormously elongated flippers, which reach nearly a third of the body length. The whole whale seems to exhibit a knobbly appearance, although in fact the knobs are confined to the short, broad snout, the chin and the sides of the lower jaw. However, the leading edge of the flippers and the trailing edge of the flukes are scalloped and very uneven and, as they are often conspicuous, since the whale is a notable acrobat, leaping out of the water and waving its flippers and flukes aloft, this adds to the knobbly appearance. The colour is basically black with a white patch of varying size on the belly and white on the under-surface of the flipper, which often creeps round the edge to appear above. The amount and pattern of white varies greatly from individual to individual, so that particular whales can be recognised from their patterns. There are 270–400 black to olive-brown (sometimes whitish) baleen plates up to 42 cm long on each side. There are only fourteen–twenty-two very wide ventral grooves which reach at least to the navel. Humpback Whales grow to about 16.2 m in length. They are nearly always infested with whale-lice and barnacles, mostly around the tubercles on the head and on the flippers. There is a very characteristic rounded projection just below the tip of the lower jaw, which also serves as a home for these fellow travellers. Humpback Whales are cosmopolitan with separate populations in the main ocean basins, where several stocks can be recognised. All have been severely depleted by whaling. The Humpback is a slow-moving whale whose migration path takes it close inshore, so, like the Grey Whales in the North Pacific, it was an easy quarry to unsophisticated whale-hunters. The early years of the great Antarctic whaling industry depended almost entirely on Humpbacks, which occurred in schools of hundreds around the ships of the pioneers. The Humpback formed a valuable catch, since its thick blubber rendered it remarkably rich in oil for its size.

3   Swimming and diving

The grace and power of a swimming dolphin or whale has to be seen to be appreciated. For how many centuries have sailors leaned over the sides of their ships to watch the dolphins gliding in the bow-wave, and effortlessly flicking away to take up another position? One can watch for hours and marvel at it, but there is a limit to the amount that we can learn from watching a living whale—for a true understanding of the mechanism whereby these animals have so elegantly solved the problem of moving through the water, we must combine observations on behaviour with anatomical and physiological studies.

We saw in Chapter 1 how whales, finding themselves in a medium both more buoyant and more viscous than air, had abandoned their conventional limbs, which acted against a solid substrate, in favour of newly evolved flattened pads of fibrous tissue, the flukes, which could be made to act against the water to provide a forward propulsive force. By simple observations, one can see that a whale swims by beating its tail up and down (a beat of surprisingly small amplitude, particularly when the whale is swimming fast), but this basic observation is capable of considerable refinement. We might start with a more detailed consideration of the flukes.

The flukes are basically horizontal planes, developed laterally on either side of the extreme end of the tail. They are of a rigid, yet somewhat elastic nature. When we come to consider the swimming movements in detail, we shall see that, in order to produce their propulsive force, the flukes have to change their angle of movement against the water—the angle of attack, as it is known—at different phases of the beat of the tail. This is achieved both by the structure of the flukes themselves and by the nature of their attachment to the tail-stock.

The flukes consist of an extremely tough and dense fibrous connective tissue, attached to the caudal vertebrae and surrounded by a ligamentous envelope extending from the tail-stock. External to this is a cutaneous layer that is not significantly different from that over the rest of the body, except that the blubber layer is almost completely absent (Felts, 1966). This structure is essentially paralleled in the dorsal fin, in those cetaceans which possess one, and provides area with little bulk, a perfect structure for a hydroplane. It is also ideal for heat dissipation. The core of the fluke serves to maintain the basic shape and this is done remarkably well. The toughness of this core is amazing. William Felts (1966) has pointed out that a cube cut out of the core can be hammered with a heavy mallet without losing its shape, while an entire whale may be suspended by a cable passed through holes cut in the flukes. The ligamentous envelope consists of bundles of fibres arranged so as to be tensed by, and hence to resist, bending in a dorsal or ventral direction. If a section is cut across a fluke, it can be seen that the virtually unstretchable ligaments have a pleated arrangement, there being fewer pleats in the dorsal layer than on the ventral side. This means that, when the fluke is raised upward (and we shall see later that this is the power stroke), only a slight extension of the ligaments is possible and the flukes maintain a flat profile, while on the downward recovery stroke the more ample pleats open up to allow the flukes to assume an upward curve, spilling water out laterally and offering less resistance (Fig. 3.1). In this very simple way the flukes are enabled to assume the functionally most efficient form solely as a result of their structure, the shape of the flukes adjusting automatically to the forces applied to them.

But, to achieve their function as propulsive organs, the flukes must be moved up and down, and this is done by movements of the tail, using the term in its strict anatomical sense as that part of the body posterior to the anus. In general, the body of a whale is a remarkably rigid structure compared with that of a terrestrial mammal. We have already seen how limited are the movements of the head, which (in most Cetacea) can do little more than nod slightly up and down and turn scarcely at all from side to side. The coalescence or marked anterior–posterior

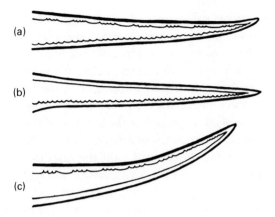

Fig. 3.1   Diagrammatic sectional view of the tail flukes of a dolphin: (a) in glide position, (b) during upward power stroke: the upper surface pleats have opened up to their fullest extent so further downward bending of the flukes is impossible and the pleats on the lower surface have closed up, (c) during downward recovery stroke: the lower pleats have opened up and the upper pleats have closed, allowing water to spill out laterally.

compaction of the cervical vertebrae leaves no functional neck, while the vertebrae of the trunk have very reduced articular surfaces in comparison with land mammals. Mobility in the entire axial skeleton is virtually confined to three points—a negligible one at the neck and two functionally highly important flexion zones, one at the base of the tail and one at the junction of the tailstock and the flukes. Slijper (1936) demonstrated this rather neatly with a small porpoise (Fig. 3.2), but the principle can be

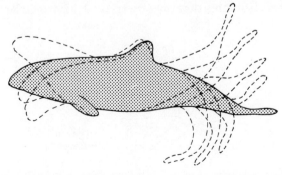

Fig. 3.2   Flexion zones in a porpoise to show the relative mobility of the various parts of the body. (After Slijper, 1936.)

67

verified by anatomical examination of larger whales, although these are a good deal less flexible than porpoises.

When a whale swims it moves its tail up and down, thus beating the tail-flukes against the water. Because it is bounded dorsally and ventrally by sharp, streamlined keels, the tail-stock itself applies little force to the water, so the power generated by the muscles is nearly all dispersed at the surface of the flukes.

If we examine the muscles that drive the tail, and hence the flukes, we can throw further light on the question of which is the power stroke in the cycle. A section cut through the root of the tail of a whale shows that the transverse processes of the caudal vertebrae divide the muscles into two major blocks. Those lying dorsal to the transverse processes—the epaxial musculature—are large and massive, while the hypaxial muscles, those ventral to the transverse processes, are less developed (Fig. 3.3). If we follow the muscle blocks forwards along the body we find that the epaxial muscles extend further forward and are attached by ligaments to all the spinal vertebrae, while the hypaxial muscles are attached to the spine only at the lumbar vertebrae, although there are other non-rigid attachments to the chevron bones and the ribs. It follows that it is contraction of the epaxial muscles that will drive the tail upwards, while contraction of the hypaxial muscles will bring it down again. If the muscles are dissected out we find that the epaxial muscles are about twice as heavy as those—the hypaxial muscles and some of the abdominal muscles—which bring the tail down.

It is clear from this that the power available from the two sets

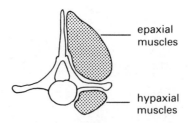

epaxial
muscles

hypaxial
muscles

Fig. 3.3   The arrangement of the axial musculature (the swimming muscles) which moves the tail in an upward direction, suggests that this is the power stroke.

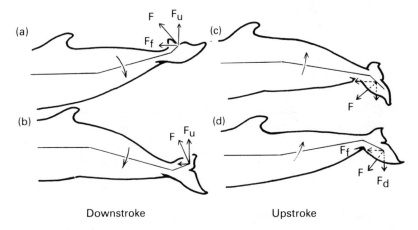

Fig. 3.4   The forces acting on the flukes of a swimming cetacean. The force F resulting from the resistance of the water to the movement of the flukes can be resolved into a forward force (F_f) and alternately upwardly and downwardly directed components (F_u and F_d).

of muscles is very different and we can designate the up-stroke as the power stroke, corroborating the evidence obtained from the structure of the flukes themselves. A power stroke and a passive recovery stroke is what we should expect—without the latter, the whale, which must rely on reciprocating movements rather than the revolution of a screw, would not proceed forward at all. Fig. 3.4 shows schematically the movements involved and the forces generated by the movement of the flukes against the water. These forces can be resolved into a forward thrust and an alternating up-and-down component.

The power that can be developed by large whales is immense. They can leap out of the water and have been known, when harpooned, to tow catcher boats of several hundred tonnes at a rate of 7.4–9.25 km per hr (4 or 5 knots). These stories are often exaggerated, of course; one hears of whales towing catchers with their engines going astern, although I cannot imagine any whale-gunner taking such a risk of the harpoon breaking out or the foreloper parting. The actual speed of a whale in the water is difficult to measure directly. A dolphin keeping pace with a ship may be stealing a ride in the ship's bow-wave. Whale-catchers often chase whales, but rarely have any accurate means of recording their speed. Large rorquals cruise at about 9.25 km per hr (5 knots) or less, but when alarmed can make off at speeds of 26–27.7 km per hr (14 to 15 knots) and can sprint at around 37 km per hr (20 knots) for short distances (Gawn, 1948). The Sei Whale, a slender and very muscular animal, has been reported to travel at as much as 64.7 km per hr (35 knots) for a short burst.

When a whale breaches clear of the water one can calculate the exit velocity it must have attained to reach its observed height. A dolphin jumping about 5.5 m above the surface would need to be travelling at about 10.5 m per sec (20 knots) just before it left the water (Lang, 1966).

The fact that dolphins, which are so very much smaller than large rorquals, are able to reach comparable speeds in the water, had puzzled mechanically minded naturalists and biologically minded marine architects for many years. The speed of a conventional ship in the water is quite closely related to the waterline length of the vessel—in rough terms, the maximum steaming speed in knots is about 2.7 times the square root of the waterline length in metres (or 1.5 times the square root in feet). Increasing the power of the engines will make very little difference to the ultimate speed—the extra power applied will be dissipated in increased turbulence around the hull or propeller. Because of this, it seemed logical to suppose that the smaller (shorter) dolphin would swim very much more slowly than the massive rorqual, yet such is clearly not the case. We need to look into this question of turbulence more closely. When a body moves through a fluid, the fluid particles nearest to it are drawn along with the body, creating a resistance known as *drag*. Layers of fluid further from the body are less affected until, at a distance from the body, the fluid is undisturbed. If the shape of the body is suitable, and the velocity not too great, the layers will glide over one another smoothly. This condition is known as *laminar flow*. As the speed of the body increases, so the drag on the fluid becomes greater and the layers can no longer glide evenly. Further increase in velocity causes eddies to form and *turbulent flow* results. The turbulence absorbs a great deal of energy, thus increasing the drag. The retarding effect of turbulence increases as the eddies occur nearer to the front end of the moving body. Streamlining creates flow-lines that push the turbulence to the rear.

The calculation of drag is complicated and depends on the viscosity of the medium, the velocity of the body and its surface area. Shape is also important and this is where the length of the moving body comes in, in a parameter known as Reynold's number. This is the product of the velocity of the body and its length divided by the vicosity of the medium. Frictional drag decreases as Reynold's number increases and the rate of decrease is much faster for laminar than for turbulent flow.

The fact that small dolphins and large rorquals can swim at about the same speed seemed anomalous, since the Reynold's number for a Blue Whale would be much greater than for a Common Dolphin. Either the Blue Whale was not using its available power or the dolphin had a surprisingly large power output.

Experiments done with a model of a dolphin towed at various speeds (Gray, 1948) in fact indicated that, to maintain the observed speeds of living dolphins, the animal's tail muscles would have to develop about ten times as much power as the muscles of more conventional mammals. As this was unlikely, the proposition became known, rather unfairly, as Gray's Paradox. Harrison Matthews, in his incisive way, remarked that it was not a paradox, but a fallacy. Gray had made his experiments on dolphin locomotion with a model of a dolphin and was well aware that the results might not truly represent what would occur with a living dolphin in the ocean.

The paradox was based on the assumption that the movement of the dolphin through the water would produce turbulence and herein lies the fallacy. Turbulence, all-important in ship design, has been eliminated in the dolphin. A condition of laminar flow exists over its surface and the power requirement for high-speed propulsion is dramatically reduced.

How is this achieved? Obviously, the streamlined form of the dolphin helps greatly (dolphins had 'bulbous bows' long before super-tankers did) but this cannot be the whole story, for Gray's rigid dolphin models, which generated turbulence, had the same shape as their living counterparts. A series of beautifully executed models in the Whale Gallery, British Museum (Natural History),

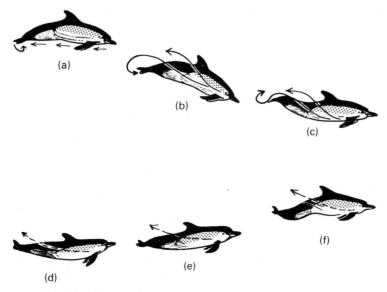

(a)

(b)

(c)

(d)

(e)

(f)

Fig. 3.5   Water flow over the body of a swimming dolphin. For explanation see text.

in London (reproduced here in Fig. 3.5), based on the work of Peter Purves (1963), explains how this is done. A stationary dolphin lies nearly horizontal in the water; when the tail is moved upwards by the epaxial musculature, water is forced from the upper to the lower surface of the flukes. As this water flow is unable to pass easily over the sharp trailing edge of the flukes, turbulence is set up and a vortex is formed (Fig. 3.5a). Continued upward movement of the flukes creates an area of low pressure on their under-side, the blades of the flukes bend down in an angle of attack and water is drawn from the surface of the head and chest. As a result the dolphin moves forwards and downwards against the hydroplaning action of the flippers (Fig. 3.5b).

Once forward (and downward) movement is established, further upward action of the flukes accelerates water obliquely over the body, past the faired edge of the back behind the dorsal fin, and the vortex at the trailing edge of the flukes is washed away (Fig. 3.5c).

The dolphin has now reached its maximum velocity on that

power stroke and the flukes have reached their greatest elevation. Their blades relax and adopt a glide position parallel with the line of motion (an automatic adjustment, as we have seen) and offer negligible resistance to the water (Fig. 3.5d).

The recovery muscles now pull the tail downwards, the movement receiving some assistance from the shape of the hydrofoil cross-section of the flukes. The flukes begin to curl upwards and spill water sideways instead of accelerating it to the rear. The buoyancy of the oil-rich head and the chest causes the anterior part of the body to rise (Fig. 3.5e). The front part continues to rise while the tail descends at about half the rate of the up-stroke; the flukes still curl upwards and the water flow over the rear of the body remains as it was during the power stroke, although without positive acceleration (Fig. 3.5f).

At the end of the recovery stroke, the position of the animal and the attitude of its tail is approximately as it was at the beginning of the power stroke. The flukes are still curled upwards but will change to the angle of attack as the power stroke begins.

This account seems complicated enough, but it in fact represents a simplification of what occurs in the living dolphin and, as far as we know, the process is basically similar in other Cetacea, although probably, in the large rorquals, laminar flow does not exist over so great a part of the body as in the dolphin—perhaps only over the anterior two thirds, whereas, in the dolphin, 90% of the flow might be laminar (Purves, 1963). Clearly, the properties of the water flow over the body are too complex to be studied with a rigid model in a constant water stream. Living animals, dye-markers, neutral-buoyancy beads, cinematography and a host of other devices have all played a role in elucidating the swimming process. Turbulence is actively avoided by washing away vortices formed by the swimming movements, and by avoiding their formation as the body moves through the water. Streamlining is of course very important in this. We noted earlier how all unnecessary projections had been eliminated from the cetacean body and the role of the blubber is very important here.

The skin and blubber are firm, but not totally rigid. It was noticed that, when a dolphin was accelerating (or decelerating) fast, or changing direction rapidly, transverse corrugation or folds at right-angles to the direction of movement would appear transiently on the surface of the body (Essapian, 1955). These marked areas where the pressure of the water at the surface of the body differed and thus represented incipient areas of turbulence. However, instead of turbulence developing, as would be the case in a rigid-hulled ship, the surface of the dolphin responded to the pressure differences by altering its shape, eliminating the turbulence even as it formed. When the dolphin is moving fast, the folds remain stationary, indicating that the pressure differences are constant, and they slope backwards.

It is possible that cetaceans have yet another way of reducing drag—they may even lubricate their passage through the water. For a long time it has been known that many fish secrete a very fine film of mucus as they swim. The mucus consists of large complexly shaped molecules and there is evidence that these can be deformed in the pressure differences in the turbulent vortices, thus dissipating large amounts of energy. The addition of traces of synthetic substances of high molecular weight, e.g. polyethylene oxide, can greatly increase the swimming speed of fish and the only logical explanation of this is that it reduces their drag. The skin of whales produces no mucus, but Harrison and Thurley (1972) showed, under the electron microscope, that the superficial layer of cells, instead of being flattened keratinised scales as in most mammalian skin, retained their nuclei almost to the surface and some of the cells appeared to contain oily droplets. Harrison concluded that the superficial cells were continually being shed into the water and it is possible that they and the oil droplets they would have released, might cause a reduction in drag, just as the mucus of a fish does.

The swimming movements of dolphins that I have described can be easily observed at an oceanarium where one can obtain clear views, both from above and, where underwater viewing windows are provided, from the side. As the dolphins circle their pool one can see the movements of the tail, the bending of the flukes in the power and recovery strokes, and even the tiny adjustments of the flippers that change the direction of swimming. From a ship, however, watching dolphins in the bow-wave, the picture is very different. For long periods a dolphin may position itself in the bow-wave, apparently motionless, yet effortlessly keeping pace with the ship. An American biologist, Alfred Woodcock, took the trouble to time dolphins free-riding in this way. He found that a dolphin in the bow-wave kept pace with a ship moving at 18.5 km per hr (10 knots) without any perceptible movement of the tail-flukes, while other dolphins, only a little further away, had to beat their tails vigorously to keep up.

How do dolphins manage to hitch free lifts in this way? The bow of a ship as it moves forward through the water creates just ahead of it and to its sides a field of positive pressure. The bow-wave that we see running away from the stern of the vessel as it cleaves the water is the release of this pressure field at the surface. If a dolphin positions itself so that its flukes lie in the pressure-field, thrust will be developed on them (recalling that the normal swimming movements depend on pressure differences generating thrust on the surface of the flukes) and the dolphin will be propelled forwards.

This method of bow-wave riding is most obvious when the dolphins are positioned a couple of metres or so beneath the surface and can be observed through a calm surface. A rather different state of affairs arises in the bow-wave itself. Here, water is being displaced by the ship's passage and welling upwards. As the wave moves forwards and outwards the water at its crest is moving fastest; if the speed of the wave is sufficient this faster moving water overtakes the water beneath it, the crest rolls over and the wave breaks. A dolphin that positions itself in the face of such a wave, with its flukes in the crest so that the forward velocity of the water acts on their underside will be propelled forwards (Fig. 3.6).

Scholander (1959) in America had tested the theory of this by suspending a hydrofoil, analogous to the dolphin's flukes, attached to a dynamometer, in the bow-wave of a ship and calculating the thrust developed. He found that at a critical angle (about 28° when the ship was moving at 14.8 km per hour [8 knots]) a strong forward thrust was developed, while at other inclinations drag was produced. Theoretical objections to this hypothesis of wave riding were developed (Hayes, 1959) on the

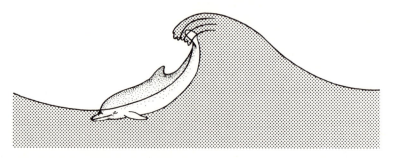

Fig. 3.6 A dolphin riding at the surface of a bow-wave. (After Backhouse and Smart, 1961.)

grounds that the dolphin would be unable to maintain equilibrium on the face of the wave and would be toppled tail-over-
head. Backhouse and Smart (1961), who were able to watch
porpoises riding in the bow-waves of fast-moving naval vessels,
pointed out that the animal would be able to use its fore-flippers
as hydroplanes to generate sufficient lift to prevent the forward
end of the body being driven into the water and the porpoise
tumbling over.

In both these cases, the dolphin or porpoise uses the pressure
of water on its flukes to drive itself forwards, just as it does when
it swims in the ordinary manner. Bow-wave riding is dependent
on the presence of ships and must thus be a recent development
(in evolutionary terms) in cetacean locomotion. However, dolphins can ride on the face of ordinary ocean waves. This is not
often observed—conditions that generate suitable waves are not
conducive to observation—but may be commoner than we
presently believe. Additionally, the great sensitivity of cetaceans to
pressure changes in the water enables them to take advantage
of small pressure differences. Small dolphins have been observed
getting a free ride in the pressure field generated by a larger com-
panion (Norris and Prescott, 1961) and the process may be important in enabling a young whale to keep in touch with its mother.

Whales use their highly developed swimming skills for a variety
of purposes, which range from large-scale migratory movements
to the meticulous positioning which must accompany courtship

in marine mammals. However, their most commonplace activities are breathing and feeding. The first requires the whale to be at the surface, while the second may require the whale to search at various depths. In consequence it is important that a whale can dive and surface again. For some whales, those that typically feed in or near the surface layer, such as the Common Dolphin, it is sufficient for them to adapt their normal locomotory movements so that they swim down to dive and up to surface, using their flippers as hydrofoils to alter their rate of descent or ascent. The larger rorquals, having relatively smaller flippers, aid their action by flexion of the whole body. If one watches a Fin Whale surface and dive again while travelling moderately fast, one sees first the snout appear, then the blow-hole (when the whale immediately breathes), then the loom of the back which seems to roll forward in the water as the whale directs its broad head downwards (Fig. 3.7). The whale then flexes the hinder end of the body, at the pelvic flexion zone, so that the flukes are sufficiently deep to have purchase for the final dive when, with an upward power

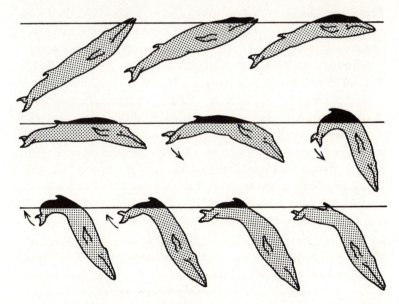

Fig. 3.7   A Fin Whale surfacing to breathe. The arrows indicate the direction of beat of the flukes. (After Gunther, 1949.)

77

stroke, the whale dips under and disappears. The last to go is the very tip of the dorsal fin.

This at last explains the function of this relatively insignificant structure. Early writers on whales had supposed the dorsal fin acted as a stabiliser against rolling, like the fin of an aircraft, but it is hard to see how such a small area could have any effective stabilising force on a body as bulky as that of a large rorqual. In fact, the dorsal fin acts to conduct away the vortex that is formed at the whale's back as it leaves the water–air interface. The humps on the back of Sperm and Grey Whales probably act in a similar way. Right whales, which lack dorsal fins, do not flex the back markedly as they dive and are in any case much slower swimmers than the rorquals and dolphins.

Rorquals can dive deeply, as evidence from harpooned whales shows, but they probably rarely do so when undisturbed and have no special modifications for doing so. Two groups of odon-tocetes, however, the Sperm Whale (and its smaller cousin, *Kogia*), and the Bottle-nosed Whales, *Hyperoodon*, both feed mainly on squid which they seem to obtain from great depths. The Sperm Whale, and perhaps to a lesser extent the others also, has developed a very complicated and ingenious method of diving and ascending again with the expenditure of very little energy.

Without doubt, the most remarkable thing about the Sperm Whale is its all-but incredible head. In a large bull, the head can make up a quarter of the length of the whale and more than a third of its weight. The vast chariot-shaped skull supports what the old whalers called the junk and the case—both oil-rich tissues, the latter a sort of cistern from which the oil can be bailed out. The spermaceti oil is peculiar. Unlike most animal oil, including the oil that is obtained from the blubber and bones of a rorqual, it is not a simple triacyl glyceride but a complex mixture of waxes (esters of higher fatty alcohols with higher fatty acids) and tri-glycerides. Above 30°C it is a clear straw-coloured liquid, but below that temperature it becomes cloudy and eventually sets to a rather soapy crystalline solid.

The case and the junk between them constitute the spermaceti organs (and a similar, but less complex organ containing sperma-ceti is found in *Kogia* and *Hyperoodon*), and, on the basis of its great size, both absolutely and relatively to the Sperm Whale's body, this must be an organ with a highly important function in the life of the Sperm Whale. Anatomists have argued about what this function is for many years and it is only recently that Malcolm Clarke, a biologist at the Marine Biological Association's laboratories at Plymouth, UK, in a series of three papers (Clarke, 1978a–c), has elucidated its role. The spermaceti organ has as its main purpose the regulation of buoyancy so that the whale can adjust its vertical position in the water column.

To find the squid on which it preys, a large Sperm Whale dives to great depths. Sperm Whales have been observed by sonar to go below 2,250 m and even deeper descents have been deduced from the presence of fresh specimens of bottom-dwelling sharks in the stomach of a Sperm Whale which was shot in an area where the depth of water was in excess of about 3,200 m (Clarke in Wood, 1972). Not all Sperm Whales go as deep as this, of course; the mean dive depth for all sizes of Sperm Whales tracked by sonar by Christina Lockyer (1977) was between 315 and 360 m, while the mean duration was about 10½ minutes. The largest whales observed dived to 1,100 m and spent periods of up to an hour below the surface.

Sperm Whales dive to hunt (animals shot on surfacing often have fresh food in their stomachs) but a characteristic and peculiar feature is that they generally reappear at the surface in nearly the same position as when they dived. This implies that the whale probably spends a large part of its time beneath the surface hanging motionless, waiting for the passing squid to come within range of its formidable jaw.

Now a Sperm Whale could not hang motionless in the water unless it had neutral buoyancy at that particular depth. If it were positively buoyant it would rise, and if it were negatively buoyant it would sink still further. One might assume that a Sperm Whale is always positively buoyant, since dead Sperm Whales float at the surface. A positively buoyant whale would have to swim to descend, using its flippers as hydrofoils to adjust its angle of descent, and would have to continue swimming movements to maintain its vertical position at a chosen depth, which would almost certainly lead to the whale moving horizontally, making

79

it unlikely that it would surface near the same place. Were a whale negatively buoyant, the same would apply, but in the opposite sense. However, if a Sperm Whale could adjust its buoyancy, it could sink or ascend, or hang motionless in the water, without swimming actions of its tail and at little energy cost.

The problem of matching its buoyancy to the water around it is not a simple one, since the whale would need to adjust continually to changing pressure as the depth increased and to changing temperature, which in the sea does not usually change evenly with depth.

Could the spermaceti organ act as a buoyancy controller? It is an observable fact that spermaceti oil changes its physical condition as it cools and congeals. This crystallisation is a gradual process because of the complexity of the mixture of waxes and fats in spermaceti, but as it takes place the spermaceti contracts and becomes denser. Malcolm Clarke had samples of spermaceti at differing temperatures subjected to varying pressures and their densities accurately determined. He found that the density increase on cooling was faster at greater pressures (Fig. 3.8). The

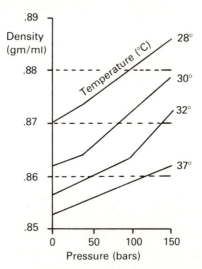

Fig. 3.8   Variations in the density of spermaceti oil at different pressures and temperatures. Density increases with cooling and also with pressure. Each additional depth increase of 10 m increases the pressure by 1 atmosphere. The density increase on cooling is fastest at the greatest pressure. (After Clarke, 1978.)

greater the density of the spermaceti, of course, the less sea-water it displaces, so the less its buoyancy. Because of the great quantity of spermaceti present (a 30-tonne whale may have 2.5 tonnes of spermaceti in its head) a variation of temperature of only a few degrees would provide a sufficient change in density for a whale to regulate its buoyancy as it dives.

The key to buoyancy control would thus seem to lie in the Sperm Whale's ability to control the temperature of its spermaceti organ. In order to understand how this may be done we need to examine the anatomy of the Sperm Whale head. This is a peculiarly difficult thing to do in practice. As mentioned earlier, the structure we might set out to dissect is gargantuan. In a big Sperm Whale it might weigh 16 tonnes or so—about the same weight as three African Elephants together. Early anatomists were tempted to use small Sperm Whale foetuses for their investigations, as they were a good deal easier to handle, but the full proportions of the spermaceti organ do not develop early in foetal life, so this approach left something to be desired. Malcolm Clarke, however, persuaded the bone-saw man at a whaling station to use his 5 m-bladed steam saw to cut the entire head of a Sperm Whale into sections 20 cm thick. From these sections, and a host of other investigations, he was able not merely to describe the anatomy of the head, but also to explain its function.

The snout contains the spermaceti oil arranged in two ways. Above is the roughly bullet-shaped case, a thick tough fibrous tissue surrounding a great mass of oily spermaceti tissue (Fig. 3.9). Beneath the case lies the junk which is composed of a series of trapezoidal blocks of spermaceti tissue separated by blocks of fibrous tissue. The junk is roughly coffin-shaped. Within and around the spermaceti organ run the nasal passages, which are certainly the most complex to be found in the whole mammalian series. The Sperm Whale's single blow-hole lies somewhat to the left of the tip of its snout and communicates with both nasal passages *via* a short common chamber. The left nasal passage runs back from this chamber, curves to pass on the left side of the spermaceti organ and enters the skull just in front of the brain case. The right nasal passage is quite different. Initially it runs

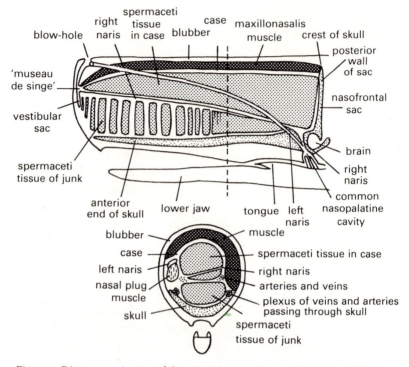

Fig. 3.9 Diagrammatic view of the arrangement of parts of the Sperm Whale's head important in buoyancy control.

forward, then widens out to form a flattened sac at the extremity of the snout, from which arises a broad flat tube which passes back through the lower part of the case to meet the left nasal passage as a narrow tube just in front of the brain case. Just before this junction the right nasal passage gives off dorsally a large sac, the naso-frontal sac, which lies against the crest of the skull. In a large Sperm Whale the part of the right nasal passage lying against the case may be more than a metre wide and its total length through the head may be more than 5 m.

The right nasal passage will thus be well adapted to act as a heat exchanger if a mechanism exists to pass water through it. Naturally, the whale cannot 'breathe' water through its nostrils while submerged, so some other form of irrigation is required. This exists in the form of a large muscle, the maxillonasalis, which runs from the crest of the skull to the tip of the case. By

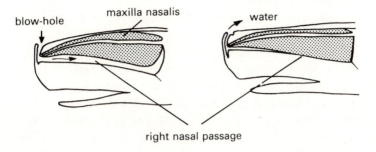

Fig. 3.10   The arrangement of the nasal passages of the Sperm Whale.

its contraction, the maxillonasalis would raise the forward end of the case, thus expanding the flattened tube of the right nasal passage which, if the blow-hole were open, would fill with water as far as the nasofrontal sac (Fig. 3.10). Relaxation of this muscle would expel the water again. An alternative, and anatomically feasible, method would be for the water to be drawn in *via* the left nasal passage and expelled *via* the right, but this seems less likely. The admission of sea-water over the potential heat exchange surface of the right nasal passage would certainly lower the temperature of the spermaceti.

An additional, and more conventional, method of heat exchange is *via* the skin, which is how whales normally regulate their internal temperature. The tissues that surround the spermaceti organ have a dense network of capillaries supplied with blood by large arteries that enter the snout from the rear. These arteries are surrounded by veins which form a counter-current heat exchanger (p. 28). This system will allow the spermaceti tissue to be cooled by exchanging heat from the warmer incoming arterial blood and the cooler outgoing venous blood. This system can maintain a temperature gradient between the snout and the rest of the body so that the spermaceti organ is normally below 34°C as opposed to the 37°C of the rest of the body. Heat can be lost through the skin of the head, either by passive conduction or a more active process in which the circulation of blood to the dermal papillae is speeded up. There is no evidence that the Sperm Whale has a capacity for localised vaso-dilation so that heat is lost only from the head and not from the rest of the body surface, but it is quite possible that the head can 'blush' independently of the rest of the animal.

Malcolm Clarke calculated the rate of heat exchange that would be possible if the whale used these two methods and found that, using both together, a Sperm Whale could adjust to neutral buoyancy in less time than it normally takes to swim to a depth of 500 m. In a dive from 200 m to 1000 m, exchanging heat *via* the snout skin alone, neutral density would be reached in 5 minutes, while, if both snout skin and the right nasal passage were used, the interval would be shortened to 3 minutes.

Exactly what happens when the Sperm Whale dives is still a matter of speculation, of course. We suppose that, as the whale descends, its spermaceti is cooled by vaso-dilation of the head skin and by irrigating the right nasal passage with water. When it has reached the desired depth, further loss of heat through the skin is prevented by constricting the arterioles to the skin papillae. Minor adjustments of buoyancy could be made by admitting small amounts of water into the right nasal passage, or by slight increases of the rate of flow of warm arterial blood into the spermaceti tissue.

Activity during the course of the dive would cause heat to accumulate in the trunk muscles; a rise of only $2°C$ would be sufficient to store all the heat necessary to bring the spermaceti back to its normal temperature of $33°C$, liquefying the wax and restoring its buoyancy. This means that a Sperm Whale which has exhausted itself chasing squid at the bottom of its dive has only to shunt the heat from its muscles to its spermaceti organ to become positively buoyant and rise passively to the surface with no extra expenditure of energy. It is not suggested that Sperm Whales normally exhaust themselves in the course of a dive— indeed they seem to be surprisingly inactive—but the advantage of such a mechanism to a diving animal is obvious.

This story of the spermaceti organ is one of the strangest that has been put forward in the whole history of cetology. It is supported by careful anatomical research and by the fit of the many calculations that Malcolm Clark made. Other theories have been put forward to explain the function of the spermaceti organ, but none has been so carefully validated as Malcolm Clarke's. Nevertheless, it is entirely possible that so complex an organ can serve more than one function (consider, for example, the relatively simple human tongue which assists with mastication and swallowing, bears the taste organs, enables us to speak and serves a not inconsiderable role in courtship) and we must not assume that, because the spermaceti organ acts as a biological ballast tank, it cannot, for example, act also as an acoustic lens in sound production (p. 134).

If a mammal is to undertake prolonged dives it must modify the normal mammalian breathing pattern. A man breathes about 15 times a minute and if his breathing is interrupted for more than about a minute or so he is in distress. Even experienced pearl and sponge divers cannot hold their breath for more than $2\frac{1}{2}$ minutes or so. Other mammals do rather better, particularly those that have adopted an aquatic habit—the Platypus can remain under water for about 10 minutes, the Musk Rat for 12, the Hippopotamus for 15 and the Beaver for 20. Some of the large seals, for example the Elephant Seal, can exceed this, but with these animals we are encountering modifications to facilitate diving that rival those of the whales.

Amongst the Cetacea, Sperm Whales and Bottle-nosed Whales are the most accomplished divers—the former being able to stay beneath the surface for 90 minutes (although, as we have seen, usually for much less) and the latter for an astonishing 120 minutes (Slijper, 1962). Rorquals rarely dive for more than 40 minutes whereas the Bottle-nosed Dolphin dives for 13–15 minutes and the Common Dolphin for only $1\frac{1}{2}$–3 minutes.

Cetaceans in general have developed a pattern of intermittent breathing, where the normal respiratory rhythm is interrupted by lengthy periods when no breath is taken—apnoea. How the whale manages to survive these periods of apnoea and carry out the necessary exchange of oxygen and carbon dioxide during the periods of breathing has excited much physiological interest.

The lung capacity of a large rorqual is great—about 2000 l in the case of a 22 m Fin Whale (Scholander, 1940)—but relative to the size of the whale this is not greatly different from the normal mammalian situation. In fact, if we compare the ratio of lung capacity to body weight we find that some whales (like rorquals and bottle-nosed whales) have substantially less, and others (like the Harbour Porpoise and Bottle-nosed Dolphin) have rather more, than conventional terrestrial mammals like man, or a horse. Whales can, however, ventilate their lungs more effectively than land mammals, up to 90% of the total capacity of the lung being exchanged at each breath (in terrestrial mammals, the tidal volume is usually between 10 and 15%). How this is achieved is not certain, but it seems likely that the very oblique diaphragm (which is a feature of seals as well as whales) and the nature of the attachment of the ribs to the sternum may facilitate this. It is important to remember that, lying at the surface of the water, the whale is effectively weightless, so the elastic recoil of the walls of the thorax after emptying the lungs will not be hindered by the weight of the ribs and chest muscles themselves. A whale out of the water, on the other hand, obviously has great difficulty in breathing.

When a whale surfaces after a dive it immediately spouts. This is an expiration (which sometimes begins even before the whale's blow-hole has quite reached the surface) and is the release of the lungful of air that the whale carried down on its dive.

The spout of a whale is often the only indication one gets of whales at sea and, to a skilled eye, the spout can tell much about the whale that made it. Most of us might hope to learn to distinguish the oblique forward spout of the Sperm Whale from the twin bushy spouts of the Right Whale, or either from the tall plume of the Fin. But telling the spout of a Blue Whale from that of a Fin, or either from a Sei, would be a task for a skilled whale-gunner and they are becoming a vanishing race.

The nature of the spout itself has been the subject of a lot of misinformation. Early prints of whales usually showed a fountain of water gushing from their brows, but I can scarcely believe that there ever was a period when sailors who encountered whales at sea were unaware of the fact that what they saw was a cloud of condensed vapour, much as their own breath steamed on a frosty morning. Whale spouts, of course, are visible in the tropics, so we cannot postulate a frosty morning to account for the visibility of the blow. However, there will nevertheless be a cooling

86

1 Indo-Pacific Humpbacked Dolphin (*Sousa chinensis*)

2 Bottlenosed Dolphin (*Tursiops truncatus*)

3 Common Dolphin (*Delphinus delphis*)

4   Killer Whale (*Orcinus orca*)

5   Minke Whale (*Balaenoptera acutorostrata*)

6 Fin Whale (*Balaenoptera physalus*)

7 Sperm Whale (*Physeter catodon*)

8 Pilot Whale (*Globicephala sp.*)

9 Sperm Whale (*Physeter catodon*)

10   Southern Right Whale (*Balaena glacialis*)

11   Beluga (*Delphinapterus leucas*)

12 Grey Whale (*Eschrictius gibbosus*)

13 Eskimo towing Whale

14   Narwhal (*Monodon monoceros*)

effect caused by the adiabatic expansion of the exhaled air as it is released from pressure in the lungs, and this is sufficient to cause the condensation of droplets from the saturated vapour. It is true that sometimes a little water will be carried up with the blow— when a whale blows close alongside a ship, drops may patter down on the deck—but this is only the water that lies about the blow-hole as the whale surfaces. Recently it has been suggested that the whale's blow may contain minute droplets of oil from the oily foam that fills the complex system of sinuses in the head (p. 115). This is possible and certainly the blow of a whale has an oily stench to it. Such oil droplets might serve as condensation nuclei for the water droplets produced by the cooling.

But to return to the respiratory pattern. The spout on surfacing is immediately followed by an inspiration, after which there is a pause, then another blow and inspiration, and so on. A Fin Whale, for example, takes about 5–20 breaths at a frequency of one a minute, between dives. Christina Lockyer (1977) found that Sperm Whales swimming quietly at the surface blew 4–7 times per minute while, after a 16½ minute dive at 10.6 m, a cow Sperm Whale, accompanied by a 4.3 m calf, blew 5 times a minute. The small calf, which surfaced with its mother, blew 9 times a minute. A 16.1 m Sperm bull blew at 2 blows a minute after a short dive of less than 5 minutes, but after a 29-minute dive blew at 10 blows a minute for nearly 11 minutes. As the old whalers knew, the whale must 'have his spoutings out' and the significance of this

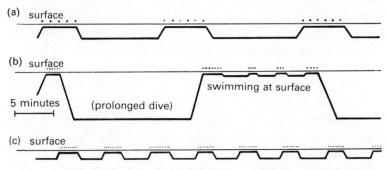

Fig. 3.11   Diving profiles of: (a) Fin Whale, (b) Sperm Whale, (c) Dolphin. (After Slijper, 1962, and Lockyer, 1977.)

will become clear later. Smaller cetaceans, such as dolphins and porpoises, usually dive for about 5 minutes or so and then surface to blow at about 6 blows a minute (Fig. 3.11).

During the period at the surface, the lungs are thoroughly ventilated and the oxygen stores in the body fully replenished in preparation for the next dive. The whale dives after an *inspiration*, taking down a lungful of air, unlike a seal which breathes out before diving. However, the oxygen in this quantity of air is far from sufficient to account for the whale's activity in the course of a dive if its physiology were the same as that of a terrestrial mammal, and some other explanation must be found for the whale's ability to survive on such a limited amount of oxygen.

One of the first things that strikes one on seeing a whale cut up is the darkness of its muscles. The meat of Sperm Whales and Bottle-nosed Whales, indeed, is almost black. The reason for this is that the whale's muscles are loaded with the dark-red protein myoglobin. Myoglobin is found in all red muscle, but whales may have concentrations of about eight–nine times as high as those in terrestrial mammals (Tawara, 1951); similar concentrations occur in other deep divers such as Elephant Seals and King Penguins. Myoglobin is a protein like haemoglobin which has an affinity for oxygen. The similarity is related to the structure—myoglobin consists of a single metalloporphyrin (haem) combined with a protein (globin), while haemoglobin consists of four such units of haem and globin combined together. The affinity of myoglobin for oxygen is intermediate between that of haemoglobin, which carries the oxygen in the blood, and the cytochrome enzyme system, which uses the oxygen in the muscle. In consequence, myoglobin takes up oxygen from the blood and stores it until it is required for use by the muscle enzymes.

The concentration of myoglobin thus enables the whale to take down with it on its dive a greatly increased store of oxygen. Nevertheless, this alone could not account for the duration of the dives. Another adaptation that whales have adopted is an increased tolerance to the accumulation of lactic acid and carbon dioxide in the blood. If insufficient oxygen is available for the complete breakdown of glycogen to carbon dioxide in the chain of enzyme-catalysed processes that lead to the production of energy in muscle, the reaction can be broken at an intermediate stage when lactic acid is produced. This happens in ourselves when we exercise violently, but the human system will tolerate only very low levels of lactic acid. When muscle metabolises like this we say it incurs an oxygen debt, since the accumulated lactic acid has ultimately to be oxidised by molecular oxygen to carbon dioxide. We pant after exercise; the whale 'has his spoutings out', and the longer he stays down, the more lactic acid he accumulates in his blood, hence the longer the period required at the surface to oxidise it to carbon dioxide and dispose of this in the blows.

Another possible mechanism that might be exploited by a cetacean to facilitate diving is the redistribution of blood flow so that only essential organs are supplied with oxygenated blood; the brain must have oxygen (it cannot accumulate an oxygen debt); the muscles, as we have seen, can do without for lengthy periods. We know that seals can control their blood flow in this way— a powerful sphincter around the posterior vena cava, where it passes through the diaphragm, contracts on diving, causing de-oxygenated venous blood to pool below the diaphragm while maintaining a flow of arterial blood to the brain. Whales do not have this sphincter muscle nor a posterior vena cava of the type found in seals. The marked slowing of the heart beat (bradycardia) which occurs when a seal dives has not been recorded in whales, either. The absence of these features does not mean, however, that whales cannot control their blood systems on diving. The extent of peripheral vaso-constriction is difficult to determine in a diving whale. The blood system in whales is complicated and the full functional significance of all its features is not understood. Among the most puzzling structures are the retia mirabilia, the 'wonderful networks' of contorted spirals of tiny blood vessels that form great blocks of vascular tissue on the inside wall of the thorax and elsewhere. How the retia function is not understood. It has been assumed that they have a role in diving—perhaps acting as a reservoir of oxygenated blood (the thoracic retia are arterial in character) for the brain. They scarcely seem large enough to contain a significant amount, but one must bear in mind that the brain of a large whale is tiny in relation to its body

size. Other suggested functions of the retia include helping to provide a steady and continuous blood flow, despite interruptions
caused by muscular or external pressure. In fact, apart from
gas spaces, pressure throughout a submerged whale will be
almost uniform, so it is unlikely that the retia function in this
way.

The spread of SCUBA diving as a popular sport has led to many
amateur divers questioning how whales manage to descend to
great depths without suffering from the effects of pressure that
limit human divers in their excursions towards the sea-floor.
There are two separate, but related effects here. The effect of
pressure on a SCUBA diver tends to compress his chest; in order
to prevent its collapse he breathes air at pressure from his tank
via his demand valve. To be able to breathe at all, his lungs must
contain air at a pressure very nearly the same as that of the water
surrounding him. A problem resulting from this is that, because
of the increased solubility of gas in liquids under pressure, nitrogen will dissolve in his blood and tissue fluids while he is at depth.
When the diver returns to the surface, unless he is very careful
to limit his time spent below and to return to the surface by careful stages, there is always a risk that the nitrogen in his blood
will bubble out, like the bubbles that appear in a bottle of soda-
water when the top is released, causing the agonising condition
known as 'the bends' if the bubbles occur in a joint capsule, or
perhaps even killing him if a bubble in the blood (an embolism)
blocks a vital artery in the heart or brain.

Whales are quite unaffected by pressure effects or the bends
and the reason for this is quite simple—unlike human divers, they
do not breathe air under pressure. A whale, as we noted earlier,
dives with its lungs full of air breathed at atmospheric pressure.
As it submerges the pressure of the water outside causes its lungs
to collapse; the abdominal viscera press against the oblique diaphragm, making it bulge into the thorax and take the place previously occupied by the air-filled lungs. As the lungs collapse, the
walls of the alveoli, the minute chambers at the end of the termi-
nal bronchioles in the lungs where gaseous exchange takes place,
thicken and the rate of gas exchange, including the solution of
nitrogen into the blood (the nitrogen invasion rate), is reduced.

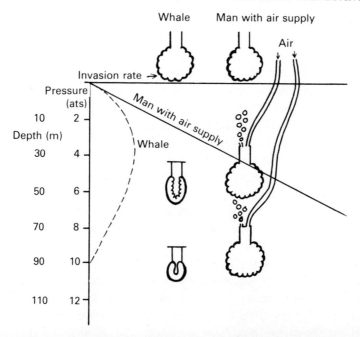

Fig. 3.12 The relationship between the invasion rate of nitrogen into the blood and pressure increase. In the whale the rate at first increases, then decreases to nil as the alveoli of the lungs collapse. For a human diver supplied with compressed air from the surface, the invasion rate steadily increases to saturation at whatever pressure is represented by the depth reached. (Adapted from Scholander, 1940.)

At a depth of 100 m (a pressure of 11 atmospheres*) the lungs have collapsed completely and the nitrogen invasion rate is zero, for the remaining air has been forced into the rigid parts of the respiratory tract, the bronchi and trachea, where little or no gas exchange can take place. In this condition the whale can safely dive deeper to whatever depths it needs to visit. Further increase of pressure will have no other effect for, apart from the minute gas spaces that still remain in the respiratory and sinus systems (there is a very important one in the middle ear, also), the whale's body is virtually incompressible, like the water round it, and the pressure acts equally in all directions.

In contrast, the human diver must continue to keep his lungs inflated as he goes deeper, so the further down he goes the greater

* 1 atmosphere = 101,325 newtons per sq m.

the invasion rate of nitrogen and the more nitrogen dissolves in his body (Fig. 3.12). His ultimate depth will be limited not only by the dangers associated with dissolved nitrogen (which he can avoid by breathing oxygen diluted with helium) but also by the poisonous effects of oxygen itself breathed under pressure. Another practical limitation is the very great amount of time that has to be spent in staging his ascent after a deep prolonged dive, in order to ensure that the nitrogen is safely flushed out of his body without the formation of bubbles.

Early physiologists failed to grasp the point that a whale could absorb no more nitrogen than the amount it took down with one breath, i.e. about four fifths of its lung capacity, and went to elaborate lengths to explain how the 'nitrogen problem' was dealt with. Perhaps the most fanciful theory was that the blood contained 'x organisms', possibly bacteria, that could absorb nitrogen (Laurie, 1933). In fact this theory was based on the examination of contaminated blood samples, hence the bacteria. More rational explanations relied on the retia to filter out gas bubbles, or for the nitrogen to be dissolved in the oil globules that are present in the blood or in the oily foam that fills the sinus system. This latter idea may be true to the extent that what nitrogen is present is probably largely dissolved in oil globules, for nitrogen is about six–seven times more soluble in fat than in water. However, the absolute quantity of nitrogen that the whale could absorb from its one lungful of air is small and probably no special mechanisms are needed for its safe disposal.

4   *The senses of whales*

The extent to which an animal can successfully exploit its environment, or compete with others, is largely dependent on the amount and quality of the information that it can receive about its surroundings. Predators in particular need to have precise information about the location and movements of their prey. We are all familiar with the large eyes, prominent ears and twitching whiskers of a domestic cat and even brief observation will show how it uses its nose to investigate its surroundings, although a cat's use of this organ is minor in comparison with a dog. Lacking an acute and discriminating sense of smell ourselves, it is difficult to appreciate the sort of information that a dog receives about its surroundings *via* its nose.

Whales are predators at two levels. The toothed whales, hunting their prey item by item, more nearly resemble the typical terrestrial predators in their sensory requirements, while the baleen whales, grazing on shoals of relatively tiny organisms engulfed *en masse*, probably have a slightly less refined sensory requirement, but both groups, in common with all other mammals, share the need to be constantly aware of incoming messages from their suroundings which, from time to time, will contain clues of special phenomena—a ship's hull that spells danger, a cuttlefish to provide a quick mouthful, another whale of the same species with whom contact must be made to satisfy a sexual drive and perpetuate the species.

The five basic senses are often reckoned to be touch, smell, taste, vision and hearing. For completeness, a physiologist might wish to subdivide some of these and to add some other senses (pain, for example, or the ability to distinguish the relative temperature of objects), but it will be convenient to consider the senses of whales in these categories.

Touch

Little is known of the sense of touch in cetaceans. At one time it was believed that the whale's skin was comparatively insensitive, but it became clear from observations on whales in captivity that even gentle caresses on the skin can be perceived and more vigorous stimulation, such as having their backs scrubbed with a yard broom, can induce a state of evident rapture in dolphins. The structure of cetacean skin, with its well developed papillary layer, could, by comparison with other mammals, provide the anatomical basis for a presumption of tactile sensation. It is likely that sensitivity varies locally, with the head being the most sensitive. Certainly the trigeminal nerve, which conveys sensation from the surface of the snout to the brain in vertebrates, is well developed, being the largest of the cranial nerves in whales. Similarly, the nerves running from the tail-flukes are also large. Both the surface of the head and that of the flukes are likely to be parts of the body where the accurate reception of tactile stimuli is significant, the head because, in going forward, it probes the environment and receives the first warning of changes in it and the tail because the water currents set up in swimming may have feed-back significance in the reflex control of swimming, so as to minimise turbulence.

This view is borne out by a study of the whale's brain (Jansen, 1950, 1953). In the cerebellum, the lobulus simplex, which receives tactile sensation from the head, is enlarged, as is the paraflocculus, which is associated with sensory input from the trunk and tail-flukes.

In our own species, the simple experiment of drawing a wisp of cotton over the skin will demonstrate that discrimination of touch is greatly increased in those parts of the body that are lightly haired. The leverage exerted by the hair shaft on the small nerve fibres wrapped round its base in the follicle increases sensitivity by orders of magnitude when compared with naked or shaven skin. As we saw earlier, whales are virtually hairless, but what hairs they do possess are concentrated in precisely those areas where an acute tactile sense will be most effective: the extremity of the chin, the margins of the jaw and around the blow-hole.

The hairs are better developed in baleen whales than in toothed whales, although they are by no means absent in the latter. Their best development of all is in the Humpback Whale, where the hairs are located on the nodules which adorn the head of this species. Each nodule has one or two associated hairs, and the nodules are arranged in rows and groups corresponding to the hair pattern in other rorquals.

Early in this century (Japha, 1907, 1912), examination of the hair follicles showed them to be complex structures corresponding to the whisker follicles of some terrestrial mammals, although they differ from the whiskers of, say, a cat, in that the vibrissae of a whale are not provided with muscle fibres so cannot be erected or moved as can a cat's whiskers. The hair follicles of a

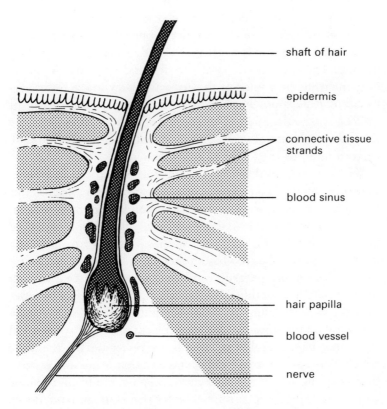

shaft of hair

epidermis

connective tissue strands

blood sinus

hair papilla

blood vessel

nerve

Fig. 4.1   Diagram of the vibrissa follicle of a whale. (After Ling, 1977.)

whale are solidly embedded in the integument, perhaps as deeply as 20 mm below the surface, while the exposed part of the hair shaft protrudes by about 12.5 mm from the follicle. The follicle (Fig. 4.1) is surrounded by a system of blood sinuses, as in all mammalian sensory vibrissae; connective tissue strands bearing nerve fibres traverse the sinus spaces and it is here one supposes that minute deflections of the vibrissa shaft, caused by slight local changes in pressure (a flow) of the surrounding water, are transformed into nerve impulses and conveyed *via* the trigeminal nerve to the brain to be interpreted.

The follicles are less elaborate in toothed whales and in some the hair degenerates late in foetal life, leaving only a small sensory crypt. It is not known whether this responds to the same type of stimuli as do the vibrissae, but it may be that odontocetes have less need to be highly dependent on a tactile sense. We cannot be certain to what use the mysticete puts its whiskers, but it seems not unreasonable to suggest that they are associated with feeding. The tiny hairs round the lips and chin may serve to keep the whale informed of the density of prey in the water surrounding it as it slowly ploughs its way through the swarm of krill or copepods. Such a function would help to explain the lesser development of vibrissae in toothed whales, which do not need to monitor their prey in this manner.

We can say little about other cutaneous sensations in whales. Like other animals, whales certainly possess a pain sense, as this is a necessary part of the self-preservation system built into an animal's body by its DNA, but it is unlikely that pain is perceived in a way similar to our own species. Whales are generally unable to groom their bodies so they have to endure the irritations of the many parasites and micro-predators that assault them. Whale-lice, modified amphipod Crustacea (Fig. 4.2) wander over the skin, nibbling away at the epidermis. These are most abundant on the slow-moving Humpbacks and right whales and the latter have developed curious excrescences on the head which, perhaps, serve to localise these ectoparasites and prevent them tickling more sensitive parts. Highly modified copepod Crustacea (*Penella* sp.) burrow into the skin and no doubt cause some discomfort, but perhaps the most common painful

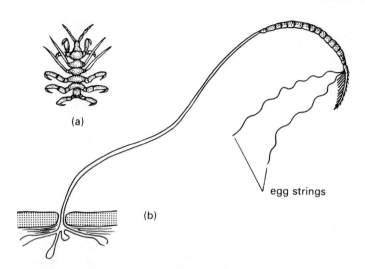

(a)

egg strings

(b)

Fig. 4.2   Parasites of whales: (a) Whale-louse *Cyamus*, a modified amphipod crustacean, lives on the skin of whales. (b) *Penella* lives with its anterior parts beneath the whale's skin and only its tassel-like abdomen, bearing egg-strings, exposed.

thing that occurs to the large rorquals is being eaten alive (in a minor way) by small sharks. Most rorquals are covered with oval scars about 110 mm long and 50 mm wide which seem to occur in generations corresponding to the whale's migration through warm waters. For a long time these were believed to have resulted from Lamprey bites but it has recently been shown (Jones, 1971) that the culprit is a small tropical shark, *Isistius brasiliensis*, which is common in both the Atlantic and Pacific Oceans. *Isistius* swims up to a whale and, facing the whale's tail, clamps its teeth in the skin; it then swings round, helped by the slip-stream of water past the whale, and neatly slices out an oval pad of skin and blubber. The wounds soon heal, but by comparison with similar relatively sized wounds on our own bodies, we might suppose them to be 'painful'. Yet the whale is quite incapable of doing anything to alleviate its suffering from this little predator.

However, we should recognise that natural selection, which ensures that, in the long term, animals do not expend energy in ways unprofitable for passing on the essential DNA, will have ensured that the whale can bear its persecution without upsetting its proper pattern of life. This equanimity which I have suggested the whale displays, in the face of what might be reckoned to be painful stimuli, is not surprising—it occurs in most wild animals. Indeed, perhaps more surprising is civilised (or pampered?) man's response to pain, which is frequently out of all proportion to the stimulus causing it. Needless to say, to suggest that whales do not feel pain as we do is no excuse for thoughtlessly inflicting suffering on whales which we would regard as likely to cause pain were similar injuries to be inflicted on us.

It is not known whether whales have a temperature sense. It is likely that they can detect a temperature gradient between their bodies and the water surrounding them. This may well have survival value in the case of those species which migrate to warmer waters to breed, but it is improbable that whales associate a warm environment with 'comfort' and a cold one with 'discomfort' as we do. In this respect the environment is recognised, not judged.

Smell and taste

Smell and the associated chemical sense, taste, are apparently little developed in whales. In the toothed whales there can be no sense of smell, since there is no olfactory organ, olfactory nerve or olfactory bulb in the brain. This was not always the case, as Miocene odontocetes are known which have a perforation in the ethmoid bone of the skull to allow the passage of the olfactory nerve and, in some of the still earlier archaeocetes, there were turbinal bones which must have supported an olfactory epithelium. Whalebone whales are a little better provided for since olfactory nerves and bulbs can be detected in foetal mysticetes, but it is not certain that they persist as functional organs in the adult.

It is not surprising that cetaceans are so deficient in a sense of smell. Sea-water is a perfectly adequate medium for the perception of olfactory stimuli and, indeed, most fishes have a very highly developed sense of smell but, when the primitive Amphibia adopted the air-breathing habit, the olfactory epithelium was incorporated into the respiratory tract and necessarily was modified to operate in air. In mammals, the olfactory epithelium is spread over the scroll-like turbinal bones at the back of the nasal passage. In this position it would not have been possible for an aquatic mammal to 'smell' the water by inhaling it over the turbinals without risk of choking and probably damaging the delicate epithelium into the bargain. With no useful function, and hence no selection pressure acting on it to maintain it, the olfactory system gradually atrophied to its present vestigial condition in the whale.

In most mammals there is present a specialised part of the olfactory system, the vomero-nasal organ. This is a small cigar-shaped organ, derived from the main olfactory epithelium and situated in the palate between the nasal cavity and the mouth. In some mammals, e.g. rodents, it opens into the main nasal cavity, but in most it communicates directly with the mouth by a duct perforating the secondary palate. The vomero-nasal organ functions as a means of smelling food already in the mouth (it has other and more complicated functions in snakes). All whales show traces of the duct in the form of two shallow grooves inside the tip of the upper jaw. Although clearly visible, they seem to have no function as there is no sensory epithelium connected with them and the reason for their persistence remains a puzzle.

Taste is little known in whales. In general, animals that swallow their food whole (as whales generally do) have little sense of taste, but it is likely that at least some sort of taste sensation is present on the tongue of most whales. It has been suggested on the basis of the size of the seventh and ninth cranial nerves and that part of the brain concerned with taste (the gustatory nucleus of the thalamus) that the cetacean sense of taste conforms to the general mammalian pattern (Kruger, 1959).

Vision

Because vision is so important a sense to ourselves, we are inclined to overestimate its significance for other animals. Few mammals rely so exclusively on sight for information about their environment as we do.

Light rays are well suited for conveying information in an environment that is sufficiently brightly illuminated. Where the environment is predominantly air, through which light is propagated with scarcely any decrement, the stimuli reaching the eye can originate from very great distances, giving early warning of the presence of prey or danger.

Most terrestrial mammals have well developed vision, but clearly mammals that are active mainly at night, or burrow underground, are less able to rely mainly on sight for information about their environment. Some nocturnal mammals, e.g. the Bush-babies, compensate for low light intensity by enlarging the eyes or developing other modifications, like reflecting layers, to make the greatest possible use of what light there is. A few burrowing mammals (Moles, Mole-rats) have virtually abandoned the eye as a means of receiving useful stimuli. One group, the insectivorous bats, have developed a sophisticated system of probing their environment in a very precise manner without relying on sight at all. Later we shall see that the Cetacea also have exploited this system, which utilises high frequency sound pulses.

The aquatic world in which whales live is much dimmer than the aerial world we are familiar with. Compared with air, water is much less transparent to light and suspended particles (mainly plankton and silt) in naturally occurring waters like the sea absorb and scatter much light. At 10 m depth in the sea, 90% of the light has been absorbed or reflected and this rises to 99% at 40 m. At 400 m it is pitch black, all the light having been absorbed. Even in the relatively well illuminated surface layers, horizontal visibility is restricted by the turbidity of the water and the absence of the large reflecting surfaces that are found in air. In consequence, the maximum range of visibility in the best circumstances is about 60 m and will often be less than this so, as Slijper (1962) pointed out, a big whale might be unable to see its own flukes!

But whales do have a visual sense and a complicated visual apparatus to go with it. In only one species, the Ganges Susu, *Platanista gangetica*, which lives by grubbing fish and crabs out

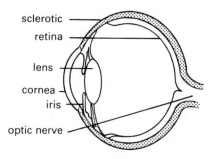

sclerotic
retina
lens
cornea
iris
optic nerve

Fig. 4.3   The human eye in diagrammatic cross-section.

of the muddy bottoms of silt-laden rivers, have the eyes de-
generated to the extent that they are probably non-functional.

Because of the differences in medium, mainly the lack of light
and the higher refractive index of water, whales' eyes have to be
built on a different plan from those of terrestrial mammals, and
it will be helpful to compare them with our own.

A human eye (Fig. 4.3) is a fairly typical mammalian eye. Its
function is to form an image from rays entering the eye and
convert that image into nerve impulses in the retina which are
then transmitted *via* the optic tracts to the brain where the
image is interpreted. Because the sense cells of the retina can
only function between certain limits of illumination, a
diaphragm, the iris, is present to control the amount of light
passing to the retina. Finally, there are various muscles, which
serve to move the eyeball, and supportive and protective tissues.

In order to form an image on the retina, a refractive system
is required. Refraction occurs when light passes from a medium
of one refractive index to another. One naturally thinks of the
lens of the eye as being responsible for refraction. But this is
only partly true. There is a big difference in refractive index
between air and the curved surface of the cornea (the transparent
front of the eyeball) and the greater part of the refraction occurs
here, while the lens, although strongly curved, is suspended in
fluids (the aqueous and vitreous humours) whose refractive
indices are only a little less than its own so that it does not form
a powerful refracting system. Its function, in fact, is the fine

focusing of the image. In order to focus correctly objects at different distances from the eye, it is necessary for the power of the lens to alter. Normally, the eye is focused for rays coming from distant objects. For near objects accommodation is achieved by the action of the ciliary muscle, which, when it contracts, relaxes the tension normally exerted on the lens by its suspensory ligament, allowing it to assume a more rounded (and optically more powerful) configuration.

As anyone realises who tries to see under water without using a face-mask, it is impossible to form a sharp image on the retina. This is because the refractive indices of water and the cornea are similar, hence the refractive system is no longer powerful enough to bring the rays to a focus on the retina—they converge behind it (Fig. 4.4) and the eye is long-sighted or hypermetropic.

Now the whale's eye, to be effective, must be able to focus under water, since it is in water that the whale will do most of its seeing. There is no refraction at all at the corneal surface in the whale, since the cornea and the aqueous (and probably the vitreous) humour have the same refractive index as sea-water (Matthiessen, 1893). By way of compensation the lens is very nearly spherical (a feature which whales share with seals and

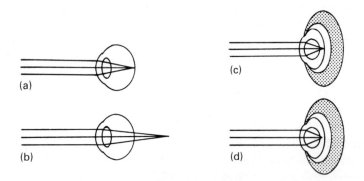

Fig. 4.4 The effect of water and air on refraction. (a) Human eye in air. Most of the refraction is at the air/cornea interface. (b) Human eye in water. There is no refraction at the cornea, hence the eye is long-sighted. (c) Whale eye in water. All the refraction is done by the spherical lens. (d) Whale eye in air. Refraction occurs at the corneal surface, as well as at the lens, hence the eye is short-sighted.

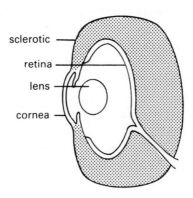

sclerotic

retina

lens

cornea

Fig. 4.5   The eye of a Fin Whale in diagrammatic cross-section.

some fish) and has a higher refractive index than that of most mammals, further increasing its power and making up for the lack of refraction at the corneal surface. Just as the human eye is defective in water, so the whale's eye in air will be very short-sighted (myopic) as refraction will now occur at the cornea. However, this problem is not so severe as it might appear. Whale eyes are, in general, large and flattened front to back (Fig. 4.5) so that the corneal surface is less strongly curved than in a human eye, causing less refraction. Further, the whale's eye is adapted to seeing in very low light intensities, so that, on emerging into the brightness of air, the iris will contract, decreasing the aperture of the pupil and, as any camera enthusiast knows, effectively increasing the depth of focus. There is also a possibility that some active accommodation may take place in odontocetes, but not in mysticetes which do not possess ciliary muscles. It is not clear how the ciliary muscle, where present, functions in whales. Since normally the contraction of the ciliary muscle causes the lens to become more rounded, and the whale lens is already nearly spherical, there is a possibility that, in whales, its action is to flatten the lens (an action similar to that which occurs in birds). The problem is not resolved, although most authorities believe that whales lack the power of accommodation (Breathnach, 1966).

From this mass of conjecture, what is certain is that many

odontocetes, at least, have acute vision in air. The aerial activities of a dolphin circus are sufficient evidence of this.

The actual performance of whale eyes at very low light intensities has not been studied, but there are clear adaptations to operation at low light levels. The most obvious of these is the presence of a tapetum lucidum, a layer of guanine crystals behind the retina. The tapetum acts as a mirror, reflecting back light which has not already been absorbed by the sense cells, so that there is a second chance for it to stimulate them. A tapetum is found in many nocturnal mammals (our most familiar sight of it is in the eyes of a cat or fox reflecting back a car's head-lamps) but it is especially well developed in whales. Another adaptation is the very large cornea which admits a wide pencil of light, combined with a highly mobile iris which can open to such an extent that there is a space left on either side of the lens. There are other highly important but less obvious adaptations in the retina itself. The sense cells of the retina in most mammals can be roughly divided into two classes, rods and cones. Cones are believed to be operative in colour vision and require a higher threshold of stimulation than rods. It is commonly observed that, in the retina of animals which are active in low light intensities, rods predominate. This is true also for whales. Not only are rods very abundant in the cetacean retina, they are also larger than the normal mammalian rod and will gather more light. The rods in a retina do not connect on a one-to-one ratio with ganglion cells and hence to the brain *via* the fibres of the optic tract. On the contrary, in the whale, many rods, perhaps 2,000 (Pilleri and Wandeler, 1964; Dral, 1977), connect with a single ganglion cell. This summation increases many-fold the chances of a ganglion cell being stimulated by a little light. The summation ratios are difficult to calculate (Dral, 1977) and perhaps the best that can be said is that the cetacean eye does have a highly summating retina, which can be regarded as a low light (scotopic) adaptation.

Cones are present in the whale's retina, but they are not very abundant. Attempts to demonstrate colour vision in the Bottle-nosed Dolphin have not been successful (Madsen, 1975). No discrimination was found between pairs of lights of white, red, green or blue. This is not very surprising. Colour vision is the exception rather than the rule in mammals and an eye as dark-adapted as that of a whale would not be expected to respond to colour.

What does a whale see out of its eyes? This, of course, will depend on the position of the eyes in the head. Our own eyes are set at the front of the head and look forward. We have a visual field of about 180°, of which 120° is covered by both eyes (Fig. 4.6), providing a wide field of binocular vision in which a sensation of depth is perceived. Some vulnerable herbivores—the rabbit is an example—have bulging eyes high up on the sides of their heads, which provide them with a full 360° visual field, with binocular fields both in front and behind. Slijper pointed out that hunted animals usually had laterally placed eyes, to give the best all-round warning, while the hunters had anteriorly placed eyes to enable them to judge the distance from their prey

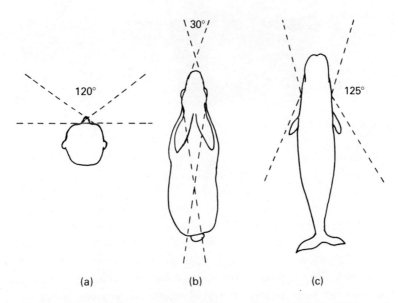

Fig. 4.6 Visual fields of: (a) Man, (b) Rabbit, (c) Sperm Whale. Both Man and the Rabbit have binocular vision, the Rabbit being able to see to its rear. The Sperm Whale has two separate visual fields and can see neither directly in front nor behind.

Fig. 4.7   A bottle-nosed Dolphin looking binocularly at an observer.

accurately. From this one might expect that whales, which are hunters, would have their eyes placed at the front. However, this would cause problems associated with streamlining, water pressure and frictional flow on the delicate surface of the eye, and we find that in fact all whales have their eyes more or less laterally placed. In some whales, e.g. the Bottle-nosed Dolphin, the eyes are sufficiently far forward to allow some binocular vision (Fig. 4.7), and this, coupled with the scanning movements they can make with their relatively mobile necks, may account for the delicate precision that trained dolphins exhibit in taking fish, etc., out of the water. In the larger whales, or those with bulbous foreheads, stereoscopic vision is impossible. The Sperm Whale has two entirely separate visual fields (Fig. 4.6), each of about 125°, on either side of the head (Fischer, 1946). The horizontal field is probably greater in extent than the vertical, because the cetacean eye is flattened. Even with an expanded horizontal field, however, the Sperm Whale is unable to see directly in front or behind, a feature often taken advantage of by the open boat whalers, as they stalked their quarry. Sperm Whales, in fact, are rather worse off than most other whales as regards sight. Their eyes weigh only a third as much as those of the Humpback Whale (Quiring, 1943). Presumably this is associated with the deep diving habit of the Sperm Whale, which finds its food at depths in which light is almost completely absent.

Whales are able to move the eyeball in the orbit and the external muscles of the eyes are well developed, although this was not generally known until Slijper pointed it out in 1958. Since that time it has been shown that *Tursiops* has the ability, unique among mammals, to move each eye independently (Dawson *et al.*, 1972).

There are other adaptations of the whale's eye which, while associated with an aquatic life, have nothing to do directly with vision. The eyes of terrestrial vertebrates require an irrigation system, the tear gland and tear duct, to wash the eye and drain away the washings. The whale's eye, continually bathed in water as it is, needs no such system and tear glands and ducts are absent. On the other hand, the water streaming past the cornea of a fast-swimming whale imposes sheer strains and a certain amount of friction and we find that the outer layer of the cornea is cornified and united to the living tissue beneath by a system of papillae, a similar situation to the structure of the body skin in whales or the skin of the human palm, also subjected to sheer strains. Glands at the outer cornea of the eyes and in the eyelids secrete an oily substance that lubricates and protects the surface of the eye. Unlike fish, but like other mammals, whales possess eyelids which can open and shut. Their chief function is likely to be to sweep clear the surface of the eye of any particle or living organism that might settle on it. A whale, after all, has no opportunity to rub its eyes to remove an irritation!

Hearing

We have seen that smell plays little part in the provision of information to a whale and that, although an acute visual sense is present, it can never function over long distances. This leaves hearing to provide information about the distant environment. Here the surrounding water provides a distinct advantage; sound travels faster (about four times as fast) in water than in air, and, more importantly, it is attenuated less in the denser medium, so that sounds can be propagated over much larger distances in water than in air. Here then is a sense that the Cetacea can exploit and they have, in fact, developed a hearing apparatus of greater complexity than is found in any other animal and they are more dependent on their hearing than any other mammal, the bats alone excepted.

For a long time, whales were believed by many scientists to be deaf, although any whaler could have told them the contrary, and, despite the lack of external ears, whales were known to have complicated internal structures. In order to understand the whale's ear it will be best to consider first some general principles.

The function of the mammalian ear (which evolved in an aerial medium) is to collect sound vibrations (which are pressure waves) in the air and convey them, in a suitable form, to the sense cells. These are the hair cells of the organ of Corti in the spiral cochlea of the inner ear. Since these were inherited from an aquatic ancestor, they have retained a watery environment and are bathed in a fluid which fills the cavity of the inner ear. The hair cells convert minute displacements of this fluid, set up by the sound vibrations, into nerve impulses which are collected in the auditory nerve and conveyed to the brain.

Additionally, it is valuable if, besides perceiving the sound, the animal can determine something about the direction of its origin. As the ears, like the eyes, are paired organs, this can be done by comparing the reception of the sound at each ear.

Another part of the inner ear, the semi-circular canals, are concerned with a completely separate sense, the sense of balance, and since these appear to function in whales exactly as they do in

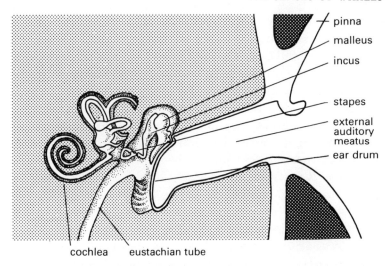

pinna
malleus
incus
stapes
external auditory meatus
ear drum
cochlea   eustachian tube

Fig. 4.8   The ear of a typical terrestrial mammal in diagrammatic cross-section.

other mammals (or other vertebrates, for that matter), I shall not discuss them further.

Let us consider how the hearing function of the ear is performed by a terrestrial mammal, the dog, for instance (Fig. 4.8).

The most obvious part of a dog's ear is, of course, the external part, or pinna. This trumpet-shaped flap of skin and cartilage is provided with muscles with which it can be pricked up or rotated to a small extent. The use a dog makes of this in locating a sound source is obvious, but it is not an essential organ for this purpose. Human pinnae are almost absent, yet we can localise sounds quite well. The funnel of the pinna narrows down to a short tube, the external auditory meatus, which is terminated by a sheet of very thin connective tissue covered by skin. This is the ear drum or tympanic membrane, and marks the division between the external and middle ear.

The tympanic membrane forms a shallow cone, its apex directed into the chamber of the middle ear. Attached along the side of the cone is the first of a train of tiny bones (derived over a long evolutionary history from parts of the gill arch and lower jaw of our fish and reptile ancestors). The first bone is the malleus (= hammer) which articulates with the incus (= anvil), which itself is connected to the stapes (= stirrup). The stapes abuts against another membrane, the oval window. The tympanic cavity in which these bones lie contains air and is connected to the throat by the Eustachian tube.

The oval window is the first part of the inner ear. This fluid-filled cavity contains the bony labyrinth—the semi-circular canals and the spinal cochlea. The cochlea is a coiled cavity in the petrous part of the temporal bone. The top of the tube is closed and it is separated for nearly all its length by a shelf of nerve cells and supporting tissue, the organ of Corti. There is thus a sort of double spiral within the cochlea, one part originating at the oval window, passing to the apex of the cochlea, and hence (because the organ of Corti does not quite extend to the top) crossing over to the other side and descending on the other side of the organ of Corti, to terminate at the round window, another membrane-covered opening in the wall of the middle ear (Fig. 4.8).

Having set the scene with rather a lot of anatomy, it is possible to begin to try to describe the functioning of this complicated organ. Sound travelling down the external auditory meatus from the pinna arrives at the ear drum and causes it to vibrate in response to the pressure waves that make up the sound. The vibrations of the drum are translated into movement of the malleus which are communicated to the incus and thence to the stapes, the footplate of which is applied to the oval window. The ear ossicles form a lever system, which reduces, to about a half, the movement of the stapes footplate (and hence the oval window) when compared with the movements of the drum. This reduction is necessary if the vibrations of sound in air (which has a large displacement amplitude) are to be effectively transferred to the fluid (perilymph) filling the inner ear, where the same frequency sound wave will have a much smaller displacement amplitude. Small muscles attached to the drum and the stapes (the tensor tympani and the stapedial muscle) have a reflex function of contracting in response to very loud sounds, thus damping the movement of the ossicles and protecting the oval window and cochlea from injury. The whole complicated apparatus has been described in electronic engineering terms as an impedance matching transformer, with automatic volume control. Essentially it converts sound waves in air to sound waves in water (or the perilymph of the inner ear) for reception by sense cells evolved in an aquatic medium.

Before leaving the middle ear the role of the Eustachian tube must be mentioned. This is another safety device. It serves to equalise pressure on either side of the ear drum, which otherwise might be ruptured by a large and sudden pressure variation.

It is not necessary to say much about the cochlea and its organ of Corti. Pressure waves in the perilymph cause movements of a basal membrane which supports the fundamental receptors, the hair cells. The hairs, when distorted, give out impulses which travel to the brain. Sounds of different frequency affect the organ of Corti in different ways, but the relationship is not a simple one—frequency discrimination is a function of the brain rather than of the ear.

Liquids are incompressible, so when the pressure waves are transmitted to the perilymph, there must be a relief system somewhere. This is the function of the round window, which bulges into the middle ear and whose movements are a counterpart of those of the oval window.

This, then, is an outline of how sound is received at the ear. Localisation depends on both ears being functional. Because there is a large difference in acoustic impedance between air and animal tissue, over 90% of sound energy is reflected from the sides of the head of a terrestrial mammal (Fig. 4.9). Only the sound which is captured by the trumpet of the pinna is transmitted to the drum and perceived in the cochlea. When a sound source is to one side of the head the ear on the opposite side is in a 'sound shadow' caused by the skull and tissues between it and the sound source, so reception at that ear is less intense. This effect will be most marked for high frequency sounds (above about 3 kHz). Another mechanism, which operates over the whole sound spectrum, depends on the finite time taken for sound to travel. A sound originating on one side takes slightly longer to reach the further ear. In the human head, a sound originating 45° to one side will take about 0.4 msec longer to reach one

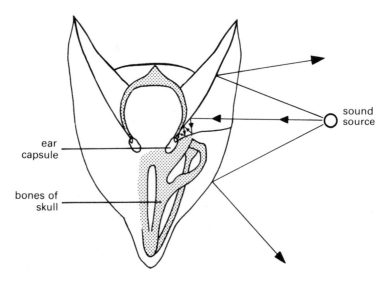

Fig. 4.9   Sound reception at a dog's ear.

ear than the other, and this difference can be detected and analysed in the brain and used to localise the source.

Where do the whales stand (or swim) in this? They have in-herited an aerially adapted aquatic ear from their terrestrial mam-malian ancestors, yet they have resumed an aquatic way of life. Since, it seems, the course of evolution never goes directly back on itself, the whales have had to re-adapt their ears to hearing in a watery medium.

Most of what we know today about the structure and func-tioning of the cetacean ear has been derived from the brilliant and inspired work of Fraser and Purves working at the British Museum (Natural History), London, (1954, 1960). What follows cannot attempt to summarise their work, but it relies heavily upon it; indeed, it would have been impossible to have written almost anything without it.

To a terrestrial ear, noises in water sound quite different. When one dips one's head beneath the surface of the sea one is aware of an increase in the level of background noise, a general distor-tion of sound and a total lack of directionality. Most of these effects are caused by sound reaching the cochlea, not by the orthodox route, *via* the pinna and auditory meatus, but directly by conduction through the bones of the head. Since there is a negligible difference in acoustic impedance between the tissues of the head and the water surrounding them, the reflections that took place from the surface of the head in air (Fig. 4.9) no longer occur and sound is absorbed over a wide surface. The sounds that are received are distorted because the drum can no longer function properly and vibrations arriving *via* the ossicles interfere with those arriving direct by bone conduction.

The first requirement of a cetacean ear, then, is acoustic isolation. This is done by the development of a very complex system of air sacs or sinuses, derived as out-pushings of the Eustachian tube (the passage whose basic function is to equilibrate pressure on either side of the ear drum). The sinuses vary in complexity and size from the more primitive whalebone whales and river dolphins to the highly specialised oceanic toothed whales and dolphins. In general five main divisions of the sinuses can be recognised: an anterior sinus which runs forward in the rostrum of the upper jaw; a pterygoid sinus, which has invaded and eroded much of the pterygoid bone and from which the anterior sinus originates; a medial sinus, near the articulation of the jaw; a peribullary sinus which envelops the tympanic bulla, the bone covering the middle ear; and a posterior sinus, which is connected with the tympanic cavity (Fig. 4.10). The sinuses are all divided up into many small pockets by strands of tissue and are richly supplied with networks of blood vessels. The presence of these sinuses goes far to explain the extraordinary appearance of the cetacean skull, in particular the erosion of the inner layer of the pterygoid.

The bones that immediately surround the inner and middle ear, the petrosal and tympanic bulla, are in most mammals an integral part of the ventro-lateral wall of the brain-case. In whales, however, they are quite separate. The bulla (Fig. 4.11) is a shell-shaped bone surrounding the enlarged tympanic cavity; the petrosal is extremely hard bone, as its name (=stony) implies. For that matter the bulla also is formed from very dense bone. The petrosal contains the structures of the inner ear. The bulla

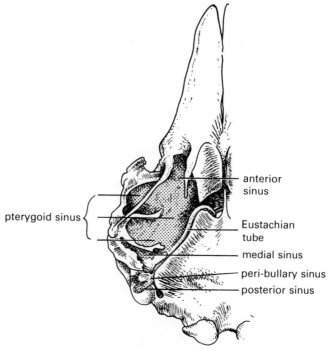

Fig. 4.10   The ventral aspect of the skull of Risso's Dolphin, to show the arrangement of the air sinuses. (After Purves, 1966.)

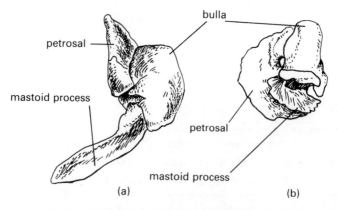

Fig. 4.11   Ear bones (bulla and petrosal) of: (a) Sei Whale and (b) a Sperm Whale.

is attached to it by one slender process in odontocetes and by two in mysticetes. The petrosal itself is attached by the mastoid and pro-otic processes to the rest of the skull. In odontocetes, the mastoid, the more important attachment, is connected by ligaments to the squamosal and occipital bones; in mysticetes, the mastoid is a long process, jammed loosely between the squamosal and occipital.

Surrounding the ear bones on all sides (apart from the mastoid) are the air sinuses, which are filled with a fine foam of gas bubbles in an oil-mucus emulsion. This foam has great resistance to compression. Fraser and Purves found that similar protein-based foams remained stable at pressures of 100 atmospheres, equivalent to a depth of nearly 1,000 m, and resumed their normal structure when the pressure was released. Clearly, the volume of the gas in the sinuses will decrease as it is compressed, but a compensatory mechanism exists here. The sinuses contain, besides the foam, a series of complex arterio-venous plexuses. When the foam is compressed as the whale dives, the blood vessels of the plexuses become engorged and take up some of the space occupied before by the foam, thus preserving the general arrangement of the tissues.

It is this foam that provides the necessary acoustic isolation for the ear. The millions of tiny gas bubbles, which persist even when the foam is highly compressed, cause it to have much the same acoustic impedance as air. Hence sound vibrations transmitted from the water to the head tissues of the whale will be reflected at the tissue–sinus interface. Minimal conduction only will occur from the skull to the petrosal and bulla *via* the mastoid process. The only unshielded route will be *via* the external auditory meatus.

In whales, the external auditory meatus is not provided with any external pinna, which is to be expected, as it would seriously interfere with the streamlining of the head. However, traces of the pinna can be found as a cartilaginous body surrounding the ear passage. The external opening of this is minute, being scarcely more than a centimetre in diameter in the largest rorquals. Leading from it is a very narrow tube which, in mysticetes, is completely closed and reduced to nothing more than a strand of fibrous connective tissue for part of its length. This condition of the external auditory meatus led many workers to assume that it was functionless and it was left to Fraser and Purves to demonstrate that this was far from the case. Using acoustic probes to measure experimentally the routes of least resistance for sound waves of known frequency, they were able to show that the sound attenuation of structures surrounding the meatus was much greater than that of the meatus itself, whether an open tube, as in odontocetes, or a strand of connective tissue, as in mysticetes.

With the function of the sinuses and the external auditory meatus revealed, we can see how whales have achieved the necessary acoustic isolation to provide each ear with one route (the traditional mammalian one) to convey an undistorted signal to the middle and inner ear. Directional binaural hearing is thus possible, based on sound shadows cast this time, not by the bones of the skull, but by the foam-filled sinuses. Sound location based on the time taken for a sound to reach each ear will be a little more difficult for whales, since the velocity of sound in water is about four times as great as in air. On the other hand, the separation of the ears is often many times greater than in terrestrial mammals!

The meatus leads to the ear drum, but in whales this is quite different from the simple membrane of most mammals. It has been transformed into a flattened triangular ligament with one apex directed inwards and attached to the first of the ear ossicles, the malleus. In whalebone whales part of the ear drum extends out towards the external auditory meatus, as a membranous sleeve, the so-called 'glove-finger' (which it much resembles). This is capped by a horny plug composed of superimposed layers of keratinised cells shed from the lining of the meatus (Fig. 4.12). These ear plugs have provided a valuable means of determining the age of whalebone whales.

Just as in terrestrial mammals, the three ossicles of the middle ear are contained in the gas-filled cavity of the bulla. There is no foam here and the bones are as free to move as in any mammal. Even at great depths, the ossicles will still be surrounded by gas, volume changes being compensated for by the engorgement of

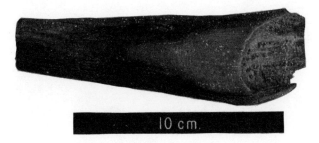

Fig. 4.12   Ear plug of a Sei Whale in section.

a body of vascular tissue, the corpus cavernosum of the bulla. Even with this compensation, however, there must still be great stresses set up in the bulla on diving, but it is probable that the massiveness of this bone provides protection while internal adjustments are made.

The bones of the middle ear of whales function in exactly the same way as do those of other mammals. However, they have to deal with vibrations transmitted through a watery medium. The displacement amplitude of sound vibrations in water is about sixty times smaller than that in air from sounds of the same intensity and frequency, while the pressure amplitude is about sixty times greater. As the cochlea of a whale is, to all intents and purposes, exactly the same as that of a land mammal, this means that the train of ear ossicles has to convert the very small displacements at the ear drum (or tympanic ligament, as it is in the whale) to substantially larger ones at the oval window. This is done by altering the leverage of the three ossicles (Fig. 4.13). The tympanic ligament is attached to the malleus at a very acute angle near to its tip. The malleus undergoes a torsional movement which is translated to the incus and results in a movement of the stapes which is about thirty times greater than that of the tympanic ligament. The final result is that the displacement of the oval window is of the same order of size in both the terrestrial mammal and the whale.

The pressure displacement at the oval window is related to the

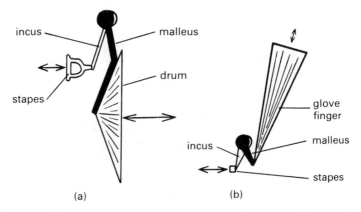

Fig. 4.13   The lever system of the ear ossicles in: (a) a terrestrial mammal, (b) a whale. The difference in arrangement of the levers compensates for the differences of displacement amplitude of sound waves in air and water.

ratio of the cross-sectional areas of the ear drum of the footplate of the stapes. In relative terms the tympanic ligament of a whale has a smaller receptive area than the ear drum of a dog. This is compensated for by a corresponding reduction in the area of the stapes footplate, so that the pressure displacement is also similar to that in the conventional mammalian ear.

These complex relationships were elucidated by Fraser and Purves with the most inspired application of mechano-physiology that has been used in the study of whales. Much more of the almost incredible process of adaptation was also revealed, as how, for example, the rotational movement of the malleus is the only one that can be transmitted to the incus, thus preventing resonant vibration from the skull being passed to the cochlea, and how the external opening of the external auditory meatus might be moved, by muscles, in and out of acoustic shadows, to facilitate binaural hearing. However, there is not space here to go further into this—the papers of Fraser and Purves cited in the bibliography can be consulted for a full account.

The Cetacea have evolved a means of isolating acoustic signals from their watery environment and converting them to a form in which they can be interpreted by a basic mammalian inner ear. The profound and meticulous adaptations that this process has required make it clear that the ear is an organ of the highest significance to the whale. The extent to which a whale uses its ears, and increases their value by producing sounds itself, forms the subject of the next chapter.

5 Vocalisations and echo-location

'The dolphin, when taken out of the water, gives a squeak and moans in air.... For this creature has a voice, for it is furnished with a lung and a windpipe; but its tongue is not loose, nor has it lips, so as to give utterance to an articulate sound.'

So wrote Aristotle (*Historia Animalium*, Book IV.9) in his usual informative manner, so it is perhaps surprising that for many centuries writers on animals, who themselves tended to make few observations, and relied on the classical authors for most of what they knew about zoology, believed whales to be mute.

People in close contact with whales could probably have corrected this belief easily enough. The under-water whistling and twittering of the White Whale earned it the name 'sea canary' from the Arctic whalers, and porpoises and dolphins can sometimes be heard to vocalise at sea. The problem in listening to whales is that they vocalise under water, and reflection and attenuation at the water–air interface makes the propagation of their vocalisations into the medium in which we can hear it difficult. An additional problem is that much of the sound that Cetacea produce is at frequencies that are inaudible to a human ear.

The impetus for the intensive study of whale sounds, together with the apparatus with which to make the study, came from the under-water defences developed during World War 2. Almost the only way to detect a submerged submarine was by listening for the noises generated by its engines and propellers. Because of the good sound-propagating qualities of water, under-water microphones, or hydrophones, could detect submarines at considerable ranges and with good directionality. Submarine listening watches became a standard defence practice and the USA in particular set up a chain of listening stations, manned continuously, to protect its long coastline.

The sea proved to be a surprisingly noisy environment and considerable difficulty was experienced in separating the sounds of intruding submarines from those of biological origin. Many of the biological sounds in the sea were of a strangely mechanical nature; sharp cracks, hums and creaks. Gradually the various sounds in the chorus from the sea were attributed to the animals that made them. It was found that shrimps could produce very loud cracks and some fish made loud groans and creaks. Some of the more complex sounds proved to be associated with the presence of Cetacea.

Because of the importance of sonic detection to defence, the USA provided strong backing for what came to be known as marine bio-acoustics, with a school of workers in the States of whom W. N. Kellogg, K. S. Norris and W. E. Scheville deserve special mention. In the three decades since these men started work, a great deal has been discovered and a fascinating story revealed. However, as with a good many other aspects of cetology, we do not yet have the whole story and much remains for research.

It is not easy to describe the sounds made by cetaceans. There are moans and whistles, trills and moos, and deep bell-like notes with great purity of tone. Additionally, and very characteristically, the odontocetes produce sounds that resemble the creaking of a rusty hinge. If these creaking sounds are analysed, it is found that they are composed of a series of very brief pulses of sound, or clicks. Each click may last for only a fraction of a millisecond to as much as 25 msec. The clicks themselves are bursts of 'noise', i.e. they do not have a particular frequency, although there may be a concentration of sound energy in one region of the frequency spectrum. Thus the click of a Rough-toothed Dolphin has a peak energy output of about 25 kHz, with some emissions as low as 2.7 kHz and some as high as 256 kHz (Norris and Evans, 1967). Dolphins can switch from clicks rich in high frequency sound to clicks with predominant low frequency components within a few milliseconds. The clicks are produced in series, or trains, of pulses with repetition rates typically around 40–50 pulses per sec but which can range from 1 or 2 pulses per sec to 525 pulses per sec (Evans and Prescott, 1962). It is when the pulse repetition rate rises to several hundred per sec that we can perceive the sound as the creak of a door hinge. Sometimes the clicks are produced in closely-separated pairs, or what appears to be a single click can be further resolved into a series of very brief pulses.

Killer Whales produce clicks that are different from those of most other delphinids. Each click consists of a narrow band component with a fundamental frequency of between 250 and 500 Hz, with higher frequency components of less amplitude. The clicks last for 10–25 msec and they are emitted in short bursts of 10–15 pulses with repetition rates of 6–18 pulses per sec. A typical train of clicks starts at around 500 Hz with the higher repetition rate and decays to about 350 Hz at the slower repetition rate (Scheville and Watkins, 1966).

Sperm Whales produce long clicks, with durations of about 24 msec, although these are complex structures comprising as many as 9 very brief clicks with durations of 2–0.1 msec. Multiple clicks of this sort are known as 'burst-pulses', using a term taken from sonar operators. These burst-pulses, or compound clicks, produced by Sperm Whales have characteristic patterns, or 'signatures', that are unique to the individuals producing them (Fig. 5.1). The repetition rates in trains of Sperm Whale clicks are relatively low compared with the smaller odontocetes; pulse rates of about 1 to about 50 clicks per sec have been recorded by Backus and Scheville (1966), although characteristically the repetition rate is in the lower part of this range.

Besides the trains of clicks, odontocetes can produce squeals and whistles which span only a narrow band of frequencies, or may be a pure tone. Sometimes these remain at one frequency, but more often they shift from one frequency to another, the complete vocalisation lasting for a second or more.

In general mysticetes do not make such complex sounds as odontocetes. Typically they produce very low frequency moans and screams with frequencies ranging from around 20 Hz in the Fin Whale (this will be below the frequency threshold of some human ears) to around 1,000 Hz in the Humpback.

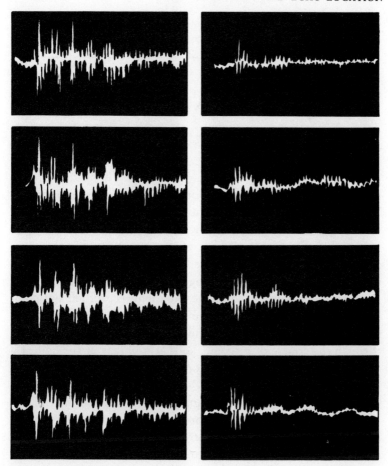

Fig. 5.1 Oscilloscope photographs of click trains from two different Sperm Whales. The essential similarity, or signature, of the clicks in the column on the left, and those in the column on the right, can be seen. (After Backus and Scheville, 1966.)

Humpback Whales seem to be especially vocal mysticetes, particularly when they are migrating in the warmer waters of their range. Their songs have become well known to many people who have listened to the recording *Songs of the Humpback Whale* made by Roger Payne (1970). The strange, haunting quality of these songs, with their echo effect resulting from the sea–air interface, has made a deep impression on many hearers.

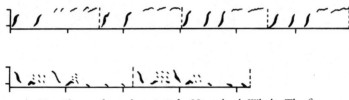

Fig. 5.2   Two themes from the song of a Humpback Whale. The first consists of four phrases, the second of only two. The frequency scale is logarithmic. (After Payne, 1970.)

Humpbacks' songs are complex and it seems that, as in the Sperm Whale, there is sufficient individual specificity in the songs to identify particular whales by their voice patterns. Each song is made up of a constant number of themes repeated in the same order. The themes are composed of phrases and the main difference between successive songs of a particular whale is the number of phrases in each theme. No theme is ever left out completely, but sometimes a whale repeats a phrase many times before going on to the next theme. Phrases may change gradually through the course of a theme, so that a phrase at the end of a theme may be quite different from what it was at the beginning (Fig. 5.2).

The means whereby cetaceans produce their sounds is not obvious. Terrestrial mammals produce sound mostly by passing air from the lungs over two strips of tissue, the vocal cords, stretched across the larynx and tensioned by very precise muscular control. Whales do not possess vocal cords, and, since their vocalisations take place under water, where there is no renewable source of air, this means of vocalising is not available to them. On the other hand, the recirculation of a small quantity of air, perhaps at considerable pressure, could provide the necessary means of generating sound energy provided there is some suitable tissue to vibrate.

The odontocete larynx, although it lacks vocal cords, is a complex structure with a well developed musculature. The anterior cartilage, the arytenoid, is greatly elongated and crosses through the lumen of the oesophagus to enter the posterior opening of the bony nasal passages, the internal nares, within

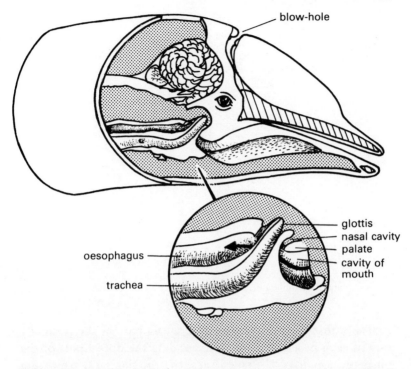

Fig. 5.3   Section of the head of a Common Porpoise, to show the relations of the larynx.

which the tip of the arytenoid is held firmly by a sphincter muscle. This results in a complete separation of the air passages from the rest of the mouth and appears to be an adaptation allowing the odontocete to feed (and perhaps to vocalise while feeding) without swamping its lungs with water (Fig. 5.3). Of course, other mammals can feed perfectly well under water—many seals habitually do this—and rely on the epiglottis to seal off the larynx, so it is perhaps permissible to suppose that the arrangement in odontocetes (the extended arytenoids are not found in mysticetes) has more to do with vocalising beneath the surface than with feeding.

At the distal end of the nasal passages through the skull, the external bony nares, are a pair of heavily muscled valves, the nasal plugs, which serve to close the nares. These plugs rest

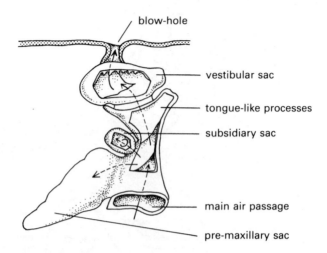

Fig. 5.4   The blow-hole and its associated diverticula in a dolphin.

against a thin membrane stretched across part of the posterior face of each narial opening. Surrounding the dorsal part of the plugs are a pair of U-shaped sacs, the tubular sacs, which are thought to assist in the tight closure of the nares by the plugs. These sacs connect with the airway by round openings on their posterior border. Dorsal to the plugs, the air passage gives off a pair of vestibular sacs, the inner margins of which form the lips of the blow-hole (Fig. 5.4).

Various sites have been suggested for the origin of the sounds made by whales. An obvious one is the larynx itself, or the lips of the arytenoid cartilage. It was early demonstrated by Bill Scheville and Barbara Lawrence (1953) that blowing through the larynx of a dead dolphin could produce sounds not entirely un-like the whistles and squeals of the living animal. Another sug-gested origin was the membrane lying across the posterior face of the dorsal narial opening. The lateral lips of the nasal plugs were another possible site. Ken Norris (1964) trained a dolphin to make clicks with its blow-hole open and was then able to peer down the airway as the dolphin clicked away. He saw fluid sputtering over the lateral edges of the nasal plugs. Although this is suggestive, it does not confirm the plugs as the site of click production, since the sputtering could be caused by the pulsation of air deeper within the nasal tract, as Norris himself recognised. Finally, the lips of the blow-hole have been put forward as a possible origin of the sounds.

The arguments put forward by the proponents of the various sites are complex. At this stage it is impossible to say with certainty that any one site is exclusively responsible for the vocalisations. Quite probably more than one site is involved; certainly the generation of the type of sounds produced by cetaceans is a complex matter which still remains to be finally explained.

What use do whales make of their vocal repertoire? The usual function of animal sounds is to advertise the presence of the animal making them and to convey a limited amount of general information about its state, whether it is angry, alarmed, sexually responsive, etc. There is little reason to doubt that whales, with their acute sense of hearing and wide range of vocalisations, use the sounds they produce in this way, though much of the evidence is conjectural. The constant whistling of a school of dolphins reminds us of the twittering of a flock of finches, or the chattering of a troop of monkeys. These are all animals that habitually move about in a group and they are believed to use their vocalisations, or contact calls, as a means of keeping members of the group in touch with each other. In the case of the finches and monkeys, visual contacts may be impeded by foliage—for the dolphins the poor visibility under water will make visual clues less effective, while, for the aquatic animal, the auditory signals will be even more efficient than they are for the animals in the aerial environment.

It is when we consider the group function of vocalisations that we see the significance of the individual signatures that Scheville discovered in the Sperm Whale's clicks. Sperm Whales are highly gregarious, with a complex social structure and, in these circumstances, the identification of particular members within the group may be of importance to its other members. Nor should we suppose that the whistles of other odontocetes are not equally as individually recognisable by other dolphins, even if sound pattern differences are not as easily demonstrable as in Sperm Whale clicks.

The Humpback Whale's songs are a different case. Here there is no complex social organisation (that we know of) but individually recognisable songs may enable pairs or groups to reform at the breeding grounds. The very great distances that sounds, particularly low frequency sounds, can penetrate in water means that the problems of locating a mate in what we suppose to be the featureless expanse of the oceans may be less than might be supposed. In fact, the ocean may well be far from featureless to a cetacean; differences in salinity or temperature, or echo patterns from the bottom or from thermal discontinuities in the water column, may be conspicuous to whales, so that what we suppose to be uniform is to them as well marked as any land mass. Even so, the ability to hear a potential mate at ranges of some tens, or perhaps even hundreds of kilometres, will have been a substantial advantage to species like some of the beaked whales, which seem always to have been rare, and is perhaps now important to species like the Blue Whale, which has become a great deal less abundant in the last half-century.

Besides serving to identify a conspecific, or a particular member of a group, the calls may provide other information. Old whalers were convinced that a wounded Sperm Whale could communicate its distress to its fellows several miles distant. More recently it was observed that a juvenile Sperm Whale that was unfortunate enough to become entangled with the propeller of the research yacht *Calypso* was soon surrounded by twenty-seven female Sperm Whales, presumably attracted by the calf's distress signals.

Some systematic observations of the effects of whale sounds on other whales have been made, mostly using the whistle vocalisations of Bottle-nosed Dolphins. John Dreher (1966) in America identified whistles of various delphinids by the contour of their pitch and found he could recognise thirty-two different patterns in the four species he studied. He used tape-recordings of six of these to play to a small group of Bottle-nosed Dolphins in a pool and analysed their response. The first whistle presented was one very commonly heard in a group of dolphins. It could be described as an 'upward glide'—a whistle that began at a lower frequency and increased to a higher one. Visually, the dolphins showed little response when this signal was played to them, but vocally their behaviour changed. They increased their own rate of vocalisation, the most common whistle being a repeat of the upward glide being played to them, although some animals produced a whistle that started high and fell to a lower frequency. It seems that the upward glide whistle represents a 'search' vocalisation and is a common response to any new stimulus; the downward glide is most often heard in a 'distress' situation. When a whistle with a rising-falling-rising contour was presented, the dolphins in the pool became highly excited and one male erected his penis. A double-humped whistle (rise-fall-rise-fall) seemed to be associated with excitement and irritation. When this was played to the animals in the pool they produced many vocalisations, including a 'distress' call, and there was a lot of thrashing about in the water. A fall-rise-fall contour whistle seemed to subdue the activity of the dolphins in the pool and their vocalisation rate dropped. A three-humped signal (rise-fall-rise-fall-rise-fall) produced great excitement, all the animals in the pool turned towards the loudspeaker and seemed to examine it closely. The vocal activity of the dolphins was higher in response to this signal than to any of the others.

What do these experiments tell us? They confirm our belief that particular vocalisations can convey more information than the simple advertisement of the presence of another dolphin, but it is doubtful if they do much more than this. Dreher used a rather complicated formula to calculate the information content of the vocalisations he studied and came to the conclusion that the whistles had an information content rather close to that of letters in English, although he was careful to point out that no connection was implied between the two systems.

It is easy to read too much into dolphin whistles and people have already begun to speak of a dolphin language. Their communication may well be more sophisticated than we know at present, but there is no evidence that dolphins possess a complex communication system, analogous to human speech, which can be used to transmit precise information. David and Melba

Caldwell (1972) studied the development of whistles in young Bottle-nosed Dolphins and found that the whistles were present on the day of birth, albeit a trifle ragged. The only change noted in an animal whose whistles were recorded regularly from birth to the age of 2 years was that the whistles became smoother. This is not what one would expect if the dolphin 'language' were of the same nature as human speech.

Much has been made of an experiment where a pair of Bottle-nosed Dolphins were separated by a barrier through which they could not see, but through which they could hear each other. One dolphin could see a pair of lights, while the other, which could not see the lights, had to press one of two plates, as indicated by the appropriate light, in order to obtain a food reward for both animals. The dolphins soon learned to do this and it was claimed that the first dolphin was using language to instruct the second as to which plate to press. This seemed a sophisticated response, but it has since been shown that it represents no more than part of the animal trainer's stock in trade and a pair of pigeons have been trained to perform the same task. As it is not usually suggested that pigeons have any special intelligence, still yet possess a language (save in the most general sense), there is no need to postulate the same for dolphins (Matthews, 1978).

What dolphins can do supremely well is to use their vocalisations and auditory sense for echo-location to provide them with detailed information about their environment under conditions when other sensory inputs are lacking. Echo-location is familiar to many people in the form of echo-sounders used to determine the distance to the bottom from the hull of a boat or, in a more refined form, as sonar used on warships to determine the range and bearing of submarines. The principle of both is the same. A pulse of sound energy is sent out and the time taken for the echo to return to the target (the sea-floor or the submarine) is measured. From a knowledge of the velocity of sound in water (about 1,500 m per sec) the range of the target can be calculated; if the sound beam emitted is sufficiently directional, the bearing also can be determined. Echo-sounders operate by using very intense short pulses of sound. The intensity ensures that the echo is loud enough to be detected and the shortness of the pulse prevents the returning echo interfering with the outgoing pulse. The clicks produced by odontocetes have exactly the characteristics that would be required for echo-locating.

The first experiments on cetacean echo-location were made in the USA. At Woods Hole Oceanographical Institute in Massachusetts, Bill Scheville and Barbara Lawrence (1956) borrowed a male *Tursiops* from an oceanarium. The dolphin was kept in a small (20 m) diameter, very murky pool, kept turbid by the silt stirred up by the dolphin's movements. If a fish was tossed in the pond the dolphin would always swim directly towards it, attracted by the splash. The investigators noticed that the dolphin spent a lot of time searching the pond for fish, emitting faint creaking noises (trains of clicks) while doing so. Suspecting that this might represent active echo-location, Scheville and Lawrence set out to test this. They found that, if a 15 cm long fish was quietly slipped a few centimetres under the water, even on a dark night, the dolphin would swim straight towards it and take it. As a refinement of the test they set up a 2.4 m long fishing net perpendicular to a skiff moored at one end of the pond. One experimenter sat at each end of the skiff, on either side of the net. After a signal, either striking a pipe suspended in the water, or a brief pulse of ultrasound, a fish was offered in a random pattern from each end of the skiff. In about three quarters of the tests the dolphin would choose the correct side of the net to swim up and take its reward. Under these circumstances it seemed certain that the dolphin was using its trains of clicks to detect the presence of the fish in the water. In these experiments, the dolphin detected the fish at ranges not usually exceeding 5 m; although occasionally it swam up to take a fish from 15 m, it is not certain that it had detected the fish at this distance.

About the same time that the Schevilles were working at Woods Hole, Winthrop Kellogg (1958) was making some experiments on the same subject at Florida State University. Kellogg had two *Tursiops*, which were kept in a specially constructed pool with a soft bottom to eliminate echoes. He constructed a maze of metal rods, 5 cm wide, hung vertically in the water 2.4 m apart, in patterns that could be varied at will. In the first 20 minutes of the test, the dolphins struck the obstacle four times, and then only with their tail-flukes as they swam past. They soon learned to avoid them completely and achieved 100% successful avoidance, even on a moonless night. In another experiment (Kellogg, 1959), he showed that the dolphins could use their click trains to discriminate between fish of different sizes. They were offered 30 cm Mullet, which they disliked, and Spotted Sea Trout of about half this size, which they preferred. On the first trial, one dolphin made four mistakes out of sixteen trials, but quickly improved on this, so that in the last 140 trials no errors were made. However, if Mullet and Sea Trout of the same size were offered, no discrimination could be made. To demonstrate that visual stimuli played no part in this discrimination, Kellogg suspended two fish, one of them behind a sheet of plate glass, which would have acted as an acoustical, but not optical, barrier. In 202 trials, the dolphin never approached the fish behind the glass plate. To eliminate the possibility of some chemical sense being involved, Kellogg devised an experiment where no food was involved. The dolphin's pool was divided by a steel net with two openings which could be closed by a sheet of transparent (and invisible while under water) Plexiglass. The dolphins were then chased from one side of the net to the other while the Plexiglass sheet was removed randomly from one opening to the other. In 100 trials, on only two occasions did the dolphins approach the sealed-off opening.

The extent to which dolphins can discriminate between artificial targets is remarkable. A female *Tursiops* called Alice was trained to submit to being blindfolded by having rubber suction cups placed over her eyes (Turner and Norris, 1966). She was then trained to distinguish metal spheres whose diameters differed from those of a standard sphere 6.35 cm across. The spheres were attached to both ends of a long horizontal bar connected to a vertical pipe, so that the position of the spheres could be alternated by rotating the pipe. The start signal was the splash of the bar being lowered into the water, in response to which the dolphin had to swim from a start point to the opposite side of the pool and press one of two levers, left or right, corresponding to the position of the standard sphere. If correct, Alice was rewarded with a fish. It was found that the dolphin could distinguish perfectly spheres that differed by 0.95 cm in diameter (15% of the standard sphere) and with 77% accuracy spheres differing by 0.64 cm (10% of the standard sphere).

During these experiments the targets could usually be successfully distinguished with a click train lasting 1.1 to 4.7 sec with pulse rates between 20 and 230 pulses per sec. Often the train began with a rate of 80–100 pulses per sec, rapidly dropping to 50–70 pulses per sec, then rising again at the end to 130–180 pulses per sec, before finally falling to 50 pulses per sec and stopping. With the simplest discrimination (between spheres of 3.18 and 6.35 cm diameter) the click series was uniform and of short duration (average about 2 sec). With more difficult problems (spheres of 4.45 and 6.35 cm and 5.18 and 6.35 cm) there was more variability in the series length. Long series, up to 4.7 sec, were more successful than short ones, as though the animal required more information to make its decision. Pulse repetition rates changed, depending on the ratio of target sizes, increasing from 65 per sec with spheres of 3.18 and 6.35 cm, to 78 per sec with spheres of 5.18 and 6.35 cm. These figures were much lower than the pulse repetition rates when the dolphin was taking a fish (about 400–500 or even 1,200 pulses per sec), but probably related to the fact that, in the experiment with the spheres, the dolphin was required to discriminate at a distance while with a fish it would swim right up to it (Norris *et al.*, 1966).

Kellogg noted that the creaking noises the dolphins produced when searching for food were made only when muddy water or darkness prevented sight being used and were always accompanied by movements of the head from side to side. For echo-location to be effective, it is essential that the sound energy produced is directional. That the click trains of dolphins had this property was demonstrated on a captive *Tursiops*. When blindfolded this dolphin emitted continuous echo-location trains but only when the animal directly faced a narrow band hydrophone could signals be detected (Norris *et al.*, 1961). As a follow-up to this experiment, sound generators were placed at suspected sites of sound production and it was found that structured directional sound fields were produced. Norris (1964) suggested how this might be effected.

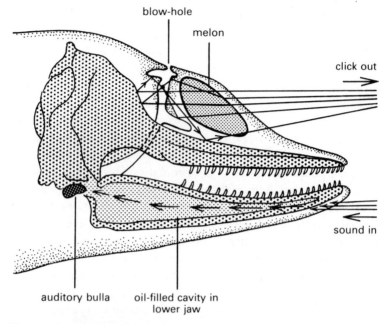

blow-hole

melon

click out

auditory bulla

oil-filled cavity in
lower jaw

sound in

Fig. 5.5 Sound propagation and reception in the head of a dolphin. The melon acts as an acoustic lens, focussing the clicks, while the oil-filled cavity of the lower jaw acts as a sound conducting pipe to the ear. (After Norris.)

Norris supposed the clicks were produced in the region of the nasal plugs. These lie in front of the concave dish formed by the dorsal surface of the upper jaw and its rising crest (Fig. 5.5) and it seems possible that the bony tissues of the skull act as a parabolic reflector, focusing the beam of sound waves produced at the nasal plugs. The complex system of air passages, in particular the tubular and vestibular sacs, would prevent sound waves being scattered randomly forward by providing further reflective surfaces to direct the sound back to the bone. An additional refinement, according to Norris's theory, is the 'melon', a fatty body that lies in front of the blow-hole and is conspicuous in many odontocetes. This contains lipids which vary in their composition depending on their position in the melon. As it has also been demonstrated that the acoustic properties of the lipids vary with their chemical composition (Varanasi et al., 1975), it is possible that the melon is, in fact, an elaborate acoustic lens which gathers up the sound waves reflected forwards from the skull and concentrates them in a narrow beam.

Norris's theory goes further and suggests that the lower jaw acts as an acoustic probe, conducting sound waves from in front of the animal directly to the inner ear. It has been shown how the ears function bilaterally, using the auditory meatus on each side to conduct sound to the very sensitive cochlea. However, echoes received from a narrow beam of sound directed ahead would not easily be received in this way. The posterior part of a dolphin's mandible consists of a greatly thinned and expanded sheet of bone (about 0.1–3.0 mm in thickness at its thinnest point in various small to medium sized odontocetes). This envelops a column of fatty tissue, the intramandibular fat body, which contains lipids similar to those of the melon. Returning echoes of the click train arrive at the tissue overlying the thin bone, the 'acoustic window' through which they pass virtually unimpeded (Norris, 1968), and are thus conducted along the fat body to the condyle of the jaw, which lies very close to the auditory bulla, where the sounds would be received.

If this ingenious theory is correct, it goes far to explain some of the otherwise puzzling structures in the head of odontocetes, as well as the side-to-side head movements of dolphins which are producing echo-location pulses—they are scanning the target with a narrow beam of sound to provide angular information. It would also explain why mysticetes do not produce echo-location clicks—they lack the requisite structures to produce them or to process the echoes they generate. On the other hand, it is possible that mysticetes may be aware of the echoes of some of their very powerful vocalisations, which could provide valuable information about their surroundings.

The echo-location of odontocetes is certainly a remarkable sense, and seems the more remarkable to the ordinary person who has little experience of interpreting echoes. However, as Professor Griffen (1958) has pointed out in his fascinating book *Listening in the Dark*, one can easily learn to use the information that echoes can provide with no special receptor apparatus (although a directional click-generator is desirable). Blind persons tapping with their sticks learn more from the echoes than most people suppose. We should not presume that because dolphins possess a refined sense of echo-location they possess also some superior mental powers. Indeed, some dolphins turn out to be remarkably poor echo-locators. Although the Common Dolphin emits typical click trains in the open sea, it may become disorientated when introduced into a tank with murky water and swim about colliding with the walls. A trained Pacific White-sided Dolphin was blindfolded and promptly ran into the walls of its pool. It took several days to learn to navigate blindfold. Similarly, a Bottle-nosed Dolphin, that paragon of the whale-trainer's art, which had been taught to press a lever on command was quite unable to find the lever when blindfolded. It was reduced to swimming round its tank, feeling for the lever with its snout (Norris, 1969). However, we should not read too much into the failures of captive specimens—gaol-birds, as Bill Scheville calls them. Their achievements are sufficiently remarkable, even without the exaggerations that some people like to confer on them.

6 Food and feeding

It was the attraction of exploitable food that lured the ancestors of the Cetacea into the marine environment. Perhaps this food was more readily available because of the recent (in geological terms) disappearance of the giant marine reptiles, the ichthyosaurs and the plesiosaurs; perhaps the early whales simply competed more effectively than the large predators already present for the food that was there. The whales did not, and still do not, exploit any unique food resource, nor do they employ any unique principle for capturing their food, although the baleen whales have specialised for filter-feeding in a manner unsurpassed by any other group of large animals.

All whales are carnivorous, in the sense that they feed on other animals, but while odontocetes have retained a fairly typical pattern of obtaining their food, by catching and eating, one at a time, prey items usually between ten or a thousand times smaller than themselves, the mysticetes browse or graze through the oceans, straining out, by the thousand, food items which are usually between a hundred million and one million times smaller than the feeding whales.

Although the odontocete feeding method is less specialised we know far less about it than we do of the feeding of the baleen whales. This is partly because far fewer odontocetes have been examined, but more because of the absence of any highly specialised anatomical adaptations in odontocetes which might give a clue to their feeding methods. In fact it seems that odontocetes depend for their feeding on the deployment of specialised behaviour patterns, which have yet to be observed and recorded.

Toothed whales feed mainly on fish and squid, although the successful and cosmopolitan Killer Whale has added a further item to the diet—the flesh of warm-blooded animals. To take any of these prey we might suppose that teeth would be highly desirable, yet we find a bewildering array of differing dentitions in odontocetes. No existing whale possesses a typical set of mammalian teeth. The most common odontocete dentition is typified by the Common Dolphin (*Delphinus delphis*) where forty–fifty slender, peg-like teeth, about 3 mm in diameter at the gum, are set along each margin of both upper and lower jaw. These teeth are all similar, or homodont, thus they cannot be divided into the usual categories of incisors, canines, pre-molars and molars. Further, the teeth in an adult dolphin represent the milk dentition, for there is no replacement of the original teeth by a permanent dentition, as is usual in mammals.

Such an array of sharp teeth is clearly well suited to the capture of agile fish or squid and we find that the dolphin's diet includes a variety of pelagic fish, such as Herring, Pilchard and Mackerel, as well as squid, which are very fast swimmers. Similar dentitions and feeding patterns are found in other oceanic dolphins. The Spotted Dolphin (*Stenella attenuata*) and the Spinner (*S. longirostris*), which occur in the tropical Pacific, both feed largely on the abundant squid, *Dosidicus gigas*, but take also several other squid species, besides numerous fish, particularly Lantern-fish (Myctophidae) and Flying-fish (Exocetidae). However, careful analysis of their diets reveals that the Spotted Dolphin feeds mostly near the surface, while the Spinner feeds at greater depths and at different times of the day (Perrin *et al.*, 1973).

These pelagic dolphins generally have slender, beak-like jaws and it is difficult to imagine that they can do much more than manipulate the fish or squid towards the throat so that it is swallowed, entire and more or less alive.

Those odontocetes that live in shallower seas and large estuaries, such as the Harbour Porpoise (*Phocoena phocoena*) or the Beluga (*Delphinapterus leucas*), tend to have a shorter rostrum with fewer teeth. The true porpoises of the family Phocoenidae have peculiar spade-like teeth with slightly lobed crowns. These could serve as a shearing device, so that porpoises at least have the option of taking bites out of their prey, although they probably swallow most of it whole. As in the oceanic forms, a wide variety of fish and squid may be taken, although some groups, such as the oceanic lantern-fishes, may not, their place being taken by bottom-dwelling fish, such as flat-fish, or demersal fish, like Cod, which inhabit the water column near the sea-floor.

Looking at the Killer Whale's teeth one has little doubt about their functional nature. There are about ten–thirteen stout teeth, some 2.5–5 cm in diameter at the gum, on each side of the upper and lower jaw. The teeth are slightly oval in cross-section, the longer axis being transverse to the teeth row. These are clearly teeth which could crush a large and active animal and which, when combined with vigorous movement of the Killer's body, could tear great chunks of flesh away. There are many accounts of Killer Whales attacking other whales and a good many of these are, no doubt, exaggerated. Harrison Matthews (1978) has recently cast some healthy scepticism on the often-repeated story of a pack of ravenous Killer Whales belabouring a wretched right whale and catching hold of its lips till the poor creature lolls out its tongue, which the Killers then seize upon and devour. This story originated from the whale-fishing off the coast of New England and was included in a paper sent by the Hon. Paul Dudley to the Royal Society in 1725 (Dudley, 1725). Since the first publication, the story has been repeated many times, although it does not appear that the events described by Dudley have been observed again. However, we should not dismiss this tale utterly. Killer Whales will certainly attack other whales. There are reliable accounts of Minke Whales being killed and eaten by Killers (Handcock, 1965) and Scammon (1874) reported them killing young Grey Whales. Scammon's observations have since been confirmed when a pack of Killer Whales was seen to kill and eat a young Grey Whale off California (Baldridge, 1972). A slow-moving right whale would seem a perfectly possible target for a school of Killers and to pull aside the lips, so as to get at the tongue, would not appear to be beyond the type of co-operative activity that one could expect from a sophisticated hunter like a Killer Whale. That the tongue of a baleen whale is a favoured morsel for Killers is known to every modern whaler. When a shot whale is inflated and buoyed at sea and left 'in flag' often it is surrounded by a pack of Killer Whales, whose first objective is always to eat the tongue. Some floating factories used to station men armed with rifles at the stern of the ship to shoot at the Killers as they worried the carcases of the whales tethered there. Every tongue taken represented the loss of five barrels of oil and this was a tax the whalers would not readily pay to the Killers. So perhaps we should reserve judgement on Dudley's anecdote. If right whales were as plentiful today as they were in Dudley's time our modern cetologists might confirm his account!

Another often-repeated yarn of the Killer's astonishing appetite and capacity stemmed from an account by Eschricht (1866), who recorded finding the remains of thirteen porpoises and fourteen seals in the stomach of a Killer Whale. Although Eschricht made it plain that the remains were only fragments, some of them very small, this was reported by Slijper (1962) as if the Killer's stomach had actually contained twenty-seven large mammals (which might have weighed something like 2,000 kg)!

But if Slijper dramatised Eschricht's account excessively, there is no doubt at all that Killers do eat smaller dolphins, porpoises and seals. They are probably not very selective, taking what is available, or perhaps exercising individual (or group) choice. In the North Pacific, Dall's Porpoise, *Phocoenoides dalli*, is said to be a favourite food item. Almost any species of seal or sea-lion is liable to Killer Whale attack. Large specimens, such as the Elephant Seal, *Mirounga* spp., or Steller's Sea-lion, *Eumetopias stelleri*, occasionally escape, bearing the characteristic parallel scars caused by the Killer's teeth, but it is unlikely that many of the smaller seals which find themselves in a Killer's jaws survive the experience. Many seals and small cetaceans are obviously intensely disturbed when they are aware of a Killer Whale in the vicinity. Naturally timid species, such as the Grey Seal, *Halichoerus grypus*, have been known to jump out of the sea and join a man on a rock when Killers are about. They have good cause to be frightened—Robert Burton has seen a Killer Whale off North Rona carrying a dead Grey Seal in its mouth!

This fear of Killer Whales evinced by other whales and seals has recently been exploited as a means of deterring these mammals away from fishing-nets where they may interfere with the fishing. Thus a 'Beluga-spooker' plays under-water recordings of Killer Whale vocalisations to keep White Whales from Salmon nets and a similar device has been experimented with to keep Cape Fur Seals, *Arctocephalus pusillus*, out of purse-seines set for Pilchards off South Africa. But those who advocate such devices as a humane means of protecting fisheries should bear in mind the possibility that, if the recorded Killer Whale sounds are broadcast too frequently, without the real and awful presence of a Killer Whale on the scene, then the seals or Belugas (which are animals eminently capable of learning) may eventually come to regard the recordings not so much as a warning than as a dinner-gong.

Besides other whales and seals, Killers also from time to time take birds. Reports are most often of penguins being captured in the Antarctic, though a variety of birds are taken in northern waters.

However, despite all this flesh-eating, for which the Killer's teeth seem so well designed, it seems that the main diet consists, as in most other odontocetes, of fish and squid. Salmon are often reported as being a major fish prey, but, off the coast of Japan, Cod and flat-fish like Halibut were, together with squid, the most abundant species found in Killers' stomachs (Nishiwaki and Handa, 1958). Probably the same is true elsewhere—Killer Whales, like other dolphins, are sufficiently intelligent to adapt their feeding behaviour to a variety of prey. Where seals congregate to breed, the Killers will hunt seals; where Salmon are massing in an estuary prior to the spawning run, the Killers will feed on Salmon. But against these conspicuous feeding behaviours, there is a normal pattern of feeding on those fish and squid that are sufficiently abundant and widespread to provide a staple diet.

Before leaving the subject of Killer Whales it is worth recalling their two smaller relatives, the Pygmy Killer Whale, *Feresa attenuata*, and the False Killer Whale, *Pseudorca crassidens*. Both these dolphins have similar stout, although smaller, teeth. The Pygmy Killer has been reported to attack other dolphins (Best, 1970) and dolphins kept together with Pygmy Killers in oceanaria in Japan showed clear fright reactions, but there are no data on actual diets. The False Killer feeds mainly on cephalopods and fish; there are no records of feeding on other dolphins or seals.

So far, the toothed whales I have been discussing have possessed what appear to be a functional dentition in both jaws. The largest odontocete of all, the Sperm Whale, has an impressive dentition of about twenty-five enormous teeth on each side of the lower jaw, but the upper jaw is devoid of any dentition at all in a functional sense. The teeth on the mandible fit into deep sockets in the upper jaw and on the inner side of these sockets may be found a rudimentary upper dentition of up to about fifteen small teeth on each side, of which few, if any, will be visible above the gum.

Because of the long commercial interest in this species there are many records of the feeding habits of Sperm Whales. The bulk of the diet is made up of medium-sized to large squid of about a metre in length, although much smaller histioteuthid squid with body lengths of only a few centimetres are also taken. Much more famous are the giant squids, the architeuthids. These are neither so massive nor as common in the Sperm Whale's diet as many people believe. Even the real giants, *Architeuthis* and *Moroteuthis*, are comparatively slim-bodied squid and most of their length (which may be in excess of 15 m) is made up by the tentacles. However, Sperm Whales do not feed only on squid; many demersal and bathypelagic (deep-water) fishes are included in the diet. It seems that Sperm Whales in the open ocean are mainly squid-feeders, but inshore populations take proportionally more fish. Near Iceland, for example, Sperm Whales feed mainly on Lumpsuckers, *Cyclopterus lumpus*, Sea Perch, *Sebastes* spp. and Angler-fish, *Lophius piscatorius* (Roe, 1969), while off the Azores a Common Skate, *Raja rhina*, makes up about a quarter of the food taken (Clarke, 1956).

If one looks at a Sperm Whale the question immediately arises: how does it get its food into its mouth? At the base of the huge wedge-shaped head lies the massive, but disproportionately slender, under-hung jaw. It would seem scarcely possible that the eyes could see what the jaw could snap at, even supposing that there were sufficient light for vision at the depths at which the whale was feeding. It has been suggested that the Sperm Whale is more a passive than an active feeder. There is evidence that the Sperm Whale swims along when feeding with its jaw hanging open (a habit which causes Sperm Whales from time to time to get entangled in submarine telephone cables). With the jaw open the dark-red tongue set in the background of the dead-white lining of the mouth and throat may act as a lure to squid. This view was first put forward by Beale (1839), (who also pointed out that Sperm Whales ate fish in shallow waters) and was revived by Slijper (1962). In support of this theory, we might note that the jiggers used by commercial squid fishermen are also patterned in red and white and do not employ any bait. Of course such a colour pattern would not be visible at depth, because of the absence of light. But squid can provide their own living light from bioluminescence and it has been suggested that a Sperm Whale, having munched a luminous squid, could retain sufficient phosphorescence to convert its mouth into a deep-water lure (Gaskin, 1967).

These methods would be less likely to apply to fish such as Lumpsuckers or Skates than they would to squid and could certainly not apply at all to inanimate objects, such as coconuts and apples, that have been found in Sperm Whale stomachs, so active feeding must be possible. Echo-location may play a part in this; it is hard to see what other senses could be used in the dark at depth. Even when the prey has been located with sufficient accuracy for it to be gripped by the jaw, it would still seem no easy matter to transfer it to the back of the mouth, so that it can be swallowed. With no functional cheeks, and only a short and rather immobile tongue, the problem might seem a difficult one. But as Robert Burton (1973) pointed out, it is one that fish-eating birds face with each meal, and it is clearly one that they have solved. Sperm Whales too must have a solution. We may suppose that it lies in the movements of the lower jaw which serve to work the prey towards the gullet. The range of movement of the jaw does not appear to have been studied, but it is presumably more complex than a single up-and-down chopping action.

Sperm Whales are not infrequently taken with the lower jaw broken and healed again at an angle (the reader may recall that Moby Dick had suffered such an injury). The part of the jaw beyond the fracture site no longer occludes against the palate and the teeth cease to have a grasping function, and are often infested with stalked barnacles. Yet the whales in this condition do not appear to be less well nourished than those with their jaws intact, so presumably the distal part of the jaw is not essential for feeding.

The Sperm Whale demonstrates what can be done with functional teeth in the lower jaw only. The remaining odontocetes have no functional teeth (from a feeding point of view) in either jaw. The beaked whales, the Ziphiidae, as noted earlier, are characterised by the possession of one or two pairs of teeth in the lower jaw, which are exposed only in the males, and not always in them. Where the teeth are exposed, it seems that they serve in sexual display or perhaps in sexual fighting. Clearly they can have nothing to do with feeding, since the females, which have the same nutritional requirements as the males, do not possess them. All the ziphiids appear to feed mainly, but not exclusively, on cephalopods. The Bottle-nosed Whale, *Hyperoodon ampullatus*, feeds on squid (*Gonatius* and *Loligo*), Cuttlefish, *Sepia* spp., and, at times, on Herring and Cod (Eschricht, 1845; Harmer, 1918); the equivalent North Pacific species, *Berardius bairdii*, eats *Gonatius*, octopus and various demersal fish (Tomilin, 1967; Pike, 1953). Little is known of the diet of the more extreme ziphiids. The extraordinary Strap-toothed Whale, *Mesoplodon layardi*, has teeth which curve over the upper jaw and appear to prevent the mouth being opened to more than a small extent. Clearly these whales (or at least the males) can eat only small prey, but, equally clearly, these suffice for their needs (although it might be pointed out that the Strap-toothed Whale is a far from abundant species).

Perhaps the strangest tooth of all is that found in the Narwhal, *Monodon monoceros*. In the embryo, two pairs of teeth develop at the front in each side of the upper jaw. The posterior pair remain rudimentary and eventually disappear, but in males the left anterior tooth develops into the beautiful, spirally fluted tusk, which may be up to 2 m in length. The right tooth, which grows to about 2.25 cm in length, remains embedded in the skull. In females, the two anterior teeth both develop like the right tooth of the male, although very occasionally the left one develops into a tusk (Mansfield *et al.*, 1975). Several skulls of Narwhals with two tusks are preserved in museums, but such animals are very rare in the wild.

The function of the male's tusk (the unicorn's horn of the ancients) is not known. Presumably it is used in some form of sexual display. Tusks are usually worn smooth at the tip but this probably results from chance encounters with the sea-floor when the Narwhal is pursuing its prey. The tusks are not used either for breaking holes in the ice or for stirring up the bottom in search of food. Narwhals appear to feed largely on Arctic Cod, *Boreogadus saida*, or Greenland Halibut, *Reinhardtius hippoglossoides*, but remains of squid and shrimps of several species are also found in their stomachs.

If we look back at the list of prey items taken by odontocetes we see that fish and cephalopods, mostly squid, make up the vast bulk. Killer Whales have developed a speciality of feeding on warm-blooded prey and many species take lesser quantities of invertebrates other than cephalopods, ranging from various sorts of shrimps, crabs, gasteropod molluscs and salps. A few species, e.g. the Ganges Susu, *Platanista gangetica*, may subsist largely on crabs or other Crustacea. Many invertebrates found in whales' stomachs have reached these 'second-hand', as it were, having been the prey items of the fish on which the whale was primarily feeding, but in many cases there is no doubt that the odontocete was taking the relatively tiny invertebrates deliberately and might in this way appear to be trespassing on the preserves of the baleen whales. However, one essential difference remains—the shrimps eaten by the odontocete are captured as individual prey items, rather than *en masse*, by sieving the sea, as does the baleen whale.

Sieving food out of the sea, or filter-feeding, is one of the basic feeding methods of the animal kingdom. Some groups, for example the sponges, feed in no other way and there are few groups which do not include at least some filter-feeders. The ancestors of the entire vertebrate series were filter-feeders and the diminutive Lancelet feeds in a similar way to the Blue Whale. Although filter-feeding is so widespread it is essentially an aquatic activity (although perhaps some birds, such as swifts and night-jars, are aerial filter-feeders, and the orb-web spiders might be included in this category), so it is not surprising to find that the mammals, basically a very terrestrial group, have exploited it only in the whales. And in the whales, filter-feeding has been carried further than in any other group, with the enormous increase in bulk of the filter-feeders that we noted in the first chapter.

Filter-feeding requires, besides a supply of food in the water, three basic features: a flow of water to bring new prey near the feeder's mouth; a filter to collect the food particles but allow the water to pass through; and a means of removing the filtered food from the filter bed and conveying it to the gut where it can be digested.

Whales provide the first requirement either by their own for-ward movement through the water, or by taking great gulps, subsequently expelling the water through the baleen. Baleen, of course, is the filter and it is a structure unique to whales. The baleen consists of a series of thin horny plates in the shape of elongated triangles set across the axis of the mouth and hanging from the margins of the upper jaw by their shortest side (Fig. 6.1). The inner edge of each plate is frayed into a fringe of

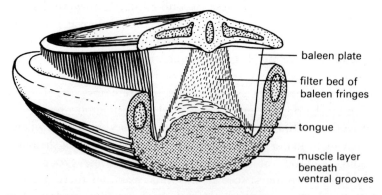

baleen plate

filter bed of baleen fringes

tongue

muscle layer beneath ventral grooves

Fig. 6.1 Sectional view of the anterior part of the head of a rorqual to show the arrangement of the baleen plates and the mouth.

coarse filaments which form a dense, yet porous, mat over the parallel edges of the baleen plates set about 6 mm apart. The plates themselves do not lie in one plane, but curve slightly backwards and are also twisted on their long axes.

The number of plates in a side of baleen varies from species to species. In the Fin Whale, there may be from 250 to 400 plates on each side, which vary in size from the smallest at the front of the jaw to the largest, about 70 cm in length, slightly behind the centre of the row, and then declining again towards the back of the mouth.

Beneath the two rows of baleen plates, the mouth is floored by the tongue. In rorquals, this is a strange organ described aptly by Mackintosh (1965) as having a consistency resembling that of a collapsed balloon partly filled with jelly. When the tongue of a dead whale rolls out onto the surface of the flensing deck, it is hard to believe that such a flabby amorphous mass could ever have been capable of co-ordinated movement. Nevertheless, the whale's tongue does contain muscles and we can be certain that, in life, these are adequate to perform the movements required of them. The tongue lies over most of the floor of the mouth and extends further back beneath the blubber over the front part of the thorax of the whale. In rorquals, but not in right whales, as we have seen, the skin and blubber of the ventral surface are furrowed by a series of longitudinal grooves extending from the chin to the navel. If a groove is sliced across, it can be seen that this belly-blubber, or 'bukk-spekk' as the Norwegian flensers called it, is richly supplied with layers of muscle fibres, so that the bukk-spekk can be salted and smoked to provide a product not unlike streaky bacon. The function of these muscles will become apparent later.

How are all these structures used in feeding? When the rorqual takes a mouthful of water and its contained plankton, the mouth is opened widely and its floor lowered, the skin of the throat expanding as the grooves open out (Fig. 6.2). The tongue may be actively retracted by its muscles, or it may be driven back towards the thorax by the pressure of water entering the mouth. The mouth closes with its floor still depressed, but then the muscles of the throat grooves contract, tautening the floor of the

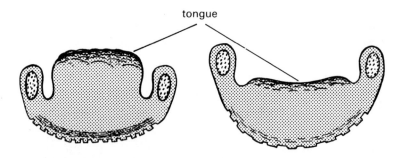

Fig. 6.2 Section of the lower jaw of a rorqual. As the mouth cavity is expanded so the accordion-pleating of the skin of the throat stretches.

mouth and driving the tongue forward, and water is forced out through the baleen fringes. Considerable pressure is created and a curtain of water has been seen to spurt out through the baleen fringe. We can now see how well the filter-bed is adapted to its task. The filaments form a layer that is supported against the considerable pressure involved by the whole width of each baleen plate, while the spacing of the parallel plates allows a rapid through-flow of water without loss of rigidity. The final process— how the filtered food is passed into the gullet—is a mystery. We cannot tell if the tongue is active in this—it scarcely seems possible that it could lick the plankton off the baleen as we can use our tongue to lick round our teeth. Perhaps a progressive wave travels backwards from the front of the tongue (aided perhaps by the throat musculature?) to drive the food backward. Planktonic organisms, like those that the whales feed on, have quite good 'flow' properties and such an action may be adequate to transfer the food to the gullet where peristaltic action in the oesophagus will take over and convey it to the stomach. It may be that a certain amount of water remains with the plankton to help it move more easily. It is difficult to see how more light can be thrown on this process; it will remain, for me, one of the more fascinating problems posed by the baleen whales.

The type of feeding described above can be termed 'gulping'. A whale can feed also by swimming slowly ahead with its mouth slightly open, allowing water to flow, from in front, into the mouth cavity and out again *via* the filter bed and the baleen plates at the sides. This is known as 'skimming', and is practised more by some species than others.

Before going on to look at how the various mysticete species employ their baleen filters, it is appropriate to look a little more closely at this remarkable substance. Baleen is unique in the mammalian series and bears no relationship at all to teeth. The early rudiments of teeth are to be found embedded in the gums of foetal mysticetes, but these are soon resorbed. It is interesting to note that the more posterior tooth buds have tri-lobed crowns, resembling the lobed cheek teeth of the archaeocetes. The baleen plates arise in the foetus as thickenings of the skin on the margins of the upper jaw. These form a series of swellings marked by a diagonal row of conical processes. These fuse to form transverse plates fringed by their papillae. Each papilla has a dermal core supplied with blood vessels and nerves, and an epidermal covering. The epidermal cells covering the papillae become cornified until they consist almost entirely of the hard protein keratin, which, by addition at the base, eventually produces a horn tube. At the same time, the spaces between the papillae produce a rather less dense horny investment which binds together the horn tubes into a baleen plate (Fig. 6.3), except at the ends, where the horn tubes protrude to form the first fringe of filaments.

At birth, the young whale has short and very soft baleen plates, but these soon harden. The baleen continues to grow throughout life, so as to replace wear at the operating surface. The tips of the horn tubes forming the fringe become finer and finer as they are worn away by friction, with the food and each other, and finally break away, but, because of continued growth of the plate and the softer nature of the covering layer, more of the horn tube is exposed, so that the fringes remain at about the same length.

The internal structure of the baleen plate—a series of tubes held together in an outer covering—provides great strength and elasticity. This property is, of course, essential to the whale; it proved also of great value to the corset-makers of the eighteenth and nineteenth centuries, and the use of 'whalebone'

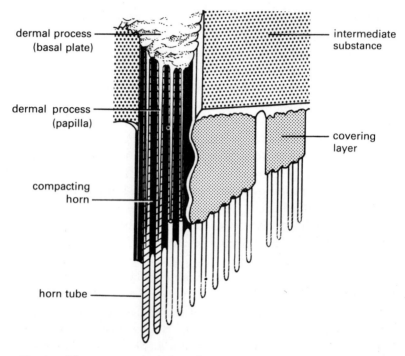

dermal process — ——— intermediate
(basal plate)   substance

dermal process —
(papilla)

—— covering
layer

compacting
horn —

horn tube —

Fig. 6.3   The structure of a baleen plate

in corsetry was relinquished only when spring steel (another
notably strong and elastic material) became readily available.

The evolutionary origin of baleen is uncertain. The most likely
explanation is that it is derived from the horny palatal ridges
that are found in many mammals. However, it is difficult to
see how so complex a structure could gradually have evolved
into an effective food-gathering apparatus. The intermediate
stages would seem to be more of an encumbrance than a feature
for positive natural selection.

The structure of the head of right whales differs from that of
the rorquals. Right whale baleen is much longer and slimmer;
in the Black Right Whale, blades are between 1.8 and 2.7 m in
length, while in the Greenland Right Whale, blades may exceed
4 m in length. To accommodate the great length of baleen, the
upper jaw of these whales is strongly arched and, to close off the
mouth cavity, the lower lip grows upwards to form an enormous

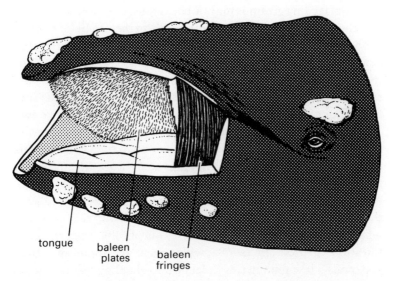

tongue   baleen   baleen
          plates   fringes

Fig. 6.4   The mouth of a right whale, showing the long baleen plates and the high lips.

scoop-like jaw (Fig. 6.4). The right and left baleen rows do not meet at the front of the mouth, as in rorquals, and the tongue is much more muscular. In the absence of muscular throat grooves, the right whale's tongue has to provide the force for driving the water out through the baleen. It is probable, however that right whales feed more by straining than by gulping, so the role of the tongue may be more to pass food from the baleen to the gullet. (Again we may ask: 'How?') Because of the great length of the baleen in right whales, the plates have to be folded backwards as the mouth closes, so that they lie on either side of the tongue. As the mouth opens again, the plates spring back to their original position. The mechanism just described forms a highly efficient system for collecting food from the sea. Similar, but not identical, devices have evolved in several other vertebrates.

Feeding in whalebone whales is a highly selective process that is concentrated in plankton-rich waters. In most species there are migratory movements between rich, but cold, feeding grounds and warmer, but relatively non-productive, breeding areas. The potential feeding grounds may be enormous, but there is evidence that the whales do not disperse randomly in them. Minke Whales, probably the same individuals, are known to return year after year to the same location in coastal waters (Gaskin, 1976) and the same is probably true of other rorquals. Whether this represents an inherited migratory pattern, or whether it is learned behaviour or part of a shared group experience, we do not know.

It is easy when describing the feeding habits of mysticetes to fall into the habit of referring solely to plankton. Plankton are those animals (and plants, although we are not concerned with these here) that float and drift passively in the water, having negligible powers of independent movement. Contrasted with this is the nekton, the active swimmers, and we find that mysticete whales can feed extensively on these, but still by using the same filtration method. In fact, a wide range of organisms, from copepods a few millimetres in length, to shoaling fish the size of herrings, are eaten by whalebone whales. Food selection is not random. Different whale species, or different age-classes of the same species, feed on different-sized prey. There is some correlation between prey size and the fineness of the baleen fringe and the mysticetes can be arranged in a series in order of decreasing size of prey and fineness of baleen thus: Grey, Blue, Fin, Humpback, Bryde's, Minke, Sei and right whales. But the order is not absolute for, as the baleen coarsens with age, a young Fin Whale might have finer baleen than a mature Bryde's Whale.

Some of the best information on whale feeding comes from the records of the biologists who accompanied the whale factory ships to the Antarctic and examined the hundreds of stomachs split open on the flensing deck. The staple diet of the whalebone whales of the Southern Ocean is composed very largely of the shrimp-like krill, which is also the staple food of the Crab-eater Seal. Krill is a member of a large group of Crustacea, the euphausiids, and, although it superficially resembles the common decapod shrimps that are familiar food items the world over, it is not closely related to them. Krill justifies its scientific name—*Eurphausia superba*—by being the largest of the euphausiids; it grows up to about 6 cm in length and dominates the zooplankton of the Southern Ocean, possibly forming about half the entire zooplankton biomass.

Besides being the main food of the whale stocks in the Antarctic, krill forms the base of the food pyramid of many other predatory species, including the Crab-eater Seals, the Antarctic Fur Seals (*Arctocephalus gazella*), several penguin species, some albatrosses and other petrels, many fish, and probably squid, whose eating habits are less well known. It was early discovered that there was a strong link between concentrations of krill and feeding whales and, for this reason, a study of the biology of krill was an important part of the work of the British '*Discovery*' scientists, who went to the Antarctic in 1925 to study the biology of whales and their environment. Work on krill is still appearing from their successors and there is currently an encouraging degree of international co-operation in trying to unravel the complicated web of which krill is such a vital strand.

Krill is widely distributed around the Antarctic, the greatest concentrations being in the Atlantic sector. It is most obvious when it occurs in swarms, which may be as much as 400 m across. In the swarms, which are found from just below the surface to depths of about 100 m, the krill are very closely packed. Precise data are still lacking, but densities of 10 to 16 kg per cu m have been claimed (Moiseev, 1970). Not all krill occur in such dense swarms, of course, and part of the stock may consist of dispersed individuals, but these are probably of less importance to the whales.

The swarming krill, on the other hand, form an ideal food for the rorquals and Fin, Blue and Minke Whales in the Southern Ocean feed almost exclusively upon it. How do these rather similar species avoid competing with each other for this food resource? It is important to answer this question, for, unless there is some ecological separation, one species would prove better adapted and more successful than the other two and would, ultimately, by the process of natural selection, replace them. In fact, we find that Blue, Fin and Minke Whales are (or, to be more precise, **were** before commercial exploitation began) successful and abundant species.

The answer is that these three whales avoid competition by two complementary methods. Each whale species concentrates its feeding on a particular size-range of krill, the Fin Whale taking krill from 30–40 mm long, the Blue Whale those from 20–30 mm, and the Minke, with the finest baleen of the series, the smallest krill, from 10–20 mm. Additionally, there is a difference in distribution, the Blue Whale tending to occur nearer the ice-edge than the Fin. Within species, there is also segregation by size, the larger and older whales arriving to feed first at the beginning of the season, with the smaller individuals arriving later and having to occupy feeding areas to the east and west of the larger animals (Laws, 1977).

In this way, predation by whales is spread over the krill stock, so that the grazing pressure is more evenly distributed and the best use is made of the resource. The system is not absolute—where krill stocks are very dense, as they usually are around the island of South Georgia (54°S, 34°W), Fin, Blue and Sei Whales all overlap and compete for the same size groups of krill.

Sei Whales seem to be more opportunist feeders. They eat a succession of organisms, from krill in the southern part of their range to calanoid copepods in the more northern parts (Brown, 1968). Humpback Whales also feed largely on krill in the Southern Ocean, while the Pygmy Blue Whales, which occur only to the north of latitude 54°S, feed on a more northerly relative of krill, *Euphausia valentini*. All these whales are gulpers and well-adapted to feeding on swarming organisms like krill. The Southern Right Whale is a skimmer and can feed on less concentrated organisms. The only adult right whale with food in its stomach examined in South Georgia waters proved to have been feeding on krill, but right whales have been observed feeding close offshore there when krill were not present in the surface waters. Probably they were feeding on copepods. Around the Falkland Islands, right whales feed on the very abundant pelagic larvae of Squat Lobsters, *Munida gregaria*, which, like krill, occur in large swarms there.

In the Northern Hemisphere, there is no one planktonic organism that dominates the ocean in the way that krill does in the south. The range of food available to the whale is more varied and it is not surprising to find that so too are their diets. Fin

Whales in the North Pacific feed on other euphausiid Crustacea, including *E. pacifica* and various species of a similar genus, *Thysanoessa*, calanoid copepods (*Calanus cristatus* and *C. plumchrus*), and fish like Capelin (*Mallotus villosus*) and Alaska Pollack (*Theragra chalcogramma*). Squid may be taken locally. In the North Atlantic, the Fin Whales have a similar diet, the euphausiids are mainly *Meganyctiphanes norvegica* and *Thysanoessa inermis*, and the calanoid, *Calanus finmarchicus*. Large quantities of fish also are taken. It is noticeable in Fin Whales that the small calanoid copepods are most often taken by the younger whales with finer baleen fringes.

The Blue Whale in the Northern Hemisphere does not accept such a wide range of food items as the Fin. As in the south, it confines itself to euphausiids. In the North Pacific, it feeds principally on *Thysanoessa inermis*, *Thy. longipes* and *Nematoscelis megalops*; in the North Atlantic, only *Thy. inermis*, *Temora longicornis* and *Meganyctiphanes norvegica* have been recorded.

The Humpback more nearly resembles the Fin in its feeding. In the Southern Ocean it feeds largely on krill, with a few warmer-water euphausiids (e.g. *Euphausia valentini*) in the northern parts of its feeding range. In the Northern Hemisphere, it takes a mixture of euphausiids and fish.

The Northern Right Whales feed largely on calanoid copepods, *Calanus plumchrus* and *C. cristatus* in the North Pacific and *C. finmarchicus* in the Atlantic, although occasional euphausiids, particularly young stages, are eaten.

The Grey Whale appears to feed largely on amphipod shrimps, which are taken from near, or on, the sea-floor. These amphipods form another of the great groups of the Crustacea, and are mostly bottom-dwellers, although some are pelagic. It used to be thought that the Grey Whale ploughed into the silt of the sea-floor, filtering out the edible organisms there, but it has recently been suggested that they use their snouts to stir up the mud and its contained animals and then filter the turbid water just above the bottom (Rice and Wolman, 1971). An interesting feature of this species is that it appears to exhibit 'handedness'. The short stubby baleen plates on the right-hand side are consistently more worn down than those on the left, and the barnacles that usually encrust the head are absent from the same side. Out of thirty-one Grey Whales examined by Kasuya and Rice (1970) only three were 'left-handed'.

The Grey Whale is one of the few baleen whales to have been kept in captivity. A young female named Gigi was kept for a year at Sea World, San Diego, USA. She was fed frozen squid and ate 900 kg a day (squid has a comparatively low nutritional value) on which she thrived. Gigi took her food from the bottom of the tank by turning on her side and sucking the squid in at the side of her mouth by depressing her tongue and expanding her throat grooves. She then expelled the excess water through her baleen. Gigi used the **left** side of her mouth, but this may have been because she was fed from this side *via* a tube when she first arrived at 'Sea World' (Ray and Scheville, 1974).

The mechanics of feeding and feeding behaviour are closely associated in the Grey Whale, because of the specialised nature of its food—no other whalebone whale is a benthic feeder. But, so far, we have not discussed the feeding behaviour of the more conventional mysticetes. David Gaskin (1976) had the opportunity to observe and film a group of Fin Whales feeding off the coast of Nova Scotia. Here, in summer, on the flood tide, swarms of *Meganyctiphanes* became concentrated in a tidal streak, often some 16 km in length. Gaskin watched a group of five large Fin Whales feeding on these euphausiids (or perhaps on the Mackerel that had come there to feed on them). A whale would advance on a swarm of *Meganyctiphanes* in a shallow upward plane until, just before breaking the surface, it would roll gently on its side (usually the right side, recalling the behaviour of the Grey Whales). As it did so, it would open its mouth widely, to 45° or more, and then, with a violent stroke of its flukes, it would turn back on its tracks in a tight half-circle. As it completed the turn, it would resume the usual upright posture of swimming and close its mouth. No doubt the lateral roll was to facilitate the tight turn, which Gaskin thought drove the prey across the arc of the whale's turning circle, so that it might more easily scoop up the euphausiids (or fish), which might be doubling back on their tracks to avoid the whale. It is hard to believe that a euphausiid, swimming as fast as possible, could in any way avoid a whale, but a Mackerel certainly could. Another possible explanation is that the tight turn might create a vortex which helped to concentrate the prey. Fin Whales do not invariably feed in this way; they have been observed feeding on an even keel but this approach seems to be used less frequently in the North Atlantic. It is, on the other hand, the normal method in the Antarctic and perhaps this is related to the greater density of prey in a krill swarm.

Humpback Whales also may roll on their sides to feed, probably for the same reason. A much more remarkable method they have been seen to use is the weaving of a snare of air-bubbles—the 'bubble net' (Wolman, 1978). To do this, the whale swims below the surface, emitting a fine stream of bubbles from the blow-hole. As it swims, it describes a circle, or a figure of eight, around a shoal of fish and a thin screen of glistening bubbles rises up like a curtain through the water. This curtain seems to alarm the fish, which concentrate in the centre of the bubble net, through which the whale rises to gulp its prey.

Although right whales feed on smaller prey, they too seem to select slicks, or streaks, of concentrated plankton on which to feed. Watkins and Scheville (1976) watched right whales at close quarters, cruising along with the tip of the rostrum just out of the water, skimming off the plankton in the slick. They use the same method to feed on plankton slicks below the surface when the water is stratified (as it often is) and have been seen feeding at a depth of about 10 m; they can probably feed deeper than this.

Most of these observations refer to whales seen feeding in coastal waters, where tidal effects can cause the plankton (and the fish feeding on them) to become concentrated. To what extent whales feed in this way in the open ocean we do not know. The dense swarms of krill in the Southern Ocean have already been mentioned and other euphausiids also form swarms. The patchiness of plankton in the open sea is very noticeable. Just how the whales locate suitable feeding patches is not known. Auditory clues may be important. The sounds produced by whalebone whales are not apparently very well adapted to precise echo-location, but they may serve well enough for plankton swarms. Perhaps all that is required is to locate a discontinuity between two water masses, which, if they are moving at different rates, or in different directions, might set up the currents that would create the plankton slicks. It is suggestive that the differences in frequency of the sounds produced by Blue and Minke Whales in the North Atlantic correlate quite well with the acoustic properties of the preferred food of these two species— the Blue eating euphausiids and the Minke mainly fish (Beamish and Mitchell, 1973). At close quarters the sinus hairs on the snout may play an important role in monitoring the water and thus serve to keep the whale's head in the plankton patch.

Energy budgets

How much does a whale eat? The difficulty of answering a question of this sort is apparent. Some information is available from the smaller cetaceans that have been kept in captivity, but it is never certain that captive animals are truly representative of the species in the wild. However, Christina Lockyer has made a serious attempt to answer this important question and to go further and provide an energy budget for some of the large whales (Lockyer, 1976). Her deductions were made on Southern Hemisphere whales; not only is a great deal of information on features like body dimensions, weights and oil contents of tissues, etc. (all necessary for calculating the energy budgets) available for these animals, but also they show well defined migratory patterns associated with summer feeding on the shoals of krill and a winter retreat to warmer waters to breed.

In general Blue and Fin Whales spend about 120 days a year feeding in the Antarctic, in which time they fatten remarkably. This was noticed very early on by the whalers, who found that whales on their arrival in Antarctic waters were lean, while towards the end of the season they produced a greatly increased oil yield. The weight of a Blue Whale may increase by about 49% during the feeding period. Much of the increase is, of course, in the blubber, but perhaps rather surprisingly the greatest percentage weight increase is in the muscle. The bones too become exceedingly oily, containing from 56–69% of oil. In fact the bone oil may constitute about 10% of the total body weight in the Blue Whale, although this vast store will not be reflected by any increase in bone weight at the end of the feeding period. Rather the reverse, in fact, since the oil replaces tissue fluid in the bones, which thus probably show a slight decrease in weight.

There are a good many measurements of the amount of food found in a whale's stomach after it has been shot, but these are often difficult to interpret. One immediate problem is that whales, like ruminants, have complex stomachs. Basically the stomach is composed of three chambers. The first, into which the oesophagus leads, is devoid of glands and is really a dilation of the oesophagus, like the rumen of a cow or the crop of a bird. The second chamber is anatomically a true stomach, being lined with an epithelium rich in glands secreting pepsin, hydrochloric acid and some lipase, which begin the digestive processes. These are continued in the third chamber, which also possesses a glandular epithelium. In some odontocetes, the stomach may be more complicated still, the third stomach of ziphiids being divided into as many as twelve chambers! Records of food found in the 'stomach' often refer only to the first chamber, the partially digested food in second and third chambers being disregarded. From what reports are available, it seems likely that a Blue Whale can take a meal of about 1,000 kg of krill and a Fin Whale about 800 kg.

The maximum quantity of food that the stomach can hold is only part of the answer to estimating the total daily food intake. Several meals a day might be taken (perhaps about four) and factors like food availability, digestion rate and energy requirement would all control food consumption. After considering all these factors, Christina Lockyer concluded that the large rorquals feed at a rate of about 4% of their body weight a day during the 120-day feeding period. The same conclusion had been reached by David Sergeant (1969) after studying dolphins and small baleen whales. He found a relationship between body weight, heart weight and weight of food consumed. He found the dolphins ate about 4% of their body weight per day and predicted that large rorquals would eat the same in the feeding season. Feeding is much reduced for the rest of the year; Christina

Lockyer estimated the rate in lower latitudes to be about a tenth of that in the Antarctic, so that the average food consumption throughout the year would correspond to about 1.5–2% body weight per day.

After careful study of the dimensions of the mouth cavity of whales, she was able to calculate the filter volume and the filter capacity (assuming a concentration of krill in the water of about 2 kg per cu m) and from all this the number of filtrations ('gulps') required to extract the daily ration. For a big Blue Whale 28 m long, weighing about 146,400 kg, the food required would be 4,124 kg per day and this could be obtained in seventy-nine filtrations. Similarly, a 22 m Fin, weighing 62,500 kg, would need 2,188 kg per day, which it could get in seventy-three filtrations. Smaller whales of either species would require proportionately more filtrations to get their daily ration. A really small whale, like a 5 m Minke, weighing only 2,041 kg, would need 71 kg of food each day but would have to take 355 gulps to obtain it. Krill densities can of course be very much more than the 2 kg per cu m used for the calculations, but these results demonstrate once again the selective advantage of increased size to the baleen whales.

The energy budgets Christina Lockyer drew up covered the developmental stages of both Blue and Fin Whales. They showed that an increase of at least 50% of body weight in the form of fat needed to be accumulated during the summer feeding period in the Antarctic and, for the pregnant females, much more, as much as 60–65% increase in body weight, in order to survive the great energy drain of lactation. Observation of the early arrival at, and late departure from, the feeding grounds by the pregnant whale support this conclusion about the great weight increase required by the pregnant females. Calculated assimilation efficiencies varied from 76% for a young adult Blue Whale to 87% for a mature female Fin Whale (suckling calves have even higher assimilation efficiencies—up to 93%—but as these are feeding only on milk they are not comparable with the adults). These very high values for growth and assimilation efficiency serve to remind us how efficient a system the whales form as harvesters of plankton in the world's oceans.

7 Reproduction and development

For any mammal, birth is a time of crisis. The newborn creature is never as well fitted to endure the stresses of the environment as its parent and mortality around the time of birth—perinatal mortality—is always a significant factor in the survival of a population. The mother is also often at risk from predators or from the accidents associated with the process of birth itself. For an aquatic mammal, there is an additional serious problem. Whales and dolphins all give birth in the water, so the young are born directly into a hostile medium, in which they can drown or lose heat at a dangerous rate.

The adoption of the aquatic medium meant that the cetacean ancestors had not only to modify their anatomy (including their genitalia) to suit them to the water, but also to evolve different physiological and behavioural patterns to make it possible for their young to be born and reared safely.

As we saw earlier, part of the anatomical adaptations to living in the sea involved smoothing away all the irregularities and protuberances of the body that were not required for locomotion and would otherwise impair the streamlining. Not many mammals have quite so obvious external sex organs as our own species, with its pendulous penis or protuberant breasts, but no other mammal is sleeker and more asexual in external appearance than the whale. It is, in fact, quite difficult to tell apart the sexes of whales, especially in the water. In neither is the sexual orifice conspicuous, but close inspection will reveal that the penial aperture, a slit-like opening, in the male is separated by about one-tenth of the body length from the anus, while the female's vulva lies immediately anterior to it. In stranded specimens, the sex may become very much more apparent, for bloating of the carcase causes the vulva to gape widely, while internal pressure may cause the penis to protrude.

The male reproductive system

The male reproductive organs in whales are relatively simple. The testes are elongated, almost cylindrical bodies lying in the abdominal cavity, just behind and lateral to the kidneys, hanging from the body wall by a sheet of tissue, the mesorchium. There is no trace of a scrotum in any whale, but at the posterior pole of the testis there may be a remnant of the gubernaculum, the strand of connective tissue that serves in most mammals to draw the testis down into the scrotum in the course of development. Whales are not the only mammals lacking a scrotum. The testes of true seals (phocids) and Sirenia are internal, but to stress that this is not a solely aquatic specialisation, so are those of elephants, sloths, armadillos and some insectivores. No one has satisfactorily explained why the majority of mammals have scrotal testes—the suggestion that the development of sperm can take place only at a temperature a few degrees below that of the body is clearly erroneous, since whales, seals, elephants, sloths, etc. all manage perfectly well with testes at body temperature. The selective mechanism that led to these vital and delicate organs being suspended between the hind-legs remains a puzzle.

Alongside the whale's testis lies the epididymis, the closely coiled mass of tubes into which the sperm are received from the seminiferous tubules of the testis. In all mammals, the epididymis acts as a storage place where sperm can be retained in an inactive state until the opportunity for their ejaculation occurs. Whales, however, make use of the next part of the reproductive tract, the vas deferens, which connects the epididymis with the urethra, as an accessory storage organ and the vasa deferentia are also much convoluted and are filled with sperm in the sexually active male. The vasa deferentia terminate in two ejaculatory ducts which open into the urethra at the base of the penis. Surrounding the junction of the ejaculatory ducts and the uretha is the only accessory gland of the male whale's reproductive system, the prostate. The prostate is a relatively, and indeed, in adult whales, absolutely, large gland. In all mammals, it secretes a fluid that makes up the bulk of the ejaculate and also activates the dormant sperm discharged from the epididymides and, in whales, from the vasa deferentia.

The penis of the whale resembles in structure that of cattle and other ruminants, as Slijper (1962) has pointed out; we shall see a similar resemblance in the placenta, when we come to examine the female system. Like the penis of the bull, the whale's penis is completely withdrawn within the general contour of the body when not erected. The flaccid penis lies on the floor of the abdominal cavity in a sigmoid curve or a single loose coil, the tip contained in a reflected fold of skin, the preputial sac, beneath the abdominal wall (Fig. 7.1). It is held in this position only by a pair of strap-like retractor muscles. As in most mammals, the body of the penis is made up of three columns of spongy tissue which can be inflated with blood. These are a pair of corpora cavernosa, fused for most of their length, but separated at the

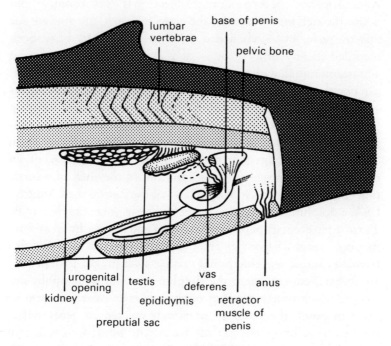

Fig. 7.1   Reproductive system of a male dolphin.

base of the penis to form two crura, which are attached, one each, to the pelvic bones and, on the underside of the penis, a poorly developed corpus spongiosum, through which the urethra runs. This is not continued over the end of the penis, causing some anatomists to doubt whether a whale has a true glans penis, but as Richard Harrison (1968) points out, this is merely a matter of definition. That part of the penis contained within the preputial sac is usually regarded as the glans.

In most mammals the penis is protruded when it becomes erect, by engorgement of the spongy tissues of the corpora cavernosa and corpus spongiosum, but these contain rather little erectile tissue in whales and it is possible that the elasticity of its tough tissue plays a more important role, the penis springing out when the retractor muscles relax. There is no baculum, or penis bone, in the whale, as is found in all seals.

A rather surprising characteristic of whales, or at any rate Bottle-nosed Dolphins, is that they seem able to erect the penis voluntarily and use it to examine objects in the environment. No doubt the rich innervation of the glans makes it appropriate for this purpose, but such a use does not appear to have been recorded in any other groups of mammals. Perhaps only an aquatic mammal, with its infinitely delicate control of movement, can position its body sufficiently precisely to use the penis in this way. Male dolphins in captivity (which are probably suffering from extreme boredom) spend a lot of time masturbating by rubbing their penes against projections in their tanks, hooking them over the rubber rings that they are given to 'play' with, or, in one case, hooking the penis over the rim of the shell of a turtle that shared the pool. At Marineland of the Pacific, Los Angeles, USA, a dolphin trainer, as a sort of 'in house' joke, taught a male *Tursiops* to erect its penis on command and carry a hoop around its pool, dangling from its erected penis. The cue used for this training routine was the trainer raising his arm; the joke proved an embarrassment when the dolphin was put in a public enclosure. Each time a member of the audience raised his arm to wave or point, the *Tursiops* obligingly erected its penis, deftly hooked up a hoop and set off round the pool (Caldwell and Caldwell, 1972).

Secondary sexual characters are comparatively little developed in male whales. The most conspicuous is undoubtedly the sexual dimorphism in size as seen, for example, in the male Sperm Whale. Other odontocetes show sexual differentiation in the development of the teeth, the Narwhal being an extreme case. Old male Killer Whales develop a very high and narrow dorsal fin. In rorquals and right whales, differences of this sort do not exist. In no whale is there any difference of colour pattern between the sexes.

The female reproductive system

The layout of the female reproductive organs in the whale (Fig. 7.2) is much more typical of the mammalian pattern. The two ovaries lie in the abdominal cavity (in much the same position as the testes in the male), each adjacent to the end of one of the two horns of the bicornuate uterus (another typical mammalian feature). The uterine horns join to form a short common uterus which connects with the vagina by a pronounced cervix (said to be absent in Narwhals and beaked whales). The vagina itself is peculiar in that its inner surface is developed into a series of annular folds projecting towards the external opening, so that they resemble a row of funnels. The function of these annular folds has not been determined but it has been suggested that they may serve to keep water from entering the uterus, or that they exert a pump-like action to prevent the loss of semen when the penis is withdrawn after copulation. The vagina opens to the exterior via the vulva but this is deeply sunken to form a genital slit. Flanking the genital slit are two other shallow slits which contain the nipples. The mammary glands lie beneath the blubber, but external to the musculature of the belly wall. They are elongated ovals in shape, extending forwards and outwards from the nipples. Each gland is composed of a series of lobules connected to a wide and capacious central duct. When inactive the glandular tissue forms only a thin layer, but this increases greatly during lactation.

The appearance of the ovaries depends on the stage of the sexual cycle and differs widely between odontocetes and mysticetes.

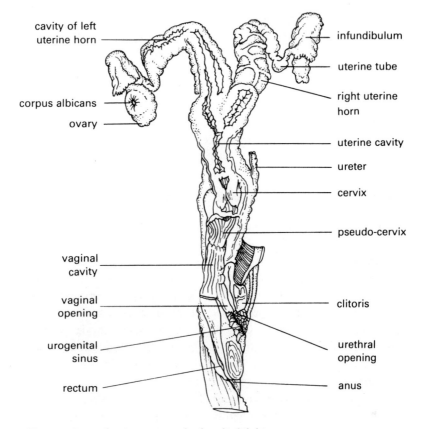

cavity of left
uterine horn

infundibulum

uterine tube

right uterine
horn

corpus albicans

ovary

uterine cavity

ureter

cervix

pseudo-cervix

vaginal
cavity

vaginal
opening

clitoris

urogenital
sinus

urethral
opening

rectum

anus

Fig. 7.2   Reproductive system of a female dolphin.

The odontocete ovary is more typical of the general mammalian
pattern. The glands are elongated ovoids, with a relatively
smooth surface, although, in pregnant whales, a bulging corpus
luteum may be present towards one pole of the ovary (Fig. 7.3).
The mysticete ovary is much less regular in outline and has even
been compared to a bunch of grapes. A more apt comparison
is with the ovary of a bird (on an enormous scale) for the surface
is studded with rounded protuberances varying in diameter from
a few millimetres to several centimetres. These are the ovarian
follicles, or the structures into which they develop, the corpora
lutea or corpora albicantia.

In order to understand the significance of these structures we

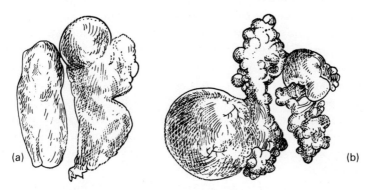

(a)

(b)

Fig. 7.3   Sections of ovaries of: (a) an odontocete, (b) a mysticete.

need to examine the female sexual cycle. The ovary of an
immature whale, like that of any other mammal, contains a large
number of undeveloped egg cells, the oocytes. With the approach
of puberty some of the oocytes become surrounded with cells derived from the ovary, which form an envelope or follicle around
the oocyte. By the time the whale is sexually mature some of these
follicles enlarge and develop a fluid-filled space in which the
oocyte, surrounded by a little cloud of attendant cells, lies,
slightly to one side. The enlargement of the follicle, which lies
near the surface of the ovary, causes it to bulge out like a blister.
With the approach of the breeding season, one of the follicles
enlarges still further and eventually bursts to release the contained oocyte, now an ovum. The ovum, which is released free
into the abdominal cavity, finds its way into the funnel-like
opening of one of the oviducts, or Fallopian tubes, where
it may be fertilised by sperm swimming up the uterine horn
towards it.

Meanwhile, in the ovary, the cells, which formed the follicle
and originally surrounded the oocyte, multiply and increase in
size to form a solid ball of secreting cells, called from its yellowish
colour the corpus luteum (yellow body). If the ovum released at
ovulation is fertilised, the luteal cells produce a hormone, progesterone, which adjusts the female system to the developing
embryo within its uterus, aids in the development of the placenta

and thus maintains pregnancy. Following the birth of the young whale, the secretory role of the corpus luteum is no longer required and the hormone-producing cells regress and are gradually absorbed, leaving in their place a hard knot of white fibrous tissue called (again from its colour), the corpus albicans. Whales are peculiar in that their corpora albicantia persist for a long time (perhaps for the life-span of the animal) and so the ovary of a mature whale will contain many follicles, perhaps a corpus luteum if the whale is pregnant and a series of corpora albicantia of different sizes, which form a record of the past ovulation of that ovary.

This character provides a very useful tool for biologists who can study the reproductive performance of whales from examination of their ovaries. Unfortunately, the situation is complicated by the fact that not all ovulations result in pregnancy. A follicle that has ovulated will always produce a corpus luteum, but if there is no embryo to develop in the uterus, the corpus luteum soon degenerates to form a corpus albicans, which is indistinguishable from the corpus albicans arising from a corpus luteum of pregnancy. There is another complication: in whales (and particularly in odontocetes, which have a long gestation period), during the course of pregnancy some follicles may develop into accessory corpora lutea which help to keep progesterone levels up (a similar phenomenon occurs in the pregnant mare). Once again, these accessory corpora lutea give rise to corpora albicantia.

Since accurate estimation of reproductive performance is an important part of the scientific basis for whale stock management, it has been necessary for scientists to make an allowance for the accessory corpora in calculating the number of ovulations that have occurred from a female whale's ovaries.

I shall return to the subject of reproductive performance later, but it is appropriate now to consider the conception and early development of a young whale. Every mammal begins its individual life when the nucleus of the sperm fuses with that of the ovum, but let us look a little further back to consider the act of mating, whereby the sperm are transferred to the female reproductive tract.

It is true, but insufficient, to say that whales copulate as other mammals do, since there is a wide range of copulatory techniques in the mammal series, from the long-drawn-out matings of some carnivores, to the almost instantaneous mounting of bulls and rams. Because whale matings take place in the water, they are difficult to observe and quantitative data about frequency and duration are almost entirely lacking. In general it seems that the actual intromission is very brief, resembling the act in cattle, although it may be preceded by a lengthy bout of courtship behaviour which some authors have referred to, rather romantically, as 'love play'. This is not surprising. Copulation always requires a degree of co-operation between the sexes. In most mammals, the male is able to determine the receptivity of the female by the odour she produces when in oestrus or on heat. Whales, lacking a sense of smell, cannot rely on this clue and must instead determine the female's response by behavioural patterns.

The courtship is sometimes very conspicuous. Humpback Whales are probably the most demonstrative. They roll, smack the water with their enormous flippers (a secondary sexual character?), crash down their flukes on the surface, and even leap right out of the water ('breach'), to fall back again with a tremendous splash. These activities do not always terminate in mating, nor are they confined to the breeding season, but they are intensified then. When the Humpbacks have reached a sufficiently high level of sexual excitement, copulation follows, usually in a side-to-side position, lying at the surface of the water (and this pattern has been observed in other rorquals). A more dramatic approach has been described, when, after a lengthy bout of courtship, the whales reared up out of the water, belly to belly, falling back afterwards, and immediately repeating the process. This type of vertical copulation has been reported also in Sperm Whales, Pilot Whales, Belugas and Harbour Porpoises, but, in general, odontocetes, like most mysticetes, copulate side to side. Male Bottlenosed Dolphins swim up from beneath their partners and mate with their bodies more or less at right angles to each other; mating lasts from two to ten seconds. When one considers that the surface of the sea is often turbulent, and that the mating whales will have little opportunity to make compensatory swimming movements to resist the buffeting of the waves, it is easy to see the functional advantage of a short period of actual intromission (and the tough, fibrous nature of the whale's penis).

Many matings in the smaller Cetacea have been observed in oceanaria. In captivity, male dolphins will attempt to mate with whatever other females are available in their enclosure, and inter-specific or intergeneric matings are common. Whether these occur in the wild or result in viable offspring is not known. This cannot be frequent, however, or the distinctions between the interbreeding taxa would break down, but an interesting report by Fraser (1940) described three odd whale skeletons from Ireland which looked as though they might have resulted from crosses between Bottle-nosed Whales and Risso's Dolphins.

But to return to the act of copulation; we suppose that, follow-ing the extrusion, rather than the erection of the penis, ejaculation takes place during the brief intromission and that this is repeated several times (this may account for the plentiful supply of sperm in the epididymides and vasa deferentia of the male). The annular folds in the vagina hinder loss of semen and eventually one sperm, more active than the rest, will enter the Fallopian tube and there penetrate the membrane of the newly released ovum and fuse with its nucleus. We know nothing of the timing of the early events of pregnancy in the whale, but it is probable that the ferti-lised egg takes a few days to move from the Fallopian tube into the horn of the uterus, whose lining, responding to the secretion of progesterone by the corpus luteum, has become modified to receive it. During this time it has developed to form a hollow ball of cells, a blastocyst. In some mammals, including seals, de-velopment is suspended at the blastocyst stage, to be resumed again after a period of 'delayed implantation'. This is not known to occur in any cetacean.

The blastocyst develops in the uterus, obtaining its nourish-ment and disposing of its wastes in the conventional mammalian way, by means of its foetal membranes, the chorion and amnion, modified to form a placenta. Mammalian placentae vary in structure, depending on how many layers of tissue separate the foetal from the maternal blood supply. The placenta of all whales studied is of the epithelio-chorial type, i.e., the epithelium of the uterine wall is in contact with the chorionic epithelium of the foetus and there has been no general erosion of either maternal or foetal tissues. This type of placenta is found also in ungulates. There are other ungulate characters in the cetacean placenta— the presence of structures where the pleats and villi of the foetal chorion fit into corresponding folds and crypts of the uterine mucosa in a complex spongy mass resembling similar struc- tures—placentomes—in cattle. The reproductive system of whales thus provides considerable support (structure of penis, type of copulation and structure of placenta) for a relationship with the ancestors of the ungulates.

In odontocetes there is a remarkable dominance of the left side of the uterus, the developing foetus occurring on that side in about 80% of cases. This is not so in mysticetes, when the foetus may be found on either side, though slightly more commonly on the right.

Development of the whale foetus is remarkably rapid, indeed the Blue Whale foetus must show the most rapid, sustained growth rate of any mammal, growing from a fertilised ovum, weighing about 0.005 mg, to a newborn whale of over 2,000 kg (an increase of 4×10^9!) in about 11 months. Growth of the embryo starts slowly and follows the general mammalian pat- tern, but by the time it is about 2.5 cm long the hind-limb buds are resorbed. After 3 months of gestation, the foetus is a miniature Blue Whale, complete with flippers and tail-flukes. Throat grooves begin to appear when the foetus is about 6 months old and less than 100 cm long, and these are soon fol- lowed by the characteristic pigment pattern. Few structural de- velopments appear in the last few months of gestation, although in this time the foetus grows greatly in size and weight, adding an astonishing 2,000 kg to its weight in the last 2 months of preg- nancy. It has been calculated that the rate of growth in the latter part of gestation is two and a half times that of most terrestrial mammals and ten times that of man and apes.

Gestation lasts from 10–12 months in those mysticetes which have been studied, but there is a wider spread in odontocetes.

The smaller toothed whales have a gestation of about 9 months (e.g. Harbour Porpoise) to 11 months (Common Dolphin) but this is extended to 15–16 months in the Common Pilot Whale, and to 16–17 months in the Sperm Whales. Despite its size, the Killer Whale does not have a long gestation—only 11–12 months.

Thus gestation periods are, in general mammalian terms, long but (except in the case of the large toothed whales) not exceptionally long. This is a consequence partly of the absolute size of whales and partly of the need to produce at birth a highly developed young whale which can swim through the water so as to breathe at the surface and follow its mother, and which can cope with the inevitable heat losses to the cold and heat-absorbent surrounding water. This last is an important factor. Whales cannot make snug nests or find protected dens for their offspring. The most that they can do is to make some compensation by migrating into warmer waters as the birth season draws near. I shall refer later to the importance of this in whalebone whales.

Not surprisingly, there are few observations of birth in the wild. The baby whale seems usually to be born flukes first—a breech birth, as the obstetrician would put it. This presents no problem, since, in the uterus, the soft flukes are tucked forwards under the belly, while the flippers lie flat against the sides, so there are no awkward projections, as there would be in the case of, for example, a young foal, born this way round. Many births of dolphins in captivity have been observed and timed and, in general, it seems a speedy process of a few minutes only.

The umbilical cord, which is short in whales, snaps during or very soon after the delivery and the young whale is then systemically independent of its mother. Its immediate need is for oxygen and for this it needs to breathe. For most newborn mammals, the stimulus to take the first breath is the build-up of carbon dioxide in the blood (because of the cutting-off of oxygenated blood supplies from the placenta when the cord breaks), coupled with the cooling of the body, especially the snout, when the young animal emerges from the birth canal. Such a reflex would have disastrous consequences for a young whale—if it breathed on being cooled, it would take in a lungful of water—so this reflex must have been suppressed before whales gave birth in the sea.

As with most mammals that produce large and advanced young, multiple births are rare in whales. In mysticetes, twins are about as common (or as rare, seeing the frequency is of the order of 1% or less) as in our own species. In odontocetes, they seem to be even rarer, although sperm whales may have about 0.66% of twin pregnancies. Triplet and quadruplet foetuses have been found in the uterus of whalebone whales on the flensing deck of whale factories, but it is very doubtful if these could have been born and reared successfully.

The mother whale shows great care and concern for her calf. This is to be expected, since in genetic terms she (or rather her DNA) has a great investment in the calf. Female whales will actively protect their calves and will attempt to drive off intruders. Old-time whalers used to take advantage of this to secure the adult whale by first harpooning the calf, whose mother would then come within range and present an easy target. An old account (Service, 1896) tells of a Harbour Porpoise that followed a fishing boat with a young porpoise in it for an hour, till the young one was put back in the sea, when both swam off together. Professor Pilleri, who has done so much research on river dolphins, has come up with a more recent account (1971) of a La Plata Dolphin (*Pontoporia blainvillei*) which, judging from tooth marks, had done its best to free its young one which had become entangled in a net.

This is perhaps standard enough behaviour for a female mammal towards its young. What is remarkable in whales is that these behaviour patterns are often shared by whales other than the young one's mother. These 'aunts' may assist the mother to help the newborn whale to the surface to take its first breath and they may help to keep off other whales in the group. In Bottle-nosed Dolphins, the 'aunt' is often the only other dolphin that the mother will allow near her calf. Female odontocetes have even been observed to help with delivery of a calf.

D. H. Brown (in Harrison, 1968) has provided a fascinating account of the birth of a Pacific Common Dolphin (*Delphinus bairdi*) in captivity at Marineland of the Pacific. The dolphin was kept in a pool with several other cetaceans of various species. She was noted to be about to give birth and the tail of the young one first became visible outside its mother's vulva at 11.50 hours. By 12.05 hours the entire hinder end of the infant had been expelled and the umbilical cord was stretched taut. At this stage there was a complication—it seemed to the observer that the dorsal fin of the baby dolphin was obstructing the progress of the birth; it appeared to have caught on the hinder margin of the vulva. At 12.15 hours, a dolphin of another genus (*Lagenorhynchus*) seized the tail-flukes of the baby in its mouth and withdrew it from the birth canal. The *Delphinus* mother carried her calf to the surface, but unfortunately it was born dead. A male Pilot Whale, another inmate of the enclosure, intervened at this stage and carried the carcase of the baby to and from the surface for 38 minutes and then rather spoiled the impression of altruistic caring thus presented by eating it! The placenta had not yet been delivered at this stage but at a little past 16.00 hours a female False Killer Whale (another member of the varied throng in this pool) seized the stub of the umbilical cord protruding from the dolphin's vulva and withdrew the placenta.

We should not read too much into this account, fascinating as it is. No doubt all these reactions were much affected by the totally artificial conditions in which these whales were imprisoned. It is highly unlikely that such a strange association of species would be found in the wild and the stillbirth may have been a direct consequence of captivity. Yet these observations do show the remarkable extent of this apparently altruistic behaviour in whales.

The fact that a newborn whale lacks blubber and has empty lungs means that it is probably negatively buoyant, so its survival will be enhanced if its mother pushes it to the surface for its first breath. Because the whale, with its relatively low reproductive rate, has such a great investment in its calf, any strategy which enhances survival will be strongly selected for. That this behaviour should spread to others in the same group in these rather social animals is not so surprising, particularly when the whales are in captivity and probably suffering from something akin to intense boredom. But this care-giving or 'epimeletic' behaviour, as it has been called, has often been seen to be extended in the wild to adult whales which have been injured and are unable to support themselves. Many people suppose that such behaviour demonstrates a sense of compassion in whales and that there is evidence of a highly organised intelligence. There is little evidence for this. In fact, whales may demonstrate the same stereotyped response in most inappropriate circumstances, as when a dolphin in captivity spent many hours pushing to the surface a small shark which it had itself killed shortly before. It is probable that the many well attested stories of dolphins saving swimmers in distress have their origin in similarly misplaced epimeletic behaviour patterns and do not demonstrate any particular link between the whale and the person saved.

The cetacean calf is suckled under water but usually close to the surface. The calf draws the nipple into its mouth between the tongue and the palate and the milk is actively ejected by muscular action from the mammary gland of the mother. Suckling takes place in short bouts as the young whale can remain submerged for a short period only. In the Bottle-nosed Dolphin this is usually less than a minute. Calves suck about two or three times an hour and continue to do so throughout the night and day. They stay very close to their mother at this time, usually swimming just behind her flipper, or sleeping under her tail-flukes. As the calf grows, so the interval between feeds become longer, but the amount of milk transferred at each feed is larger. Slijper (1962) suggested that about 600 l of milk might be produced daily by a large whale but a more cautious estimate (based on observed weight gains) of 90 kg per day for a Blue Whale and 72.3 kg per day for a Fin Whale was given by Tomilin (1946). In Blue and Fin Whales, lactation lasts about 6–8 months, in the smaller rorquals (Minke, Bryde's, Sei) about 4–5 months. Most odontocetes suckle for about a year or even longer.

Whale milk is very rich. The samples that can be expressed from the nipples of a dead lactating whale are thick and creamy. Although Slijper claimed it often had a fishy, oily taste, the only sample I have tried was very palatable, with a nutty, rather than a fishy, taste. It would have gone well with strawberries. In Blue and Fin Whales, milk fat and protein together constitute up to 50% of the milk, compared with an equivalent value of 10–20% in most terrestrial mammals. Christina Lockyer (1976) calculated that, in an average sample of Blue or Fin Whale milk, containing 36% fat, 13% protein, 1% mineral ash and the remainder water, the calorific content of the milk would be about 4,137 kcal per kg, or a total energy input of about 372,330 kcal per day for a Blue Whale calf and 299,105 kcal per day for a Fin Whale calf— values which might make a weight-conscious reader recoil. During its suckling period of about 7 months the Blue Whale calf will put on about 17 tonnes weight, at a rate of 81 kg per day, equivalent figures for a Fin Whale calf being 11.5 tonnes at 53 kg per day.

Conception, parturition and the rearing of a calf are not isolated events in a whale's life. They form part of a recurring cycle whereby each female produces a series of calves to give natural selection the raw material to work on. Not surprisingly, the details of the cycle are best known in those species which have been exploited by the whaling industry and for which abundant material is available. The picture is complicated by the fact that the industry, which has provided the material on which our knowledge of the whale's reproductive cycle is based, has itself altered some of the key factors in the cycle, for instance, age at first pregnancy and pregnancy rate. Nevertheless, the pattern remains reasonable clear.

N. A. Mackintosh devised a clever diagram (Fig. 7.4) to depict the movements of a typical adult female Fin Whale in the Southern Hemisphere and her experiences in a normal period of two years. In the figure, the upper vertical scale represents the geographical location and is marked in degrees of latitude, while the lower vertical scale shows the length of the foetus or calf in metres. The horizontal scale represents time. The female whale begins the period with a northward journey from the Antarctic feeding grounds in about April (thicker line at upper left of figure); mating takes place in warm waters, probably between 20° and 30° S, in about June. Because of the uncertainties of the location of Fin Whales outside the whaling grounds, this is shown as a broken line—this convention of a broken line for less certain

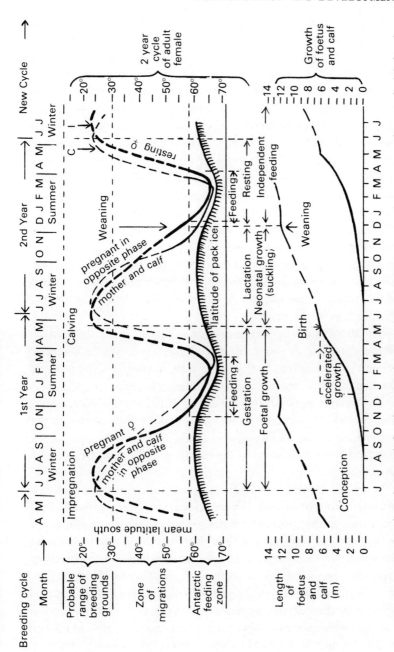

Fig. 7.4 The seasonal cycle in the Fin Whale. The upper diagram represents the migrational movements of a typical adult female, by latitude and season. The lower figure shows the growth of the calf. (After Mackintosh, 1965.)

features is used throughout. Later, as a pregnant female, the whale moves back towards the Antarctic. There is evidence that the pregnant females arrive on the feeding grounds earlier than the nursing or resting females and they may leave earlier. On the feeding grounds, the whale develops its enormous food store in the blubber and bones and then leaves on a northward migration again in the autumn (March–April). Arriving in warmer waters she gives birth, then makes a more leisurely southerly migration with her calf at heel (or rather 'at flipper'). The calf is weaned at 6–7 months, while still in the food-rich southern waters. Later, as a resting female, she returns again to the breeding grounds for pairing and so on. The family unit is a single cow and a bull, as far as we know, and we have no knowledge of whether the cow mates with the same bull year after year or is quite promiscuous. The whole cycle takes two years, so in any one year about half the adult female population will be in one phase and half in the other. The events of the opposite phase are shown as the thinner line in the figure.

The growth of the foetus or calf is shown in the lower part of the diagram. A point of special interest is the 'accelerated growth' of the foetus in the latter part of pregnancy, following the arrival of its mother on the feeding grounds.

The movements of the male Fin Whales parallel those of the females. However, not all whales will follow precisely this pattern, so there is coming and going over a large part of the year and some whales even appear to spend the winter in high latitudes.

In the Northern Hemisphere, the seasons are reversed, so that the northern whales travel south to warm waters to breed at the same time as the southern whales are travelling south, but to the colder seas for feeding. There is thus very little opportunity for the whales from different hemispheres to mingle on the breeding grounds, even if they were to use the same areas. There is little chance of a whale remaining in the breeding areas for protracted periods as they do not appear to feed there.

Other whalebone whales mostly show similar cycles. In Humpbacks the migratory movements are very well known (Fig. 7.5) since these whales swim much closer to the coast on these

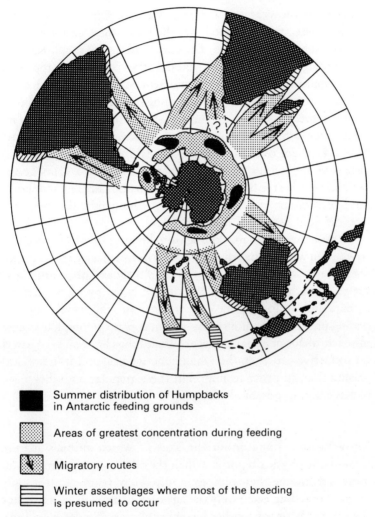

■ Summer distribution of Humpbacks
in Antarctic feeding grounds

▨ Areas of greatest concentration during feeding

▨ Migratory routes

⬛ Winter assemblages where most of the breeding
is presumed to occur

Fig. 7.5   The migration paths of southern Humpback Whales.

migrations than do the balaenopterids. Lactation in the Humpback lasts for 10½–11 months and is followed by a very short
resting phase, yet, like the other rorquals, they produce one calf
every two years.

Sperm whales have a quite different cycle. The females and
the younger males are found in temperate or tropical waters

throughout the year and occur in schools. Ohsumi (1971) has studied these and concluded that the basic organisation was the 'nursery school', composed of mature females and suckling calves and immature whales of both sexes. As the young males approach sexual maturity they leave the nursery school and form loose 'bachelor schools'. During the breeding season, mature bulls contend for the possession of the females in the nursery schools. These are normally matriarchal in organisation but the mature bulls take them over as 'harem schools' for a limited period. A harem master serves an average of fourteen cows. Outside the breeding season the largest of the bulls do not associate in schools but live a solitary existence. It is mostly these old bulls that stray into the cold waters of high latitudes.

Because there is no marked seasonal migration of the breeding cows, as in whalebone whales, there is not such a clear-cut breeding pattern. Mating takes place in the winter and pregnancy lasts for $14\frac{3}{4}$ months. The Sperm Whale calf is fed by its mother for 2 years and, following the end of lactation, the female enters a resting phase of 8–9 months, which makes up a complete breeding cycle of about 4 years. Sperm Whales thus have an even lower reproductive rate than the whalebone whales, and it is not surprising that, in order to maintain these populations, they need to have a long potential life-span.

Knowing something about the ages at which animals mature sexually or physically, or at which they die, is clearly important in understanding their biology. Only a few years ago, the only method of telling accurately the age of wild animals was to mark them at birth, or some other recognisable age. Whales, of course, present their own special problems for this technique.

Whales have been marked ever since the old harpooners of the open-boat whaling days made a practice of marking their harpoons, so that if a whale escaped, it carried an identifiable iron in it. Deliberate marking, however, dates from 1920 when a Norwegian biologist hit upon the idea of shooting copper lances into whales. This did not prove very successful and a fresh attempt was made by scientists of the 'Discovery' Committee in 1926 off

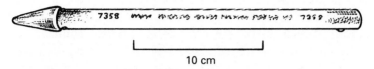

10 cm

Fig. 7.6 *'Discovery'* pattern whale mark.

South Georgia. The first whale-mark resembled a gigantic draw-ing-pin, with a head of about 7.5 cm in diameter. The pin was designed to stick in the blubber by three small barbs on its point, while the head would be conspicuous on the body of the whale. These, too, were unsuccessful. The next type of mark, which is similar to that used today, consisted of a tube of stainless steel about 25 cm in length which could be fired from a 12-bore shot gun (Fig. 7.6). The mark is embossed with instructions to the finder to return the mark, with details of the circumstances in which it is found, and offering a £1 reward. The mark is fired into the blubber of the whale's back and frequently ends up in the epaxial muscle mass. The injury is said not to inconvenience the whale much, but the mark would certainly seem large enough to cause considerable pain when embedded in the muscle. Ideally, the mark is discovered when the whale is stripped of its blubber on the flensing deck. If this is the case, detailed measure-ments can be taken and specimens secured. More often, the mark is overlooked at flensing and is not recovered till the meat cookers are cleaned out, by which time it is usually too late to associate the mark with a particular whale. However, such marks can still provide valuable information on the migration patterns. Most often, of course, the mark is not recovered at all. Of rather more than 5,000 marks applied by *'Discovery'* scientists to whales between 1926 and 1939, only 370 were ever found and returned. Their low rate of return (which has been similar for other whale marking schemes) and the great cost of chartering a whale-catcher or other boat to apply the marks, has discouraged the development of this potentially very valuable research tool.

Fortunately other methods were available for age-determina-tion. Around the middle of this century, two seal biologists, R. M. Laws working on Elephant Seals in the Antarctic, and V. B.

Scheffer, working on Fur Seals in the Pribilof Islands, discovered independently that the canine teeth of seals carried a natural record of their age in the form of incremental annual layers, sometimes visible externally as a series of ridges on the root of the tooth, but always capable of being revealed by examination of cross-section of the teeth.

This discovery was of the greatest importance in elucidating age-specific factors in the biology of the seals, but more than this, it proved to be a method of general application in the study of mammals and now a common approach to age-specific problems is to try to find some hard structure (usually a tooth) which may contain incremental layers.

For the Sperm Whale this was not much of a problem. The enormous teeth showed clearly a pattern of concentric rings of light and dark, or translucent and opaque, dentine. These could be even more clearly demonstrated by etching the cut surface of the tooth and staining the resulting ridges (Fig. 7.7). It was much more difficult to demonstrate that each pair of rings constituted an annual increment. For some time it was believed that two sets of rings were formed each year. However, long-term recoveries of whale-marks suggested that two sets could not be formed in

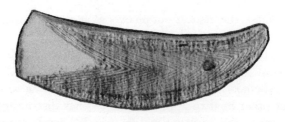

Fig. 7.7　Sectioned Sperm Whale tooth, showing growth layers.

a single year, since nine out of fifteen long-term recoveries gave values, for the number of tooth layers divided by the elapsed time in years since marking, of 2.0 or less; four of the returns had values of less than 1.5 layers per year. Since some layers must have been present when the marks were applied, the accumulation rate seems most likely to be one set per year (Gambell, 1976) and this is generally, although not universally, accepted. Why the dentine is deposited in this differential manner is unknown—presumably it relates to differences in the rate of calcification at the time, which may be associated with climatic or dietary factors, but even animals living in very equable environments are known to produce layered patterns in their teeth.

This method of age determination is not, of course, available for whalebone whales, because of their lack of teeth. However, there are other structures which contain natural records. It was early noticed that the surface of the baleen plates showed a pattern of ridges. The Norwegian cetologist, Johan Ruud (1940, 1945), showed that these represented seasonal variation in the formation of the plate in the gum. Unfortunately, the baleen plate wears away on the exposed edge, so that only about five years' growth are represented, too short a period to be of much value in following events in the whale's life history.

A much more promising structure for the indication of age, surprisingly enough, is the horny plug that lies in the cavity of the external auditory meatus. If one of these plugs is cut longitudinally, it reveals a series of light and dark layers. The formation of these layers is a matter of some interest. The plug in fact consists of the shed cornified cells of the epithelium lining the meatus. The 'glove finger' that extends part of the ear drum, also secretes ear wax, and the shedding of cornified cells alternates with the secretion of wax so the layered structure of the plug is built up. The alternation of light, horny, and dark, waxy, layers would seem to correspond with the regular feeding migrations, to and from cold water shown by most rorquals, but the same structure is present in the ear plugs from Bryde's Whales, which stay the year round in warm water.

Just as with Sperm Whale teeth, so with the ear plugs, there has been controversy about the rate of accumulation of the layers. It was first thought that two sets of layers were formed each year, but recoveries of whale-marks showed this could not always be the case (Gambell, 1976). Careful study of the histology of the ear plug by Roe (1967) showed fairly conclusively that one set is formed each year, although there remain some puzzling cases— a Humpback marked as a yearling was recovered five years later with twelve growth layers in the ear plug (Chittleborough, 1960). Perhaps we have to conclude that the rate of layer formation is different in Humpbacks from that in Fin Whales, or perhaps it is only young Humpbacks that are different. (Another possibility, of course, is that of human error in recording the details of the whale at the time of marking.)

Even were there no controversy about the rate of accumulation of layers in ear plugs or teeth, there would still remain difficulties of interpretation—the later layers in old animals are often difficult to resolve. But ages derived from ear plugs and teeth, supplemented by length measurements and corpora lutea counts, give a very good estimate of the age of whales and this enables us to say a great deal about their life histories. Perhaps the most surprising thing about the great whales is that they are not as long-lived (even in the absence of a whaling industry) as their immense size might suggest. Whales, like most other mammals, become sexually mature before they reach physical maturity, as defined by the fusion of the epiphyses of the vertebral centra. In the Fin Whale, for example, puberty occurs at around 6–7 years in males and females, when they are 19.4 and 20 m long respectively. Physical maturity is not reached until the male is 20.9 m long and the female 22.5 m—these values are for Southern Hemisphere Fin Whales—by which time the whales may be aged 15–20 years. The maximum age reached by a Fin Whale is not known—the effect of the whaling industry has been to reduce the *average* age very markedly—but a large rorqual between 25 and 30 years old is probably nearing the end of its natural expectation of life.

Male Sperm Whales reach puberty at around 20 years, become harem masters first at around 25 years and mature gradually between lengths of 15.4 m and 16 m, corresponding to ages 35–

45 years. Female Sperm Whales become sexually mature at about 10 years and physical growth stops at a length of about 11.1 m, corresponding to an age of 28–29 years (Best, 1970). Sperm Whales have a much greater potential life span than rorquals, as would be expected from their lower reproductive rate.

Age at sexual maturity is a particularly important factor in determining the reproductive potential of an animal. Clearly, the earlier it matures, the greater its potential number of offspring. As sexual maturity in females is closely associated with physical size, a young whale that grows faster will become sexually mature earlier. One reason for faster growth might be less competition for food; a possible reason for this might be a reduction in the absolute numbers of whales, leaving more krill for the survivors.

The layers in the ear plugs consist of two types—the earlier layers are irregular and often diffuse, while later layers are more compact and evenly spaced. Christina Lockyer (1972, 1974) showed that the transition between the two types of layer corresponded to the attainment of sexual maturity. A similar pattern can be found in the dentine layers in seal teeth.

This observation has allowed us to follow changes in this important parameter in exploited whales over the years. Fig. 7.8 shows the changes in mean age at sexual maturity in Southern Fin Whales by year classes (year of birth). Although there is a

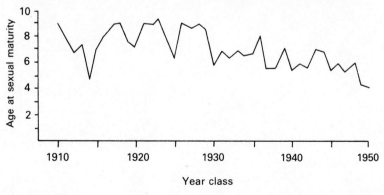

Fig. 7.8 Changes in age at sexual maturity in the Southern Fin Whale. (After Gambell, 1977.)

185

good deal of variability, or 'noise' as it has become fashionable to call it today, it is clear that, from a mean age of sexual maturity of about 10 years for whales born up to about 1930 there has been a decline to about 6 years for the 1950 year class. A similar decline has been noted in Sei Whales. The hypothesis that removal of their fellow whales has allowed better feeding and enhanced growth would seem to fit here, since the Antarctic whaling industry reached a peak in the 1930s.

The significance of these changes, and an associated increase in pregnancy rates, which together constitute a density-dependent response, will be appreciated when the management strategy of 'maximum sustainable yield' exploitation is considered.

8 Whale brains and intelligence

Most people make their first close contacts with whales through visiting an oceanarium and watching one of those remarkable displays, most often given by Bottle-nosed Dolphins or, if one is lucky, by a Killer Whale. No one can fail to be impressed, and often entertained, by the antics that a clever trainer can persuade his charges to indulge in. Such trainable animals, we say to ourselves, must possess a high degree of intelligence. When we discover their echo-locating ability and their complex vocalisations these faculties reinforce our impression.

There is no aspect of an animal's biology that is more difficult to investigate than its mental processes. However, a logical approach to the further study of this topic in Cetacea will be to look at the anatomy of the whale brain—the organ of mind. It is nearly three hundred years since John Ray first described the brain of the whale. Since that time much has been published—a recent bibliography of the central nervous system of cetaceans listed 212 titles and did not claim to be exhaustive. Much careful effort has gone into research. While the early anatomists had to be content with the superficial examination of brains from whales washed up on shore, usually far gone in decomposition before the investigator could arrive on the scene, the modern scientist can anaesthetise a porpoise and perfuse its brain with a preservative selected to reveal those structures he wishes to study. Not one, but several, whale brains have been embedded in nitrocellulose (to strengthen them) and serially sectioned into slices 0.035 mm thick from end to end, the slices mounted on glass, stained and examined microscopically. Well preserved specimens of brains of the large whales are still hard to come by, but a very great deal of material has been collected and examined from the smaller odontocetes and the neuro-anatomist now has much on which to base his conclusions.

The brains of the larger cetaceans are the largest known brains of any animal. Sperm Whale bulls have brains weighing between 9.2 and 6.4 kg, with an average weight of 7.8 kg (Kojima, 1951). Whalebone whale brains are only slightly smaller; a series of seven Fin Whale brains weighed between 7.9 and 6.0 kg, averaging 6.9 kg (Jansen and Jansen, 1969). Further brain weights are given in Table 8.1. The largest recorded brain weight of a land

Table 8.1   Brain Weights for Various Cetacea*

	Brain weight (kg)
Odontocetes	
Sperm Whale	7.80 (average of 16)
Killer Whale	6.05
Pilot Whale	2.66
Beluga	2.26 (average of 3)
Bottle-nosed Dolphin	1.54 (average of 12)
Common Dolphin	0.88
Harbour Porpoise	0.52
Mysticetes	
Fin Whale	6.93 (average of 7)
Blue Whale	6.19 (average of 2)
Humpback Whale	7.50
Sei Whale	4.46 (average of 12)
Black Right Whale	2.75
Minke Whale	2.65

* From values given by Jansen and Jansen, 1969, and Morgane and Jacobs, 1976.

mammal is that of the Indian Elephant, with a brain that weighs about 7.5 kg. In comparison, a human brain weighs about 1.3–1.7 kg.

The whales' brain is a peculiar shape, being foreshortened and very wide transversely, characteristics more marked in odontocetes than in mysticetes (Fig. 8.1). This recalls the telescoping of the skull that has taken place in the course of cetacean evolution, but it is likely that the two phenomena are not related. In the

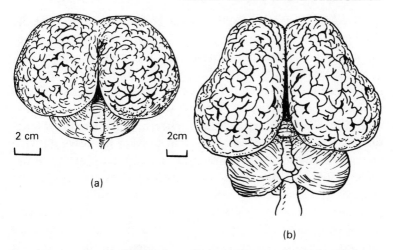

Fig. 8.1   Dorsal view of brain of: (a) Harbour Porpoise, (b) Minke Whale.

case of the brain, what has happened is that, besides the enlargement that has taken place, the axis of the fore-brain has been
rotated forwards and downwards, so that it lies at right-angles
to the axis of the mid-brain. This contrasts with the normal mammalian pattern, where the axes of the various parts of the brain
and the spinal cord all lie more or less in the same line, but is
similar to the situation in the human brain (Fig. 8.2). We might
explain the latter as a result of the upright posture of man, but
clearly the same explanation will not serve for the whale.

The most striking feature of the cetacean brain is the great development of the cerebral hemispheres, which, besides being
large in absolute size, are complexly folded, the extent and depth

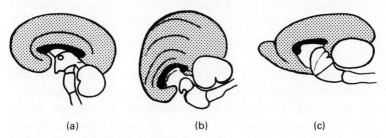

Fig. 8.2   The brain axis in: (a) Man, (b) a cetacean, (c) a seal. The corpus callo-
sum is hatched. (After Flannigan, 1972.)

189

of the folding approaching the condition found in man. Here the similarity ends, for the pattern of the folding bears no resemblance at all to the human condition, being more similar to that of carnivores and ungulates (Harrison and King, 1965). What one sees when one looks down at the cerebral hemispheres is the cerebral cortex, or neopallium. This consists of a cellular layer ('grey matter') a few millimetres thick, beneath which is a great mass of connecting nerve fibres ('white matter'). The fibres serve to convey nerve impulses between the various parts of the brain, bring impulses from the sense cells and convey them to the muscles and glands. The cells carry out the neural activities of correlation and association. Increase in the size of an animal will increase the number of fibres to and from its effector and sensor systems, and this will necessitate an increase in the number of cortical co-ordinating cells. But, because the cortical cells are arranged as a rind on the surface of the hemisphere, they will increase only as the square of the linear dimension, while the fibre population will increase more nearly as the cube. In order that the cortical cells can keep pace with the increasing number of fibres as size increases, it is necessary for the cortex to fold in on itself, producing the familiar patterns of sulci and gyri. This increase in the complexity of the convolutions of the cortex is well seen if we compare the brains of the rat and the horse (Fig. 8.3)—the former has a nearly smooth brain, while the latter exhibits a high degree of folding, yet horses display no evidence of a higher mental capacity than rats. It is the simple increase in bulk that has necessitated the more complex brain of the horse. As cetaceans are large mammals, one would expect their brains to exhibit complex folding and this is indeed what we find. The porpoise is considerably smaller than the horse, but its brain is just as convoluted, if not more so, than the horse's brain.

We have rather little information about the functional organisation of the cortex in the whale. The visual, auditory and sensory motor regions occupy a relatively smaller proportion of the cortex than they do in lower mammals. A large part of the cortical surface appears to be given up to association areas where higher orders of co-ordination take place. Interesting in this respect is a unique cetacean feature, the introduction of a lobe not

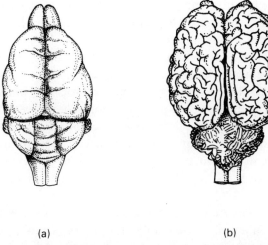

(a)   (b)

Fig. 8.3   The surface of the brain of: (a) a rat, (b) a horse, to show how increasing body size affects the folding. The horse is not more intelligent than the rat, but its brain shows many more convolutions.

seen in other mammals in the architecture of the cerebral hemisphere. This is known as the paralimbic lobe, since it lies between the limbic and supralimbic lobes. According to Morgane (1978), the functional significance of the paralimbic lobe is to provide a continuum of all the specific sensory and motor areas which in man are distributed throughout the supralimbic lobe.

In terms of microscopic structure, the cetacean cortex shows the usual mammalian pattern of six layers of cortical cells. Morgane has identified some thirty–forty types of cortical area, identifiable by the peculiarities of the arrangement of their cells. It is logical to suppose that the different spatial patterns correspond to different cortical functions, and it is usually accepted that a high diversity of cortical areas corresponds to a higher development of the brain. There are, for example, more than fifty such areas described for the human cortex.

The only other part of the brain visible from above is the cerebellum. This is more obvious in the mysticete than in the odontocete brain. In both groups, however, it is highly developed. I have mentioned earlier the importance of parts of the cerebellum in receiving tactile stimuli. Other parts are comparatively reduced in size. This has been interpreted as reflecting the relative lack of need of an acute sense of balance in an animal which floats in a buoyant medium, when compared with a terrestrial mammal. However, it seems to me that it is not so much a matter of a whale being indifferent to its equilibrium, which is assessed from messages arriving from the semicircular canals in its inner ear, as that it has more important information derived from sensors on its skin, particularly the flukes. The whale, and particularly the dolphin, as an active swimmer in a medium which itself may be in motion, needs to orient itself to the water mass, rather than to the comparatively irrelevant concept of a level horizon.

A high degree of muscular co-ordination is obviously important in swimming and, presumably, this process would be carried out in the cerebellum and various ganglia and brain nuclei, although precisely how they operate is unknown.

The importance of the auditory sense is reflected in the great development of the parts of the brain involved in sound perception and processing—the cochlear nucleus, the inferior colliculus and some other centres. Not surprisingly, in view of their echo-locating faculty, the odontocetes have these centres better developed than the mysticetes.

Cetaceans have the usual array of cranial nerves, with the important exception that the olfactory nerve is missing in the odontocetes (there may be a few vestigial fibres present in Sperm Whales and *Hyperoodon*). The optic nerves and the group of cranial nerves that control the muscles which rotate the eyeball and move the eyelids follow the usual mammalian pattern. The optic nerve in *Tursiops* has only about one tenth as many fibres as in a visually oriented mammal like man, but, on the other hand, there are more fibres present than in the cat (Morgane and Jacobs, 1972). In the river dolphins, *Inia* and *Sotalia*, the optic nerve is reduced while in *Platanista* it consists of only a few hundred fibres. This little dolphin is devoid of a sense of sight, its eyes lacking lenses.

The fifth cranial nerve, the trigeminal, is very highly developed and is the largest cranial nerve in mysticetes and second in size only to the auditory nerve in odontocetes. This is probably a response to the relative size of the head in mysticetes and the important role it plays as a bearer of tactile sense organs in both groups. The seventh, or facial, nerve, is also large, probably for the same reason. This nerve also provides motor fibres which run to the muscles of the blow-hole, the nasal plugs and the muscles in the walls of the air sacs. It is thus likely to be involved in the production of vocalisations.

As mentioned earlier, the eighth cranial nerve, the auditory nerve, is of the highest importance in whales. This nerve carries fibres from the cochlea and also from the vestibular part of the inner ear and is thus concerned with both hearing and the sense of balance. In the Bottle-nosed Dolphin, there are about 67,900 cochlear fibres in the auditory nerve, more than twice as many as in man, and substantially more than the 50,000 or so found in the cat, a terrestrial mammal with a very acute sense of hearing (Morgane and Jacobs, 1972).

It is difficult to summarise this. We see whales as mammals with large brains (some with exceedingly large brains) and most of the enlargement has taken place in the most highly evolved part of the brain, the neocortex. The cortex is complexly folded and is made up of many areas with their own characteristic cell patterns. It seems possible, from the structure of their brains, that cetaceans have larger areas of cortex available for the co-ordination of neural activity, or for the higher mental functions. Sensory inputs related to hearing and tactile stimuli are important to whales in interpreting their environment. There is nothing fundamentally different in the cetacean brain from the standard mammalian pattern, although some parts which are well developed (e.g. the paralimbic lobe) are not found in other mammals.

These facts have been used in two quite different ways by opposing schools of cetologists. There are those who claim that the size and complexity of the whale's brain supports the assertion that whales are intelligent animals, second only to man in their mental powers, and are at a different level of mental organisation from the lower mammals. On the other hand, there are those who deny this, pointing out that there is little which is special in the whale's brain and that their behavioural patterns do not support the idea of an active intelligence. Rather few people seem to occupy a middle ground in this debate.

The arguments are likely to continue. Intelligence defies useful definition even in our own species. It is futile to attempt to apply human concepts of intelligence to an animal that inhabits a medium so utterly different from our terrestrial world as does the whale, that obtains most of its information about its surroundings from tactile organs on or in its skin, and from the reverberating sounds in its environment (which odontocetes supplement by adding their own clicks to provide information-rich echoes), and which, lacking any form of manipulative appendage, can express itself only by the motor patterns of swimming movement and by vocalisations. This last point is particularly important in a practical assessment of intelligence. The development of mental processes in the human species was closely associated with the use of the hand for manipulation. No whale, however intelligent it might be, could attempt to modify its environment in the way that man so effectively does.

If whales are *not* intelligent, the great size of the whale brain is a puzzle. Professor Harry Jerison of the University of California, Los Angeles, USA, considers brain size a matter of prime importance in assessing mental ability. The function of the brain is performed by its neurones; the larger brain contains more neurones and hence should be able to perform more complex functions. There are about 10,000 million neurones in a human cortex; some whales have 30,000 million neurones in theirs (Jerison, 1978). Larger animals may be expected to have larger brains, as there will be more sensory cells from which to receive information and more muscles and glands to control. This is the difference we noted earlier in the comparison of the brains of the rat and the horse. But some animals have gone further than this, with an additional relative enlargement of the brain over and beyond what can be accounted for by increase of body size. This phenomenon has been labelled 'encephalisation'.

Encephalisation is a feature of some, but not all, vertebrates. Fish and reptiles show scarcely any encephalisation in the course of their evolution, but birds and mammals do. The higher pri-

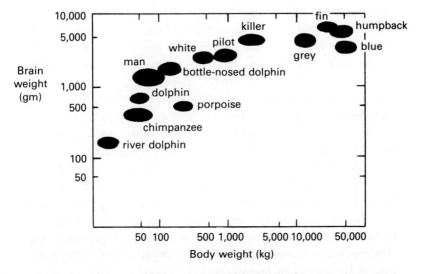

Fig. 8.4 Comparison of brain weights and body size for various cetaceans, Chimpanzee and Man. (Modified from Jerison, 1978.)

mates and Cetacea both show a high degree of encephalisation and, if one plots brain weights against body size (Fig. 8.4), one finds that the values for Cetacea overlap those for Man and Chimpanzees. Jerison considers that this increase in the size of the brain is related to the handling of an increasing load of information from the sense organs and the feed-back processes within the brain. The capacity to handle these data, which he calls biological intelligence, he regards as related to brain size.

Perhaps what Professor Jerison defines as biological intelligence is not very similar to the concept of intelligence as we use it to describe our own mental abilities. Can we learn anything from the behaviour of Cetacea that might lead us to suppose them intelligent?

There is no doubt that whales, or at any rate dolphins, can be trained to carry out remarkably complicated routines. But so too can troupes of performing dogs in a circus, and the example quoted (p. 130) of pigeons being trained to carry out a task which received acclamation when it was performed by dolphins, goes far to demonstrate that the performances of trained animals tell us more about the intelligence and patience of their trainers than of the animals they train. On the other hand, it is a noticeable feature of dolphins that they do not always have to be **taught** tricks. They will, if allowed, develop and vary their own routines. Suffering, as they must do, from the narrow restrictions of their pools, it is almost as though these 'gaol-birds' are experimenting with the development of new stimuli to train the white-coated attendant at the pool-side to give them another piece of fish. An imitative response is strongly developed in dolphins. A Bottle-nosed Dolphin was placed in a pool containing a Spinner Dolphin. When the Spinner jumped clear of the water and made its characteristic spin in response to the trainer's signal, the Bottle-nosed Dolphin immediately leaped out of the water and made a crude but recognisable spin. It could not have seen a Spinner Dolphin before, yet its immediate response was to imitate the complex motor pattern of the Spinner. Imitativeness is characteristic of the higher primates also.

Dr John Lilly considers that dolphins make attempts to mimic human speech, although other workers have failed to observe this (Alpers, 1960). Lilly has been very impressed with the gentleness and co-operativeness of dolphins and this has struck other workers. Nearly all the dolphins used in performances could, if they wished, inflict serious injury on their trainers. Killer Whales might well regard a man as a suitably sized prey item, yet there are no accounts of a Killer Whale turning on its trainer in the pool and devouring him. On a couple of occasions a trainer has been forcibly seized by the arm or leg and compelled to do what the whale wanted, rather than what he (or she) wished to do, but no serious injuries were inflicted, despite the fact that it would have been the easiest thing in the world for the Killer to have crunched off the limb in its mouth.

But even Bottle-nosed Dolphins are not always quite docile, particularly the males. Beaky, the Bottle-nosed Dolphin that frequented the Isle of Man and the south-west coast of England and Wales between 1972 and 1978, abducted two women and a child, carrying them off against their will, one of the women enthroned on its nose, like a ballerina (Webb, 1978). However, these alarming exploits were the exception and not the rule in the behaviour of this wild, but very sociable, dolphin which seemed to seek out the company of men, or perhaps I should rather say, women. Beaky had become separated from his own herd of dolphins, or perhaps had been actively cast out, and his behaviour had become fixed on humans and their artefacts. It is remarkable that he seemed able to differentiate between men and women. To the latter he showed overt sexual behaviour, which did not cease if they encouraged him. To a man he would make similar sexual advances, rubbing his body against him and hooking his erect penis round his waist, but if the man rubbed back, Beaky's behaviour stopped abruptly, seeming to demonstrate that it represented the imposition of male dominance rather than sex, *per se*. To children, Beaky was reported to exhibit no sexual behaviour. How he distinguished the sexes (or the children, for that matter) remains a mystery, like so much else in the perplexing field of dolphin behaviour.

The large amount of sexual behaviour seen in whales—mostly in captivity, but at times, as in the case of Beaky, in the wild— has been taken by some people as evidence of an elevation of sex from a simply reproductive function to some role akin to 'love' in humans. It is true that in few mammals does sex play so large and continuous a role as in the human species (and this is not necessarily evidence of higher mental abilities), but there are cases of other group-forming mammals, lions for example, where a high level of sexual behaviour relates to the maintenance of group structure. This is probably part of the explanation of the sexual behaviour seen in whales, but it must be remembered that, in the case of captive animals, sexual behaviour may occur because the captives have little else to do. Elaborate courtship behaviour is another matter. As noted earlier, the courtship of whales may be necessitated by the nature of their aquatic environment.

Lilly (1977) believes that dolphins have a complicated language and feels that the fundamental requirement for testing cetacean intelligence is to discover a means of communicating with them. Animal psychologists are already experimenting with the use of AMESLAN (American Sign Language for the Deaf) in an attempt to communicate with apes. A similar study with dolphins would

have to use auditory, rather than visual, signs and Lilly is developing a computer-based programme to enable him to investigate
this further at his research foundation at Malibu.

Should we pay regard to the many tales, some dating from antiquity, of dolphins coming to the rescue of drowning men?
Antony Alpers, in his charming book on dolphins (Alpers, 1960)
has recounted many of them. The earliest and best known is the
story, told by Herodotus, of the poet Arion who, while on a journey to Corinth about 600 B.C., was cast overboard by pirates,
but was rescued and brought safely to shore by a dolphin. The
story of Arion may well be a myth, but there are plenty of more
recent well authenticated accounts of similar exploits involving
swimmers in distress and helpful dolphins. I have already referred
to the care-giving or epimeletic behaviour of dolphins and this
has a ready enough explanation in terms of ordinary genetic survival values. I think that epimeletic behaviour can be behind most
of the accounts of dolphins aiding swimmers in distress. The
many stories of dolphins giving rides to boys recall Beaky's
exploits; these do not seem to indicate especially high levels of
intelligence, rather a play activity of running off with the play-
thing, such as may be observed in a cat or a dog.

A feature of cetacean behaviour that seems to demonstrate a
startling lack of intelligence is what happens when they become
stranded on the shore. Some whales strand, of course, because
they are sick or old and incapable of proper locomotion. Others
may be the victims of unfamiliar surroundings—a deep-ocean
cetacean like a Blue Whale, on finding itself in shoal water, may
be incapable of processing the information it receives about its
surroundings or fail to appreciate its significance and consequently runs ashore. But there are many examples of schools of
dolphins, for example Pilot Whales, seeming to swim deliberately ashore. When kind-hearted people have attempted to haul
them back into the sea, the rescued dolphins have at once swum
back to strand alongside their companions on the beach. It has
been suggested that the animals are responding to the distress calls of the others on the beach, or the rallying calls of the
leader. This may be so, but cases have been recorded of solitary
stranded animals that refused to swim away from the beach when

repeatedly moved out to sea (Wood, 1966) and it is unlikely that these could have been responding to auditory signals (unlikely, but not impossible, for as we have seen, sounds can travel vast distances in the sea).

Various explanations have been offered to account for mass strandings. It has been suggested that dolphins approaching a gently sloping sandy or muddy bottom find their echo-locating pulses reflected *away* from them and, hence, presume they are in deeper water than is actually the case. It seems very unlikely that this is in fact so for there are plenty of examples of dolphins swimming close in to the shore without subsequently stranding. Similarly, the behaviour of returning to the beach after being towed out, shows that they can orient *to* the beach and, if to it, why not *away* from it?

Another theory put forward is that stranded whales are suffering from infestations of nematode worms in their air-sacs or middle or inner ear. Nematodes are common, and generally harmless, parasites in the pterygoid sinuses but Francis Fraser (1966) found it possible to suppose a situation where abcesses and inflammation had caused the breakdown of the air-sac system so that it no longer reflected sound and the isolation of the essential organ of hearing was disrupted, causing the whale to lose its sense of direction. But it strains credulity to suppose that all members of a stranded group (which may number hundreds) could be affected in this way and, again, there is the question of the return to the place of stranding.

An even less likely explanation suggests that the milling about of the whales near the shore stirs up so much sand and mud that they cannot see to navigate and hence strand. But, in fact, stranding dolphins, unless *driven* ashore, are not often reported as milling about. Some accounts speak of them swimming directly, almost in a purposive fashion, to the place when they strand (Hubbs, 1966). And if the water is murky, why do the dolphins not echo-locate their way back out to sea?

Mass panic, as in a drive-fishery, is another matter, although we may be rather puzzled that slapping the water with an oar or clacking two stones together under the surface, should cause cetaceans to panic to such a degree that they swim in to strand, rather than turn beneath the boats of their pursuers and swim away to freedom. Indeed, in the course of the Faroes drive fishery for pilot whales, if one of the school does swim outside the wall of encircling boats, it may swim back to rejoin its companions, and meet its death.

I know of no convincing and general explanation of mass strandings and the events which may follow. In none of these cases can the behaviour of the dolphins be described as in any way intelligent—indeed, in most it seems quite the opposite—but there remains a chance that, where we do not understand the explanation, it might just possibly be concerned with a higher mental process of which at the moment we know nothing.

It is difficult to know what conclusions to draw from all this. I do not know of a single properly authenticated episode wherein the behaviour of a cetacean could be described as intelligent, as we might use the term of some human behaviour which involved a choice of several actions, the choice involving foresight and an estimation of hypothetical consequences. On the other hand, there are plenty of examples where cetaceans seem to behave very much in the manner of other herd animals, a flock of sheep in a panic, perhaps, which are not usually thought of as intelligent. Because dolphins are imitative and easily trained, and one of the commonest seen in captivity, the Bottle-nosed Dolphin, has a built-in smile on its face (Tavolga, 1966), we tend to endow them with qualities which they do not possess.

On the other hand, the large size of the brain, with its highly developed cortex, seems to me to indicate the possibility of higher mental functions. There are aspects of cetacean behaviour which we do not understand at all—stranding behaviour is an example—which may relate to unknown mental processes.

If it were to be shown that cetaceans had a language with which they could communicate detailed and precise information to each other—and no one has yet come near to showing that they can—then I would regard this as good evidence of intelligence, in a human sense, since no other species approaches this condition. The possession of a developed language would facilitate abstract thought patterns in the mind and could go a long way to explaining the complexity of the cetacean nervous system.

My belief is that cetaceans are not intelligent. The odontocetes, as active social hunters, have the plasticity of behaviour that characterises other social carnivores which can obtain their daily sustenance in a small part of each twenty-four hours. With time on their hands, as it were, they fill in the rest of the day with 'play', or types of behaviour which do not seem directly related to the ordinary vital processes of feeding, reproducing and caring for their young. Sexual activity becomes elaborated and divorced from a purely reproductive function, serving also to maintain the social bonding.

But, even if cetaceans are not, as some suppose, second only to man in mental ability, this is no reason to value them less, exploit them inhumanely, or contemplate their extermination with equanimity. Whales will not be less attractive to watch, less stimulating aesthetically, or less significant in the ecology of the oceans, if they are on the mental plane of more familiar terrestrial mammals, rather than that of man himself.

9 Man and whales—the first contacts

Primitive man owed much of his success, and even his very survival, to his ability to utilise food as he found it and to act as a scavenger. It was probably in this way that he first encountered whales. A stranded whale would have provided an exceedingly valuable resource to a wandering band of Stone Age savages, particularly in high latitudes, where people had to contend with a climate that necessitated warm clothing and were dependent on the protection of a dwelling that could, at the worst of the seasons, be heated. Only a couple of centuries ago a people of Stone Age culture, the Inuit Eskimos, coped with this sort of environment. Inuit culture was relatively sophisticated but they lived self-contained lives that demanded no more of their environment than would have been available to the earliest colonists of the far north. Their basic requirement was a supply of seals, which provided them with meat, skins for clothing and the vitally important blubber. Blubber could be eaten and, consisting as it did almost entirely of fat, provided an exceedingly rich energy source. Equally, it could be burnt in a simple stone lamp, giving heat and, most importantly, light. Life during the long Arctic winter would surely have been insupportable without some form of lighting to enable the manufacture of stone and ivory implements and the preparation and maintenance of the fur clothing that alone made life possible outside. Seals were the mainstay of most of these peoples, but certainly whales would not have been neglected if they were found. The local people may well have gathered round a beached whale carcase and feasted on it for many days, weeks, or even months. Any prejudice about eating stale meat is not generally marked in primitive peoples and Inuit in particular seem to relish meat even more as it goes rotten. Sinews could be extracted, after first stripping off the blubber, for use as lashings and bones used for implements or structural work. The blubber might either be carried away to more permanent settlements or used on the spot.

Such activities would leave little or no trace in the archaeological record but, from time to time, the skeleton of a large rorqual—too large to have been captured deliberately by man, and therefore presumably a stranded specimen—has been found in association with stone axes and stone adzes which it is logical to presume were used to cut up the carcase and strip off the blubber respectively.

Bones of whales are commonly found at prehistoric sites. In the comparatively treeless regions of the high Arctic, or islands like Orkney and Shetland, whale ribs provided rafters of a convenient length and a suitable curvature and the vertebrae of the larger whales provided convenient stools or work-tables and were used in that way in a good many settlements. The porous nature of whale bone renders it easily worked with stone implements (unfortunately it also means it is not very well preserved in many cases) so that it was a favoured medium for small fabricated products and works of art.

Stranded whales continued to have economic significance long after the Stone Age ended and more complex communities had sprung up. This significance was still recognised very much later in England, where, since at least the fourteenth century, the law has reserved cetaceans for the Crown. The law (Statute Praerogativa Regis, 17 Edward II [1324]) states that, although the Crown has sovereign dominion over the sea which encompasses the British Islands, it has no general property in the fish therein except whales and sturgeon. These are Royal Fish and belong to the Crown. The chief merit of the prerogative nowadays is that stranded Cetacea are reported by the Coastguards to the Receivers of Wreck, who inform the British Museum (Natural History) of the stranding. Since 1913, records have been kept of the numbers and species of whales stranded on the British coasts, and the collection of the Museum has benefited accordingly.

To return to our primitive people, the scavenging of beached carcases would soon have suggested the idea of hunting whales at sea, either to kill them directly, or to strand them deliberately by driving them ashore. Certain species are more readily driven than others and the one that has formed the basis of most drive-fisheries in the North Atlantic is the Pilot Whale, *Globicephala melaena*. Pilot Whales naturally occur in large schools, often numbering several hundreds, and not infrequently swim near to the shore. The fishermen of Shetland discovered centuries ago that, by bringing their boats between the school and the open sea, and splashing the water with their oars, or throwing stones into the sea, the whales could be driven into one of the voes. Once the leading whales had been stranded the remainder were easy to capture, since all would follow the leader to their death.

Pat and Ursula Venables (1955) have made a useful summary of Pilot-whaling in Shetland. A strict code of rules existed for the conduct of a drive and for the division of the spoils after-wards. Shares were divided according to age and the final division, obviously a highly complicated matter, was supervised by the 'Baillie' who also received a share. These shares, however, came to less than one third of the total. One third went to the Admiral of the County and another to the laird on whose lands the whales were beached. And, inevitably, the minister of the par-ish came in for his tenth-share, or tithe. A revolt against these claims was finally successful but, by this time, 1888, the drive-fishery was almost at an end. The last organised drive was on 7 February 1903 in Weisdale Voe, when eighty-three whales were killed. Pilot Whales are still seen off Shetland, but not in large numbers, nor do they come close to shore. Why this change has taken place is uncertain. It may be associated with subtle changes in ocean currents or it may be that a local stock of whales has been exterminated. Some very large kills were made in the nine-teenth century, the largest being the astonishing total of 1,540 whales killed in the Bay of Quendale on 22 September 1845, allegedly in the space of 2 hours!

At least in the later years for which we have records, the Shet-landers seem to have made but sparse use of the whales they drove ashore. Oil was almost the only product used, although, during a great famine in 1740, the meat was eaten by the crofters.

In the Faeroe Islands on the other hand, the meat of the Pilot Whale, or 'grindhval' as it is known there, has always been esteemed a delicacy. This is one of the few localities in the world where a drive fishery for this species persists, and we are fortunate that many careful eye-witness accounts exist. Some of the best of these are by Williamson (1948, 1960). Pilot-whaling plays a more important part in the culture of the Faeroese than it does in their present economy and the 'grind' and its aftermath is a social occasion of some importance, so when the cry of 'Grind-aboð' goes up there is great activity.

Boats that take part in the 'grind' have to be properly equipped and manned. Important parts of the gear are the whaling lance ('hvalváken'), the hooks used for making fast the carcases ('sóknaronglar') and white stones attached to short lines ('kast'), which are thrown into the water repeatedly as a means of shepherding the whales. The 'grindaformadur' in charge of the drive must choose the 'grindaplás' when the whales will be driven ashore carefully, remembering that the whales will not be driven against the tide, but are said to like to swim against the wind. Once the whales are driven ashore they are lanced or finally killed by severing the spinal cord at the neck with a knife.

The division of the catch is different from the Shetland system being based essentially on whales rather than on parts of the whale and most of the whale is used for food.

The average annual catch of Pilot Whales in Faeroe for the decade 1961–1970 was 1,392 (Mitchell, 1975). This is slightly lower than it had been in earlier years, but the indications would seem to be that a catch of this size is sustainable, so unless the intensity of hunting increases or there is some other change in the whales' environment that affects their numbers, the 'grind' could continue indefinitely.

Other drive-fisheries for Pilot Whales have existed elsewhere in the North Atlantic, for example Newfoundland, where the fishery was active from 1947 to 1964, with catches reaching 10,000 in 1956, and Cape Cod from the mid-eighteenth century to the 1920s, when, in the late 1800s, the annual catch was around 2,000 to 3,000 whales.

Drive-fisheries for other species of small cetaceans are wide-spread but usually follow a similar pattern of cutting off a school of whales with small boats, thus driving the animals into confined waters where they are beached. Dolphins in particular were important to the Pacific islanders as, before the introduction of pigs by white explorers in the eighteenth century, they provided, together with fruit bats and human flesh, the only red meat that the islanders could obtain. Their teeth were used for ornamentation and for currency and were of particular significance for purchasing brides, a value that was well exploited by the Sperm-whalers who cruised the Pacific in the last century.

But let us return to our Stone Age hunters in northern Europe. It is but a short step from using boats in a drive-fishery, where the whales are killed on shore, to killing the animals at sea from the boats and bringing the carcases back. Indeed, there is no way of telling whether drive-fisheries did in fact precede killing at sea. The antiquity of this type of hunting is very great. There are Stone Age rock engravings in northern Norway, mainly on the coast from Møre to Finmark, which clearly depict the animals hunted at that time and some include the figures of men in canoes (Fig. 9.1). Exactly the same equipment that was used to take the larger kinds of seals would be suitable to take the smaller kinds of whales, as shown by the recent tradition of the Inuit.

Franz Boas' book on the Central Eskimos, first published in

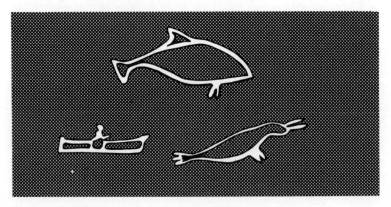

Fig. 9.1   Stone-age rock engravings from Rødøy, Norway.

1888 (Boas, 1964) gives a good account of the basic hunting gear used with little modification by all the tribes from Greenland to Alaska. The kayak, or skin canoe, was a very light craft made up of a framework of thin wooden (or bone) laths and ribs over which was stretched a waterproof covering of three or four Ring Seal skins. The hunter sat in a central cockpit, into which he laced himself, so that it was impossible for the boat to be swamped, though it might be capsized rather easily. The kayak was out-fitted with its paddle, a scraper for ice, a harpoon and its line, to which a seal-skin float was attached, the receptacle for the line, a bird-spear with its throwing board, and a couple of lances. The harpoon was used mainly for the hunting of seal and walrus, but was also the weapon employed when small whales were to be taken.

After harpooning his prey the hunter would make no attempt to remain attached to it. The end of the harpoon line was attached to a float made of the inflated skin of a seal. The resistance of the float prevented the animal from diving and hindered its swimming. Further resistance could be provided by attaching a sea-anchor, made of a wooden hoop with a seal or deer skin stretched over it, to the line. After the wounded animal had tired itself out a little it would be lanced with an 'anguvigang'. The equipment used was simultaneously primitive and sophisticated and could be used to take the smaller Cetacea, such as Narwhals and White Whales. However, the Inuit, in past times, by the co-operation of several families, were prepared to tackle even the Greenland Right Whale.

The great depredations by European whalers led to right whales becoming so scarce that this type of hunting became extinct, but a sort of large whale hunting has persisted in Alaska.

This type of fishery, where the harpoon line was attached to a buoy which could be cast over the side once the whale had been fastened, considerably reduced the risk associated with attacking the large whales and this was fully exploited by some primitive peoples. Perhaps the best documented of these were the Indians of the west coast of Vancouver Island and the northern part of the coast of the State of Washington. Waterman (1920) has described the whaling activities of the Makah Indians of Cape

Flattery. The Makah would set off to kill large whales from 8–49 km offshore in large dug-out canoes fashioned from red cedar logs (Chinook canoes) and crewed by eight men. The equipment consisted of an enormous harpoon with a shaft of up to 5.5 m long, a line of whale sinew and a seal skin float.

The harpooner led the expedition from the bow of the canoe. When a whale was sighted the paddlers would paddle the canoe up to it and the harpooner would drive the huge harpoon as deeply into its side as possible. Immediately the man behind the harpooner on the starboard side (all whales were harpooned on that side) would bend another line and float onto the end of the harpoon line and toss this clear over the side. As the whale went down so successive lines of 10–20 m of heavy spruce root fibre ropes and floats were bent on. As many as thirteen floats might be attached to one line; last of all was a small float attached to a long, very light line. This would bob to the surface quickly, or might not submerge, and gave the Indians an indication of the whereabouts of the whale. As soon as it rose again another harpoon was planted. Meanwhile signals were made to other boats in the vicinity that a whale had been fastened and assistance invited in return for specified parts of the captured whale. A wounded whale which had been struck a number of times often could not get below the surface, though it might be hours before the Indians could get sufficiently near to it to lance it with a bone-pointed 'butuysk'. Occasionally a whaler would climb onto the dying whale's back to deliver the *coup de grace* at close quarters.

When the whale was dead a diver went over the side and fastened a line to its lower jaw; this was then passed through a hole cut in its upper lip and made fast to the tow line. Towing the whale thus kept a strain on the lower jaw, so that it stayed shut, a matter of some importance if the whale were to be towed head-first, a more hydrodynamically efficient method than that used by modern whalers. If the whale showed a tendency to sink, it was buoyed up with floats, perhaps as many as twenty being needed to keep it afloat.

The Grey Whale was the kind most often hunted, but the Makah would also pursue Sperm Whales, right whales, Humpbacks and perhaps even Fin and Blue Whales. Killers were also regularly taken by the West Coast Indians.

When the whale was eventually towed to shore, which might take a couple of days or more, it was beached and ceremoniously divided up. After proper measurements had been taken (from the blow-hole to the hump or fin, as appropriate), the 'saddle' (that part below the hump or fin) was removed first. This belonged to the hunter, but could not be eaten by him, because it was taboo, and was set up on a rack, suitably decorated with eagle down and feathers. Portions were distributed to the first boat to bring assistance and, after all the proper rewards had been handed out, the hunter would distribute the rest as he thought fit until he had given all of it away, keeping none for himself— a form of potlatch ceremony that was so characteristic of the North-West Indians. Only the blubber and the oil extracted from it was eaten, the meat and bones being left on the beach.

For the Makah Indians to hunt whales successfully it was not sufficient to have the right equipment, knowledge and skill. 'Power' was also required and this could only be obtained by the observance of complicated ceremonies. There were many customs associated with the attainment of power for whaling— taboos on sex, eating whale-meat, etc.—and customs such as these were perhaps more significant in the regulation of primitive hunting than is often realised. The whales which the Makah and their neighbours hunted were on their main migration route between the feeding and breeding grounds. The effect of the requirement for elaborate preparations for a hunt would have been to restrict the hunting pressure, allowing a better opportunity for the hunters and their quarry to stay in balance and ensure that the resource (the stock of whales) was not over-harvested.

The type of whaling carried on by the Makah was probably matched on the other side of the Pacific where similar conditions of a whale migration route close to shore are found. There is some evidence of this from bone engravings from Sakhalin. The natives of the Aleutian Islands, Kamchatka and the Kurile Islands were said to have killed whales with poisoned lances. The whales were stabbed and then abandoned in the expectation that in two or three days the bodies would be cast up on the shores of one of the islands.

A sophisticated whaling industry developed quite early in Japan. Prior to about 1600, the Japanese were whaling in their coastal waters using small rowing boats, harpoons, lines and lances, very much as the Europeans were doing at the same period. During the seventeenth century, however, a method of whaling using heavy nets was developed. This required a fleet of boats and a small army of labour, so it could only be organised by wealthy, feudal barons, such as those who ruled the Japanese at that time. We know about Japanese net-whaling mainly through the vivid and detailed prints that have survived, for example *Illustrations of Whaling* by Yosei Oyamada, (1829). Harrison Matthews (1968) reproduces some marvellous plates from it and quotes extensively from the text and I have based my description mainly on that.

Watch towers were set up on high ground overlooking the sea and when a whale was sighted the boats would be launched. The whaling nets, heavy large-meshed rope nets each about 33 m square, were carried in six net-boats, each 13 m long and 3.5 m in beam, which operated in three pairs. Whales were driven towards the net-boat pairs by a fleet of twenty driver boats, 13 m long by 2.2 m in beam, each propelled by eight oars and with a crew of ten. When a whale approached one of the net-boat pairs, they would be rowed apart, at the same time casting their nets. The whale would be driven on and would, with luck, entangle itself in one of the nets. This would break away from its moorings—it served only to entangle the whale, not to confine it—and the whale would then be lanced from the driver boats. right whales, Humpbacks and occasionally Fin Whales could be easily taken in this way, but Grey Whales were reckoned to be too fierce and destructive to be taken with nets. They were lanced to death, being surrounded by swarms of driver boats. When the whale was half-dead, a man would jump on its back and cut a hole in the snout with a long knife. Through this hole a rope from one of the boats would be passed. In order to prevent the whale sinking when dead, other ropes were passed under its belly and made fast to a boat on either side, which were then joined with a spar, so as to create a raft or pontoon, which would tow the whale back to the whaling station.

Once on shore the whale was dragged up with huge capstans and stripped of its blubber. The blubber was minced and tried out for oil, as was the crushed bone. After the oil had been extracted the bone meal was used as a fertiliser. Nearly all other parts of the whale were used for food (a trend that has continued in Japan to the present day), except for the liver, possibly because its Vitamin A content is sufficiently high to cause symptoms of poisoning (Ash, 1964).

The last Japanese net-whaling took place in 1909. As far as I know the only other net-fishery for large whales was one that flourished for a time in New Zealand where Humpbacks were caught in this way. From 1890 to 1910, a Mr H. F. Cook at Whangamumu, in the Bay of Islands, hunted whales with nets and lances. Later he acquired a modern whale-boat with a proper cannon and gave up the old method (Tønnesen, 1967). Matthews (1968) reports that this minute industry was exported to Tonga by emigrants from the New Zealand station and that a small net fishery for Humpbacks still survives there.

10 The right whale fishery: the beginnings of commercial whaling

Primitive whaling probably had little effect on large whale stocks, not because the means used were inefficient, but because the populations who hunted the whales were few in number. As the tide of civilisation spread across Europe, whaling came to be based on a commercial, rather than a subsistence economy, and the whales were open to exploitation.

The great whaling industry of the twentieth century originated, probably from a drive-fishery, in the Basque country of the Bay of Biscay, where Black Right Whales were very common. By the twelfth century, Basque whaling was economically important to the region.

As the industry developed it became necessary to look further afield for whales and the Basques responded by building larger offshore vessels. However, their range was limited by the need to tow the carcase of the whale back to shore for processing. By the sixteenth century, the Basques were voyaging away as far as Newfoundland, mainly for the cod-fishing, but also to catch right whales. By the end of the sixteenth century, it had become customary to try the blubber out on board the ship, but the fire risk associated with this was considerable. Black Right Whales seem to have been reasonably abundant off Biscay at least until the mid-seventeenth century and the industry continued in a sporadic fashion as late as the end of the eighteenth century.

The next chapter of whaling was presaged in 1553, when an expedition, under Hugh Willoughby, was sent out from England to discover a route to China by the North-East Passage.

Willoughby's expedition did not get to China, but reached Archangel and, on the way, claimed to have sighted Spitsbergen. The resulting trade with Archangel led to the formation of the Muscovy Company which, amongst its other interests, took up the whaling trade. In 1577, the Muscovy Company secured the services of a number of experienced Basque whale-men and were granted a twenty-year monopoly in British whaling.

Henry Hudson in 1607 and 1608, while continuing the search for the North-East Passage, noted the abundance of whales. These, however, were in the open sea around latitude 74°–75° N and so beyond the reach of the whalers with their limited means. However, in 1610, Jonas Poole explored and charted the seas round Spitsbergen and was sufficiently impressed to name one of the features 'Whale Bay'. As a direct consequence, the Muscovy Company, in 1611, fitted out two ships, the 60 ton *Elizabeth*, which Poole had used the previous year in his exploration, and the 160 ton *Margaret*, under Thomas Edge, which was the first whaler to kill the Greenland Right Whale in Spitsbergen and thus started a new era.

The first season could scarcely be counted a success. Thirteen right whales were killed and the blubber tried out, but the *Margaret* was destroyed by drifting ice floes and the *Elizabeth*, who took off her cargo, stowed it so badly that she capsized. The *Hopewell* of Hull took off the crews and brought home part of the cargo.

In 1612, the first Dutch whaler, and also a Basque vessel from San Sebastian, reached Spitsbergen, each piloted by an ex-employee of the Muscovy Company. A period of conflict began between the Muscovy Company, and almost everyone else, ably led by the Dutch. In 1613, the Dutch sent out a small whaling fleet to Spitsbergen and were repulsed by seven heavily armed vessels of the Muscovy Company. The following season the Dutch retaliated by sending four warships out with their whaling fleet. This intolerable situation was terminated by an agreement in 1618, to divide up the grounds between the contenders, namely the English, Danes, Dutch, Hamburgers, Spanish and Basques.

By 1618, the Dutch had become the indisputable masters of the European whaling trade (Jackson, 1978) and, in 1642, felt so confident that they declared the trade open to all whereas the

Greenland Company (as the Muscovy Company was now known) still endeavoured to affirm its monopoly. The chief contestants were ships from other English ports, and ships from York and Hull succeeded in breaching the monopoly when, after a fracas, it was agreed that the total English whaling tonnage should be 3000, of which ships from York and Hull should be entitled to provide one fifth. With no profit to be found in the monopoly, the trade was eventually opened to all British subjects in 1673.

The Dutch, on the other hand, reached the peak of their whaling activities around 1670. Bay-whaling had begun to fall off before 1640 but the Dutch moved their hunting grounds to the pack-ice to the north, hunting the whales in the open sea and flensing them alongside in whatever shelter could be afforded by the ice. They stowed away the blubber in casks, trying it out on returning from the voyage. For ice-whaling, larger ships were used than had been customary for the bay-whaling and a longer season could be expected, since bay-whaling could not be started before March (on account of the ice) and was over by the end of April, when the whales left. At the ice, however, whales were always to be found and the season was limited only by the endurance of the ships. The Dutch, and the Hamburgers, who had invested heavily in this trade and were now a dominant whaling state, were eager to take advantage of this, while the English whalers allowed the trade to slip away from them.

While the English whaling trade languished, whale oil was still an important item of commerce and the demand was satisfied by imports from the continent, mainly from Holland, and from the colonies where early in the seventeenth century, the New England colonists had started taking right whales. In 1712 they took the first Sperm Whale and started a new and extensive branch of the whaling trade. A main market for whale oil had been the soap industry. Traditionally this had used tallow, but whale oil was cheaper, although it did not make such good soap. However, in the eighteenth century, whale oil was adopted on a large scale in the textile industry to scour wool prior to spinning, particularly wool for the coarser cloths, such as the military serges that were in such great demand in Europe, at least until 1815. Another important developing use for whale oil was for street and factory lighting. The other product from the Greenland Right Whale, its remarkably long and flexible baleen, was in great demand for stiffening ladies' garments.

The government was anxious that Britain should be a producer in this lucrative trade and also that the whaling industry should be a training ground for seamen, and as an encouragement in 1750 instituted a bounty of £2 a ton for whale-ships. This was a considerable inducement as it meant an average-sized whaler would net £600 simply by fitting out—no mean sum in those days.

Increased demand for oil and the bounty system stimulated a resumption of British whaling at a time when the Dutch and Hamburgers were faltering. The British were still less skilful than the Dutch, but were improving. 1783 to 1808 was a boom period for British whaling. With the end of the American War of Independence there was an end to the cheap importation of colonial oil from New England and the British were quick to fill the gap. While in the 1770s the Dutch fleet was still larger than the British, by the mid-1780s the British fleet was double that of the rest of Europe together. War with Holland led to the British government providing cruisers to convoy the whalers and attack Dutch ships. In 1798, Dutch whaling was practically destroyed and never regained its position.

The most prosperous period for the British began around 1795. Now all the crews were British—there was no longer any need to depend on Dutch or Basque harpooners or line managers.

Part of the reason for this new expansion was to be found in the move to new grounds. Spitsbergen was practically deserted by 1820 and the whalers had moved to the Davis Straits. There was no great change in the technology involved, although the voyages tended to last a month or two longer. What was important was that new grounds and virgin stocks were being exploited. The whales, in general, were larger (the older classes of the population not having been removed by heavy fishing, as in the Greenland seas) and were found in greater concentrations at the ice edge. This meant that a full cargo could, if conditions were right, be obtained more speedily in Davis Straits than in Greenland.

Prior to the War of Independence, the American whale-fishery was well developed and the prospect of the rebellion (which was not universally popular in the colony) was viewed with some dismay by the whalers. Some left New England to set up a whaling industry in Newfoundland, others came to Europe. One family, Samuel Enderby and his sons, arrived in London in 1775. Enderby was largely responsible for establishing the southern whale-fishery for Britain. The Southern whalers followed the American tradition of searching the Atlantic, but they extended the range and whaled in the bays of South America and South Africa and the island groups like the Falklands.

The southern whalers were keen to spread beyond the South Atlantic, but the monopoly of the East India Company, which reserved to the Company all trade east of the Cape of Good Hope (and, by implication, west of Cape Horn), hindered them. However, by 1789, an Enderby vessel, the *Emilia*, was ranging the South Pacific looking for whales and returned with a full cargo. The Australian grounds were a rich hunting area for both right whales and Sperm Whales, but the East India Company's monopoly hampered British whalers from taking full advantage of the opportunities offered, while the Yankee whalers were able to move in and reap most of the benefit. Not until 1813 was the Company's monopoly ended, and by then it was almost too late to save the British southern whale-fishery.

Between 1791 and 1800, the value of the products of the southern whale-fishery, which employed fewer ships, was considerably greater than that of the northern fishery, though the latter produced more oil after 1797. This was the result of the inclusion of the more valuable sperm oil in the southern cargoes. But the southern fishery was soon in danger. The early profits that could be reaped from virgin stocks were soon taken and southern voyages become protracted and less profitable.

The end of the Napoleonic wars in 1815 was not followed by a period of great economic expansion as in 1783. However, whaling at first continued to be relatively profitable. The bounty which had been initiated in 1733 was finally ended in 1824 and oil prices declined. Rape seed oil prices fell and this pulled whale oil prices down. An added threat was the introduction of coal gas as an illuminant. In 1809, the Gas Light and Coke Company was established in London and the days of whale oil-fuelled street lamps were over. The only bright light on the horizon for the whalers was the renewed interest in whalebone for ladies' corsetry, which helped to improve profits. Despite this, however, the British whaling fleet declined by a quarter between 1821 and 1822 (Jackson, 1978).

Whalers were getting noticeably scarcer in the north. Vessels were now reaching the limits of their endurance in the Davis Straits. 'Rockhopping'—hugging the coast-line in unknown waters, hoping to find a previously unknown resort of the whales —was the order of the day. Whaling had always been dangerous and these tactics increased the risk. In 1830, ninety-one whalers set out to Davis Straits. Nineteen were lost, twenty-one returned clean, and the rest were mostly severely damaged. The total catch was 161 whales!

The southern fishery was not in a much better state. Ships encountered a hostile reception in many waters, particularly by the Spanish in South America, and, in particular, competition with the Yankee whalers in the Southern Hemisphere was proving too much for the British. In 1818, there were 200 American whalers; in 1838 there were 700. Another factor was the development of bay-whaling in Australia. It was cheaper to set up a shore station in a bay than to hunt pelagically and many of the whaling owners did just this. As the proportion of the British ships declined, so the imports of Australian whale oil increased.

Tasmania was the headquarters of the Australasian whaling trade. Right whales were plentiful there and bay-whaling began in about 1815. Just as everywhere else, the local stocks were soon exhausted and small vessels, mostly brigs, were fitted out to cruise further afield. In 1837, seven vessels and twenty-four boats worked out of Hobart and took 207 whales. The industry was highly important to the young colony; in 1838 the value of oil and bone was £137,000, which compared favourably with the £172,000 received in the same year for wool. By 1840, bay-whaling was declining rapidly, but offshore Sperm-whaling was well established. The first deep-sea whaling barque left Hobart in 1829 and, for the next forty years, the sperm-fishery flourished, with Tasmanian ships visiting every part of the Pacific and regularly passing through the Bering Straits to hunt in the Arctic. In 1850, there were thirty-five deep-sea whalers and the trade was second only to the United States. By 1862, the number of vessels had declined to twenty-five and continued to fall off. The last Hobart whale-ship was fitted out in 1894 and continued to make voyages, with varying success, until she was withdrawn in 1900 (Villiers, 1974).

In England, by the 1840s, owners were selling out of the southern trade. In 1849, Enderby's, the greatest of the British South Sea companies, left London to set up the Southern Whale Fishery Company, a bay-whaling concern in the Auckland Islands, off New Zealand. (It was a failure.)

The British Arctic fishery declined from all ports except the Scottish ones. Peterhead was still an active whaling port, but they succeeded only by combining harp-sealing with whaling. The jute industry which had developed at Dundee, was a large consumer of whale-oil, and kept the Dundee fleet active. Steam was introduced in 1857. Hull went in for large iron screw-steamers, but these proved underpowered, and very vulnerable to the ice, and were soon abandoned. Scotland, on the other hand, developed heavily built wooden ships fitted with auxiliary steam power. Initially these were very successful and certainly eased the labour and danger of whaling to a large extent, but little could be done to help with the root of the problem—the growing scarcity of whales. Whalers were making up their cargo with seals, White Whales, Bottle-nosed Whales, Walrus and Polar Bears. Fashion came to the rescue again when whalebone corsets came into great demand by the *haut-monde* and ultimately, by all who could afford them. In 1906, whalebone reached a peak price of £3,000 a tonne, and the bone from one or two whales could pay for a voyage, as at that time the expense of fitting out an Arctic whaler was reckoned to be £3,500 (Lubbock, 1937). In 1905, the value of whalebone landed at Dundee was eight times that of the oil (Jackson, 1978).

However, by now the great Greenland Whale was nearly extinct. The last two Arctic whalers to sail from a British port, the *Morning* and the *Balaena*, sailed from Dundee in 1913 but returned home empty. The Greenland whale-fishery was dead.

11   The yankee whalers: the sperm whale fishery

The whaling carried on by the American settlers and their descendants from New England, the Yankees, developed a technique, a literature and a cult of its own. The technique was refined over a couple of centuries, and reached a perfection unmatched elsewhere (though it stopped short of an economical use of the whale).

The first whaling from New England was carried on by the Indians, probably in much the same manner as in the north-west. It is uncertain whether the colonists learnt their whaling from the Indians or from other Europeans engaged in the trade, the Basques, the English or the Dutch. According to Captain John Smith (in Scammon, 1874) the New England colonists had begun whaling prior to 1614, although it was the middle of the seventeenth century before whaling became of importance. However, for many years before that, stranded whales, or drift whales as they were called, had been utilised. Long Island seems to have been the first to organise whaling expeditions. Small boats were fitted out to cruise along the coast, searching for Black Right Whales, killing those they found and towing the carcases to shore to be flensed and tried out. The operation must have been very similar to Basque whaling in its early stage. Just as with the Biscay coasts, the whales near the shore were soon reduced and it became necessary to pursue the survivors further out to sea. By 1748, the colonists were using sloops and schooners of about 50 tons equipped with two whale-boats and with a crew of thirteen.

Islanders had an advantage in this type of fishery and it was the people of Nantucket Island who originated the great whaling enterprise which eventually was to spread to all the oceans of the world, excepting only the Antarctic. This first whaling, as on the mainland, was in boats from the shore. Initially the Nantucketers lacked expertise, so they secured the services of experienced Cape Cod whalers to teach them the best methods of killing right whales and boiling out the oil. The Nantucketers, lacking any lofty heights from which to spy out whales, erected tall spars fitted with cleats on either side, up which lookouts climbed to watch for whales. When a spout was seen, the boats were immediately launched and set off to intercept the whale and kill it. The carcase was towed back to shore for processing.

This type of whaling lasted over fifty years, but, just as with all other such enterprises, it was eventually abandoned because of the scarcity of whales within range. As early as 1712 or 1713, sloops were being fitted out at Nantucket for voyages east to Newfoundland, or south to the Gulf Stream, to search for whales. By 1746, the Nantucketers were equipping larger schooners and brigs up to 130 tons, which could voyage to the coast of Africa or even to the ice of Baffin Bay, reaching as far as 81°N in open seasons. These vessels, like the Arctic whalers from Europe, brought the blubber back for trying out.

Although all the initial whaling centred on right whales, in 1712 an event occurred at Nantucket that was to change the main effort of the Yankee whalers. Captain Christopher Hussey was cruising offshore in an open boat, looking for right whales, when a strong north-easterly gale swept him a considerable distance offshore. When the wind died away he found himself in sight of a school of whales, which surprised him by having only a single bushy spout, which arched forwards from the whale, instead of the characteristic forked double spout of the right whale. They were Sperm Whales. Hussey killed one and towed it to the shore where it was tried out (Stackpole, 1953).

This was the first Sperm Whale captured at sea by the Yankees, although dead Sperm Whales had been found washed up on shore on at least one earlier occasion at Nantucket. The oil of the Sperm Whale was clearly quite a different product from that of the right whale. In the early days almost every possible medicinal quality was ascribed to it. Its lasting value, however, lay in its excellent quality as an illuminant. Sperm oil burnt with a bright, clear flame and without the disagreeable odour that was associated with ordinary whale oil. From the solid spermaceti the purest and finest candles could be made, which were vastly superior, both in brilliance and fragrance, to tallow candles; only later was the great value of sperm as a lubricant to be discovered.

Hussey's discovery showed that Sperm Whales were to be found at no great distance from Nantucket and by 1715, Nantucket had six sloops of about 30 tons fitted out for cruises of six weeks or so, or until they found a whale and killed it, when they would return home with the blubber. By 1730, there were twenty-five whaling vessels based at Nantucket and the trade was still expanding. In 1755, Joseph Russel built the first sperm oil factory at Bedford, Massachusetts, later to become known as New Bedford, and destined to be, after the decline of Nantucket, the main port of the Yankee whaling trade.

The trade was soon producing more oil than could be consumed locally and the surplus was exported to England. The same bounty that encouraged English whalers applied equally to the colonials and this was a powerful stimulus to the American industry.

Larger vessels meant longer voyages and, by 1774, some of the vessels, by now mostly ships or barques, were crossing the Equator and fishing Sperm Whales on the Brazil Banks. Soon afterwards the enterprise was extended to the Falkland Islands. No fewer than 360 vessels of various kinds, amounting to 33,000 tons and employing 4,700 men were engaged in the fishery, which, between 1771 and 1775, produced oil annually to the value of £75,000, most of which was sperm (Starbuck, 1878).

Such an extension of range across tropical seas necessitated a change of technology. At least as early as 1762, the Yankees introduced the practice of boiling out the blubber at sea in a try-works built on the deck and this soon became universal throughout the fleet.

Although the trade was booming in 1775, the American War of Independence temporarily ruined it. When the war started, the British blockaded the whaling ports, immobilising the whaling fleets, and Nantucket, which by this time was almost solely dependent on whaling, almost starved and the condition of the islanders became so grave that the British Admiral agreed to allow twenty-four of their ships to go to sea to hunt whales. However, the end of the war saw a rapid revival of the American fleet. Despite the loss of colonial preference in England, cargoes of sperm could still be disposed of profitably for there was scarcely any other supply.

Samuel Enderby's ship, the *Emilia*, had pioneered the way into the rich Sperm Whale grounds of the Pacific when she rounded Cape Horn in 1789 and, in 1791, six whalers from Nantucket followed. These ships were of only about 250 tons, but they whaled successfully along the coast of Chile and, a few years later, were followed by vessels extending the grounds northwards to Peru and westwards along the Equator.

A market for whale oil and sperm opened in France in 1789, which afforded relief to the Yankees, since Britain had recently put a tax on foreign oil, which had caused a slump in the price of American sperm. However, the French Revolution in 1793 closed that market as well. Neither was the American whaling industry immune from harsh treatment at home. Privateers, mainly French, were constantly seizing the slow-moving whale-ships on the high seas and insurance became prohibitive. In consequence, Congress passed the Embargo Act in 1807, which ordered all whaling vessels to stay in port because the USA had no navy with which to protect them (Ommanney, 1971). Finally, the outbreak of war in 1812 struck American whaling another hard blow. Many ships were taken as prizes or destroyed in port by the British fleet, but the trade picked up rapidly with peace in 1815, although there were only forty Yankee whaling vessels afloat by then. By 1821 this number had increased to eighty-four. The discovery of new and very rich Sperm-whaling grounds was an added impetus.

By 1839 there were 557 vessels, mostly ships and barques, in the American whaling fleet, 169 of them from New Bedford, and seventy-seven from Nantucket. Nantucket was falling out of the whaling trade because of the increasing size of the ships and a sand bar that was beginning to build up at the mouth of the harbour.

By 1842 the American fleet numbered 652 and the combined fleet of the rest of the world only 230 vessels. The Americans were undoubtedly masters of the whaling trade and Yankee whaling continued to expand. The first Bowhead (as the Greenland Right Whale was called by the Yankees) to be taken in the North Pacific was killed on the coast of Kamchatka in 1843. In 1847, the breeding grounds of the Bowheads in the Sea of Okhotsk were discovered, while, in 1848, Captain Roger, in the *Superior* of Sag Harbour, passed through the Bering Straits to be the first man to capture Bowheads in the Arctic Ocean on that side of the North Pole. (An American whale-ship had passed Bering Straits in 1819, but little is known of its success there.)

Whaling voyages now often lasted for up to 4 years, or more, the ship off-loading oil to send home in a merchantman. For whaling in the North Pacific, the whalers made their base at San Francisco, from where they could attack Bowheads in the Bering Sea, Grey Whales on their annual migration up and down the coast between their feeding grounds in the Bering Sea and their breeding grounds in Scammon's Lagoon, and Sperm Whales on the Japanese Ground and around Hawaii. Pacific whaling received a set-back in 1849, when a great many of the vessels were deserted by their crews, eager to join the 'Forty-niners' in their rush to the Californian gold fields. Further west, the grounds off Australia, Tasmania and New Zealand were hunted by vessels from New England who travelled by way of the Cape of Good Hope.

The Civil War dealt unkindly with the whalers. Many of the whale-ships, nearly all of which came from northern ports, were captured and burnt by Confederate cruisers and, as if the efforts of their enemies were not sufficient, the Government in 1861 purchased forty laid-up whalers (the famous 'Stone Fleet') filled them with rocks and scuttled them at the mouths of Charleston and Savannah harbours to prevent the privateers and blockade runners using these ports.

Even these reverses, severe though they were, did not shatter the whaling trade. 1876 was perhaps its peak, when it employed 735 vessels totalling 233,000 tons. However, two factors were at work that were to end Yankee whaling. One was the discovery of petroleum, which was to take over from sperm oil as a cheaper and as efficient illuminant. The other, just in all other fields of whaling, was the growing scarcity of whales. The Bering Sea–Arctic Ocean fishery suffered its worst ever catastrophe in 1871 when the fleet was beset by the ice and thirty-four out of forty-one vessels were lost. The crews, miraculously, were all saved and landed at Honolulu, but the American Arctic whaling never recovered. It was in 1880 that the first American steam whaler went north, but it was too late to hope for reasonable Bowhead catches.

The same condition that depressed the market for whale oil in Britain operated in the USA. Sperm-whaling might still show a modest profit, since no substitutes had been found for sperm oil for some forms of lubrication and for cutting oils, but right whale oil fell to very low prices. The petroleum age had arrived.

The last of the Yankee square-rigged whale-ships to put to sea was the barque *Wanderer*, built at Mattapoisett, Massachusetts, in 1878. She sailed on 25 August 1924 from New Bedford and was wrecked the following day on Cuttyhunk Island, almost within sight of the harbour, in a severe north-easterly gale. When the schooners *John R. Manta* of Provincetown and *Margarett* of New Bedford returned to New Bedford in 1925, the epoch of the Yankee whalers had ended.

A lasting memento of that period is the splendid old whale-ship *Charles W. Morgan*, built at New Bedford in 1841 and now on display at the Marine Historical Association at Mystic, Connecticut.

A more living memento also lingers. Even today a small, but flourishing sperm-whaling industry, using open boats the Yankee way, still exists in the Azores, and Dr. Robert Clarke, a British cetologist who has devoted his life to the study of the Sperm Whale, has written an excellent account of this (Clarke, 1954). The sea around the Azores, or the Western Isles Ground, as it was known to the Yankees, provided a hunting ground for the deep-sea whale-ships till the end of the industry. Perhaps the Azoreans had first learned to whale from the Basques—at any rate they use the term 'cachalote', which is of Basque origin, for the Sperm whale—but the present trade is entirely American in origin. The Yankee whalers regularly called at the Azores (and the Cape Verde Islands) for crew on their way out. The recruits from the Azores quickly showed themselves to be natural born whalers and many rose to officer rank in the Yankee whale-ships; some even became captains.

Once on board the ships it was natural to use the Azoreans to help establish the various shore-based whaling enterprises that were set up. The Azoreans were active in the lagoon-fishing for Grey Whales in California, as they were in the Sperm-whaling off Tasmania and the Humpback-fishing in Cook Strait.

The present shore-fishery in the Azores seems to have started at Fayal around 1832. This was abandoned after a time, but taken up again in the 1850s. From Fayal the trade spread to other islands of the group and, at one time or another, all the larger islands supported some whaling. When Clarke was in the Azores in 1949 there were modern factories on four islands and boats stationed on all save Corvo.

Up till 1894, all the whale-boats used in the Azores were imported from New Bedford, but in that year the first local boats were built and, by 1900, all the boats were built in the islands. Save for the ropes, try-pots and the modern factory machinery and motor boats, all the whaling gear used is made in the islands.

The Azoreans, though they adopted the idea of using motor boats for towing the whale-boats in 1909, relinquished the use of swivel guns, shoulder guns or darting guns to kill whales and put their reliance wholly in hand harpoons and lances.

By 1910 the Azores catch of sperm oil contributed 72.3% of the world total, but this declined to 3.8% by 1915 and, although Azores whaling picked up after the war, other Sperm Whale fisheries increased still further, so it never again became so important on a world scale.

The Azorean open-boat whaling industry is an interesting survival. It represents a low-technology, reasonably efficient use of a resource. Its worst feature is its uncontrolled use of the stock of whales without reference to what might constitute a sustainable yield. To many people, the killing of female whales, accompanied by their calves, is distasteful. However, there is good reason to believe that heavy exploitation of males only might have an adverse effect on the social organisation of the whales, and killing family units in a controlled manner could be the most rational way of utilising Sperm Whales. In any case, the pressure on Sperm Whales today is not from open boats and hand harpoons, but from the modern whale-catchers and the 75 mm harpoon gun.

12   *The modern whaling industry*

Throughout the latter half of the nineteenth century, it was clear to the whalers, particularly those who operated in the Arctic hunting right whales, that the major factor restricting the profitability of their industry was the shortage of whales. Yet, paradoxically, there were whales in plenty around their boats, long before they reached the hunting grounds off Greenland or in the Davis Straits. Right whales were 'right' because they were the ones which, using the technology developed by the Basques, could be successfully hunted and captured. The other whales, those that appeared in such remarkable numbers, were the rorquals. Rorquals were *not* 'right' whales because they swam too fast to be pursued by a row-boat and if one could, by chance, be approached when asleep or unawares, on feeling the harpoon it would dash off at great speed, taking the line out so fast there was no chance of following. On the rare occasions when one of these whales was killed, it would probably sink, dragging the boat down with it, if the line were not cut. The Makah Indians and the Japanese had solved this problem with floats or rafts, but the Arctic whalers and the Yankees, almost without exception, had never attempted this solution. The established whalers therefore generally ignored the substantial stocks of rorquals on their doorstep and continued to scour the ocean for the last surviving specimen of the 'right' whale, the Sperm Whale and the Humpback, which, when killed in shallow water, as was usually the case in bay-whaling, might either float at once or would rise to the surface after a few hours as the carcase bloated.

One American whaler, Thomas Welcome Roys, however, in 1856, made a trip towards Spitsbergen in the brig *W. F. Stafford*, which was equipped with a sort of rocket-gun of Roys' own construction. This was not a new idea; William Congreve had thought of this more than thirty years earlier. The rocket harpoon, equipped with an explosive grenade head and four claws designed to fasten the whale-line firmly to the whale, was fired from an iron tube, supported on the shoulder of the boat-steerer from an 11.6 m whale-boat. Roys patented this device in London in 1857 and an improved version (with Lilliendahl) in 1865.

On W. F. *Stafford's* first trip, no Greenland whales were seen but they shot a total of fifty-two whales, none of which was saved.

In 1860 Roys formed a company with Gustavus Lilliendahl, a pyrotechnist of New York and, in 1865, they set up a shore station at Seydisfjord on the east coast of Iceland. The venture did not prosper, however. Roys withdrew in 1866 and the company eventually became bankrupt and ceased business (Johnsen, 1959). Two other companies whaled a little using Roys' method but the results were disappointing and by 1872 the method had been entirely displaced by a new technique developed in Norway.

Up to the middle of the nineteenth century the Norwegians had been more concerned with sealing. A wealthy sealing skipper, Svend Foyn, impressed with the abundance of rorquals which he encountered on his voyages to and from the sealing grounds, looked anew at the problem of how to harvest them and came up with a solution that was to endure with relatively little change for the rest of the whaling industry's history. This was to mount a harpoon gun, large enough to fire a harpoon which would kill or disable a whale, in the bows of a vessel which, in turn, was fast enough to pursue a rorqual and buoyant enough to hold it at the surface when dead.

The harpoon gun probably called for the least innovation. By the 1860s, when Foyn began experimenting, harpoon guns were already well developed. However, as they had to be mounted in the bows of a lightly built whale-boat they remained small and with no other role than that of fastening to the whale. The darting gun, which fired a bomb as well as a harpoon, worked on an entirely different principle. Roys' rocket gun, though not mounted, came near to what was needed and certainly influenced Foyn. Foyn was not restricted in the size of his harpoon gun, since it was his intention to mount it on the bows of a substantial vessel. However, even a large harpoon was insufficient to deal a lethal blow to a big rorqual without the use of explosives, and the successful introduction of this idea took a little time.

The whale-catcher, as such vessels came to be called, was a completely new concept. The first voyage of *Spes et Fides*, as Foyn's first whale-catcher was called, was not successful and the following year Foyn returned to seal hunting, but continued his experiments with whaling gear. In 1866, he sailed *Spissa* (as *Spes et Fides* was known) to Iceland to study at first hand Roys' and Lilliendahl's technique. He was clearly impressed with the four-clawed harpoon, which opened like the ribs of an umbrella within the whale, the steam winch for hauling in and the rubber 'accumulator' over which the line passed. This was a device which served to take the shocks out of the whale-line, by the elasticity of the rubber straps. All three devices were to become integral parts of modern whaling techniques. Foyn also experimented with whaling from a row-boat, after Roys' example, but soon abandoned this. He continued his experiments in 1867 and 1868, developing a heavier harpoon with an explosive head in which he was aided by Pastor Esmark, who like Lilliendahl, was interested in fireworks. Foyn, though no mean engineer, lacked knowledge of chemical matters and Esmark supplied this. In 1868, Foyn caught a total of thirty whales, the majority from *Spissa* but some from row-boats fitted with harpoon guns. In 1869, he purchased a site at Vadsø, in Varanger Fjord and obtained a second catcher, *Fiskeren*, little more than half the size of *Spes et Fides*. There followed another poor season, with only fifteen whales, but Foyn was not discouraged and the following year enlarged his station and had a modest success with a catch of thirty-six whales, largely due to improvements to the explosive grenade. Foyn patented his catching methods in 1872 and obtained a monopoly for 10 years. His success was sufficient to encourage an independent company from Tønsberg to start whaling, with the whale-catcher *Jarfjord*, in Varanger Fjord in 1877. This led to considerable friction and eventually litigation over the breach of Foyn's monopoly. *Jarfjord* continued to whale, however, and Foyn granted concessions under his patent to several companies. By 1880, there were eight companies operating in north Norway with twelve steam catchers. By 1886, the number of companies had increased to nineteen. The largest yearly catch at this time had reached nearly 1,300 whales, comprising Blue, Fin, Sei and Humpback (Brown, 1976).

The success of these ventures, and local shortages of whales, led to the establishment of whaling stations outside Norway. The first foreign station was set up in Iceland in 1883 and, by 1897, eight more stations were operating there. In 1894, a station was built in Faeroes and another in 1898. Far away in the Pacific, the first Norwegian-style whaling station was built in Japan in 1895. With Norwegian gunners, this flourished and, in 1899, the first locally built whale-catcher, the *Choshu Maru I* was launched. On the west side of the Atlantic, two modern stations were built at Newfoundland in 1898, to be followed by many others. The main expansion in the early years of the twentieth century was in the north-east Atlantic, however, and, between 1903 and 1905, a number of stations opened in this region.

The stimulus for this was the disquiet that had been expressed in north Norway by the Cod-fishermen, who, until whaling had begun, had pursued the sole trade of that region and believed that the activities of the whalers were driving the Cod away from their shores. In 1903, as a result of pressure from the fishermen, a law prohibiting whaling in Norway was passed and in 1904 whaling ceased. Thus interest was shifted to other grounds at no great distance.

Sidney Brown (1976) has reviewed the history of the development of modern whaling in the north-east Atlantic. In 1903, two Norwegian companies, each with one whale-catcher, started work in Ronas Voe in the Shetland Isles. In the first season the boats caught 127 whales and by 1906 nine whale-catchers were at work. Fin Whales made up 67% and Sei Whales 30% of the catch, with very small numbers of Blue, Humpback, right, Sperm and Bottle-nosed Whales.

Whaling started again in 1920, after the war, but by 1929, the catch had dropped to eighty-five whales and the enterprise was abandoned. The total catch in Shetland from 1903 to 1929 was 6,823 whales.

In 1904, another Norwegian company started whaling with three catcher boats from Bunaveneader in West Loch Tarbert in the outer Hebrides. Here also Fin and Sei Whales made up most of the catch (54% and 20% respectively) but Blue Whales were more numerous at 15% and there were large numbers of right and Sperm Whales. As in Shetland, there was an interruption during the war years, but whaling was resumed in 1920 and continued till 1928 when poor catches caused closure, after a total of 2,759 had been taken since its inception in 1904. Surprisingly, Bunaveneader had a brief recrudescence in 1950 when a company with a single whale-catcher started work and secured two Blue Whales and thirty-three Fin Whales in the first season. The following year four Blue and thirteen Fins were taken, but the company ran out of money and was dissolved.

In Ireland, whaling began in 1908 at Iniskea Island in County Mayo and another station opened in Blacksod Bay (also in County Mayo) in 1910. Results were good to start with, but soon fell off. Again the catches (up to 1914) consisted mainly of Fin Whales (63%) with a fair proportion of Blue (14%) and Sei (13%). The Blacksod station whaled in 1920 and 1922 before closing finally. A total of 895 whales was taken.

Spitsbergen was another area to which the displaced Norwegian companies (or their successors) moved. The first company in the field there (not counting a short-lived attempt in 1890) was A. S. Ørnen, named after its new and well equipped whale-catcher. Ørnen hired a wooden steamer, the *Telegraf*, of 737 tons gross and rigged her up with boilers to cook out blubber from the whales which *Ørnen* was to bring to her as she lay anchored in a sheltered fjord. *Telegraf* was thus the fore-runner of a new type of whaling-ship, the floating factory. There were problems with weather and ice and the processing capacity but the season's catch amounted to fifty-seven whales, of which forty-five were Blue.

The following year a new catcher, *Hauken*, was ordered and another ship, *Admiralen*, substituted for *Telegraf*. *Admiralen* was much bigger, 1517 tons, and was properly equipped with processing apparatus on a permanent basis. 1904 proved a fine season; the two catchers between them caught 113 Blue, thirty-three Fin and eight Humpback Whales.

Admiralen was joined that season by another floating factory from Sandefjord and, in 1905, five other companies followed suit with floating factories, besides two land stations which were set up. Whaling continued in Spitsbergen until 1912 and a total of 2180 whales were taken, of which about 60% were Blue Whales (Tønnesen, 1967). By the time of the collapse of the Spitsbergen whaling, the main focus of the industry had shifted from the far north to the south.

By the turn of the century, the Antarctic was the last undisturbed refuge of the great whales although it had not been totally neglected by the whalers. Several expeditions came back with tales of the immense numbers of rorquals they had encountered, but there was little enthusiasm in Europe at the prospect of whaling in the Antarctic. The supply of northern rorquals, except in the immediate vicinity of Finmark, had not yet been greatly depleted and the prospect of the huge transport operation, involving both supplies and oil, that would be needed to support an Antarctic industry, was enough to deter most Norwegian firms, which in general lacked capital. The oil market was stagnant and hence the prospect of putting a large extra supply of oil on the market would only further depress the price (Jackson, 1978).

In 1901–03, C. A. Larsen took *Antarctic*, a modified sealing barque, south as Otto Nordenskjöld's expedition ship on his voyage of exploration. When *Antarctic* was crushed in the ice and sank in February 1903, Larsen, with the rest of the expedition, was rescued and taken to Buenos Aires, where he found businessmen who took a different view of Antarctic whaling. Capital seemed to be less of a problem and a local market for some of the oil to be produced was expected. Larsen believed, with justification, that once he was established in the Antarctic, whales would be so numerous that he would need to cook out only the blubber, thus producing a better quality and more saleable oil than that from the northern fishery, where for some time bones had been cooked up in an attempt to maximise oil production from a limited catch.

Larsen formed his company, the Compañia Argentina de Pesca, and, on 16 November 1904, arrived at a snug harbour on the northern side of South Georgia which he had previously inspected with *Antarctic*. The expedition consisted of the new whale-catcher *Fortuna*, an old wooden transporter, the barque *Louise*, and a small schooner *Rolf*. The Norwegian crew of sixty men worked from 05.00 until 20.00 hours, building the huts to live in and the whaling factory.

The first year's operation resulted in a catch of 183 whales, predominantly Humpbacks, and also Fin, Blue and right whales. It was scarcely necessary to go outside the limits of Cumberland Bay (of which Grytviken itself was a small cove) to find Humpbacks in plenty.

The success of the first season at Grytviken, which was to be measured in terms of the whales taken, rather than the profits made, was followed by even better results in 1905–06. In that year, 399 whales were caught, of which no fewer than 288 were Humpbacks and sixteen right whales. Profits increased even more, since some investment capital had been paid off and the price of oil improved as a result of the expanding soap industry requiring more animal fats of good quality.

By this time, therefore, other companies were becoming interested in Antarctic whaling. When Larsen was in Sandefjord in the spring of 1905, buying new equipment for Grytviken, his comments encouraged Christensen, who by this time was chief shareholder of A. S. Ørnen, to send *Admiralen* south when the Spitsbergen season ended. *Admiralen* and her two catchers, *Ørnen* and *Hauken* started their southern whaling at New Island, in the Falkland Islands, where they obtained forty whales, mostly Sei. Seven of these actually swam up to the catchers as they lay moored during bad weather and were shot without moving the boats! At the end of January, they moved to Admiralty Bay on the south side of King George Island in the South Shetlands where, between 27 January and 22 February, they shot fifty-eight whales, twenty-four of which were big Blue Whales. The weather deteriorated at the end of February and the expedition moved back to Falkland, where they took another eighty-five Sei Whales.

Meanwhile, a Norwegian from Sandefjord, Amandus Andresen, who had settled at Punta Arenas in the Straits of Magellan, had as early as 1903 mounted a harpoon gun on a small tug and, on New Year's Eve, shot the first whale taken there, a Humpback. In 1905 he founded the Chilean whaling company, Sociedad Balleneria de Magallanes, which in 1906 began whaling off the South Shetland Islands with its floating factory *Gobernador Bories* (built at the same Framnes factory as *Admiralen*) (Tønnesen, 1967, 1970).

Thus were the foundations of Antarctic whaling laid by an Argentinian, a Norwegian and a Chilean company. Despite the flags and the origin of the capital, these companies were basically Norwegian, and Antarctic whaling was, and was to remain till Japan entered the field in 1934, a Norwegian trade.

Initially the emphasis was on floating factories. For establishing a whaling plant in as hostile an area as the Antarctic floating factories offered substantial advantages. Suitable ships could be purchased cheaply and converted and the expense of building a shore station eliminated. The floating factory could arrive with all her stores for a season and travel back with the cargo of oil at the end. Suitable deep-water anchorages with some protection from ice were not frequent, but the almost completely enclosed Port Foster at Deception Island—the breached cone of an old volcano—was one of the most perfect anchorages that could be imagined and was soon crowded with floating factories and their attendant catchers. Given such an anchorage, and a good supply of fresh water, a floating factory was reasonably suitable for cooking oil out of blubber.

If operating costs were greater in the Antarctic, so was the productivity of the catchers. For the first six seasons of operations in the Antarctic, the average production per catcher was over three times as great as that of an Arctic catcher (Table 12.1) in terms of the barrels of oil produced. The difference was even greater in numbers of whales killed. In that period, an Antarctic catch averaged 168 whales per season, while in the Arctic it was only a little over forty-two.

By 1911, seven stations were operating in South Georgia as well as ten in the South Shetlands, while some expeditions were attempting to establish themselves in the less suitable South Orkney Islands, and one even tried, without success, to set up a floating factory at the South Sandwich Islands. Once installed, the advantages of a shore station over a floating factory were

Table 12.1   Production Statistics for Antarctic and Northern Whaling, 1905–10. Six Barrels of Oil Equal One Ton

Season	Whale catchers	Whales caught	Oil production, barrels/catcher
Antarctic			
1904–05	1	95	2,870
1905–06	5	712	3,820
1906–07	8	1,112	3,465
1907–08	14	2,312	4,340
1908–09	21	4,125	4,500
1909–10	37	6,099	4,259
Northern Oceans			
1905	82	3,536	1,318
1906	79	2,766	1,027
1907	80	3,432	1,251
1908	81	3,248	1,177
1909	78	3,958	1,440
1910	83	3,448	1,354

* From Tønnessen, 1967.

immediately apparent (Fig. 12.1). There was ample space and an unlimited supply of fresh water for generating steam. Processing was simpler and less hazardous. At this time the floating factories flensing their whales in the water alongside from a 'jolle' (a sort of large flat-bottomed wooden boat). Conditions were notably better for the crews, who were not compelled to live so close to their work as on the factory ships. In South Georgia, all but one of the stations were shore stations, though several had started as floating factories till the shore plant was ready. The early whaling plants, whether shore stations or floating factories, were all closely tied to the shore—the shore stations necessarily so and the floating factories because they needed shelter and a large supply of fresh water. It followed from this that, irrespective of where the whales were caught, they all had to be brought back to the shore to be processed and this meant that the activities of the whaling companies could be controlled by the country from whose territory, or territorial waters, they operated. At that time all Antarctic whaling was conducted within the area known as the Falkland Islands Dependencies. (It so happened that Argentina and Chile also claimed some or all of the area as well, but neither tried to exercise any control over the whaling.)

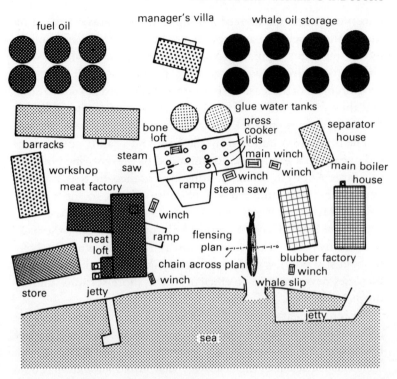

Fig. 12.1 Plan of a whaling shore station.

Fortunately, the administration of the Falkland Islands was aware of the risks of uncontrolled whaling and took steps to limit the expansion of the industry. This was done by restricting the number of leases available for shore stations, or of licences issued to floating factories. Each expedition was limited to two or three catchers, though some expeditions increased their catcher fleet by obtaining an additional lease. Thus, when the British whaling firm of Christian Salvesen and Company established their station at Leith Harbour in South Georgia in 1909 they were limited to two catchers. However, Salvesen's formed a new company, the South Georgia Company, and obtained a lease for Allardyce Harbour, further to the west in South Georgia, also with two catchers. No attempt was made to build a station at Allardyce Harbour and all four catchers operated from Leith (Vamplew, 1975).

Besides the limitations on the number of catchers, the Falkland government also introduced a number of regulations restricting the whaling itself. It was forbidden to take right whales (though, by the time this regulation was brought in, right whales were already very rare) or whales accompanied by calves. It was made a requirement of the lease of shore stations granted in 1909 or after that they should utilise all the parts of the whales they killed—the wasteful dumping of skrots (the flensed carcases) was to cease.

The limitations imposed by the Falkland Islands government did not prevent (and were not intended to prevent) the build-up of a large Antarctic whaling industry. Catchers increased in size and horse-power and brought in more whales to increasingly efficient factories. Waste, which was characteristic of the early years (one South Georgia station habitually used only the back blubber from the whale, towing away the skrot with the belly blubber still on it), was gradually eliminated, though the floating factories never became so efficient as the shore stations, and oil output increased.

Despite the easy availability of whales on the new Antarctic grounds, expansion of the industry would never have taken place had it not been for a great increase in the demand for whale oil. This was the result of the discovery that liquid animal oils could be converted to solid fats of a desired hardness by the process of hydrogenation. The Normann process for doing this using a nickel catalyst was patented in 1902 and 1903, but it was some time before the process was perfected.

Hardened whale oil could be used both to produce hard soap (the oil previously had produced only soft soap) and margarine, which was becoming increasingly popular as a cheap substitute for butter. Between 1909 and 1913, the demand for whale oil increased enormously at the expense of other animal fats. An important by-product in the manufacture of soap was glycerine which assumed the utmost importance as the basis of nitro-glycerine for explosives as the war clouds gathered. Although the increased outlet improved the market for the whalers, the complexity of the hydrogenation process meant that the trade fell into the hands of a few very large companies, like Lever Brothers and Van der Bergh, who were eventually to have a major influence over the economics of whaling (Jackson, 1978).

13 Modern whaling: the final phase

There was one more move for the whaling industry to take to encompass its final ruin. The seeds for this were sown in the 1912–13 Antarctic season. When the floating factories arrived at the South Orkneys in November they found the pack-ice still invested the islands and they were unable to bring their ships into the harbour. As they lay waiting at the ice-edge in fine, still weather, the whales were there in plenty, blowing all around the ships, and rubbing against their sides. It was M. T. Moe, captain of the *Tioga*, who first decided to try to flense a whale alongside in the open sea, and his attempt was soon followed by other factories. This was the first attempt at real pelagic whaling in the Antarctic and although work at the ice-edge in fine weather was not very different from work near the shore, the ships were not well-adapted for it. However, this period of flensing at sea made the gunner on one of the catchers, Petter Sørlle, think seriously about the further possibilities of whaling in this way.

As the market for whale oil improved an increased interest in Antarctic whaling ensued. The government of the Falkland Islands, however, refused to grant more licences on account of its conservation policy. There was already evidence of a decline in some whale stocks on the catching grounds at that time. In South Georgia, in the 1910–11 season, Humpbacks formed 95% of the total whale catch; by 1917–18 this had fallen to a mere 2% of the total. In the same period the average number of whales of all species caught per catcher per season fell from 207 to 102. Always it was the Humpbacks that were the first to be eradicated (ignoring the very scarce right whales, which soon disappeared), but significant changes occurred also with Blue and Fin Whales.

South Georgia had its maximum Blue Whale catch in 1915–16, when 3,026 were taken; catches thereafter declined.

The Colonial Office commissioned an interdepartmental report into research and development in the Falkland Islands Dependencies, to examine the state of the whaling industry and decided it was in the best interests of the industry to set up a biological investigation of the whales and their environment. This was to be the '*Discovery*' Investigations (so called after their expedition ship), which was to add so much to our knowledge of the Southern Ocean and its stocks of whales. To finance the investigation, the Falkland Islands government increased the tax on whale oil.

Not surprisingly, the search for a means of evading the restrictions on the number of licences and the payment of oil-duty intensified and there was also the threat of reduced catches to urge the whaling companies to seek other fields.

Meanwhile, Petter Sørlle, thinking about the best means of processing whales in the open sea, had decided that the problem of outboard flensing would be solved by bringing the whales on deck; the operation thereafter would be the same as at a shore station. He designed a ramp at the stern of the ship, its lower end below the water line, up which the whale could be hauled. This was not an entirely original suggestion; patents had been taken out for similar schemes in 1904 and 1905, but nothing had come of them. Sørlle patented his idea in 1922 and the ship-owner H. G. Melson of A. S. Globus, seeing its possibilities, purchased an old steamer of 12,000 tons, built in 1898, and refitted her with Sørlle's stern-slip, a long sloping ramp leading from the water beneath a stern-bridge to a flensing deck aft. She was renamed *Lancing* after a famous four-masted sailing barque that the company had previously owned.

Lancing left Framnaes in June, 1925, bunkered at Barry, and then, accompanied by five whale-catchers, arrived off the Congo in July. The intention was to try out Sørlle's invention with Humpbacks on their breeding grounds in more sheltered waters, before the final test in the rigorous conditions of the Antarctic. In three months *Lancing* took 294 Humpbacks, from which were cooked out 9,268 barrels of oil. The Antarctic season that followed proved the effectiveness of the stern-ship but, nevertheless, production was not as great as had been hoped. A total of 17,184 barrels (2,910 tonnes) of oil was obtained, including some taken on the Patagonian coast (Naess, 1951). Nevertheless, *Lancing* showed what could be done in the open sea and other companies were quick to follow suit. To evade Sørlle's patent, various techniques were tried, none of which was successful and, eventually, the stern-slip became standard practice for factory ships, as these pelagic vessels were called to distinguish them from floating factories.

The first non-Norwegian factory ship was the 12,398 ton *Southern Empress*, owned by Lever Brothers and considered to be the first modern factory ship to have adequate processing plant in relation to the number of catchers employed.

The development was very rapid. In 1925–26 there were two expeditions operating pelagically, together producing 56,814 barrels (9,652 tonnes) of oil. By 1930–31 there were forty-one factories (mostly equipped with stern-slips) with 205 catchers, which killed about 37,500 whales and produced 3,420,410 barrels (579,120 tonnes) of oil (Brown, 1963).

As Gordon Jackson pointed out, expansion could hardly have come at a worse time. Markets were everywhere filled with raw materials and extra production saturated them but, despite the ominous signs, the whaling industry invested more and more in their fleets. 140,000 tons of new construction were ordered and 250,000 tons of laid-up steamers were converted into factories and transporters (Jackson, 1978). 'We should get as large a share as possible for ourselves and this country by greatly extending our operations now without licences' wrote Harold Salvesen in his report on the viability of pelagic whaling in 1928 to the firm that was to become the dominant British interest in the whaling industry.

It was bitterly ironic that the debut of *Lancing* and the totally uncontrolled expansion that was to follow coincided with the start of the '*Discovery*' Investigations. The chance of a whaling industry regulated by a strong national power, on the basis of a proper biological understanding of the whale stocks disappeared before it was properly born. The lack of a single effective controlling power was to bedevil all future attempts at the rational control of the industry.

At first the increase in the efficiency of the new pelagic fleets pushed down production costs, so that, although the market price fell, profits still rose. But the outcome was inevitable. The market was glutted and whale oil became almost unsaleable. In 1931–32, the Norwegian whaling fleet did not sail for the Antarctic, but stayed at its anchorage in Norway.

It is just possible that the events of the early 1930s might have resulted in some lessons learned and some regulations introduced had whaling remained exclusively in Norwegian and British hands. In 1932–33, when whaling resumed, the companies agreed voluntarily to limit production with quotas for catches and oil production for individual expeditions. The intention was to stabilise oil production at about 2.5 million barrels, which it was felt was appropriate for the market (the status and possible future of the whale stock was not considered at all). However, these good intentions came to nothing when, in 1934, Japan entered Antarctic whaling (having purchased a factory ship and catchers from a Norwegian company) to be followed in 1936 by Germany. By 1937–38 production had risen to 3.25 million barrels. In the final season, before the outbreak of war in 1939, there were thirty-four factory ships in the Antarctic (twelve Norwegian, nine British, six Japanese, five German, one USA and one Panamanian) with 270 catchers. They took about 36,600 whales and produced some 2.7 million barrels of oil.

It had been clear to even the most optimistic whalers for some years that the whale stocks could not long withstand this sort of onslaught, let alone further expansion. In 1931, the League of Nations drew up an International Convention for the Regulation of Whaling. This did not come into effect till 1935, largely as a result of the UK's tardiness in ratifying it, and, as Sidney Brown has pointed out, it was already nearly obsolete when introduced. Neither Japan nor Germany were parties to it and so were quite unaffected by its provisions. The industry's own production agreements provided limitations which extended beyond those of the Convention. The industry (which was concerned with limiting **oil** production, so as not to destroy the market) set

1
Blue

2
Fin

2.5
Humpback

6
Sei

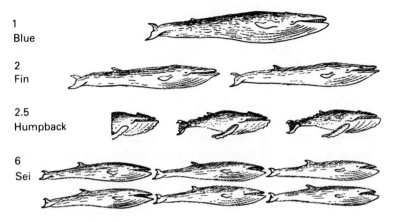

Fig. 13.1   The Blue Whale unit.

quotas in terms of Blue Whale Units (BWU). In general working terms, a Blue Whale would produce as much oil as two Fin Whales, two and a half Humpbacks or six Seis, so a Blue Whale Unit was defined in these terms (Fig. 13.1). From the point of view of limiting oil production the Blue Whale Unit was an admirable concept; for the conservation of whale stocks, it was a disaster. Because large whales yielded more oil than smaller ones, minimum lengths for the taking of Blue and Fin Whales were set down by the industry and the opening date of the Antarctic whaling season was set so as to obtain the best output of oil. These last regulations tended to maximise oil production, but they also ensured more efficient production, thus maintaining profits with a limited maximum production.

In 1937 another agreement, the International Agreement for the Regulation of Whaling, was signed in London by Norway, the UK and Germany, but not Japan. This adopted some of the points of the industry's agreement, including limitations of catching season and minimum lengths for Blue and Fin Whales, to which were added Humpback and Sperm. The following year Humpbacks, now greatly reduced, were protected in the Antarctic, and a sanctuary was established between longitudes 70°W and 160°W, where no whales were to be killed. (A cynic might point out that it was no coincidence that the industry had taken practically no whales from this area anyway.)

The intervention of the war in 1939–45 provided a breathing space for the whales. Whaling in the Antarctic was greatly reduced and 30 factory ships were sunk.

Whaling resumed in 1945–46, when six Norwegian and three British expeditions whaled pelagically in the Antarctic. By the following season the USSR, South Africa and the Netherlands had entered the field while General McArthur, the US supreme commander in Japan, arranged for the Japanese to send an expedition south. By 1950–51 there were no fewer than twenty factory ships of average gross tonnage 15,000, accompanied by 473 catchers of average horse-power 1774. Working to a limit of 16,000 BWU, this fleet accounted for 32,566 whales.

This catch limit, expressed in BWU, was agreed in 1944 under the arrangements existing then, but in December 1946 the representatives of fourteen governments (Argentina, Australia, Brazil, Canada, Chile, Denmark, France, Netherlands, New Zealand, Norway, Peru, the USSR, UK and USA) signed the International Convention for the Regulation of Whaling. This convention established the International Whaling Commission (IWC), consisting of delegates of all the countries adhering to the convention, which would be the executive body of the convention. The regulations laid down that right whales and Grey Whales (the convention was not concerned solely with the Antarctic) should be protected absolutely; Humpbacks should be protected in the Antarctic; certain areas were to be out of bounds for taking certain species of whales; the Antarctic pelagic season should be from 22 December to the 7 April; no whales below designated minimum lengths should be taken; shooting of whales accompanied by calves should be prohibited. Finally, an Antarctic catch quota of 16,000 BWU was set. This quota was probably not far above the maximum sustainable yield of the combined stocks of whales when whaling started again after the war (Gulland, 1976), but because it took no account of the varying degree of protection which each stock of each separate species required, it allowed a depleted stock to be still further reduced while the industry remained economically viable on another more abundant stock or species (Gambell, 1977). No provision was made for independent, i.e. international, inspection of the operation and the IWC had no power of enforcement. Any member of the Commission who objected to a proposed decision could opt out of it within the subsequent 90 days, and would thus be unaffected by that ruling.

The extent to which the rulings of the IWC were observed is debatable. Even had all the regulations been scrupulously observed with a quota set at 16,000 BWU the result was inevitable. Blue Whale stocks declined sharply while the industry lived off Fin Whales; later, in the 1960s, the Fin Whale catch crashed while the Sei Whale (virtually unfished pelagically in the Antarctic prior to the late 1950s) took the strain. By the mid 1960s the Sei Whale catch declined catastrophically and, in desperation, the remaining factories in the 1970s turned to the tiny Minke Whales (Fig. 13.2).

The situation that confronted the IWC almost as soon as it was formed was an increasing fleet chasing a decreasing stock of whales. The response of the commission was to set up a Scientific Sub-Committee to examine the quota of 16,000 BWU and advise on the state of the stocks of Humpbacks. At the initial meeting of the IWC in 1949, almost its first action was to relax

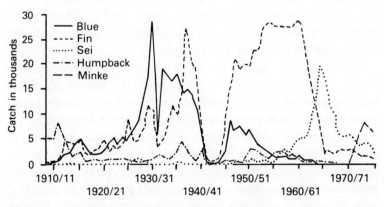

Fig. 13.2 Annual catches of baleen whales in the Antarctic. The curves show how Humpbacks, Blue Whales, Fin Whales, Sei Whales and finally Minke Whales were successively exploited. (After Gambell, 1976.)

the total ban on taking Humpbacks and allow a quota of 1,250. This was honoured more in the breach than the observance, since the first three seasons of Humpback catching after the war resulted in catches of 2,117, 1,630 and 1,545. It was unfortunate, and not only for the wretched Humpbacks, that the IWC was so early seen to be ineffective in controlling catches. The Scientific Sub-Committee reported in 1953 that Humpbacks should be protected by limiting the hunting season to only three days, and that the quota should be reduced to 14,500 BWU. This aroused strong opposition from some whaling nations and it was 1956 before the reduction came into effect. But the quota was still far too high and, because it was, international nations competed against one another, leading to over-investment in catchers. Between 1946–47 and 1961–62, the number of catchers increased from 382 to 657 and their average horse-power from 1233 to 2723 (Brown, 1963).

A move was made to introduce national quotas but agreement could not be reached, and Norway and the Netherlands withdrew from the Convention. This led to the abandonment of the quota system from 1959–60 to 1961–62. However, the whaling nations set themselves quotas outside the Convention so that catching was not totally unrestricted. Despite this, catches rose to the highest ever catch of 16,433 BWU in 1960–61. Norway rejoined the Convention in 1960 and the Netherlands in 1962. The quota in that year was set at 15,000 BWU, perhaps as an inducement. This was, however, clearly too high, for in fact only 11,306 units were taken in the season.

From 1962 onwards Antarctic catches declined steeply as the stocks collapsed. In 1963, a Committee of Three (later Four) Scientists, chosen from people with experience of population dynamics, but not previously connected with the whaling industry, reported. They recommended complete cessation of catching Blue and Humpback Whales and a reduction in the Fin Whale catch to 5,000 animals, or less, if the current sustainable yield was to be maintained, and an even greater reduction if it were to be increased to a maximum sustainable yield of about 20,000 whales. The IWC responded by reducing the 1963–64 quota from 15,000 to 10,000 BWU and providing protection for

Humpbacks everywhere in the Antarctic and for Blue Whales in most of it.

In 1964, the IWC were unable to agree a quota, but, outside the Convention, a quota of 8,000 BWU was arranged; only 6,986 units were obtained (Brown, 1970).

The last British factory ship, *Southern Harvester*, whaled in the 1962–63 season and at the end of the following season the solitary Dutch factory withdrew. (The last shore station at South Georgia closed at the end of that season also.) In 1964–65 there were four Norwegian, seven Japanese and four Russian factories with 172 catchers in the Antarctic. Norway stuck it out till 1967–68, when its last factory *Kosmos III*, was retired, leaving only three Japanese and three Russian factories with eighty-four catchers for the 1968–69 season. It was a bitter blow for Norway, and particularly for the county of Vestfold where the whaling towns of Tønsberg and Sandefjord were situated. The Norwegians had founded modern whaling in both the north and south and now it was all over as far as they were concerned.

At last in 1972–73, the IWC did what its Scientific Sub-Committee had begged for almost from its inception—it abolished the Blue Whale Unit. Blue Whales had been totally protected in 1967 but the unit system lingered on. In 1972–73 separate quotas were set for Fin, Sei, Minke and Sperm Whales. It is difficult to understand why it took the Antarctic whaling nations so long to accept individual species quotas, since in the North Pacific such a system had been in use since 1968 (Gambell, 1977). Had it been introduced in the Antarctic earlier, the catastrophic declines might have been recognised sooner and perhaps even averted.

In 1975, the IWC introduced a fresh concept of regulation in the New Management Policy (NMP). This divided whale stocks into three categories: Protection Stocks—those which were more than 10% below the level giving the maximum sustainable yield (MSY), calculated on principles derived from the study of fish populations; Sustained Management Stocks—those where stock levels were between 10% below and 20% above the level giving the MSY; and Initial Management Stocks—those whose abundance was more than 20% above the MSY level (Gambell, 1977).

No catching was to be allowed from Protection Stocks; quotas were to be set for Sustained Management Stocks to keep them near the MSY level; quotas for Initial Management Stocks should be designed to bring them gradually towards MSY levels (May, 1978). This last provision would, incidentally, mean that if a pristine whale stock were to be discovered, it should be deliberately reduced to about one half to two thirds of its size, since it would then theoretically render the maximum *sustainable* yield.

The theory underlying this policy and the calculations on which it is based are described in a very comprehensive paper by Ray Gambell (1976), the present secretary of the IWC. Gambell presents an account of the stock structure of the commercially hunted whales, their reproductive and life history parameters, and the various methods used to assess their populations. These are necessarily complicated mathematical models. Age composition data are used for recruitment and mortality estimates, reproductive data for estimates of recruitment, while behavioural observations help to interpret estimates based on sightings and are particularly helpful with Sperm Whales, which have a complicated social structure.

There are six main techniques of assessment but the subject is a complicated one, and anyone wishing to investigate it further should refer to Gambell's paper. An easy to understand account of the basic principles and the older methods is to be found in Mackintosh (1965). The more modern methods, which make use of complex mathematical models, have become available only since the introduction of powerful computers, and computer programs now form part of the IWC reports.

Calculation of catch quotas is now a highly specialised art. It is sad that the reduction of stocks allows the experts to apply their skills only to depleted populations. In the 1979–80 Antarctic season and the 1980 season for the rest of the world, more than 75% of the permitted catch was made up of Minke whales; another 14% of Sperm Whales (Table 13.1).

The Sperm catch was to be taken from shore stations on the east and west coasts of South America (Brazil, Chile and Peru), the North Atlantic (Iceland and Spain) and the North Pacific (Japan and Korea). Only Minke Whales were to be hunted pelagically. It had originally been intended that all pelagic whaling should

Table 13.1   Whaling Quotas for 1978/79 and 1979/80 Antarctic Seasons and 1979 and 1980 Seasons Elsewhere

	1978/79	1979/80
Southern Hemisphere		
Bryde's Whale	—	264
Minke Whale	6,221	8,102
Sperm Whale	4,857	580
	1979	**1980**
North Atlantic		
Fin Whale	470	624
Sei Whale	84	100
Minke Whale	2,552	2,543
Sperm Whale	685	273
Greenland Humpback Whale	10†	10†
North Pacific		
Bryde's Whale	454	479
Minke Whale	400	1,361
Sperm Whale	3,800*	1,350*
Grey Whale	178†	179†
Alaska Bowhead Whale	18 (27)**	18 (26)**
Total	19,747	15,883

† aboriginal catch.
* quota for males only: to allow for gunner errors a 'by-catch' of 11.5% of females included in total is permitted.
** aboriginal catch: figures in brackets refer to whales struck; the lower figure to whales landed. Hunting must cease when either of these figures is reached.

be suspended (such a suspension is called a 'moratorium' by whale-conservationists, despite the fact that what this word really means is the time allowed to postpone payment of a debt), but the Minke was excluded from the 'moratorium' to avoid problems with some IWC members and because of evidence of increasing Minke stocks in the Antarctic.

Another major step taken at the same meeting of the IWC in London in July 1979 was to establish a 40 million square mile (103,600,000 sq km) sanctuary in the Indian Ocean (everything north of the Equator and west of 100°E, including the Arabian and Red Seas and the Gulf of Oman, and south from the equator between 20° and 130°E to 55°S). This could have considerable conservation value, particularly for Sperm Whales, if it is respected.

The whole story is a sad one. The body set up to protect whale stocks, the IWC, failed to do this as completely as most people would wish, though the actions it took certainly retarded the slaughter and allowed a greater harvest of whales to be taken than would otherwise have been the case. But it is difficult to see what other course of action the IWC could have taken. Voluntary agreements, like the whaling convention, cannot be enforced in a Draconian fashion. Unpopular proposals were received with threats to withdraw from the Convention and these threats were put into effect on more than one occasion. Compromise was the price paid for whaling to continue within some limits, even if it was recognised that these limits were too broad. An economic control, based on the regulation of the number of catchers used, might have had more chance of success, but it was never given an opportunity to be tested at the critical post-war phase, partly because of the acute world shortage of edible fats at that time.

Now the damage is done. It remains to be seen whether whale stocks will ever recover to the point at which exploitation will again be practicable or profitable.

14 The present and the future for whales

For most of the history of man's interaction with whales, the predominant view has been that the whales were a resource to be harvested. Things began to change in the 1950s. Whaling was at a peak and a number of books appeared describing the dimensions of the slaughter and the likely effect it would have on whale stocks. No one can be sure how the whaling issue first was brought to the attention of the conservationists. The origin of the conservation movement itself is obscure, but certainly by the mid-1960s there was a growing public awareness of the need for the conservation of the earth's resources. The term 'ecology' took on a special meaning and semi-political pressure groups were set up. A very potent stimulus for this, at least in Europe, was the appearance on television of a series of excellent wildlife programmes which brought the conservation issues to a far wider public than had ever been reached before. The result of these pressures was a more general acceptance of the proposition that man's use of nature should be a rational one, and that the world's resources were not to be squandered by a minority.

The application of these new concepts to whaling was prompt. It was clear that whaling control was industry-oriented, not ecosystem-oriented. Even the principle of harvesting only the sustainable yield of the whale stocks, which was what most of the scientists wished to work towards, did not appeal to all the whaling industrialists. If the natural growth rate of a species is smaller than the prevailing bank rate interest, the rational entrepreneur will harvest that species either to extinction or to some feasible economic low level. In this way he will maximise his profit over a given time (Clark, 1973).

As this view of whaling was probably shared by many of the companies, it is not surprising that the IWC found regulation a difficult task. But with the advent of the conservationist lobby, pressures other than those of the whaling industry began to be applied. Nations with no direct whaling interest were free to accede to the Whaling Convention, and hence to vote at the IWC. As more and more nations dropped out of active whaling, so the balance of the IWC changed. Some nations which, as whalers, had been intractable in agreeing necessary quota reductions, now they whaled no more, appeared on the side of the conservationists. Other states joined out of a desire to influence the IWC in the direction of conservation.

The NMP was the product of a better scientific evaluation of the whale situation, but it was not uninfluenced by conservationist pressure. The NMP was still a policy designed for exploitation—this is explicit in its aim to set quotas so as to bring stocks to the level at which they will provide the MSY. If this level could be calculated with sufficient precision from what is known of existing stock levels, and if the response of the whale stocks to known levels of exploitation could be accurately predicted, it would be difficult to oppose the NMP on scientific grounds. There is no doubt that it represented a great advance on the old method of setting quotas.

In fact, both the conditions to be fulfilled, if the NMP is to be satisfactory, are challenged. A basic problem in whale research today is obtaining sufficiently precise information about stock size of whales. Most of the data are based on calculations derived from catch/catching effort ratios and the recoveries of marked whales. Unfortunately it is not easy to quantify 'effort' and the situation is complicated by the absence of any catching effort at all in relation to protected species. This means, for example, that only by infrequent sightings do we have an indication that stocks of Antarctic Blue Whale are responding to the protection they have enjoyed since 1967. The same difficulties apply to the mark recovery method—this requires a fair number of returned marks to give results of even approximate precision. Inevitably, the absence (or great reduction) of a whaling industry means a shortage of material for the scientists to work on, ranging from sightings per catcher's day's work to ear plugs. This has been used as an argument for maintaining at least some kind of whaling activity in the Antarctic as the only practical means of obtaining data on the whales.

The IWC has responded to doubts about the precision of the data which it uses to calculate quotas set under the NMP, by setting quotas for management stocks 10% below those calculated to be at the MSY. In some cases zero quotas are set pending further information.

A more serious objection to the NMP is that it may not be theoretically sound. Many scientists doubt whether single-species population models, like those on which the whale quotas are based, are appropriate today for the rational harvesting of marine resources. Others go further than this and suggest that whale populations may not behave in the manner required by the theory on which MSY calculations are based. It is difficult to obtain convincing evidence on this one way or the other, but clearly, if whales do not conform to this expectation, then the whole theory on which their population management is based collapses.

With this in mind, scientists, backed by the conservationists, called for caution and a re-examination of the data. The ultimate in caution was, of course, to cease whaling altogether. This was formally proposed in 1972, at the UN Conference on the Human Environment in Stockholm, and put again to the IWC meeting in that year. The motion, which was passed easily at Stockholm (where no scientific evidence was available), was rejected at the IWC, where the Scientific Committee considered total cessation unnecessary, four nations voting for it, six against and four abstaining. The following year, it was put again when eight voted for, five against and one abstained. Despite the majority in favour, the proposal was not adopted since it required a three-quarters majority to become effective. It was not until 1979 that the 'moratorium' came into effect by eighteen votes to two (Japan and the USSR) with three abstentions (Brazil, South Korea and Spain). Even this was a weakened motion, for it applied only to factory ship whaling, leaving the shore stations still free to whale (though in fact the same IWC meeting greatly reduced the shore station quotas).

With a conservatively administered NMP giving combined quotas of some 5,000 whales less in 1979/80 than in 1978/79 (Table 13.1), a 40 million square mile sanctuary in the Indian Ocean, and an awareness of the need to investigate the theoretical background on which its policies are based, it might be thought that the IWC was performing its role in a way that should satisfy most conservationists. However, there still remain matters which cause justifiable concern to many reasonable people. The International Union for the Conservation of Nature and Natural Resources (IUCN) has asked for a mandatory requirement for a truly independent observer system wherever whaling is carried out; tighter control of the transfer of whaling ships, gear and technology to non-IWC member states, and exhaustive examination of alleged infractions of the regulations (IUCN, 1979).

These are important points, but even more serious is an issue over which the IWC has no control whatever. This concerns the taking of whales by states not party to the International Whaling Convention. Currently, all the major whaling nations are members of the IWC (though this was not the case only a few years back). There are some non-member countries which whale locally from their shores. Thus at the 1979 IWC meeting it was felt necessary to ask China not to take right whales. Of greater concern is the operation on the high seas of small catcher-factories, the so-called 'pirate whalers', of which the best-known was the m.v. *Sierra*.

Any whaling by such vessels imperils the data base on which the IWC attempts to manage whale stocks, besides the direct harm it does to the stocks themselves. However, the situation now seems hopeful. South Africa, which in the past has provided crews and facilities for the pirate whalers, in June 1979 amended her Sea Fisheries Act so as effectively to prohibit pirate whaling. Perhaps even more telling will be Japan's formal banning of all imports of whale products from non-IWC nations. This should close the market to the pirate whalers (if the ban is enforced) and thus drive them out of business.

A type of whaling which is under the international control of the IWC and the national control of a very conservation-minded nation, the USA, is the continued hunting, off Alaska, of the Bowhead Whale, which seems to be the only whale species in real danger of extinction. The perilous state of all right whales has been recognised by the protection afforded to them since the 1931 Whaling Convention. Despite this protection status the IWC rules allowed hunting by aboriginal peoples and Bowhead whaling is the modern version of Inuit whaling. It is still conducted from the skin-covered boats, the umiaks, though these may be equipped with outboard motors for towing and, in place of the old stone- or shell-pointed harpoons, shoulder-guns and bomb-lances are used.

Whaling had almost disappeared from Alaska by the middle of this century, though the tradition still persisted at Barrow, Wainwright and Point Hope. During the years 1946–1970 an average of about ten Bowheads were taken by Inuit in Alaska. Between 1970 and 1976 this jumped to an average of twenty-nine with the largest take, forty-eight struck and landed, in 1976. It is difficult to isolate the factors responsible for this increase in whaling activity. Although whale meat is undoubtedly highly valued and relished by the Inuit, it is not clear that this is subsistence hunting. An editorial comment in *Orca* magazine (1, i, 1979: p. 19) suggested it constituted trophy hunting. Prowess as a hunter had traditionally been very important in Inuit society and the Bowhead was the greatest triumph of all. Since modern technology and firearms made the Polar Bear an easy quarry, it was only against the Bowhead that the aspiring hunter could pit his skill.

The increasing take alarmed the IWC and, at its June 1977 meeting, the Scientific Committee recommended a cessation of Bowhead whaling in Alaska. This proposal excited vigorous opposition from a very vocative group of Inuit and their activities finally secured a quota of twelve landed or eighteen struck (i.e. harpooned or struck with a bomb lance, but not subsequently brought ashore or on ice and butchered). A research programme was started by the US and, at the 1978 IWC meeting, it was announced that there were at least 2,254 Bowheads and that twenty-nine calves had been counted. Even with this discouraging evidence, the USA, responding to Inuit pressure, still asked for a Bowhead quota, in order to secure Inuit cooperation so as to enable the US to comply with the IWC rulings! Nick Carter (1978) reported that the US referred repeatedly to Inuit cultural and nutritional necessities. Eventually, with support from the USSR and Norway, the USA secured a quota of eighteen landed or twenty-seven struck. The quota for 1980 is eighteen landed or twenty-six struck.

To me, Bowhead whaling at the present time with the present stocks is quite indefensible. Regrettably, it seems possible that, even without whaling mortality, the Bowhead population has been reduced to such a level that recruitment is insufficient to replace those dying naturally, so the population will slowly dwindle away. Even if this is not the case, it is to me clearly wrong to hunt such a small population. The need for whale meat to maintain nutritional standards could, and should, be met in other ways. There is evidence that not all the meat is consumed by the villages which hunt the whales, but that large quantities are flown out to Inuit in Anchorage and Fairbanks. This does not accord with the normal idea of subsistence whaling.

The argument for the retention of Bowhead whaling on cultural grounds is not convincing. Bomb-lances and outboard engines are not part of Inuit culture. While whaling is undoubtedly socially important, it is now more a challenging sport. Members of modern Inuit whaling crews may live in a large town like Fairbanks or Anchorage and travel to Barrow or Point Hope for a whale-hunting holiday (McVay, 1979).

Furthermore, Inuit Bowhead whaling is extremely inefficient. Between 1970 and 1976, it was calculated that four times the annual average catch of twenty-nine whales, were struck and lost, perhaps to die later at sea. The Bowhead is peculiarly at risk because its migration path takes it close to the shore. If the Inuit continue to ignore the long-term prospects in favour of selfish short-term gains the USA will have to face up to their responsibilities under both the IWC and their own Marine Mammal Act. Domestic minority problems should not be allowed to prevent proper conservation practice. Bowheads are threatened with extinction and on this ground I maintain they should not be hunted. Others would go further and claim that no whales

grenade   claws   leg

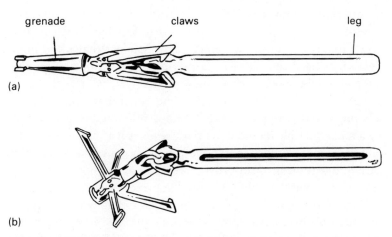

(a)

(b)

Fig. 14.1　Modern whaling harpoon: (a) with grenade in place and claws closed, (b) after explosion of the grenade, claws opened.

should be hunted, for not only are their populations depleted, but the method of hunting is inhumane in the extreme.

The explosive harpoon currently in use (Fig. 14.1) is about 1.5 m long and weighs 55 kg. It consists of a head with four barbs, to which the explosive grenade is screwed, and a leg. The grenade weighs about 9–10 kg and contains a bag of 400 g of black powder. This is ignited by delayed action fuses which are activated by the firing of the harpoon. Modern guns are platform-mounted breech-loaders as far as the cartridge is concerned; the harpoon is loaded down the muzzle. The guns are equipped with glycerine and spring recoil and run-out cylinders. The very nature of the explosive harpoon ensures that, properly placed, death will occur in a very short time and my own impressions from the whaling at South Georgia coincided with those of Ash (1964) on board a factory ship—when death was not instantaneous, the death struggle lasted a few minutes only in nearly all cases. But some careful studies have been made which do not bear out these impressions. Peter Best (1975) found that in hunting Sperm Whales off South Africa, an average of 1.6 harpoons was used for each whale killed, and the median time of death ranged from 2 min 10 sec to 4 min, depending on the gunner. 77% of the whales died within 15 min, but only 15%

in less than 1 min. Ohsumi (1977) found that, for a Japanese expedition, the average time of death for Fin Whales was 6.12 min, for Sei Whales 4.0 min and for Minke Whales 3.72 min. Even if, as has been claimed, the shock of the explosion numbs the pain of the wound, these figures could not be acceptable in slaughtering any other mammal. The Australian inquiry into whaling (Frost, 1978) concluded that death was brought about by a most horrible method and that, when it was not instantaneous, it occurred most inhumanely and, because such was the case in a significant proportion of the total, the inevitable conclusion was that the techniques used at present were not humane.

Various other means have been used for killing whales in place of the conventional harpoon, for example harpoons carrying phials of prussic acid or a charge of compressed carbon dioxide, which, it was planned, would expand on discharge, thus killing the whale with a fatal embolism and inflating it at the same time, but none have proved more satisfactory. Experiments have also been carried out with electrical harpoons but no improvement in death-times was shown and, in some cases, animals which appeared dead became active again when the current was switched off and then had to be shot with a conventional harpoon. Conductor leads between the harpoon and the whale-catcher were another problem, as was the safety of electrical equipment on the deck of a steel ship at sea. Proposals have been made to use anaesthetic or immobilising drugs to kill whales, but the eventual use of the whale products for human consumption would seem to preclude this.

The switch of hunting to smaller species of whale for meat production has seen the introduction of the 'cold grenade' technique. This uses a harpoon equipped with a non-explosive grenade. It is not difficult for a modern catcher to winch up to a harpooned Sei or Minke Whale, even if it is still alive. The Japanese have used carefully placed electrodes to electrocute a still-living whale, but often Minke Whales are killed by the harpoon alone, even though a smaller, 50 mm harpoon is generally used. The 'cold grenade' causes far less damage to the back meat, the prime product, than does the explosive grenade, hence its use, but it is even less humane than the explosive harpoon.

If whaling is to continue it would certainly be appropriate to research a more humane way of killing, but the prospects of a satisfactory solution are not bright.

With so many objections to the continuation of whale-hunting is it practicable to suggest that it should be abandoned absolutely? Are whale products essential to the world's economy or to any significant part of it? With increasing human populations and chronic famine in many parts of the world, it is difficult to claim that any food source is superfluous. However, it is possible that one food source, for example, whale products, could be replaced by another, perhaps at a lower energy cost. The traditional whale products in the west, oil and meat meal, can be, and in general have been, replaced by vegetable and fish oils, and by fish meals. Baleen whale oil in 1973 comprised only 4.3% of the total world production of animal oils from marine sources and the proportion has certainly declined since then. Nor is whale meat meal an important product. In terms of resource utilisation, the economics of hunting marine creatures, whether they be whales or fish, converting them into meal and then feeding this product to chickens or pigs, so that their flesh may be eaten by man, are very shaky, although this practice is likely to continue for some time.

Whale meat for direct human consumption is another matter, or course. The Japanese have claimed that whale meat is a vital part of their diet, but in fact it made up only 0.9% of the total protein consumption (2.1% of animal protein consumption) in Japan in 1972 (FAO, 1978). One might reasonably conclude that, although baleen whale products are a valuable resource (and were at one time much more valuable), they are not a vital or irreplaceable resource.

Sperm Whale products are used mainly as oils for industrial purposes, the meat and bone being generally converted to meal; small quantities are, however, used for pet-food or even for human consumption. Sperm oil has great value for specialised forms of lubrication, particularly where the lubricant has to remain effective over a wide range of temperatures and pressures. Spermaceti was recently widely used in the cosmetics industry as a base for various creams and lipsticks. Sperm oil, in both unrefined and refined states, is of great value in dressing leather to produce the soft supple finishes that are used for clothing and certain types of upholstery. For nearly all, if not quite all, of its applications, substitutes can be found for sperm oil, although these may be more expensive. Currently there is no single product that can substitute for all the uses of sperm oil. The most promising alternative is the oil that can be extracted from the Jojoba bean (the fruit of a desert shrub, *Simmondsia chinensis*). This is chemically similar to sperm oil and could perhaps be a satisfactory replacement. Unfortunately Jojoba is a slow grow-ing plant and the development of high yielding economic strains is likely to take a considerable time.

It is often argued that the whaling industry is important in generating employment and income for a large number of people and, for this reason, its abandonment cannot be countenanced. However, were whaling to cease, it is likely that re-deployment to other fishing activities could take place. As it happened, the withdrawal of Norway from Antarctic whaling was achieved without severe economic consequences for the whaling com-munity, as the ex-whalers found employment in other branches of industry. In any case, it does not follow that money can be made out of whales only by killing them. Attention has been drawn recently to the considerable industry based on whales, but causing the deaths of few, if any of them. This has been called the 'low-consumptive use' of whales (as opposed to the high-con-sumptive whaling industry). It consists of uses such as the exhibi-tion of dolphins in oceanaria, whale-watching cruises, television and film programmes about whales, and so forth (this book could be regarded as part of that industry). Low-consumptive uses of whales are important, without doubt, but in no sense could they substitute for the employment and income generated by com-mercial whaling, as different countries and communities are in-volved in whaling on the one hand and most low-consumptive uses on the other. If successful management policies were de-veloped, low-consumptive uses could, of course, co-exist with a high-consumptive industry without detriment to either.

If world opinion, market trends or some other reason caused the final abandonment of whaling, would the prospects for the remaining whales then be rosy? It is all too easy to suppose that, providing an adequate 'breeding stock' remains, total protection will guarantee the increase of a stock to around its original level under full protection. This is far from the truth in practice. On land, habitat destruction is often the main barrier to re-establishment. In the sea one might suppose this was impossible, except in some land-locked areas where silting or pollution may occur. In a sense this is true; the seas remain as a physical habitat, largely unchanged by man. But despite this, within the last one hundred years man has wrought great changes in the sea by the vast harvests reaped by his fishing industry. The North Sea today is biologically very different from the North Sea of a century ago. The Herring, for example, once a dominant member of the fish fauna, is now virtually absent from large areas. On the other side of the Atlantic, similar intensive exploitation of the Capelin, an important constituent of the diet of Fin, Humpback and Minke Whales off Newfoundland, is under way. If the Capelin are reduced to the same level as the North Sea Herring, what then is the chance for the whales?

Perhaps we can see the situation most clearly in the Antarctic, as we can with so many problems associated with whales, for there we have a long history of data collection and analysis and a relatively simple environmental situation. By far the most important item in the diet of the Antarctic whalebone whale is krill, mostly *Euphausia superba*, but with some *E. crystallo-rophias* as well. Not only whales feed on krill. The Crab-eater Seal, the most abundant seal in the world, subsists entirely on krill which is nearly as important in the diet of several penguin species, while other birds, fish and squid also eat large amounts.

The initial stocks of whalebone whales in the Antarctic (i.e. those prior to the establishment of the whaling industry) were estimated to consume, each year, nearly 190 million tonnes of krill; the existing stocks, now much reduced by whaling, account for nearly 43 million tonnes (Laws, 1977a). A first assumption from this might be that there are 150 million tonnes of uneaten krill available each year in the Southern Ocean. This, however, is far from the truth. The 'surplus' of krill left by the whales was available to other species and they took advantage of it. This

WHALES

effect was first noticed in relation to penguins when Sladen (1964) suggested that the observed increase in abundance of Adelie (*Pygoscelis adeliae*) and Chinstrap (*P. antarctica*) Penguins was the result of more food being available because of the decline of the whalebone whale stocks. Similar increases have been noticed in some other penguins and also in Crab-eater Seals.

It seems then that the place of the whales in the complex food webs of the Antarctic has been to some extent usurped by other krill consumers. Nor is it simply seals and birds that have taken the whale's place. Presumably fish and squid have benefited similarly and, even within the whales themselves, there have been changes. Because the whale species were selectively hunted, the larger Blue Whales being taken before the Fins, which were followed by the Sei and finally the Minke, a similar competitive situation existed within the whale species. This is shown most clearly by the Sei Whale. Sei Whales were not significantly hunted until the 1960s and yet their pregnancy rates had risen since the mid-1940s and the age at maturity has fallen (Gambell, 1973). Both of these factors are indications of increased food availability. We thus deduce that Sei Whale stocks were increasing to take the place of the depleted Blue and Fin Whales, though they have since been reduced by hunting. The same thing has happened with the Minke Whale, where current abundance in the Antarctic is probably greater than it was prior to the beginning of whaling.

It is not surprising that these changes have taken place. Nature abhors a vacuum and, if a gap is left in the ecosystem, some opportunistic species will fill it. Once the delicate balance has been disturbed the next equilibrium is unlikely to be the same as the previous one. The inevitable conclusion we must draw is that, even if all killing of whales in the Southern Ocean were to cease, we could not expect the Blue Whale, for example, to regain its previous numbers. It is possible, of course, that if the Blue Whale is a more efficient krill predator than the Sei Whale or the Crab-eater Seal, eventually the original position will be restored, but this is far from certain and, in any case, might take many centuries to come about. Because of the great difficulty in obtaining accurate information we have little idea of whether in fact

Blue Whales in the Antarctic have increased since they were first protected in 1966.

Looking at this as a management problem of the sort familiar to those who maintain terrestrial wildlife reserves, we might conclude that the best way to achieve an increased Blue Whale population would be to reduce the abundance of its competitors and start killing Crab-eater Seals, penguins and other whale species. Fortunately for the latter, this is not a practicable course.

It seems to me very doubtful, even if whaling were to be totally abolished tomorrow, whether anyone alive today could expect to travel to the Antarctic and see whales (of whatever species) in the sort of abundance that so impressed the early pioneers.

Yet another difficulty lies in the path of recovery for the Antarctic whales. This is the development of a commercial fishery for krill. Because krill form dense swarms they can be successfully located and caught by conventional fishing methods and the last decade has seen a great increase of interest in this huge resource (the amount of krill eaten each year by Crab-eater Seals exceeds the total world fisheries catch by man). Catches currently are small in terms of the resource, within 100,000 tonnes a year, but should these increase in an uncontrolled manner, then all krill consumers, whales, seals, birds, fish, etc., would be at risk.

Currently no fisheries agreement regulates krill fishing in the Antarctic, but a treaty is being negotiated (The Antarctic Marine Living Resources Convention) which, if successfully carried through, would enable a control to be exerted which would protect the ecosystem as a whole, not merely one or a few components of it.* This ecosystem approach, in contrast to the species approach which has dominated most fisheries management policies, becomes more and more essential as our exploitation of the ocean's resources becomes more intensive. Without appropriate regulation a fully developed krill fishery could strike the remaining whale stocks as hard a blow as ever the whalers did. Least affected of all may be the consumers of deep-water oceanic squid, the Sperm and Bottle-nosed Whales. Protection for Sperm Whales could well result in a reasonably rapid recovery of the

---

* This Convention was signed at Canberra in May, 1980.

stocks. So far, however, the only case where protection has resulted in a demonstrable increase to something like the original numbers has been the Eastern Pacific stock of Grey Whales.

It is rash to attempt to prophesy what the future will hold for whales. Perhaps currently the prospects are better than they have been for some time. The IWC is today a far more effective body than it has been in the past, with a composition that ensures it is not dominated entirely by the whaling industry and an active awareness of the need for sound management policies to conserve whale stocks. Public interest has been aroused in whales to an extent that would have been inconceivable a decade ago and this interest has been expressed as vigorous activity by many conservation groups. Although pressure for whale conservation is not evenly distributed throughout the world, a sufficient number of influential nations are involved to ensure that the effect of their opinion spreads world-wide.

The final question is whether man's use of marine resources in general will be governed by rational plans. If we do not soon agree codes which will ensure the integrity of the marine eco-system as a whole we may find that the result will be changes of such a profound nature that the sea itself is unable to provide whales (and other groups of equal importance and interest) with the necessary environment in which to live and flourish. This would be the ultimate tragedy in man's relations with the whale.

Bibliography

Alpers, A. (1960) *Dolphins* John Murray, London.

Aristotle *Historia Animalium* Translated by Thompson, D. W. (1910), Clarendon Press, Oxford.

Ash, C. (1964) *Whaler's Eye* George Allen & Unwin, London.

Backhouse, K. M. and Smart, P. J. G. (1961) 'The mechanism of wave-riding in porpoises' *Proc. Zool. Soc. London.* **136**, pp. 197–200.

Backus, R. H. and Scheville, W. E. (1966) '*Physeter* clicks.' In *Whales, Dolphins and Porpoises* Norris, K. S. (ed.), pp. 510–28. University of California Press, Berkeley and Los Angeles.

Baldridge, A. (1972) 'Killer Whales attack and eat a Gray Whale' *J. Mammal.* **53**, pp. 898–900.

Beale, T. (1839) *The Natural History of the Sperm Whale* (Reprinted 1973.) The Holland Press, London.

Beamish, P. and Mitchell, E. (1971) 'Ultrasonic sounds recorded in the presence of a Blue Whale, *Balaenoptera musculus' Deep-sea Res.* **20**, pp. 375–86.

Best, P. B. (1970) 'The Sperm Whale (*Physeter catodon*) off the west coast of South Africa. 5. Age, growth and mortality' *Investl Rep. Div. Sea Fish. Un. S. Afr.* No. 79, pp. 1–27.

Best, P. B. (1975) 'Death-time for whales killed by explosive harpoons' *Rep. Int. Whal. Commn* No. 25, pp. 208–14.

Boas, F. (1888) 'The Central Eskimo' *A. Rep. Bur. Am. Ethnol.* No. 6 (Reprinted 1964.) University of Nebraska Press, Lincoln.

Boyden, A. and Gemeroy, D. (1950) 'The relative position of the Cetacea among the orders of Mammalia as indicated by precipitin tests' *Zoologica N.Y.* **35**, pp. 145–51.

Brodie, P. F. (1975) 'Cetacean energetics, an overview of intraspecific size variation' *Ecology* **56**, pp. 152–61.

Brown, S. G. (1963) 'A review of Antarctic whaling' *Polar Rec.* **11**, pp. 555–66.

Brown, S. G. (1968) 'Feeding of Sei Whales at South Georgia' *Norsk Hvalfangsttid.* **57**, 6, pp. 118–25.

Brown, S. G. (1970) 'A decade of decline in Antarctic whaling, 1959–69' *Polar Rec.* **15**, pp. 198–200.

Brown, S. G. (1976) 'Modern whaling in Britain and the north-east Atlantic Ocean' *Mammal Rev.* **6**, 1, pp. 25–36.

Burton, M. (1965) *Systematic Dictionary of Mammals of the World* Museum Press Ltd, London.

Burton, R. W. (1973) *The Life and Death of Whales* Andre Deutsch, London.

Caldwell, M. C. and Caldwell, D. K. (1972) 'Behaviour of marine mammals.'

In *Mammals of the Sea: Biology and Medicine* Ridgway, S. H. (ed.), pp. 419–65. Charles C. Thomas, Springfield, Illinois.

Carter, N. (1978) 'Report on the International Whaling Commission's Thirtieth Annual Meeting, 26th–30th June 1978' *International Society for the Protection of Animals*, 17 pp (Mimeo.)

Chittleborough, R. G. (1960) 'Marked Humpback of known age' *Nature, Lond.* 187, p. 164.

Clark, C. W. (1973) 'The economics of overexploitation' *Science N.Y.* 181, pp. 630–4.

Clarke, M. R. (1978a) 'Structure and proportions of the spermaceti organ in the Sperm Whale' *J. Mar. Biol. Ass. U.K.* 58, 1–17.

Clarke, M. R. (1978b) 'Physical properties of spermaceti oil in the Sperm Whale' *J. Mar. Biol. Ass. U.K.* 58, pp. 19–26.

Clarke, M. R. (1978c) 'Buoyancy control as a function of the spermaceti organ in the Sperm Whale' *J. Mar. Biol. Ass. U.K.* 58, pp. 27–71.

Clarke, R. (1954) 'Open boat whaling in the Azores. The history and present methods of a relic industry' *Discovery Rep.* No. 26, pp. 281–354.

Clarke, R. (1956) 'Sperm Whales of the Azores' *Discovery Rep.* No. 28, pp. 237–98.

Davies, J. L. and Guiler, E. R. (1957) 'A note on the Pygmy Right Whale, *Caperea marginata* Gray' *Proc. Zool. Soc. Lond.* 129, 579–89.

Dawson, W. W., Birndorf, L. A. and Perez, J. M. (1972) 'Gross anatomy and optics of the dolphin eye (*Tursiops truncatus*)' *Cetology* 10, 1–12.

Dral, A. D. G. (1977) 'On the retinal anatomy of Cetacea (mainly *Tursiops truncatus*).' In *Functional Anatomy of Marine Mammals* Harrison, R. J. (ed.), 3, pp. 81–134. Academic Press, London, New York and San Francisco.

Dreher, J. J. (1966) 'Cetacean communication: small group experiment.' In *Whales, Dolphins and Porpoises* Norris, K. S. (ed.), pp. 529–41. University of California Press, Berkeley and Los Angeles.

Dudley, P. (1725) 'An essay on the natural history of whales' *Phil. Trans. Roy. Soc. Lond. Ser. B* 33, 387, pp. 256–69.

Elsner, R., Pirie, J., Kenney, D. and Schemmer, S. (1974) 'Functional circulatory anatomy of cetacean appendages.' In *Functional Anatomy of Marine Mammals* Harrison, R. J. (ed.), 2, pp. 143–59. Academic Press, London, New York and San Francisco.

Eschricht, D. F. (1845) 'Undersögelser over hvaldyrne. 1. Bemaekninger over Cetologiens tidligere og naervaerende skjebne' *K. Dansk. Vidensk. Selbsk. Nat. Math. Afh.* 11.

Eschricht, D. F. (1866) 'On the species of the genus *Orca* inhabiting the North Sea.' In *Recent Memoirs on the Cetacea* Flower, W. H. (ed.), Ray Society, London.

Essapian, F. S. (1955) 'Speed-induced skinfolds in the Bottle-nosed Porpoise, *Tursiops truncatus*' *Breviora Mus. Comp. Zool.* No. 43, pp. 1–4.

Evans, W. E. and Prescott, J. H. (1962) 'Observations on the sound production capabilities of the Bottlenose Porpoise: a study of whistles and clicks' *Zoologica N.Y.* 47, 3, pp. 121–8.

FAO (1978) *Mammals in the Seas*. Report of the FAO Advisory Committee on Marine Resources Research Working Party on Marine Mammals, 1. Food and Agriculture Organisation of the United Nations, Rome.

Felts, W. J. L. (1966) 'Some functional and structural characteristics of the ceta-cean flipper and flukes.' In *Whales, Dolphins and Porpoises* Norris, K. S. (ed.), pp. 255–76. University of California Press, Berkeley and Los Angeles.

Flannigan, N. J. (1972) 'The central nervous system.' In *Mammals of the Sea. Biology and Medicine* Ridgway, S. H. (ed.), pp. 215–46. Charles C. Thomas, Springfield, Illinois.

Fraser, F. C. (1940) 'Three anomalous dolphins from Blacksod Bay, Ireland' *Proc. Roy. Irish Acad.* **45B**, 17, pp. 413–55.

Fraser, F. C. (1966) [Discussion on navigation in Cetacea.] In *Whales, Dolphins and Porpoises* Norris, K. S. (ed.), p. 602. University of California Press, Berkeley and Los Angeles.

Fraser, F. C. and Purves, P. E. (1954) 'Hearing in cetaceans' *Bull. Brit. Mus. Nat. Hist. Zool.* **2**, pp. 103–16.

Fraser, F. C. and Purves, P. E. (1960) 'Hearing in cetaceans' *Bull. Brit. Mus. Nat. Hist. Zool.* **7**, pp. 1–140.

Frost, S. (1978) *Whales and Whaling* Report of the Independent Inquiry conducted by the Hon. Sir Sydney Frost, 1. Australian Government Publishing Service, Canberra.

Gambell, R. (1973) 'Some effects of exploitation on reproduction in whales' *J. Reprod. Fert.* (Suppl.) **19**, pp. 533–53.

Gambell, R. (1976) 'Population biology and the management of whales.' In *Appl. Biol.* Coaker, T. H. (ed.), 1, pp. 247–343. Academic Press, London, New York and San Francisco.

Gambell, R. (1977) 'Whale conservation: role of the International Whaling Commission' *Marine Policy* **Oct.**, pp. 301–10.

Gaskin, D. E. (1976) 'Evolution, zoogeography and ecology of Cetacea' *Oceanogr. Mar. Biol. Ann. Rev.* **14**, pp. 247–346.

Gray, J. (1948) 'Aspects of locomotion of whales' *Nature, Lond.* **161**, p. 199.

Griffen, D. R. (1958) *Listening in the Dark* Yale University Press, New Haven, Connecticut.

Gulland, J. A. (1976) 'Antarctic baleen whales: history and prospects' *Polar Rec.* **18**, pp. 5–13.

Gunter, E. R. (1949) 'The habits of Fin Whales' *Discovery Rep.* No. 25, pp. 113–42.

Hancock, D. (1965) 'Killer Whales kill and eat a Minke Whale' *J. Mammal.* **46**, pp. 341–2.

Harrison, R. J. (1968) 'Reproduction and reproductive organs.' In *Biology of Marine Mammals* Andersen, H. T. (ed.), pp. 253–348. Academic Press, New York and London.

Harrison, R. J. and King, J. E. (1965) *Marine Mammals* Hutchinson University Library, London.

Harrison, R. J. and Thurley, K. W. (1972) 'Fine structural features of delphinid epidermis' *J. Anat.* **111**, pp. 498–500.

Hayes, W. D. (1959) 'Wave-riding dolphins' *Science N.Y.* **130**, pp. 1657–8.

Howell, A. B. (1930) *Aquatic Mammals* Charles C. Thomas, Baltimore.

Hubbs, C. L. (1966) [Discussion on navigation in Cetacea.] In *Whales, Dolphins and Porpoises* Norris, K. S. (ed.), p. 605. University of California Press, Berkeley and Los Angeles.

IUCN (1979) 'IUCN's statement to the IWC. 9 July 1979' *IUCN Bull.* New Series, 10, 8/9, p. 75.

Jackson, G. (1978) *The British Whaling Trade* Adam and Charles Black, London.

Jansen, J. (1950) 'The morphogenesis of the cetacean cerebellum' *J. Comp. Neurol.* 93, pp. 341–400.

Jansen, J. (1953) 'Studies on the cetacean brain. The gross anatomy of the rhombencephalon of the Fin Whale [*Balaenoptera physalus* (L.)]' *Hvalråd. Skr.* 37, pp. 1–32.

Jansen, J. and Jansen, J. K. S. (1969) 'The nervous system of Cetacea.' In *The Biology of Marine Mammals* Andersen, H. T. (ed.), pp. 175–252. Academic Press, New York and London.

Japha, A. (1907) 'Uber die Haut nord atlantischer Furchenwale' *Zool. Jb. Abt. Anat. Ontog. Tiere* 24, pp. 1–40.

Japha, A. 'Die haare der Waltiere' *Zool. Jb. Abt. Anat. Ontog. Tiere* 32, pp. 1–42. Translated by Sinclair, D. A. (1972), *Techn. Transl. Nat. Res. Council. Can.* No. 1537.

Jerison, H. J. (1978) 'Brains and intelligence in whales.' In *Whales and Whaling.* Report of the Independent Inquiry conducted by the Hon. Sir Sydney Frost, 2, pp. 159–95. Australian Government Publishing Service, Canberra.

Johnsen, A. O. (1959) *Den Moderne Hvalfangsts Historie. 1. Finsmarksfangstens historie 1864–1905* H. Aschehoug & Co. (W. Nygaard), Oslo.

Jones, E. C. (1971) '*Isistius brasiliensis*, a squalid shark, the probable cause of crater wounds on fishes and cetaceans' *Fishery Bull. Fish. Wildl. Serv. U.S.* 69, p. 791.

Kanwisher, J. and Sundnes, G. (1966) 'Thermal regulation in cetaceans.' In *Whales, Dolphins and Porpoises* Norris, K. S. (ed.), pp. 397–409. University of California Press, Berkeley and Los Angeles.

Kellogg, W. N. (1958) 'Echo ranging in porpoises. (Perception of objects by reflected sound is demonstrated for the first time in marine animals)' *Science N.Y.* 128, pp. 982–8.

Kellogg, W. N. (1959) 'Size discrimination by reflected sound in a Bottlenose Porpoise' *J. Comp. Physiol. Psychol.* 52, pp. 509–14.

Kojima, T. (1951) 'On the brain of the Sperm Whale (*Physeter catodon*)' *Sci. Rep. Whales Inst. Tokyo* No. 6, pp. 49–72.

Kruger, L. (1959) 'The thalamus of the dolphin (*Tursiops truncatus*) and comparison with other mammals' *J. Comp. Neurol.* 111, pp. 133–94.

Lang, T. G. (1966) 'Hydrodynamic analysis of cetacean performances.' In *Whales, Dolphins and Porpoises* Norris, K. S. (ed.), pp. 410–32. University of California Press, Berkeley and Los Angeles.

Laurie, A. H. (1933) 'Some aspects of respiration in Blue and Fin Whales' *Discovery Rep.* No. 7, pp. 363–406.

Laws, R. M. (1977) 'Seals and whales of the Southern Ocean' *Phil. Trans. Roy. Soc. Lond. Ser. B.* 279, pp. 81–96.

Lilly, J. C. (1977) 'The cetacean brain' *Oceans* July/Aug., pp. 4–6.

Ling, J. K. (1974) 'The integument of marine mammals.' In *Functional Anatomy of Marine Mammals* Harrison, R. J. (ed.), 1, pp, 1–44. Academic Press, London and New York.

Ling, J. K. (1977) 'Vibrissae of marine mammals.' In *Functional Anatomy of*

Marine Mammals Harrison, R. J. (ed.), **3**, pp. 387–415. Academic Press, London and New York.

Lockyer, C. (1972) 'The age at sexual maturity of the southern Fin Whale (*Balaenoptera physalus*) using annual layer counts in the ear plug' *J. Cons. Perm. Int. Explor. Mer* **34**, 2, pp. 276–94.

Lockyer, C. (1974) 'Investigation of the ear plug of the southern Sei Whale, *Balaenoptera borealis*, as a valid means of determining age' *J. Cons. Perm. Int. Explor. Mer* **36**, 1, pp. 71–81.

Lockyer, C. (1976) 'Growth and energy budgets of large baleen whales from the Southern Hemisphere' *Advisory Committee on Marine Resources Research Scientific Consultation on Marine Mammals. ACMRR/MM/SC/41* 179 pp. (Mimeo.)

Lockyer, C. (1977) 'Observations on diving behaviour of the Sperm Whale, *Physeter catodon.*' In *A Voyage of Discovery* Angel, M. (ed.), pp. 591–609. Pergamon Press, Oxford and New York.

Lubbock, B. (1937) *The Arctic Whalers* Brown, Son and Ferguson, Glasgow.

Mackintosh, N. A. (1965) *The Stocks of Whales* Fishing News (Books) Ltd., London.

Madsen, C. J. (1975) 'Tests for color vision in the bottlenosed dolphin, *Tursiops truncatus*' Ph.D. thesis. Univ. Hawaii, Honolulu (quoted in Dral, 1977).

Mann Fischer, G. (1946) 'Ojo y vision de las ballenas' *Biologica, Santiago* **4**, p. 23.

Mansfield, A. W., Smith, T. G., and Beck, B. (1975) 'The narwhal, *Monodon monoceros*, in eastern Canadian waters' *J. Fish. Res. Bd. Can.* **32**, 7, pp. 1041–6.

Mathiessen, L. (1893) 'Uber den physikalisch-optischen Bau der Augen Knölwal und Finnwal' *Z. Vergl. Augenheilk.* **7**, p. 77.

Matthews, L. H. (1952) *British Mammals* New Naturalist Series, Collins, London.

Matthews, L. H. (1978) *The Natural History of the Whale* Weidenfeld and Nicolson, London.

May, R. M. (1978) 'Whaling: past, present and future' *Nature, Lond.* **276**, pp. 319–22.

McVay, S. (1979) 'Another perspective [Bowhead whaling.]' *Orca* **1**, 1, pp. 13–15.

Melville, H. (1851) *Moby Dick, or the Whale* (Reprinted 1962.) W. W. Norton and Co. Inc., New York.

Mitchell, E. D. (1975) 'Review of biology and fisheries for smaller cetaceans' *J. Fish. Res. Bd. Can.* **32**, 7, pp. 875–1242.

Mitchell, E. (1975) 'Porpoise, dolphin and small whale fisheries of the world' *IUCN Monogr.* No. 3 International Union for the Conservation of Nature and Natural Resources, Morges.

Moiseev, P. A. (1970) 'Some aspects of the commercial use of krill resources of the Antarctic seas.' In *Antarctic Ecology* Holdgate, M. W. (ed.), **1**, pp. 213–6. Academic Press, London and New York.

Morgane, P. J. (1978) 'Whale brains and their meaning for intelligence.' In *Whales and Whaling* Report of the Independent Inquiry conducted by the Hon. Sir Sydney Frost, **2**, pp. 199–220. Australian Government Publishing Service, Canberra.

Morgane, P. J. and Jacobs, M. S. (1972) 'Comparative anatomy of the cetacean nervous system.' In *Functional Anatomy of Marine Mammals* Harrison, R. J. (ed.), 1, pp. 117–244. Academic Press, London and New York.

Naess, Ø. (1951) *Hvalfangerselskap Globus A/S 1925–1950*. Privately published, Larvik.

Nishiwaki, M. and Handa, C. (1958) 'Killer Whales caught in the coastal waters off Japan for recent 10 years' *Sci. Rep. Whales Inst. Tokyo.* 13, pp. 85–96.

Norman, J. R. and Fraser, F. C. *Giant Fishes, Whales and Dolphins* Putnam, London.

Norris, K. S. (1964) 'Some problems in echolocation in cetaceans' In *Marine Bio-acoustics* Tavolga, W. N. (ed.), pp. 317–36. Pergamon Press, New York.

Norris, K. S. (1969) 'The echolocation of marine mammals.' In *The Biology of Marine Mammals* Anderson, H. T. (ed.), pp. 391–423. Academic Press, New York and London.

Norris, K. S. and Evans, W. E. (1967) 'Directionality of echolocation in the Rough-tooth Porpoise, *Steno bredanensis* (Lesson)' *Proc. 2nd Conf. Mar. Bio-acoustics*. New York, pp. 305–16.

Norris, K. S., Evans, W. E. and Turner, R. N. 'Echolocation in an Atlantic Bottlenose Porpoise during discrimination.' In *Les Systèmes Sonars Animaux, Biologie et Bionique* Busnel, R. G. (ed.), pp. 409–37. Laboratoire de Physiologie Acoustique, Jouy-en-Josas.

Norris, K. S. and Prescott, J. H. (1961) 'Observations on Pacific cetaceans of Californian and Mexican waters' *Univ. Calif. Publs Zool.* 63, pp. 291–402.

Norris, K. S., Prescott, J. H., Asa-Dorian, P. V. and Perkins, P. (1961) 'An experimental demonstration of echolocation behaviour in the porpoise, *Tursiops truncatus* (Montagu)' *Biol. Bull. Mar. Biol. Lab. Woods Hole* 120, 2, pp. 163–76.

Ohsumi, S. (1971) 'Some investigations on the school structure of the Sperm Whale' *Sci. Rep. Whales Inst. Tokyo* 23, pp. 1–25.

Ohsumi, S. (1977) 'A preliminary note on Japanese records on death-times for whales killed by whaling harpoon' *Rep. Int. Commn Whal.* No. 27, pp. 204–5.

Ommanney, F. D. (1971) *Lost Leviathan* Hutchinson and Co., London.

Payne, R. S. (1970) *Songs of the Humpback Whale* [Gramophone record.] SWR-11, CRM Records, Del Mar, California.

Perrin, W. F., Warner, R. R., Fiscus, C. H. and Holt, D. B. (1973) 'Stomach contents of porpoises, *Stenella* spp. and Yellowfin Tuna, *Thunnus albicorus*, in mixed-species aggregations' *Fishery Bull. Fish. Wildl. Serv. U.S.* 71, pp. 1077–92.

Pike, G. C. (1953) 'Two records of *Berardius bairdi* from the coast of British Columbia' *J. Mammal.* 34, pp. 98–104.

Pilleri, G. (1971) 'Epimeletic (nurturant) behaviour by the La Plata Dolphin, *Pontoporia blainvillei*' *Invest. Cetacea* 3, 1, pp, 74–6.

Pilleri, G. and Wandeler, A. (1964) 'Ontogenese und funktionelle Morphologie des Auges des Finwals, *Balaenoptera physalus* L. (Cetacea, Mysticeti, Balaenopteridae)' *Acta Anat.* (Suppl. 50) Addendum 1, 57, 74 pp.

Purves, P. E. (1963) 'Locomotion in whales' *Nature, Lond.*, 197, pp. 334–7.

Purves, P. E. (1966) 'Anatomy and physiology of the outer and middle ear in cetaceans.' In *Whales, Dolphins and Porpoises* Norris, K. S. (ed.), pp. 320–80. University of California Press, Berkeley and Los Angeles.

Quiring, D. P. (1943) 'Weight data on five whales' *J. Mammal.* 24, pp. 39–45.

Ray, G. C. and Scheville, W. E. (1974) 'Feeding of a captive Gray Whale, *Eschrichtius robustus*' *Mar. Fish. Rev.* 36, p. 31.

Ray, J. (1671) 'An account of the dissection of a porpoise' *Phil. Trans. Roy. Soc. Lond. Ser. B* 6, pp. 2220, 2274.

Rice, D. W. and Wolman, A. A. (1971) 'The life history and ecology of the Gray Whale (*Eschrichtius robustus*)' *Am. Soc. Mammalogists Spec. Publs.* No. 3, 142 pp.

Roe, H. S. J. (1967) 'Seasonal fluctuation in the ear plug of the Fin Whale' *Discovery Rep.* No. 35, pp. 1–30.

Roe, H. S. J. (1969) 'The food and feeding habits of the Sperm Whales (*Physeter catodon*) taken off the west coast of Iceland' *J. Cons. Perm. Int. Explor. Mer* 33, pp. 93–102.

Romer, A. S. (1945) *Vertebrate Palaeontology* University of Chicago Press, Chicago.

Ruud, J. T. (1940) 'The surface structure of the baleen plate as a possible clue to age in whales' *Hvalråd. Skr.* No. 23, pp. 1–24.

Ruud, J. T. (1945) 'Further studies on the structure of the baleen plates and their application to age determination' *Hvalråd. Skr.* No. 29, pp. 1–69.

Scammon, C. M. (1874) *The Marine Mammals of the Northwestern Coast of North America together with an Account of the American Whale Fishery* (Reprinted 1968.) Dover Publications Inc., New York.

Scheffer, V. B. (1969) *The Year of the Whale* Souvenir Press, London.

Scheville, W. E. and Lawrence, B. (1953) 'Auditory response of a Bottle-nosed Porpoise, *Tursiops truncatus*, to frequencies above 100 kc'. *J. Exp. Zool.* 124, pp. 147–66.

Scheville, W. E. and Lawrence, B. (1956) 'Food finding by a captive porpoise' *Breviora Mus. Comp. Zool.* 53, pp. 1–15.

Scheville, W. E. and Watkins, W. A. (1966) 'Sound structure and directionality in *Orcinus* (Killer Whale)' *Zoologica N.Y.* 51, 2, pp. 71–6.

Scholander, P. F. (1940) 'Experimental investigations on the respiratory function in diving mammals and birds' *Hvalrådets Skr.* No. 22, pp. 1–131.

Scholander, P. F. (1959) 'Wave-riding dolphins: how they do it' *Science N. Y.* 129, pp. 1085–7.

Scholander, P. F. and Scheville, W. E. (1955) 'Counter-current heat exchange in the fins of whales' *J. Appl. Physiol.* 8, pp. 279–82.

Scholander, P. F., Walters, V., Hock, R. and Irving, L. (1950) 'Body insulation of some Arctic and tropical mammals and birds' *Biol. Bull. Mar. Biol. Lab. Woods Hole* 99, pp. 225–36.

Sergeant, D. E. (1969) 'Feeding rates in Cetacea' *Fiskdir. Skr. Havundersøk.* 15, pp. 246–58.

Service, R. (1896) 'Mammals of Solway' *Ann. Scott. Nat. Hist.* 20, pp. 201–10.

Sladen, W. J. L. (1964) 'The distribution of the Adelie and Chinstrap Penguins.' In *Biologie Antarctique* Carrick, R., Holdgate, M. W. and Prévost, J. (eds), pp. 359–65. Hermann, Paris.

Slijper, E. J. (1936) 'Die Cetaceen' Dissertation. *Capita Zoological, Utrecht* 7.

Slijper, E. J. (1962) *Whales* Hutchinson, London.

Stackpole, E. A. (1953) *The Sea-Hunters: The New England Whalers during Two Centuries, 1635–1835* J. B. Lippincott Co., Philadelphia and New York.

Tavolga, M. C. (1966) 'Behavior of the Bottlenose Dolphin (*Tursiops truncatus*): social interactions in a captive colony' In *Whales, Dolphins and Porpoises* Norris, K. S. (ed.), pp. 718–30. University of California Press, Berkeley and Los Angeles.

Tawara, T. (1951) 'On the respiratory pigments of whales' *Sci. Rep. Whales Res. Inst. Tokyo.* 3, p. 96.

Tomilin, A. G. (1946) 'Lactation and nutrition in cetaceans' *Dokl. Proc. Akad. Sci. USSR Biol. Sci.* 52, 3, pp. 277–9.

Tomilin, A. G. (1967) *Cetacea. Mammals of the U.S.S.R. and Adjacent Countries* Israel Programme for Scientific Translation, Jerusalem.

Tønnesen, J. N. (1967) *Den Moderne Hvalfangsts Historie. 2. Verdenfangsten 1883–1914* Norges Hvalfangstforbund, Sandefjord.

Tønnesen, J. N. (1970) 'Norwegian Antarctic whaling, 1905–68: an historical appraisal' *Polar Rec.* 15, pp. 283–90.

Vamplew, W. (1975) *Salvesen of Leith* Scottish Academic Press, Edinburgh and London.

Varanasi, U., Feldman, H. R. and Maluis, D. C. (1975) 'Molecular basis for formation of lipid sound lens in echolocating cetaceans' *Nature, Lond.* 255, pp. 340–3.

Venables, L. S. H. and Venables, U. M. (1955) *Birds and Mammals of Shetland.* Oliver and Boyd, Edinburgh and London.

Villiers, A. (1974) *Vanished Fleets. Sea Stories from Old Van Diemen's Land* Patrick Stephens, Cambridge.

Walls, G. L. (1942) 'The vertebrate eye and its adaptive radiation' *Cranbrook Inst. Sci. Bull.* No. 19.

Waterman, T. T. (1920) 'The whaling equipment of the Makah Indians' *Univ. Washington Publs Anthrop.* 1, 1, pp. 1–67.

Watkins, W. A. and Scheville, W. E. (1976) 'Right whale feeding and baleen rattle' *J. Mammal.* 57, pp. 58–66.

Weast, R. C. (ed) (1976–1977) *C.R.C. Handbook of Chemistry and Physics* C.R.C. Press, Ohio.

Webb, N. G. (1978) 'Women and children abducted by a wild but sociable adult male Bottlenose Dolphin (*Tursiops truncatus*)' *Carnivore* 1, 2, pp. 89–94.

Williamson, K. (1948) *The Atlantic Islands: a Study of Faeroe Life and Scene* Collins, London.

Williamson, K. (1960) 'Ca'ing the whale' *Scott. Field,* June 1960: 44–5.

Wolman, A. A. (1978) 'Humpback Whale.' In *Marine Mammals of Eastern North Pacific and Arctic Waters* Haley, D. (ed.), pp. 47–53. Pacific Search Press, Seattle.

Wood, F. G. (1966) [Discussion on navigation in Cetacea.] In *Whales, Dolphins and Porpoises* Norris, K. S. (ed.), p. 604. University of California Press, Berkeley and Los Angeles.

Wood, G. L. (1972) *The Guinness Book of Animal Facts and Feats* Guinness Superlatives Ltd., Enfield.

Index

Numbers in *italics* refer to pages containing black and white illustrations. Numbers in **bold** refer to colour plates.